SPINAL CORD INJURY

THE REHABILITATION INSTITUTE OF CHICAGO PUBLICATION SERIES

Don A. Olson, Ph.D., Series Coordinator

Spinal Cord Injury: A Guide to Functional Outcomes in Physical Therapy Management

Lower Extremity Amputation: A Guide to Functional Outcomes in Physical Therapy Management

Stroke/Head Injury: A Guide to Functional Outcomes in Physical Therapy Management

Clinical Management of Right Hemisphere Dysfunction

Clinical Evaluation of Dysphagia

Spinal Cord Injury: A Guide to Functional Outcomes in Occupational Therapy

Nursing Rehabilitation of Spinal Cord Injury

Rehabilitation Institute of Chicago
PROCEDURE MANUAL

SPINAL CORD INJURY

A GUIDE TO FUNCTIONAL OUTCOMES IN OCCUPATIONAL THERAPY

Judy P. Hill, OTR

Sharon Intagliata, MS, MPA, OTR/L
Occupational Therapy Series Editor
Director of Occupational Therapy
Rehabilitation Institute of Chicago

AN ASPEN PUBLICATION®
Aspen Publishers, Inc.
Rockville, Maryland
Royal Tunbridge Wells
1986

Library of Congress Cataloging-in-Publication Data

Hill, Judy P.
Spinal cord injury.

Bibliography: p.
Includes index.
1. Spinal cord — Wounds and injuries — Patients — Rehabilitation — Standards.
2. Occupational therapy — Standards. 3. Physically handicapped — Care and treatment.
4. Self-help devices for the disabled. I. Title.
RD594.3.H55 1986 617'.482044 86–25852
ISBN: 0–87189–604–4

Editorial Services: Lisa J. McCullough

Library of Congress Catalog Card Number: 86–25852
ISBN: 0–87189–604–4

Printed in the United States of America

1 2 3 4 5

Table of Contents

Series Preface

In recent years, occupational therapy has entered a dynamic new phase in its development as a health care profession. As advances in medical technology have enabled people to survive increasingly more catastrophic illnesses or trauma, we have been faced with many new demands. These demands have challenged us to learn new techniques and specialized skills to keep pace with the rapid changes taking place throughout the field of rehabilitation. Although these scientific advancements have had a significant impact on the rehabilitation treatment process, the basic tenets of our profession have not changed. As occupational therapists, we continue to assist individuals to engage in meaningful and productive activity. This role has been and will continue to be a critical component in the effort to enhance the health and well being of our patients and to aid them in returning to the mainstream of society.

Since the Rehabilitation Institute of Chicago was founded in 1954, our Occupational Therapy Department has grown considerably in size. Along with the growth in numbers has come an evolution in the theoretical approaches, technology, and specialization of skills being used in our clinic. Accordingly, it was felt that developing uniform standards of clinical care would help to ensure a consistent and comprehensive approach to our occupational therapy treatment of patients with similar diagnoses.

Our department's Quality Assurance Committee encouraged the development of these standards. The committee recommended that the standards be written in a format that would facilitate our monitoring of the appropriateness and effectiveness of our treatment programs in an ongoing manner. The format developed focuses on (1) systematically identifying significant behavioral indicators in the recovery process and (2) defining and describing the concepts, evaluation protocol, and treatment planning methods relevant to each patient's condition.

This volume describes our treatment approach to spinal cord injury and is the first in a series of three volumes to be completed by the Occupational Therapy Department at the Rehabilitation Institute of Chicago; the two subsequent volumes will be devoted to standards for the treatment of stroke and head injury. The standards that serve as the foundation of each volume were compiled by clinical supervisors and senior staff members with input from our entire department; therefore, each volume represents a culmination of the ideas and efforts of many talented occupational therapists who have devoted their clinical expertise and creative wisdom to our department. The process of developing and refining these standards has solidified our collective rationale for treatment. The standards have been useful to us in orienting new staff and students to general treatment techniques as well as to therapeutic procedures that may be unique to our facility. They have also enabled us to begin to measure the results of our efforts in relationship to the functional achievements of those we serve.

Our objective in producing these manuals for dissemination outside the Institute is to share the results of our efforts in a format that will be useful to other practicing clinicians. In recognition of the fact that every patient presents a unique neurological, psychosocial, and motivational picture, our standards are not meant to be prescriptive. Rather, they have been written in a way that will enhance the clinical problem solving and judgment that is the foundation of professional practice. It is our hope that occupational therapy students and clinicians will use these manuals as resources to supplement their own treatment planning processes.

Sharon Intagliata, MS, MPA, OTR/L
Director of Occupational Therapy
The Rehabilitation Institute of Chicago

Preface

This guide offers a comprehensive description of occupational therapy for the spinal cord injury (SCI) patient at the Rehabilitation Institute of Chicago (RIC). As such, it is intended to be a guide to treatment for occupational therapy students and new therapists as well as a contribution to the documented literature on SCI to share with more experienced therapists. It does not attempt to include all possible treatment techniques that may be used by the occupational therapist with the SCI patient, but those techniques commonly used with positive outcomes by therapists at RIC. Nor does it include units on functions not performed by occupational therapists at RIC, although therapists in other facilities may be responsible for these functions. Driver's training, for example, is provided through the Vocational Rehabilitation Department at RIC. Wheelchair prescription and transfer training are provided by physical therapists. It is hoped that occupational therapists in other facilities who are responsible for teaching these skills will utilize other volumes in the RIC series on SCI as references for these areas.

The units are organized according to functional skills and treatment interventions rather than level of SCI. Within each unit, reference is made to methods appropriate for various levels of injury. This organization was chosen because of individual variations in SCI persons. A person with a C6 lesion may utilize methods for feeding commonly used by persons with C5 or C7 injuries as well as methods used by others with a C6 lesion. It is believed that the therapist will benefit from considering the methods used by SCI patients at different functional levels to accomplish a task and choosing, with the patient, the most appropriate method for them rather than assuming that all patients with a C6 injury will perform tasks in the same way. This is a performance-oriented, rather than dysfunction-oriented, approach that aids in problem solving when the most probable method is not successful.

Frequent reference is made to the need for coordinating efforts with other professionals in the treatment process and the necessity for patient and family participation in goal setting and treatment planning to achieve optimal outcomes. The concept of team, patient, and family collaboration is as important as specific methods in achieving successful outcomes.

Judy P. Hill, OTR/L
Clinical Supervisor,
Occupational Therapy

Acknowledgments

The preparation of this guide was a departmental rather than an individual project. Many people, in addition to the editor and unit authors, contributed to compiling the information and preparing it for publication. Katy Allen, former director of occupational therapy education at RIC; Kathy Okkema, clinical education specialist in the RIC Occupational Therapy Department; Shari Intagliata, director of occupational therapy at RIC; Dr. Gary Yarkony, Director of Rehabilitation, Midwest Regional Spinal Cord Center; Ruth Ann Watkins, vice president of allied health services at RIC; Pam Buckley, head nurse for spinal cord injury at RIC; and Craig Heckathorne of the Northwestern University Rehabilitation Engineering Program, all offered valuable and constructive suggestions in their editing of the drafts of the manuscript. Many supervisors and senior staff therapists at RIC contributed to writing the standards of care for SCI that were the foundation for this guide. They include Chris Chapparo, Judy Ranka, Beverly Meyers, Mary Jo Pelland, Barbara Flemming, Ruth Gordon, Pam DiPasquale, Diane Berman, and Paula Dolph. Oscar Izquierdo of the RIC Biomedical Media Department contributed many hours and excellent suggestions for making the photographs enhance the text. Vicki Willard of the RIC Occupational Therapy Department and Jerry Schoendorf of RIC's Biomedical Media Department assisted with the illustrations. Leatrice Campbell of the RIC Word Processing Department expertly and efficiently typed the many drafts of the book. Lou Carpino, director of therapeutic recreation at RIC, reviewed and made helpful suggestions for the Leisure Skills unit. He also compiled the leisure resource list.

A special "thanks" goes to all the occupational therapy interns and staff members who have contributed to the treatment methods and equipment utilized for SCI patients at RIC. Carl Gulbrandsen, whose name is listed after some devices, is a retired engineer from Quaker Oats Company who has volunteered many hours of his time in designing and fabricating equipment for the RIC OT department.

Finally, I extend my gratitude to the persons with SCI who contributed their time for the photographs in this guide, who tried our treatment ideas and equipment, who gave us feedback about our treatment programs, and who offered so many ideas and solutions of their own. It is to them that this guide is dedicated.

Unit 1

Introduction

Karen Kovich, OTR/L

ABBREVIATIONS

ADL—Activities of daily living
A—Assisted
BFO—Balanced forearm orthosis
C—Cueing
C1–C8—Cervical spinal levels 1 to 8
D—Dependent
DIP—Distal interphalangeal joint
ECS—Environmental control system
ECU—Environmental control unit
F (F+)—Fair (fair plus)
G—Good
HO—Hand orthosis
I—Independent
I/E—Independent with equipment
I/E/S—Independent with equipment and setup
I/O—Independent with orthosis
IP—Interphalangeal joint
L1–L5—Lumbar spinal levels 1 to 5
LE—Lower extremity
LSEO—Linear shoulder-elbow orthosis
MMT—Manual muscle test
MP—Metacarpophalangeal joint
N—Normal
OT—Occupational therapy
P (P−)—Poor (poor minus)
PIP—Proximal interphalangeal joint
PNF—Proprioceptive neuromuscular facilitation
PT—Physical therapy
RE—Rehabilitation engineering
RIC—Rehabilitation Institute of Chicago
ROM—Range of motion
S2–S4—Sacral spinal levels 2 to 4
SCI—Spinal cord injury
SOMI—Sternal occipital mandibular immobilizer
T—Trace
T1–T12—Thoracic spinal levels 1 to 12
UE—Upper extremity
W/C—Wheelchair
WDFH—Wrist-driven flexor hinge
WHO—Wrist-hand orthosis

DEFINITIONS

Assisted—Physical assistance required for completion of activity.

Cues—Verbal cues and directions required to complete activity with or without equipment. This definition is not usually used as a goal but rather to describe current status during training.

Dependent—Patient requires complete physical performance of activity by care giver.

Direct selection—Method of input in which one selection indicates one item; for example, through typing on the computer keyboard.

Halo—A method of externally stabilizing the cervical spine through a body jacket with upright supports affixed to the skull.

Hardware—Refers to the computer and peripherals, including monitor, printer, disk drives, mouse, Koala pad, and cards inserted inside the computer. Does not include software or any cables attached to the cards inside the computer.

Independent—Activity can be completed without aid of equipment or physical assistance.

Independent with equipment—No physical assistance necessary for setup or completion of activity, including equipment application.

Independent with equipment and setup—No physical assistance necessary to complete activity. Physical setup of patient, equipment, and activity necessary.

Independent with orthosis—Patient utilizes orthosis for activity, without other equipment, setup, or physical assistance.

Keyboard emulator—Alternative input method providing transparent access to the computer, which permits use of standard software while bypassing the standard keyboard.

Latching—Refers to switch activation in which a device remains on when the switch is activated and released and goes off only when a switch is activated the second time.

Long sitting—Sitting with knees extended.

Momentary—Refers to switch activation in which a device is activated only when the switch is held on and turns off when the switch is released.

Paraplegia—Paralysis of the lower extremities due to injuries of the spinal cord.

Peripherals—Refers to equipment attached to the computer via interfaces, namely cables. Includes disk drives, monitor, printer, and Koala pad.

Quadriplegia—Paralysis of all four extremities due to injuries of the spinal cord.

Short sitting—Sitting with knees bent, as in a chair.

Software—Programs that tell the computer what to do, provided in the form of floppy disks, hard disks, and cassette tapes.

SOMI—A method of externally stabilizing the cervical spine through a body jacket with upright supports that limit flexion, extension, and rotation of the neck.

Tenodesis hand function—Active prehension and release through active extension and active or passive wrist flexion. The wrist movement mechanically applies force to the finger flexors and extensors.

USING THE GUIDE

This book was written to assist the therapist in developing expectations and treatment goals. Information presented is based on functional level, which includes the physical, social, and emotional variances among individuals as well as level of injury. These factors are not related to the injury level, but they profoundly affect functional achievement.

After some units, summary charts are included that begin with goal levels for each task. These goals outline expected levels of function in daily living skills. Indicators, which are listed in the second column, include the level of the lesion and are used in determining the appropriate goal to be set. Indicators are descriptors of patient performance and represent levels of function prerequisite to achieving the stated goal.

In determining the appropriate goal, the therapist should not feel limited to the indicators listed. Psychological status, related medical problems, and many other pertinent factors deserve individual consideration. Often these factors are of great importance in allowing a person to meet a goal.

Recommended intervention is also outlined in the summary charts. This information provides an outline of the equipment and setup that may be used to meet the desired goal, while the training process is described more completely in the text.

CONSIDERATIONS IN PROVIDING EQUIPMENT

Initially after spinal cord injury (SCI), patients are dependent in many of the daily living skills until they are shown how to perform familiar tasks in new ways. Equipment and adaptations are essential in accomplishing these tasks.

For most of the daily living skills addressed in this book, ways of accomplishing a task are outlined on the basis of the patient's functional level and equipment options. Some of the equipment is commercially available, while much has been designed over the years by staff, students, and patients at the Rehabilitation Institute of Chicago (RIC).

Equipment suggestions are not intended to be all-inclusive, and should not be interpreted as the best or only way to accomplish a task. They are meant to illustrate problem-solving skills to the therapist and to provide a working knowledge of options available to the patient.

Therapists should not assume sole responsibility for deciding equipment options. The patient's expectations, goals, and preferences, and those of their loved ones, must be considered. The primary function of the therapist is to present equipment options and discuss with the patient individual factors that may enhance or hinder his performance of a given task. Recommendations can then be made on the basis of mutual goals and expectations.

Involving the patient in the decision-making process is a vital step in rehabilitation that may be overlooked by therapists. Frequently, equipment is not used after discharge because the therapist has failed to take into account the patient's goals or motivation to perform a given task. This can prove costly to the patient and may misdirect therapy from tasks more meaningful or important to the patient.

Discussing options and deciding on equipment are only the beginning of rehabilitation. A therapist must also facilitate the patient's development of insight and problem-solving skills so that the decision-making process can continue throughout his lifetime.

CLINICAL PRESENTATION OF SPINAL CORD INJURY

Spinal cord injury is one of the major injuries treated in rehabilitation centers throughout the country. More than 10,000 SCIs result in quadriplegia or paraplegia each year in the United States alone. Seventy percent of these spinal injuries are the result of automobile or sports-related accidents.

Fracture dislocation is the most common injury to the cervical spine, with dislocation usually occurring at the C5 to C6 level. Anterior dislocation occurs most frequently, resulting from hyperflexion of the neck, often in diving or automobile accidents. The vertebrae may be fractured and dislocated, with articulating surfaces damaged at the level of the lesion. Compression fractures, gunshot or stab wounds, vascular occlusions, and compression due to internal disease processes may also result in SCI. Compression fractures occur from vertical stress on the spinal column, with the most common site at C5 to C6. The vertebrae are compressed and decreased in height, with portions narrowing the spinal canal. Gunshot or stab wounds damage the cord by direct penetration or through laceration of the cord by bone fragments, resulting in vascular damage. Spinal cord function can also be disrupted by hemorrhage, aneurysm or arteriovenous (AV) malformations in vessels supplying blood to the spinal cord, or the blockage of these vessels by thrombi or emboli.

Intrinsic or extrinsic compression of the cord due to tumors, osteoarthritis, spondylosis, arachnoiditis, or syringomyelia may also cause permanent damage to the spinal cord.

Incomplete Lesions of the Spinal Cord

Traumatic injury may result in complete or incomplete lesions of the spinal cord. A complete lesion is defined as loss of all motor and sensory function. With incomplete lesions, any combination of neurologic function may be retained. These injuries most often fall into one of several categories.

Brown-Séquard's syndrome occurs when a hemisection of the cord results in ipsilateral paralysis and loss of postural sense, with contralateral loss of pain and thermal sense. Clinically, the extremities with motor function intact have marked deficits in sensation and those with the best sensation have less motor function.

Anterior cord syndrome is caused by damage to the anterior aspect of the cord. It results in paralysis and loss of pain and temperature sense below the level of the lesion, with preservation of touch, proprioception, and vibration.

Central cord syndrome occurs after injury to the centrally located structures in the cervical cord. This clinically results in greater motor deficits in the upper extremities (UEs) than in the lower extremities (LEs).

Lesions of the conus are frequent and result from damage of the twelfth thoracic and three upper lumbar vertebrae. Lesions of the cauda equina are often incomplete, with the most common clinical picture being a loss of both sensory and motor function. The nerve roots have potential for regrowth if they are not physically divided.

Paralysis

The loss of voluntary function of the skeletal muscles is one of the primary signs of SCI. The designation of the level of an SCI is determined by the most caudal normally functioning myotome segment. In complete injuries, all control of muscles innervated by nerve roots below the level of lesion is lost. In incomplete injuries, muscle function depends on which spinal fibers remain intact.

Initially after injury there is a period of spinal shock that may last from 1 day to 6 or 8 weeks. Spinal shock refers to a state of diminished excitability of the spinal cord secondary to sudden withdrawal of a predominantly excitatory influence from supraspinal centers. During this period, muscles are in a state of flaccid paralysis. As spinal shock subsides, muscle function and reflex activity begin to reappear.

Sensation

Spinal cord injury results in loss of sensation according to dermatomal distribution. In complete lesions of the spinal cord, all modalities of sensation are absent below the level of injury. With incomplete injuries, sensation may be intact, impaired, or absent in all or some of the modalities.

Altered Body Functions

Alteration in autonomic function, including control of bowel and bladder, respiration, temperature, and sexual function, occurs in both complete and incomplete spinal injuries. During the period of spinal shock the bladder is flaccid, and catheterization is necessary. As shock subsides, reflex activity may return in the bladder. Urologic tests are used to determine the best form of bladder management for each patient. Bowel control is absent because of loss of voluntary control of the sphincters. Bowel function can be controlled through the establishment of a regular bowel program (unit 11). Respiration and vital capacity may be reduced because of paralysis of the diaphragm and intercostal and abdominal muscles. Loss of temperature control occurs below the level of the lesion. The autonomic mechanisms of vasoconstriction to conserve heat and vasodilation to lower body heat no longer operate. Consequently, the patient's body tends to assume the temperature of the outside environment.

Remaining reproductive function is determined primarily by the level and completeness of the lesion. The ability to achieve an erection or ejaculate may be affected in the male. Ovulation and the ability to become pregnant are usually not altered in the female; however, delivery may require special precautions. Regardless of reproductive function, individuals with SCI can and do engage in fulfilling sexual and intimate relationships.

Abnormal Tone

As stated earlier, after injury flaccid paralysis occurs for a variable time period, often up to 8 weeks. There is a gradual increase in spasticity, primarily in the flexor groups, during the first 6 months after injury. This is followed by an increase in extensor spasticity 6 to 12 months after onset, at which time a leveling off of abnormal tone usually occurs.

Related Disorders

Pressure Sores

The loss of blood supply to an area due to prolonged pressure over a bony prominence is the most common cause of a decubitus ulcer. Muscles that normally pad these areas may be atrophied, and the patient may be unaware of the problem because of sensory loss. Other factors contributing to decubitus ulcers are moisture leading to skin maceration and cold leading to vasoconstriction in the affected area. Other causes are abrasions or burns that initially go unnoticed because of sensory loss.

Symptoms include a reddened or darkly discolored area that does not blanch on pressure, blisters, or an actual opening in the skin. The therapist should watch for pressure areas that may arise from new orthoses or adaptive equipment and should instruct the patient and family on safety when using hot or cold objects. The therapist should also assist patients in pressure relief, or provide reminders if they are able to do so independently.

Autonomic Dysreflexia

Autonomic dysreflexia, or hyperreflexia, may occur in lesions above T6. A dangerous increase in blood pressure can be caused by bladder distension from inadequate urinary drainage, bowel distension from impaction or suppository insertion, or skin irritation secondary to tight clothing, leg bag straps, or pressure sores. The increase in blood pressure may rapidly lead to a cerebrovascular accident or death if not relieved.

Common symptoms of autonomic dysreflexia include sudden onset of a pounding headache, sweating, nausea, and bradycardia. If symptoms occur when the patient is prone or supine, elevation to a sitting position is recommended. Having the patient recline will result in a further increase in blood pressure. The urinary drainage system should be checked, as emptying a full leg bag or straightening kinked tubing may relieve symptoms. The patient will need catheterization or immediate medical attention if the symptoms cannot be quickly relieved through these methods.

Orthostatic Hypotension

Orthostatic hypotension is caused by a lack of tone in abdominal and LE musculature, leading to pooling of blood in these areas with a decrease in blood pressure. This usually occurs in the sitting position, with symptoms being dizziness or loss of consciousness, nausea, and pallor. If these symptoms occur, the wheelchair (W/C) is locked and the patient tilted back until the symptoms subside. Bringing the patient slowly into the upright position can assist in avoiding orthostatic hypotension, as can elevating the feet. Abdominal binders, corsets, or elastic hose may be used to prevent orthostatic hypotension while building sitting tolerance.

Respiratory Deficiency

Patients with lesions in the cervical or thoracic area will have diminished respiratory function because of the lack of full innervation of the diaphragm and the abdominal and intercostal muscles. Patients with respiratory deficiency may display low energy and tolerance for activity, shallow coughing, and congestion. Familiarity with the procedures for a manual assistive cough and suctioning is important.

Respiratory Dependency

Patients with lesions above C4 require assistance in respiration from external sources secondary to lack of innervation of the diaphragm and respiratory accessory musculature. These patients are dependent on a respirator or phrenic nerve stimulator, and usually require the placement of a tracheostomy tube. Because the tube is placed below the vocal cords, vocalization is not possible unless a fenestrated tracheostomy tube, which can be temporarily plugged with the cuff deflated, is used.

Heterotopic Ossification

Heterotopic ossification, also called ectopic bone, is an abnormal calcification around a joint that can occur in SCI patients. It is most frequently found in the hip joint, but is occasionally found in the proximal joints of the UEs.

Symptoms of heterotopic ossification include limitations in range of motion (ROM), redness, pain, and swelling around a joint. Often the bony formation can be palpated around the joint. Symptoms should be reported to the physician and treatment continued according to prescription. Therapists may be involved in bed and W/C positioning as well as passive ROM in order to minimize loss of ROM.

Posttraumatic Syringomyelia

The etiology of cysts that form on the spine is unknown. Clinically the patient may present with decreasing strength or sensation in areas innervated at or above the original level of injury. Should these symptoms occur, the physician should be notified.

Edema

Factors that contribute to edema are dependent positioning of the extremities, resulting in uneven fluid distribution, and lack of muscle tone to assist in venous return. Orthoses, clothing, and equipment straps can contribute to edema. An edematous extremity should be elevated to allow gravity to assist with venous return. Mobilizing the extremity (e.g., alternating flexed and extended positioning of fingers) may facilitate venous return. This can be accomplished through the use of flexion loops on splints or flexion gloves.

Prognosis

Prognosis for recovery from SCI depends on whether the lesion is complete or incomplete. If no sensation or motor function is present below the level of the lesion, the injury is considered complete. If the lesion is incomplete, sensation and motor function are present below the level of the lesion. A widely used indicator of incomplete lesions is sacral sparing, the presence of perianal sensation, voluntary toe flexion, and sphincter control, giving evidence of transmission of impulses across the injured area.

Prognosis for recovery varies. As long as function continues to reappear and grow stronger, the chance for additional recovery is good. Once a plateau is reached, prognosis for further recovery is guarded.

Once presented with the facts about the severity and type of SCI, the therapist has only a small portion of the information needed to effectively treat the patient. Knowledge of innervated musculature and sensation alone provides only broad indicators of the patient's potential for recovery.

An individual's motivation, determination, socioeconomic background, education, family support, acceptance of disability, and problem-solving ability prove to be invaluable assets or limiting factors in determining the outcome of rehabilitation. A therapist must carefully assess the patient's status in each of these areas before determining a course of treatment.

Unit 2

Evaluation

Annette Russell Farmer, OTR/L

The evaluation process begins the day the patient is admitted and continues throughout the hospitalization. During each treatment session the occupational therapist is informally assessing progress toward the functional goals. Patient and family involvement is encouraged in determining these goals.

The initial evaluation consists of gathering data from the medical record, which includes the patient's age, sex, date of injury, level of injury, medical history, physical findings, psychosocial status, cognitive status, family status and involvement, education, vocation, hobbies, medications, and living accommodations. Observations of the patient's interactions with family, staff, and other patients; interviews with the patient and family; and specific evaluation procedures are all components of the initial evaluation process.

The evaluation process continues throughout the hospitalization. Monitoring strength, ROM, sensation, and activities of daily living (ADL) will allow the occupational therapist to upgrade or downgrade the patient's goals appropriately.

A complete reevaluation is performed at the time of discharge. Psychosocial status and the patient's readiness to return to community living are also evaluated at this time. This reevaluation not only accurately records the patient's status at discharge but can be compared to the status at admission to give patient, family, and staff a measure of their accomplishment.

If initial goals or subsequent goals have not been met, plans for a home program or follow-up therapy can be made to continue working on these goals.

The occupation therapy (OT) evaluation comprises the following categories:

1. psychosocial
   - status that may prevent or assist the patient from participating in goal setting
   - understanding of condition
   - level of motivation
   - ability to solve problems
   - ability to verbally direct others to meet needs
   - family involvement
   - discharge plans
2. sensation
   - protective
   - discriminative
3. head and neck ROM
4. UE ROM
5. head and UE motor control
   - muscle tone
   - strength

6. wrist and hand function

   - grasp/release and pinch measurements
   - object manipulation abilities
   - standardized coordination tests

7. trunk control
8. deformity control

   - positioning
   - splinting
   - inhibitory or serial casting

9. ADL

   - feeding
   - simple hygiene
   - general hygiene
   - bowel and bladder care
   - dressing
   - communication
   - mobility
   - home management
   - home accessibility
   - community skills
   - leisure pursuits

PSYCHOSOCIAL

Psychosocial skills are evaluated to determine the patient's ability to participate in treatment and to cope with the disability and the effects it may have on future plans. Interviews with the patient, the patient's family, and significant others are conducted to identify previous life-styles and roles. Observations of the patient's motivation, coping mechanisms, problem-solving skills, ability and willingness to verbally direct others, and family involvement contribute to the information base for realistic goal setting.

SENSATION

Sensation in the UEs is evaluated to determine areas of sensory impairment as it might affect hand function and for prevention of secondary trauma. Two types of sensation are routinely assessed: protective responses and discriminative responses. Protective responses are assessed through sharp/dull or temperature discrimination. Sharp/dull assessment is performed with a safety pin. The patient's vision is blocked and directions are given for the patient to identify the sharp or dull side of the pin as light to moderate pressure is applied. Temperature discrimination is assessed with identical metal containers, one filled with warm and the other with cold water. Vision is blocked and the patient is asked to identify the containers as hot or cold as each is applied to the UE with moderate pressure and then removed.

Two-point discrimination and proprioception (position sense) are evaluated to determine discriminative abilities. Two-point discrimination is evaluated in the fingertips with an aesthesiometer started at 3 mm. The points are slowly moved apart until the patient can accurately discriminate between one and two points. Vision is blocked during the procedure. If two-point discrimination is impaired or absent or if the injury is incomplete, proprioception is assessed in the shoulder, elbow, wrist, and hand. Vision is blocked and the tester maintains manual contact on the bony prominences of the UE to minimize sensory input. The patient is asked to position the opposite extremity in the same position as the one the tester is holding. If the patient is unable to accurately place the extremity in the correct position, he is then asked to indicate the direction of movement, for example up, down, in, or out at the shoulder or bending or straightening the elbow.

HEAD AND NECK ROM

Head and neck ROM is evaluated to determine head and neck limitations that might interfere with sitting, the use of equipment such as the W/C and the mouthstick, and performance of self-care skills. Rotation, lateral flexion, protraction, and retraction are measured. Evaluation of head and neck ROM is postponed if the patient is wearing a cervical spine orthosis (SOMI or halo).

UPPER EXTREMITY ROM

Upper extremity ROM is evaluated to determine limitations that may influence equipment selection or the patient's ability to perform self-care skills. ROM measurement is performed according to the guidelines in Trombly & Scott's *Occupational Therapy for Physical Dysfunction* (Appendix C).

HEAD AND UE MOTOR CONTROL

When evaluating head and UE motor control, two areas are assessed. Muscle tone is evaluated to identify the presence of spasticity or flaccidity in individual muscles that may render manual muscle testing unreliable. Muscle tone in the UE is evaluated by performing a quick stretch in flexion or extension at each joint and determining minimal, moderate, or maximum tone by the amount of resistance and range in which it is elicited. Manual muscle testing is performed to identify areas of muscle weakness and imbalance. Standard manual muscle-testing procedures are used according to the methods described in Kendall *et al* and Rancho Los Amigos (Appendix C). This information is used to determine the treatment emphasis needed to maximize function or to suggest the need for assistive or adaptive equipment.

WRIST AND HAND FUNCTION

An evaluation of wrist and hand function determines the degree to which the patient will be able to hold and manipulate objects in daily tasks. This information can also be utilized to suggest the need for equipment (e.g., orthoses, utensil cuff, and typing stick) to substitute for limited skills. Grasp/release and pinch measurements indicate functional abilities and are used as an adjunct to manual muscle testing to provide objective measurement for use in charting progress and comparison to standardized norms. The test procedures and norms for grasp/release and pinch measurements used were developed by the Occupational Therapy Department at the University of Wisconsin, Milwaukee, by Mathiowetz (Appendix C).

Object manipulation abilities determine the patient's ability to perform functional skills. Standardized tests of coordination such as the 9-Hole Peg Test, Minnesota Rate of Manipulation, Jebson Taylor Hand Function Test, Purdue Peg Board, and Crawford Manual Dexterity Test as well as clinical observations of the patient's actual activity performance may be utilized.

TRUNK CONTROL

Clinical observations and performance evaluations are used to assess trunk control. The amount of trunk stability and mobility is directly correlated with the patient's ability to perform functional tasks. Balance or trunk control is evaluated in the W/C or on a bed or mat. When evaluating trunk control in the W/C, the occupational therapist assesses the patient's ability to reposition in the W/C and to use UEs to maintain balance during an activity. The patient is evaluated for his ability to maintain a position using both UEs for support, using one UE for support while engaging the other in activity, or to use both UEs in a task while maintaining balance. These abilities are also assessed in supported and unsupported long and short sitting. Patients with injuries at T4 and below may be assessed in kneeling and standing. The ability to change positions—mobility—is also assessed to determine whether the patient needs both UEs, one, or neither to support himself and maintain control during movement.

DEFORMITY CONTROL

Analysis of the evaluations of sensation, UE ROM, head and UE motor control, and wrist and hand function indicates the potential for deformity and need for intervention. Positioning, orthotic management, or casting may be indicated.

ACTIVITIES OF DAILY LIVING

Activities of daily living are evaluated to establish the patient's ability to perform functional tasks. Adapted techniques or equipment may be indicated initially. As skills improve it may be necessary for the occupational therapist to upgrade techniques or equipment. Supplemental evaluations may be required, depending on the findings from the initial evaluation.

1. Environmental control unit (ECU) evaluation. This evaluation is performed when physical limitations require compensation to control the environment (unit 17).
2. Sensory integration evaluation. When concomitant or pre-SCI brain damage is suspected, sensory integrative functioning is evaluated to determine the patient's ability to process tactile, motor, and visual information. These skills affect not only one's understanding of the environment but also the ability to interact appropriately with it.
3. Prevocational assessment. Prevocational assessment is performed in conjunction with a voca-

tional rehabilitation counselor, depending on the patient's potential for employment or continuing education. Areas of assessment include communication skills, object manipulation skills, office equipment use, self-care needs on the job, and work-related behaviors. Information about the patient's previous vocational pursuits is gathered through interview.

4. Safety assessment. This assessment is performed during ADL in the home and community to determine the patient's safety awareness.
5. Support system training assessment. Observations of and direct interaction with the patient, family, and friends are used to gather information about the social systems to which the patient will return. This assessment is conducted throughout the hospitalization to determine the outside support the patient is receiving. It includes observations of the frequency of visits and the amount of involvement others have in the patient's care. It includes the family's ability to learn patient care tasks, such as passive ROM or verbal cueing in ADL.

SUMMARY

Evaluations are performed at admission, during hospitalization, and at discharge. Complete evaluation procedures are performed at admission and discharge. Reevaluation in goal areas occurs during the hospitalization through observation of functional performance or specific evaluation procedures such as manual muscle testing or sensory testing. A patient with an incomplete injury or a rapidly changing muscle picture may require more frequent assessment in order to upgrade the treatment plan appropriately and to objectively chart progress.

Before the patient's discharge from RIC, the team establishes a recheck date to monitor and reevaluate the patient's status. The therapist may choose to perform a complete reevaluation during the recheck; however, very often this is not necessary. A screening evaluation is then performed around the level of lesion (two levels above and two levels below) to determine ascending or descending signs in changes in muscle strength or sensation. Patient and family interviews are utilized to monitor ADL status. Upgrading of home programs, determining the need for further follow-up therapy as an out-patient or in the home setting, and assisting the patient and family in problem areas may occur at this time.

The initial evaluation form included in this chapter has been completed as it would be for a typical C5 to C6 quadriplegic male (Exhibit 2–1). The diagnosis, onset, age, medical history and status, reason for referral, and date of referral are filled out with information taken from the medical record and the physician's orders.

The assessment area includes a brief summary of evaluation findings. For a discharge evaluation, Assessment is lined out instead of Discharge Summary and a statement is made that reflects the patient's status at discharge and summarizes progress during the hospitalization.

Under Goals, a summary of the long-term functional goals for the current hospitalization is made. At discharge, achievement of initial goals is stated and remaining goals are indicated. The areas checked under General Plan indicate the treatments that will be used to achieve the goals. On the discharge evaluation form, General Plan is lined out and the treatments that will be needed after discharge are checked. The number of group and individual treatments planned per week is indicated. SCI patients at RIC are usually seen for six to twelve 1-hour sessions of OT per week.

The types of equipment that it is projected will be needed to accomplish the individual's goals are checked. For the discharge evaluation, Anticipated Equipment Needs is lined out and the equipment that was actually provided is checked.

Sections II through VI on the evaluation form are filled out utilizing the goal statements for each from the goals listed in unit 3. For example, under Functional Skills, wrist and hand function, the wrist and hand function goal 1 from unit 3 (no wrist or hand function present) is used under Observations to describe the current status along with statements referring to indicators for setting the goal. For this patient, those statements include zero wrist extensor strength on the left and poor minus wrist extensor strength on the right. Wrist and hand function goal 3 (tenodesis hand function) is set for the right UE and goal 1 (no wrist hand function expected) is set for the left. Information about other indicators used to set these goals is listed in other sections of the evaluation form. There is no spasticity in wrist and hand musculature documented in the Manual Muscle Examination section. Limited assisted arm

Exhibit 2–1 Initial Evaluation Form

REHABILITATION INSTITUTE OF CHICAGO

OCCUPATIONAL THERAPY DEPARTMENT

SPINAL CORD INJURY EVALUATION

Patient Name ______

RIC Number XXXXX

Physician ______

Date 5/16/86

[X] Inpatient [ ] Outpatient

[X] Initial [ ] Re-evaluation and Plan [ ] Discharge Evaluation and Plan

Period Covered From 5/13/86 to 5/16/86

I. MEDICAL

Diagnosis C_{5-6} Quadriplegia Onset 4/2/86 Age 39

Medical History and Status Patient was reported in good health until a motor vehicle accident 4/2/86; currently spine stable in SOMI brace.

Reason for Referral Evaluate and treat UE strength, ROM, ADL. Provide orthoses. Consider ECU evaluation

Date of Referral 5/13/86

Assessment/~~Discharge Summary~~: Patient displays C_5 function bilaterally, P-radial wrist extensors right only. ROM limited and painful left shoulder. Patient attempted feeding one time in acute hospital with deltoid assist sling and wrist brace on right. He is dependent in all ADL.

Goals: Patient to be I to I/E in most feeding, simple hygiene, communication and meaningful leisure pursuits, will require assistance with dressing, bathing, bowel and bladder care.

General Plan/~~Follow up~~

[X] Strength and Coordination
[X] Self-Care
[X] Orthotics
[X] Functional Mobility
[ ] Homemaking
[X] Community Living Skills

Treatment: 12 times per week [X] Individual [X] Group

Anticipated Equipment Needs/~~Equipment Provided~~

[X] Environmental Control Unit
[ ] Balanced Forearm Orthosis(es)
[X] Definitive Orthosis(es)
[X] Temporary Orthosis(es)
[X] Communication Equipment
[X] Self-Care
[ ] Positioning
[ ] Homemaking
[ ] Mouthstick

RIC # 2-013 203-10

MEDICAL RECORDS

Exhibit 2–1 continued

REHABILITATION INSTITUTE OF CHICAGO
OCCUPATIONAL THERAPY DEPARTMENT

SPINAL CORD INJURY EVALUATION

II. COGNITIVE COMMUNICATIVE - SENSATION

Pain/Temperature

N - Normal
I - Impaired
A - Absent

	LEFT	RIGHT	
C_4	N	N	C_4
C_5	N	N	C_5
C_6	I	I	C_6
C_7	A	A	C_7
C_8	A	A	C_8
T_1	A	A	T_1

Two Point Discrimination In Fingertips

Normal: .3-.6 cm.
Functional: .6-1.2 cm.
Absent: 1.2... cm.

	LEFT	RIGHT	
C_6	A	F	C_6
C_7	A	A	C_7
C_8	A	A	C_8

Observations

Proprioception normal shoulder and elbow bilaterally, impaired wrists, absent fingers.

Goal/~~Prognosis~~: Functional UE sensation bilaterally. Visual compensation for residual deficit to prevent skin compromise.

Plan: Sensory simulation through structured functional activities. Instruct in areas of sensory deficits and protective compensatory techniques.

III. PSYCHOSOCIAL

Observations: Patient displays limited coping skills and participates well in individual treatment. He is cooperative and motivated. Articulates general goals related to previous roles but becomes tearful when discussing specifics. Does not interact with other patients. Very dependent and demanding on wife. Patient states his goals are to return home and do what he can for himself

Goal/~~Prognosis~~: Patient to demonstrate coping for functioning in a controlled environment and behaviors supporting independent participation in treatment.

Plan: Involve patient and wife in specific goal setting. Encourage patient to talk with other SCI patients, Quad group involvement.

IV. FUNCTIONAL SKILLS (See manual Muscle Testing, Range of Motion, and Activities of Daily Living Forms for Specifics)

Upper Extremity Strength

Observations: C_5 musculature P-F on the left; F on the right, Radial wrist extensor P-right. No other wrist or hand musculature palpable. Endurance poor (5-6 muscle contractions) bilaterally.

Goal/~~Prognosis~~: C_5 musculature in G-N range bilaterally. F+ radial wrist extension right.

Plan: UE and wrist strengthening through exercise and bilateral functional activities with BFO's with elevating proximal arms. RIC splint with wrist extension assist for the right.

Range of Motion

Head and neck ROM not tested because of SOMI.

Observations: UE ROM within normal limits except shoulders with minimal limitations in flexion and abduction on the right; moderate limitations and pain with flexion, abduction and rotation left.

Goal/~~Prognosis~~: Normal UE ROM. Prevent deformity.

Plan: Daily passive and active assisted ROM. Mobilize left scapula during ROM. Orthotic intervention.

THERAPIST ______________

Exhibit 2–1 continued

REHABILITATION INSTITUTE OF CHICAGO
OCCUPATIONAL THERAPY DEPARTMENT
SPINAL CORD INJURY EVALUATION

PATIENT NAME: ----------------
RIC #: XXXXX
PHYSICIAN: ----------------
DATE: 5/16/86

Arm Placement

Observations: Assisted limited arm placement at present. Without assistive device patient can achieve partial hand to mouth pattern left, full hand to mouth pattern right but fatigues after 3-5 repetitions.

Goal/~~Prognosis~~: Unassisted limited arm placement bilaterally with endurance for repeating hand to mouth and table top 20-30 times in succession.

Plan: UE strengthening through functional activities with BFO with elevating proximal arm and exercise.

Wrist/Hand Function

Observations: No wrist hand function available at present. P-radial wrist extensor right.

Goal/~~Prognosis~~: Tenodesis hand function right. No hand function expected left.

Plan: Wrist strengthening right. Assistive exercise and RIC splint with wrist extension assist to train tenodesis.

Head, Neck, and Trunk Control

Observations: Head and neck control not tested because of SOMI. No trunk control currently. Patient requires external support while using one or both UE's in tasks.

Goal/~~Prognosis~~: Limited trunk stability

Plan: Lateral trunk supports initially. Instruct patient in substitutions for trunk musculature through scapular, UE, and head (when SOMI removed) movements.

Activities of Daily Living

Observations: Patient dependent in most ADL. Beginning training in self feeding using BFO's, temporary WHO's.

Goal/~~Prognosis~~: I-I/E most feeding, basic hygiene, communication, leisure, and UE dressing. A-D bathing, bowel and bladder care, LE dressing, community skills, and home management.

Plan: Feeding group. AM care program, provide equipment. Home assessment, Quad Group and Community Re-entry Group.

V. VOCATIONAL/EDUCATIONAL

Observations: Patient works as foreman in a construction firm. Mostly office based but some construction site work. Has worked for present company since age 20. Completed high school. Patient drove to work.

Goal/~~Prognosis~~: Patient able to describe 2 realistic vocational options by discharge.

Plan: Consult with vocational rehab. counselor. Discuss vocation applicable skills with patient.

VI. COMMUNITY PLANNING

Observations: Patient plans to return to home living with wife. House has 2 steps to enter. Patient not sure if wheelchair will fit through doorways inside.

Goal/~~Prognosis~~: Entrance and limited indoor areas to be accessable to patient by discharge.

Plan: Home assessment form. Consider need for home visit. Home pass 4-6 weeks. Community Re-entry Group for developing problem solving skills. Provide patient/wife with home accessability resources.

MEDICAL RECORDS

Exhibit 2–1 continued

REHABILITATION INSTITUTE OF CHICAGO
OCCUPATIONAL THERAPY DEPARTMENT
ACTIVITIES OF DAILY LIVING EVALUATION

SPINAL CORD INJURY EVALUATION

O (circle) DISCHARGE STATUS; ✓ - INITIAL STATUS; X - GOAL: (D) Dependent; (A) Physical assistance required; (C) Verbal cues required; (IS/E) Independent after set up/Equipment (optional); (IE) Independent with equipment; (IO) Independent with orthoses; (I) Independent. * indicates activity performed at standing/ambulating level. (NA) Not applicable.

FEEDING:	D	A	C	IS/E	IE	IO	I
drink/straw				√			X
drink/cup	√X						
finger feed	√						X
utensil feed		√			X		
cut food	√				X		

SIMPLE HYGIENE:	D	A	C	IS/E	IE	IO	I
wash face	√						X
brush teeth	√				X		
shave	√				X		
make up	NA						
dry hair	NA						
donn glasses	NA						
floss teeth	√				X		
comb hair	√				X		
wash hands	√						X
clean glasses	NA						
deodorant	√				X		
hard contacts	√	X					
ear care	NA						
denture care	NA						
nail care	√X						
set hair	NA						
soft contacts	NA						

GENERAL HYGIENE:	D	A	C	IS/E	IE	IO	I
bathing UEs	√				X		
bathing body	√	X					
bathing LEs	√	X					
wash hair	√				X		
feminine	NA						

BOWEL & BLADDER:	D	A	C	IS/E	IE	IO	I
empty leg bag	√				X		
change leg bag	√X						
catheterize	√X						
irrigation	√X						
digital stim	√X						
suppository	√X						
cleansing	√X						
toileting	NA						

DRESSING:	D	A	C	IS/E	IE	IO	I
UE on	√						X
UE off	√						X
LE on	√X						
LE off	√X						
shoes on	√X						
shoes off	√X						
fasteners on	√				X		
fasteners off	√				X		
accessories on (watch)	√				X		
accessories off	√				X		
socks on	√X						
socks off	√X						

COMMUNICATION:	D	A	C	IS/E	IE	IO	I
write	√				X		
type	√				X		
phone	√				X		
turn page	√						X
tape recorder	√				X		
mail	√				X		

MOBILITY:	D	A	C	IS/E	IE	IO	I
bed cont.	√				X		
turn in bed	√	X					
drive	√X						
ambulation	NA						
wheelchair (electric)	√						X

COMMUNITY SKILLS:	D	A	C	IS/E	IE	IO	I
money	√				X		
shopping	NA						
mobility	√						X

LEISURE:	D	A	C	IS/E	IE	IO	I
table games	√				X		
crafts	NA						
TV	√				X		
radio	√				X		
tape recorder	√				X		
phono	√				X		
sports (spectator)	√						X
gardening	NA						
smoking	NA						

HOME MANAGEMENT:	D	A	C	IS/E	IE	IO	I
food prep-hot	√			X			
food prep-cold	√			X			
set table	√			X			
daily cleanup	√	X					
cleaning	NA						
laundry	NA						
iron	NA						
food shop	√	X					
child care	NA						
seasonal clean	NA						

HOME ACCESSABILITY:	D	A	C	IS/E	IE	IO	I
entrance (2 steps)	√				X		
exit	√				X		
temp. regul.	√						X
utilities	√						X

Time Considerations for Activity Performance: None at present.

Equipment Used: BFO, WHO with utensil slot, bent utensils, long straw, wheelchair cup holder.
See Equipment Checklist Attached ☐.

THERAPIST ______________________

Exhibit 2–1 continued

REHABILITATION INSTITUTE OF CHICAGO
OCCUPATIONAL THERAPY DEPARTMENT
MANUAL MUSCLE EXAMINATION OF THE UPPER EXTREMITIES

PATIENT NAME: ---------------------
RIC #: XXXXX
PHYSICIAN: ---------------------
DATE: 5/16/86

SPINAL CORD INJURY EVALUATION

5/14/86 ← Left	SHOULDER GIRDLE		Right → 5/14/86
P	ANTERIOR DELTOID	C5-6	F
P	MIDDLE DELTOID	C5-6	F+
P	POSTERIOR DELTOID	C5-6	F
NT	UPPER TRAPEZIUS	C2-4	NT
NT	MIDDLE TRAPEZIUS	C2-5	NT
NT	LOWER TRAPEZIUS	C2-4	NT
0	SERRATUS ANTERIOR	C6-7	P
NT	RHOMBOIDS	C5-6	NT
0	PECTORALIS MAJOR - STERNAL	C7-T1	0
P–	PECTORALIS MAJOR - CLAVICULAR	C5-7	F
0	LATISSIMUS DORSI	C7-8	0
P–	INTERNAL ROTATORS	C5-T1	P
P	EXTERNAL ROTATORS	C5-6	F
	ELBOW		
F	BICEPS	C5-6	G
F	BRACHIORADIALIS	C5-6	F+
0	TRICEPS	C7-8	0
F	SUPINATORS	C5-6	F+
0	PRONATORS	C6-7	T
	WRIST		
0	FLEXOR CARPI ULNARIS	C7-8	0
0	FLEXOR CARPI RADIALIS	C7-8	0
0	PALMARIS LONGUS	C7-8	0
0	EXTENSOR CARPI RADIALIS LONGUS	C6-7	P–
0	EXTENSOR CARPI RADIALIS BREVIS	C6-7	T
0	EXTENSOR CARPI ULNARIS	C7-8	0
	HAND		
0	1 FLEXOR DIGITORUM PROFUNDUS	C8-T1	0
	2		
	3		
	4		
	1 FLEXOR DIGITORUM SUPERFICIALIS	C8-T1	
	2		
	3		
	4		
	1 EXTENSOR DIGITORUM COMMUNIS	C7-8	
	2		
	3		
	4		
	1 LUMBRICALES	C8-T1	
	2		
	3		
	4		
	1 DORSAL INTEROSSEI	C8-T1	
	2		
	3		
	4		
	1 PALMAR INTEROSSEI	C8-T1	
	2		
	3		
	ABDUCTOR POLLICIS LONGUS	C7-8	
	ABDUCTOR POLLICIS BREVIS	C8-T1	
	ADDUCTOR POLLICIS	C8-T1	
	FLEXOR POLLICIS LONGUS	C8-T1	
	FLEXOR POLLICIS BREVIS	C8-T1	
	OPPONENS POLLICIS	C8-T1	
	EXTENSOR POLLICIS LONGUS	C7-8	
	EXTENSOR POLLICIS BREVIS	C7-8	

GRADE: N = normal; G = good; F = fair; P = poor; T = trace; 0 = zero

(S) indicates spasticity present

MEDICAL RECORDS

Exhibit 2–1 continued

REHABILITATION INSTITUTE OF CHICAGO
OCCUPATIONAL THERAPY DEPARTMENT

SPINAL CORD INJURY EVALUATION

PASSIVE JOINT RANGE MEASUREMENTS

LEFT								RIGHT		
			5/13/86	DATE			5/13/86			
			NT	PROTRACTION	0-4″	Neck	NT			
			↓	ROTATION	0-90		↓			
				FLEXION	0-35					
			0–100	FLEXION	0-180	Shoulder	0–140			
			0–40	EXTENSION	0-40		0–40			
			0–120	ABDUCTION	0-180		0–150			
			0–60	INT. ROTATION	0-80		0–80			
			0–45	INT. ROTATION	0-60		0–60			
			0–90	HORIZ. ABD.	0-		0–100			
			0–20	HORIZ. ADD.	0-		0–30			
			0–150	FLEXION	0-150	Elbow	0–150			
			0–80	SUPINATION	0-80		0–80			
			0–80	PRONATION	0-80		0–90			
			0–90	FLEXION	0-80	Wrist	0–85			
			0–75	EXTENSION	0-70		0–75			
			0–25	ULNAR DEV.	0-30		0–25			
			0–20	RADIAL DEV.	0-20		0–20			
			0–50	MP FLEXION	0-50	Thumb	0–50			
			0–90	IP FLEXION	0-80		0–75			
			0–70	ABDUCTION	0-70		0–70			
			0–90	MP FLEXION	0-90	Index F.	0–90			
			0–30	MP EXTENSION	0-45		0–30			
			0–90	PIP FLEXION	0-100		0–100			
			0–70	DIP FLEXION	0-80		0–80			
			0–90	MP FLEXION	0-90	Long. F.	0–90			
			0–30	MP EXTENSION	0-45		0–30			
			0–100	PIP FLEXION	0-100		0–100			
			0–90	DIP FLEXION	0-90		0–90			
			0–90	MP FLEXION	0-90	Ring F.	0–95			
			0–30	MP EXTENSION	0-45		0–30			
			0–100	PIP FLEXION	0-100		0–100			
			0–90	DIP FLEXION	0-90		0–90			
			0–90	MP FLEXION	0-9	Little	0–95			
			0–35	MP EXTENSION	0-45		0–30			
			0–100	PIP FLEXION	0-100		0–100			
			0–90	DIP FLEXION	0-90		0–90			

DOMINANCE: PREMORBID: right
PRESENT: right

PREHENSILE STRENGTH:

LEFT					RIGHT			
			NA	CYLINDRICAL GRASP	NA			
			NA	3-POINT PINCH	NA			
			NA	LATERAL PINCH	NA			
			5/13/86	DATE	5/13/86			

THERAPIST ______________________

Exhibit 2–2 Equipment Checklist

Rehabilitation Institute of Chicago
Occupational Therapy Department
Spinal Cord Injury

NAME: ______________________
RIC #: ______________________
THERAPIST: ______________________

Equipment Checklist

ORTHOTIC

_____ BFO
_____ WHO (long opp.)
_____ WHO (cable dr.)
_____ WHO (myoelectric)
_____ WHO (battery dr.)
_____ WHO (RIC tenodes.)
_____ WHO (wrist dr. FH)
_____ WHO (resting)
_____ WHO (cock-up)
_____ HO (short opp.)
_____ OTHER (   )

FEEDING

_____ Orthosis _____
_____ Utensil slot
_____ Utensil cuff
_____ Bent utensils
_____ Built-up utensils
_____ Finger ring utensils
_____ Swivel utensils
_____ Spork
_____ Kni-fork
_____ Quad quip knife
_____ Adapted knife
_____ Long straw
_____ Straw holder
_____ Plate guard
_____ Dycem
_____ Sandwich holder
_____ OTHER (   )

ORAL-FACIAL HYGIENE

_____ Orthosis _____
_____ Utensil slot
_____ Utensil cuff
_____ Electric toothbrush
_____ Built-up toothbrush
_____ Tooth-paste caps
_____ Wash mitt
_____ Long-handled comb/brush
_____ Built-up brush/comb
_____ Handled brush/comb
_____ Finger-ring brush
_____ Little octopus
_____ OTHER (   )

CATH./BOWEL MANAGEMENT

_____ Deluxe cath clamp
_____ Double loop clamp
_____ Finger ring clamp
_____ Elastic leg bag straps
_____ Adapted posey
_____ Sup-a-sert

SUPPORT/POSITIONING

_____ Lateral trunk supports
_____ Lap board

HOMEMAKING

_____ Long-handled dust pan
_____ Pail on wheels
_____ Long-handled feather duster
_____ Reacher
_____ Socket switch

OTHER EQUIPMENT

WHEELCHAIR PROPULSION

_____ Wheelchair gloves
_____ Orthosis
_____ T-bar hand cont.
_____ Built-up hand cont.
_____ Lap-board cont.

COMMUNICATION

_____ Orthosis _____
_____ Mouthstick
_____ Utensil slot
_____ Penholder on orthosis
_____ Utensil cuff
_____ Built-up pen
_____ Figure-eight penholder
_____ Elastic penholder
_____ Felt-tip pen
_____ Typing-stick
_____ Finger-ring typing stick
_____ Electric typewriter
_____ Keyguard
_____ Adapted tape recorder
_____ Touch tone phone
_____ Spar telephone arm
_____ Line interrupter
_____ Dialing stick
_____ Speaker phone
_____ Envir. Cont. Unit

DRESSING

_____ Orthosis _____
_____ Velcro closures
_____ Button hook
_____ Zipper pull/button hook
_____ Loops on pants
_____ Removable loops
_____ Dressing stick
_____ Reacher
_____ Loops on socks
_____ Sock donner
_____ Long-handled shoe horn
_____ Heel guard
_____ Wrap-a-lace
_____ Kno-bows
_____ Elastic laces

AVOCATION

_____ Orthosis _____
_____ Utensil slot
_____ Penholder on orthosis
_____ Mouthstick
_____ Bookholder
_____ Electric page turner
_____ Built up tools
_____ Tall checkers
_____ Handle on sanding block

COOKING

_____ Orthosis _____
_____ Table top oven
_____ Electric fry pan
_____ Electric mixer
_____ Lap board
_____ Dycem
_____ Handles on bowls
_____ Cutting board with nails
_____ Socket switch
_____ Handle stabilizer
_____ Hot mitts
_____ Mirror over stove
_____ Electric can opener
_____ ZIM Jar opener

placement is present bilaterally, as documented in the Arm Placement Section. On the discharge evaluation form, observations include a statement on whether the initial goal was met as well as a description of the status at discharge. Goal is lined out and the prognosis for maintaining or improving skills is stated at discharge. Statements made under Plan in sections II through VI describe the types of treatment that will be used to achieve the goals. Unit 4 describes general considerations in establishing the treatment plans and units 5 through 17 describe specific plans for equipment and training to accomplish functional goals.

The ADL chart is designed to give a total picture of current abilities and goals in specific ADL skills. The patient's initial level of performance is indicated with a check and goals are indicated with an X. Where the goal is to maintain current status a combined check and X mark is used. Activities that the patient does not need to perform are marked NA. For the discharge evaluation initial status checks and goal Xs are transferred to the discharge evaluation form and circles are used to indicate status at the time of discharge. In this way, all goals that were met show a circled X on the discharge evaluation. The amount of time that it takes the patient to perform activities is summarized in the box provided. Equipment utilized to accomplish tasks can be listed in the space provided or an equipment checklist can be attached (Exhibit 2–2).

The Manual Muscle Examination and Passive Joint Range Measurement sections of the evaluation form are used to document specific muscle strength, spasticity, goniometric measurements of passive ROM, dominance, and prehensile strength. The same copy of these sections of the form is used to record initial, interim, and discharge status. A duplicate of these sections with initial evaluation results is kept in the medical record until discharge. At that time the original of these sections, which contains initial, interim, and discharge recordings, is submitted to the medical record along with the originals of the first four pages of the discharge evaluation.

This evaluation form is used to document initial and discharge evaluations. For progress notes and follow-up rechecks, a simplified or narrative form is used.

Unit 3

Setting Goals

Annette Russell Farmer, OTR/L

After the initial evaluation process, long-term goals are set that can be accomplished during the initial rehabilitation stay, averaging 2.5 months for quadriplegics and 1.5 months for paraplegics at RIC. Longer term goals are discussed with the patient and family when it is believed that, because of changing status, psychosocial factors, or medical complications, goals will be accomplished after discharge or on subsequent rehabilitation hospitalizations. Short-term goals are set to break the long-term goals into components that can be achieved in 1- to 2-week periods. Short-term goals are then used to guide treatment activity selection.

The goals listed in this and following units are considered realizable during the initial rehabilitation unless otherwise stated. That is not to say that all goals are equally prioritized by patients and their families for initial rehabilitation. Setting and achieving basic self-care goals, such as feeding, simple hygiene, urinary management, dressing, and communication skills are often prioritized by the patient and therapist, while goals in home management, leisure, and community skills may be given lower priority initially. Often this may be appropriate, but there are times when, because of the patient's life-style or culture, leisure, community, vocational, or home management goals are more important to the patient and family than self-care. The patient's former life-style and personal priorities should be taken into consideration in determining the goals. The goals that are set by the therapist and the patient should be monitored on a regular basis to ensure appropriateness and appropriate alterations made to accurately reflect changes in the patient's status.

This unit is intended as a general guide to setting treatment goals. Goals for specific levels of injury and indications for setting them are included in Table 3–1. (Specific treatment recommendations are outlined in the units that follow. The unit or units in which treatment recommendations are found for a particular goal are indicated in parentheses next to the goal heading.) Goals for each patient must be determined on an individual basis. The ADL Outcome Scales in Appendix 3–A can be used to establish specific ADL goals. The indicators for setting the ADL goals are included in the charts under Factors in the first four rows of each chart page. These include the following:

- level of injury
- head and UE control
- wrist and hand function
- trunk control

The numbers in the rows following each factor refer to the motor goal identified by that number in the earlier sections of this unit. For example, the indicators for

TABLE 3–1 Setting Treatment Goals

Goals	*Indicator*
Psychosocial	
Participation in Treatment	
1. Behavior allowing for therapeutic intervention. Definition: Patient allows therapist to provide a minimum of treatment (e.g., promoting safety and maintenance of function through positioning, splinting, etc.), although patient does not actively participate.	1. Combative 2. Angry 3. Manipulative 4. May have previous history of psychological dysfunction or associated head injury
2. Behavior promoting participation in structured, supportive, one-on-one treatment environment	1. Uncooperative 2. Passive 3. Limited carry-over 4. Limited decision-making responsibility
3. Behavior supporting independent participation in treatment	1. Cooperative 2. Directive 3. Motivated 4. Sets own goals 5. Shows follow-through with treatment-related tasks
Coping with Disability	
1. Limited coping skills	1. Difficulty adjusting to present environment 2. Unable to participate in future planning 3. Difficulty maintaining previously established relationships 4. Unable to direct and accept assistance appropriately (e.g., patient may have outbursts in response to offer of assistance) 5. Lacks awareness of and confidence in self as a sexual being
2. Coping adequate for functioning in a controlled environment	1. Actively involved in therapies; coping with present situation but unable to direct future plans 2. Maintains involvement in previously established social systems; initiation and termination of relationships may be inappropriate 3. Inconsistently directs others 4. Limited acceptance of necessary assistance 5. Aware of self as a sexual being but lacks confidence
3. Coping adequate for realistic future planning and positive social interactions	1. Actively involved in identifying options and directing plan for future 2. Initiates, sustains, ends personal relationships appropriately 3. Accepts and directs necessary physical assistance; redirects unnecessary assistance 4. Patient aware of and confident in self as a sexual being
UE Sensation	
1. No UE sensation expected; maintain skin integrity through visual compensation	1. Complete C4 or higher injury 2. Absent protective (sharp/dull) and discriminative sensation (two-point discrimination; position sense)
2. Proximal UE sensory awareness	1. Complete C5 or incomplete higher injury 2. Minimally impaired to normal protective (sharp/dull) sensation in C5 and above dermatones 3. Minimally impaired to normal position sense present in the shoulder and possibly elbow 4. Two-point discrimination absent in hand
3. Functional UE sensation	1. Complete C6–C8 or incomplete higher injury 2. Minimally impaired to normal protective (sharp/dull) sensation in C6 and above dermatones 3. Minimally impaired to normal position sense in shoulder, elbow, wrist, thumb, and index finger 4. Two-point discrimination 0.5 to 1.0 cm in thumb and index, possibly other digits
4. Normal UE sensation	1. Complete T1 or T2 or incomplete higher injury 2. Minimally impaired to normal protective and discriminative sensation throughout UEs

TABLE 3–1 continued

Goals	*Indicator*
Head, Neck, and UE ROM (unit 6)	
1. Subfunctional ROM expected; compensation for ROM deficits. Definition: Range not adequate for use of available muscle strength or interfering with care provided by self or care givers; for example, shoulder ROM interfering with patient being dressed by care giver, or neck ROM interfering with mouthstick use.	1. Any level injury 2. Extended immobilization 3. Severe spasticity 4. Heterotopic ossification 5. Pain 6. Secondary diagnosis such as arthritis
2. Functional ROM. Definition: Range adequate for performance of functional tasks by self or care giver. At the elbow, a 20°–30° flexion contracture may be considered functional to put weak biceps at a mechanical advantage when full elbow extension is not needed for depression transfers.	1. Active motion limitations secondary to denervation combined with existing passive limitations of motion 2. Moderate to severe spasticity 3. Moderate to severe pain
3. Normal ROM	1. Existing normal passive ROM 2. Minimal UE spasticity 3. Potential for full active ROM 4. Potential for reconstructive surgery
Head and UE Motor Control (unit 5)	
1. No head control expected; no goal. Definition: Patient unable to move head and neck. External support is required for patient to support head.	1. C1–C2 injury 2. Subfunctional ROM of head and neck 3. No neck musculature innervated
2. Limited head control in gravity-eliminated position. Definition: Patient able to rotate head. May require external support.	1. C2–C3 or incomplete C1 injury 2. Functional head and neck ROM 3. T to P neck musculature
3. Limited head control. Definition: Full active ROM in all planes of head and neck movement except extension. Endurance may be poor.	1. C3–C4 injury 2. Functional head and neck ROM 3. P to G neck musculature strength
4. Functional head control and limited scapular control. Definition: Patient demonstrates full active ROM in all planes of head and neck movement with good endurance. Patient demonstrates scapular elevation and retraction that may assist in repositioning trunk and UEs. No functional arm placement is present.	1. C4–C5 injury 2. Functional ROM 3. Zero to T deltoid, biceps, brachioradialis; T to F trapezius 4. Moderate spasticity
5. Assisted limited arm placement. Definition: Patient can abduct, flex, and extend shoulder and flex elbow through partial range of motion in gravity-eliminated position. Equipment may enable tabletop and hand-to-mouth arm placement patterns.	1. C4–C5 injury 2. Functional ROM 3. T to P deltoids, biceps, brachioradialis, clavicular pectoralis 4. Limited endurance 5. Mild spasticity 6. Willing to use BFO, overhead sling, etc., to enhance function
6. Unassisted limited arm placement. Definition: Patient can abduct, flex, and extend shoulder to 90° against gravity or resistance and flex elbow through full range against gravity or resistance. Hand to tabletop, top of head, back of neck, mouth, opposite shoulder, and backward reach available without equipment.	1. C5–C6 injury 2. Functional ROM 3. P to F or above deltoids, biceps, brachioradialis, clavicular pectoralis 4. Moderate to no spasticity in scapular, shoulder, elbow musculature
7. Full arm placement. Definition: Full shoulder flexion, abduction, extension, elbow flexion, extension against gravity or resistance. Full overhead and behind back arm placement in addition to those patterns available under limited arm placement.	1. C7 or incomplete higher injury 2. All shoulder, scapular, elbow musculature in F to N ranges 3. Normal UE ROM 4. Minimal to no spasticity in the above muscles
Wrist and Hand Function (units 5 and 6)	
1. No wrist or hand function expected; prevent deformity. Definition: Patient has no functional grasp, release, or wrist stability.	1. Complete lesions at C5 or above 2. No palpable wrist or hand musculature 3. Moderate to severe spasticity in wrist or hand musculature 4. Subfunctional ROM in wrist and hand 5. Associated injuries or other complications 6. No arm placement 7. Patient not motivated to use assisted hand function
2. Assisted hand function. Definition: Grasp or pinch and release available through orthotic assistance.	1. C5–C6 or incomplete higher injury 2. Zero to P radial wrist extensors or other hand musculature

TABLE 3–1 continued

Goals	Indicator
	3. Minimal to no spasticity 4. Limited assisted or better arm placement 5. Patient motivated to use assistive devices to achieve active hand function 6. Functional sensation in at least one hand if goal is for bilateral hand function
3. Tenodesis hand function. Definition: Active prehension and release through active wrist extension and active or passive wrist flexion causing a pull on extrinsic finger flexors as the wrist is extended and on extrinsic finger extensors as the wrist is flexed.	1. C5–C7 or incomplete higher injury 2. P (initially), F (later) or better radial wrist extensors 3. Minimal or no spasticity in wrist and hand 4. Limited assisted or better arm placement 5. Functional sensation in at least one hand if goal is for bilateral hand function
4. Limited (natural) hand function. Definition: Functional active grasp and release, lateral pinch. Limited object manipulation.	1. C8 or incomplete higher injury 2. Extrinsic finger musculature, wrist musculature, P (early after onset or incomplete) to F (later post onset) or better 3. Moderate to no spasticity in wrist and hand 4. Limited assisted arm placement or better 5. Functional to normal sensation
5. Normal hand function. Definition: Active grasp, release, and manipulation skills with scores on standardized tests within normal limits for age and sex group.	1. T1 or lower injury and incomplete higher injury 2. Intrinsic, extrinsic and wrist muscles in F or above strengths 3. Mild to no spasticity in wrist and hand musculature 4. Normal sensation
Trunk Control (units 5 and 6)	
1. No trunk control or stability expected; stable upright positioning through equipment. Definition: External support required for upright positioning (lateral trunk supports can be used for positioning in W/C).	1. C4 or higher injury 2. No trunk and limited scapular musculature innervated
2. Limited trunk stability. Definition: Stability in sitting with UE, W/C, or bed support. External support may be necessary to free both UEs for function. Limited trunk mobility through use of both UEs, one as a stabilizer, one as a mobilizer. (Example: In leaning forward to empty leg bag, patient stabilizes with one arm behind W/C pulls self forward with other arm; returns to upright pulling with arm behind W/C and pushing with other arm as possible.)	1. C5–C6 injury 2. Partial innervation of scapular musculature (latissimus dorsi, serratus anterior, rhomboids); adequate to maintain upright position in sitting through substitution
3. Trunk stability. Definition: Stability in sitting adequate for freeing both UEs for activity. Forward flexion from short sitting will still require UE stabilization.	1. C8 or lower injury
4. Limited trunk control. Definition: Functional active trunk mobility in sitting. Able to flex forward from short sitting without UE assist. UE stabilization required for higher positions. Emergency or household ambulation is possible and ADL training at ambulatory level may be indicated.	1. T6 or lower injury
5. Full trunk control. Definition: Functional trunk control in all positions. One or both UEs may be freed for function in all positions. Household to community ambulation is expected unless there are interfering factors (obesity, cardiac problems, etc.). Functional training at ambulatory level may be indicated.	1. T12 or lower injury
Deformity Control (unit 6)	
1. Prevent neck deformity (flexion, extension, rotation contracture)	1. C1–C4 injury 2. Disease process complications (arthritis) 3. Zero to P neck musculature
2. Prevent, support, or reduce glenohumeral subluxation	1. C1–C5 injury 2. Rotator cuff musculature, deltoids below F strength.
3. Promote proper spinal (trunk) alignment for stability to free UEs for function	1. C4–C5 injury (C6 injury initially) 2. Unable to use both UEs in function while maintaining trunk stability 3. Zero to G scapular and shoulder musculature 4. Unable to shift weight to relieve pressure

TABLE 3–1 continued

Goals	*Indicator*
4. Prevent UE extension contractures	1. C4 or higher injury, incomplete injuries 2. Extensor spasticity, spasm 3. Zero to P flexor musculature
5. Prevent elbow flexion, forearm supination contracture (secondary wrist extension contracture may also occur)	1. C5–C6 injury 2. Biceps spasticity 3. Recumbent positioning 4. Zero to P triceps
6. Prevent wrist drop	1. C5–C6 or higher injury 2. Zero to F wrist extensors
7. Prevent intrinsic minus, flat hand (MP hyperextension, PIP flexion)	1. C8 or higher injury 2. Zero to P intrinsics 3. May be more severe if extrinsic extensors and flexors innervated (C7–C8) 4. May be exaggerated in higher injuries (C4–C5) if wrist not supported, secondary to pull on extrinsic extensors
8. Promote balanced, moderate shortening of finger flexors and extensors for tenodesis hand function	1. C5–C7 injury 2. P to N wrist extensors 3. Zero to T finger musculature
9. Maintain thumb abduction, opposition	1. C8 or higher injury 2. Zero to F thumb abduction, opposition

setting a goal of independence in propelling an electric W/C with proportional control include

- C5 level of lesion
- head and UE control goal 5 or 6 (assisted limited arm placement or unassisted limited arm placement)
- wrist and hand function goal 1 or 2 (no hand function or assisted hand function)
- trunk control goal 2 (limited trunk stability)

Psychosocial status (motivation, adjustment, coping), length of time since injury, and medical stability factors are not listed under the indications to avoid repetition. They are, however, important factors that may influence goal achievement in a positive or negative manner. With these indicators considered, the goals in this unit can be used as flexible guidelines in projecting and planning treatment outcome.

SUMMARY

The establishment of initial goals lays the foundation for the OT program. When the patient and family are first engaged in helping to set goals, it may be difficult for them to state which goals are important to them because they are not sure what is possible. The therapist can offer an array of possible goals and then assist the patient and family in prioritizing them. A discussion of the previous daily routines of the patient and the family members can be helpful in considering goals. While learning what will be possible for the SCI patient, family members often recall previous activities that the patient engaged in, thus generating additional goals.

Long-term goals are generally set for the duration of the hospital stay. Occasionally they may extend into the postdischarge period. Goals are based on head and UE control, wrist and hand function, trunk control indicators, and level of injury.

Appendix 3A

Activities of Daily Living Chart

<u>FACTORS</u>

Level of Injury		C_1	C_2	C_3	C_4	C_5	C_6	C_7	C_8	T_1	T_2	T_3	T_4	T_5–T_{11}	T_{12}	L_1
Head and UE Control	G O	#1	#1–2	#2–3	#3–4	#5–6	#6	#7	---	---	---	---	---	---	---	>
Wrist and Hand Function	A L	#1 ---	---	---	--->	#1–2	#2–3	#3–4	#4	#5	---	---	---	---	---	>
Trunk Control	S	#1 ---	---	---	--->	#2	--->	#3	---	---	---	---	---	#4	#5	->
<u>ACTIVITIES</u> FEEDING																
Drinking - Straw		IES ---	---	---	---	--->	IE-I	I ---	---	---	---	---	---	---	---	>
Drinking - Cup		D ---	---	---	--->	IES	IE-I ---	--->	I ---	---	---	---	---	---	---	>
Finger Feeding		D ---	---	--->	D-IES	IES-IE	IE-I ---	--->	I ---	---	---	---	---	---	---	>
Utensil Feeding		D ---	--->	D-IES ---	--->	IES-IE	IE-I ---	--->	I ---	---	---	---	---	---	---	>
Cutting Food		D ---	---	---	---	D-IES	IE ---	--->	IE-I	I ---	---	---	---	---	---	>
SIMPLE HYGIENE																
Wash Face		D ---	---	---	--->	IES	I ---	---	---	---	---	---	---	---	---	>
Brush Teeth		D ---	---	---	--->	IES	IE ---	--->	I ---	---	---	---	---	---	---	>
Shave		D ---	---	---	--->	IES	IE ---	--->	I ---	---	---	---	---	---	---	>
Make-Up		D ---	---	---	--->	IES	IE ---	--->	I ---	---	---	---	---	---	---	>
Dry Hair		D ---	---	---	---	--->	IE ---	--->	I ---	---	---	---	---	---	---	>
Don Glasses		D ---	---	---	--->	D-I ---	---I ---	---	---	---	---	---	---	---	---	>
Floss Teeth		D ---	---	---	---	--->	IE ---	--->	I ---	---	---	---	---	---	---	>
Comb Hair		D ---	---	---	---	--->	IE ---	--->	I ---	---	---	---	---	---	---	>
Wash Hands		D ---	---	---	---	--->	I ---	---	---	---	---	---	---	---	---	>
Clean Eye Glasses		D ---	---	---	---	--->	I ---	---	---	---	---	---	---	---	---	>
Deodorant		D ---	---	---	---	--->	IE-I ---	--->	I ---	---	---	---	---	---	---	>
Apply Hard Contacts		D ---	---	---	---	--->	D-IE ---	--->	I ---	---	---	---	---	---	---	>
Ear Care		D ---	---	---	---	--->	IE-I ---	--->	I ---	---	---	---	---	---	---	>

FACTORS

Level of Injury		C_1	C_2	C_3	C_4	C_5	C_6	C_7	C_8	T_1	T_2	T_3	T_4	T_5–T_{11}	T_{12}	L_1
Head and UE Control	GOALS	#1	#1–2	#2–3	#3–4	#5–6	#6	#7	---							>
Wrist and Hand Function		#1 ---			--->	#1–2	#2–3	#3–4	#4	#5 ---						>
Trunk Control		#1 ---			--->	#2	------>	#3	---				--->	#4	#5	>
SIMPLE HYGIENE (cont)																
Denture Care		D ---				--->	IE-I ---	--->	I ---							>
Nail Care		D ---				--->	D-IE	IE	I ---							>
Set Hair		D ---					--->	IE	I ---							>
Soft Contacts		D ---						--->	I ---							>
GENERAL HYGIENE																
Bathing UEs		D ---			--->	IES	I ---									>
Bathing Trunk/Body		D ---				--->	A-IE	IE	I ---							>
Bathing LEs		D ---				--->	A-IE	IE	I ---							>
Wash Hair		D ---				--->	IE ---	--->	I ---							>
Feminine Hygiene		D ---				--->	A-IE ---	--->	I ---							>
BOWEL AND BLADDER CARE																
Empty Leg bag		D ---			--->	D-IE	IE ---	--->	I ---							>
Change Leg bag		D ---				--->	IE ---	--->	I ---							>
Self Catheterization		D ---				--->	IE ---	--->	I ---							>
Irrigation		D ---				--->	IE ---	--->	I ---							>
Digital Stimulation		D ---					--->	IE	IE-I	I ---						>
Suppository Insertion		D ---					--->	IE	IE-I	I ---						>
Cleaning		D ---					--->	I ---								>
Toileting		D ---					--->	I ---								>
DRESSING																
UE and Trunk on		D ---			--->	A	I ---									>
UE and Trunk off		D ---				--->	A-I	I ---								>
LE on		D ---				--->	A-I	IE-I	I ---							>
LE off		D ---				--->	A-I	IE-I	I ---							>
Fasteners on		D ---				--->	IE ---	--->	IE-I ---							>
Fasteners off		D ---				--->	IE ---	--->	IE-I ---							>
Accessories		D ---				--->	IE ---	--->	IE-I ---							>
COMMUNICATION																
Write		D ---	--->	IES ---	--->	IES-IE	IE-I ---	--->	I ---							>
Type		IES-IE ---				--->	IE-I ---	--->	I ---							>
Telephone		IES-IE ---				--->	IE-I ---	--->	I ---							>
Page Turning		IES ---			--->	IES-IE	I ---									>
Tape Recorder		IES ---				--->	IE-I ---	--->	I ---							>
Manage Mail		D ---			--->	A-IE	IE-I ---	--->	I ---							>
MOBILITY																
Bed Controls		IE ---				--->	IE-I	I ---								>
Movement in Bed		D ---			--->	A	IE	I ---								>
Pneumatic Wheelchair		I ---														>

FACTORS

Level of Injury		C_1	C_2	C_3	C_4	C_5	C_6	C_7	C_8	T_1	T_2	T_3	T_4	T_5–T_{11}	T_{12}	L_1
Head and UE Control	GOALS	#1	#1–2	#2–3	#3–4	#5–6	#6	#7	---							--->
Wrist and Hand Function		#1 ---			--->	#1–2	#2–3	#3–4	#4	#5	---					--->
Trunk Control		#1 ---			--->	#2	--->	#3	---				--->	#4	#5	>
MOBILITY (cont)																
Tongue or Chin Control		I ---														--->
Control Wheelchair		I ---														--->
Short Throw Switch					A-I	I ---										--->
Proportional Control		D ---			--->	I	I(community) ---									--->
Manual Wheelchair		D ---			--->	A-I	I(household)			I(community) ---						--->
Emergency Ambulation		D ---											---	A-IE ---		--->
Household Ambulation		D ---												--->	IE --	>
Community Ambulation		D ---													--->	IE
COMMUNITY SKILLS																
Money Handling		D ---				--->	IE ---	--->	I ---							--->
Community Mobility		AE ---						--->	A-I ---						--->	I
Shopping, Personal		A ---				--->	A-IE ---	--->	A-I ---							--->
Driving		D ---			--->	D-IE	IE ---									--->
LEISURE PURSUITS																
Smoking		IES ---				--->	IE-I ---	--->	I ---							--->
Table Games		IES ---				--->	IE-I ---	--->	I ---							--->
Crafts		D ---	---	IES ---		--->	IES-IE ---	--->	IE-I	I ---						--->
TV		IE ---				--->	IE-I ---	--->	I ---							--->
Radio		IE ---				--->	IE-I ---	--->	I ---							--->
Tape Recorder		IES ---				--->	IE-I ---	--->	I ---							--->
Phonograph		D ---				--->	IE-I ---	--->	I ---							--->
Gardening		D ---			--->	A-IES ---		--->	I ---							--->
Sports Participation		D ---			--->	IES	IES-IE ---	--->	IE ---							--->
HOME MANAGEMENT																
Food Prep., hot		D ---				--->	A	A-IE	IE-I	I ---						--->
Food Prep., cold		D ---			--->	A	IES-IE ---	--->	I ---							--->
Meal Service		D ---				--->	A-IE ---	--->	IE-I ---							--->
Daily Clean-up		D ---				--->	A-IE	IE	IE-I	I ---						--->
Cleaning		D ---						--->	A-IE ---							--->
Laundry/Ironing		D ---				--->	A-IE ---	--->	IE-I ---							--->
Food Shopping		D ---				--->	A ---	--->	A-IE ---							--->
Child Care (infant)		D ---				--->	A ---	--->	I/E ---							--->
Seasonal Cleaning		D ---						--->	A ---							--->
HOME ACCESSIBILITY																
Entrance/Exit		D-IE ---						--->	IE-I ---							--->
Temperature Regulation		D-IE ---						--->	IE-I	I ---						--->
Utilities		D ---			--->	D-IE	IE-I ---	--->	I ---							--->

Unit 4

Treatment Planning

Jessica Presperin, OTR/L

Treatment planning requires a comprehensive, systematic approach involving the patient, family, friends, and staff. After a thorough initial evaluation, long- and short-term goals are established. The treatment plan is then formulated to assist in the achievement of these goals. Reassessment is continuous throughout the rehabilitation process. This allows for new short-term goals to be set and for changes in long-term goals to be considered. The treatment plan thus becomes a general account of the patient's progress.

INVOLVING THE PATIENT

For rehabilitation to be most effective, an effort by both the patient and staff is needed. The therapist should attempt to involve the patient as soon as possible in treatment planning. Initially, however, the patient may not be psychologically prepared for involvement in decision-making and may work best in a structured, supportive setting.

When planning treatment, the therapist must be aware of the total impact that a permanent injury may have on an individual. As the rehabilitation process begins, the patient becomes aware of the effect that the physical losses of sensation and movement have on his life. Changes in mobility, control, and independence may be accompanied by changes in relationships, career plans, and life roles. Body image and self-esteem become critical factors as the individual learns about, and reacts to, the outcome of his disability.

The therapist should explain all aspects of the patient's treatment plan to enable him to understand how they will meet his needs. The patient should be given the opportunity to contribute to the process by prioritizing realistic goals and establishing a workable treatment plan. Each person has a unique set of needs that must be integrated into the treatment plan. What may be low on the priority list for the therapist may be a high priority for the patient.

INVOLVING THE FAMILY AND FRIENDS

The family plays an important role in a patient's rehabilitation and should be considered when setting goals and planning treatment. The treatment plan should be developed to establish and implement goal-oriented problem-solving techniques that allow patient and family to follow through with the program and manage care in the home setting.

It should not be taken for granted that the family and friends will immediately take on a supportive role for the patient. Each person must first pass through an emotional period characterized by various combinations of grief, anger, overprotection, denial, rejection, and high expectations. Other specific reactions may include

- fear of reinjuring or physically hurting the disabled person
- knowledge of the increased responsibility for physical care
- awkwardness in assuming bowel and bladder care
- discomfort resulting from role reversals
- denial of the effects and permanence of injury
- anxiety regarding financial burdens
- difficulty adjusting to the reactions of others
- apprehension in considering the possibility of the need to move

The therapist should be aware of the family dynamics, explain goals and treatment, and involve each individual as much as possible.

IDENTIFYING FACTORS INTERFERING WITH GOAL ACHIEVEMENT

When planning treatment, the therapist must be able to identify factors interfering with goal achievement. Physical factors include

- decreased strength
- decreased ROM
- decreased sensation
- pressure sores
- spasms
- abnormal tone
- decreased endurance
- age
- obesity
- decreased endurance
- medical complications
- deformities
- impaired respiration
- premorbid physical involvement

The treatment plan must take these into consideration, with efforts made to alleviate or compensate for the problems.

Psychosocial factors, as stated previously, are critical in the determination of a treatment program. The patient's involvement and motivation are required for the rehabilitation program to be a success. The treatment plan should change to accommodate the psychological needs of the patient. For instance, a patient may need to spend an hour discussing the impact of his injury and how he feels about it instead of performing strengthening activities previously planned. The therapist should be perceptive and flexible in response to these needs.

Motivating the patient to participate in goal setting and treatment is a high priority for the therapist. Knowing how to motivate the patient is the key for successful involvement. Unfortunately, there is no sure way to do this because each patient is unique. Some are internally motivated by their own needs to meet goals, others are motivated by peers or loved ones, and still others become motivated only by seeing the negative effect of nonparticipation. Sometimes interim discharge from the rehabilitation hospital can help the patient and his family to realize the permanent implications of life with an SCI and to identify concrete goals and plans to be accomplished in further rehabilitation.

Cultural factors greatly influence the rehabilitation process. Behaviors and values determine how a patient will respond to therapy, equipment, goals, the rehabilitative setting, and the therapist. Similarly, religious beliefs, life roles, traditions, and time management all influence the way a person will respond to disability. To develop a program that will prove successful, the therapist must know the patient's background.

Cognitive factors must be considered when planning treatment. Some patients may learn new methods of performing ADL in one trial. Others may require weeks of practice and a breakdown of the activity into small steps in order to be successful. The patient may have suffered a closed head injury or anoxia or may have had preexisting learning problems. The therapist must be aware of any resultant cognitive and behavioral deficits.

Environmental limitations may interfere with successful goal achievement. A patient may be independent in W/C propulsion in a hospital or on a paved street, but may have difficulty negotiating a dirt road or maneuvering in the confines of a mobile home. Stairs, doors, terrain, weather, transportation, and the general accessibility of the discharge environment must be considered in treatment and equipment planning.

The financial situation of each patient must also be considered. It is frustrating for the patient (as well as the therapist) to train on an expensive piece of equipment and then to be denied funding. The therapist should be aware of the financial status of the patient, the potential for funding, and alternative resources before involving the patient in an intensive training program with costly equipment.

COMPONENTS OF AN OCCUPATIONAL THERAPY PROGRAM

An integrated program allows the patient to experience diverse treatment methods to achieve goals. The therapist can coordinate treatment in the OT department by offering various individual or group interventions. By determining the needs of the individual, the therapist can select programs that will be optimal for meeting patient needs. After the level of injury, the psychological state, and the therapeutic techniques that work best have been considered, the patient is scheduled for various treatment programs. The treatment programs at RIC include

- Individual therapy, which allows the occupational therapist to work on a one-to-one basis with the patient. Activities include goal setting, orthotic fabrication, ADL training, strengthening, equipment ordering or fabrication, community activities, and family teaching.
- The a.m. care programs, in which the early morning hours are used for assisting the patient in practicing ADL, including oral and facial hygiene, dressing, bathing, catheter care, and feeding.
- The feeding group, which offers the patient the opportunity to practice feeding skills learned in individual OT. The patients are set up with feeding equipment and minimal assistance is provided during the meal.
- The quadriplegic group, which offers opportunities to practice skills learned during individual therapy. Group activities are preplanned each week, with activities ranging from strengthening, practicing ADL, gross motor games, cooking, and community activities. Goals, feelings, and ideas are discussed.
- Community reentry groups, established for paraplegics and quadriplegics to assist in the transition from the rehabilitation setting to the home. The groups focus on intensive community skills, independent planning, problem solving, and adapting to the outside environment.
- The avocational group, in which patients work individually on craft projects. This assists in the achievement of such goals as strengthening, equipment use, problem solving, and leisure skills development.

WORKING WITH THE TEAM

The team members collaborate in developing the treatment plan, with goals prioritized in a logical sequence. Activities can be coordinated so as not to overstress the patient but to optimize his functioning. The team should set goals and treatment activities to complement each other. For instance, before a dressing program is introduced, OT may work on UE strengthening activities while physical therapy (PT) is working on bed mobility. PT may have an individual walking in the parallel bars while OT has them practice homemaking skills while standing at the counter.

Communication with the team is a critical part of treatment planning. The team must agree on long-term goals and coordinate the information relayed to patient and family. Double messages and conflicts of interest must be avoided.

END OF TREATMENT

Once the long-term goals of the therapy program have been successfully met or have been determined to be unachievable, the patient is ready to be discharged. This may be difficult because of the psychological impact that discharge may have on both the patient and the therapist. Accordingly, the discharge should be planned in such a way as to minimize this impact. It is best to address the subject of discharge openly throughout the rehabilitation stay.

SUMMARY

Treatment planning is based on goals determined by the patient, his family, and the therapist. Once goals are established, the physical, psychosocial, cognitive, and environmental factors preventing goal achievement are identified. Remedial or compensatory treatment methods are planned to address each factor interfering with goal achievement. In this manner, both patient and therapist have a clear, goal-oriented understanding of the purpose of each treatment activity. The OT treatment plan is then integrated into the total care plan.

Unit 5

Building Strength Through Function and Function Through Strengthening

Judy Hill, OTR/L

As occupational therapists, we utilize functional activities to enhance performance, including motor performance. In SCI, the partial or full severance of innervation to muscles results in a sudden decrease in the motor skills—strength, endurance, and coordination—necessary to perform daily tasks. Maximization of residual muscle activity for use in ADL is an important early remedial goal in OT with this population.

STRENGTHENING ACTIVITIES

Specific strengthening activities are introduced early in rehabilitation to prevent atrophy of weakened muscles, maximize strength and endurance for beginning participation in ADL, and maximize the potential for long-term functional performance. Although exercise may not be considered a functional activity in the traditional sense of the term, for many young and active people exercise is a regular and important activity of daily living. Both exercise and strengthening through participation in self-care tasks and leisure activities are considered in a well-integrated OT program. The specific focus or method is based on individual interests and life-style, the specific muscle picture [it may not be possible to engage a trace (T) muscle in a functional task], and equipment availability.

Questions to consider in planning strengthening programs include:

- Was exercise a regular component of the patient's life-style?
- Which activity might be the most meaningful to the patient?
- Is exercise through performance of routine tasks set up with a strengthening component [feeding with a balanced forearm orthosis (BFO), for example] too frustrating?
- Would performing the task in an easier fashion with less of a strengthening component be more acceptable to the patient?
- What strengthening activities is the patient doing in PT?
- Is spasticity, muscle tightness, or contracture present that may require modification of the strengthening program?
- What muscles and patterns of motion require strengthening for functional goal achievement?

ENDURANCE

Endurance is as important as muscle strength in the performance of functional tasks. Most ADL require the repeated performance of motor patterns. In feeding, for example, the hand to tabletop and mouth patterns must be repeated 20 to 50 times. The repetition does not need to occur in rapid succession, but the endurance must be available for successful completion of the task.

COORDINATION

Coordination of muscle function into movement patterns and learning new movement patterns with which tasks can be completed is the third component to be considered in muscle-strengthening programs after SCI.

Often, tasks will be performed by motor patterns that are less refined than those used before injury. Writing, for example, is performed largely by wrist and hand musculature on the foundation of a stable UE in the able-bodied population. The patient with C5 to C6 quadriplegia must learn to achieve the fine distal control needed for writing by using the grosser musculature of the shoulder, elbow, and forearm.

Altered or reduced sensory feedback as a result of spasticity and sensory loss can make the relearning process more difficult.

MOTOR LEARNING DEFICITS

Patients who have had a head injury as well as SCI—a situation that occurs more frequently than has been recognized—may have even greater difficulty in learning to coordinate new motor patterns, though strength and endurance are adequate. It is important for the therapist to recognize when motor learning problems are present in order to avoid setting expectations too high. Goals and expected time to accomplish them may have to be altered. Family education regarding the specific deficits and verbal and manual cues that may be necessary during task performance are crucial for carry-over of activities when motor learning deficits are present.

STRENGTHENING HEAD AND NECK MUSCULATURE

Strength, endurance, and coordination of head and neck musculature are specifically addressed in cases of C4 to C5 and higher injuries and are generally achieved

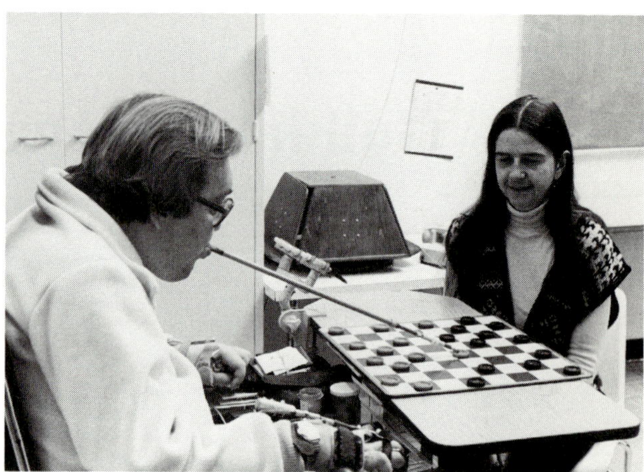

Figure 5–1 Playing checkers with a mouthstick to strengthen neck protraction, rotation, flexion, and extension.

through mouthstick activities. Head and neck stability is necessary for engaging in mouthstick activities in the upright position. Activities can then be introduced that demand controlled protraction, rotation, flexion, and extension of the head and neck against minimal resistance (Figure 5–1).

Page turning with a mouthstick requires rotation and resisted protraction (enough force must be exerted to "grab" the page). A nonskid tip for the page-turning device and page holders on the book support that offer little resistance will allow the patient to exert less force while using the device.

Typing with an electric typewriter requires protraction combined with various degrees of rotation, flexion, and extension. Access to the entire keyboard requires good range of motion and control. The telescoping mouthstick (unit 8) can help to compensate for limited range in reaching the entire keyboard; however, the longer the mouthstick the more force the patient will have to exert to depress the key. Mouthstick typing offers resistance to neck flexors (Figure 5–2). By slanting the typewriter the resistance is transferred to protraction (Figure 5–3). The amount of force required to depress the keys is adjustable on many typewriters.

Painting on paper, canvas, or ceramic greenware with a mouthstick offers little resistance, but a fair amount of coordination is required in all motions. Writing requires even more controlled coordination.

When neck muscle strength is not adequate for supporting the head in an upright position, most of the above activities can be performed with the patient semireclined to strengthen head rotators and flexors. Magnetic games can be introduced on a slant board.

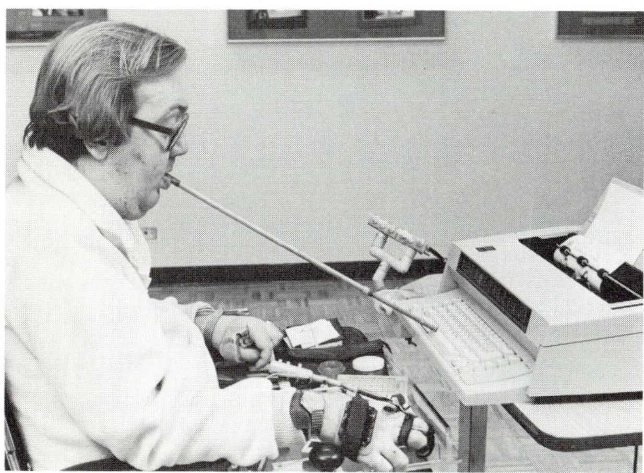

Figure 5–2 Resistance to neck flexors is provided by mouthstick typing on a flat surface.

Figure 5–3 With the typewriter slanted, resistance is to protractors.

SCAPULAR ELEVATOR STRENGTHENING

For trapezius strengthening and muscle reeducation in C4 quadriplegia, BFOs or linear shoulder-elbow orthoses (LSEOs) (Figure 5–4) are introduced to the patient with good motor learning abilities. Limited arm placement can be achieved through skilled control of the scapular elevators and retractors (Figures 5–5 and 5–6). This is a good example of a situation where, although strengthening and improving coordination in the scapular elevators can be accomplished with an arm support system, a mouthstick may be preferred by the patient for ease and speed of performance in functional tasks such as typing.

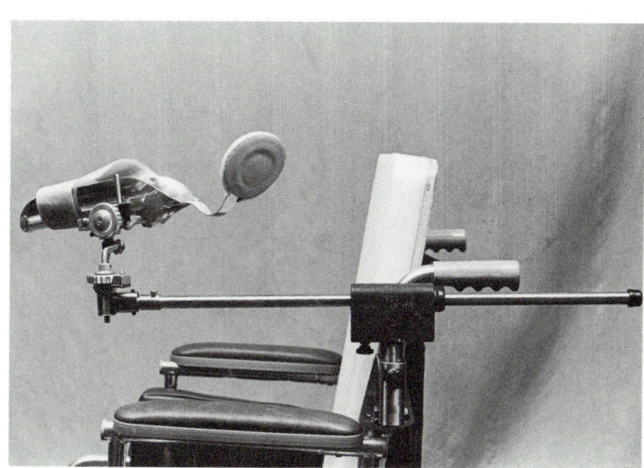

Figure 5–4 The linear shoulder-elbow orthosis.

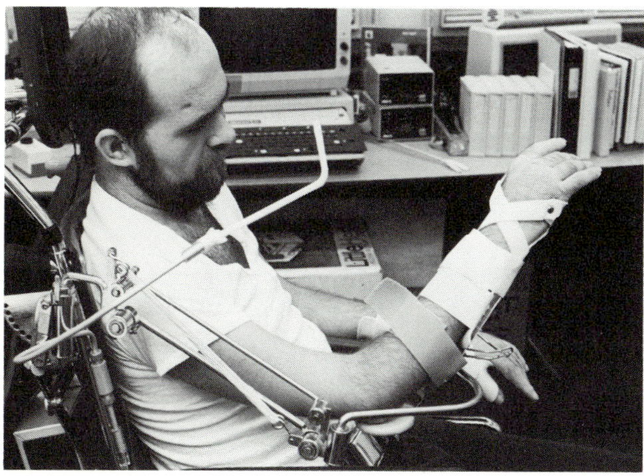

Figure 5–5 Using scapular elevator relaxation to elevate the hand, flex the elbow and externally rotate with a BFO.

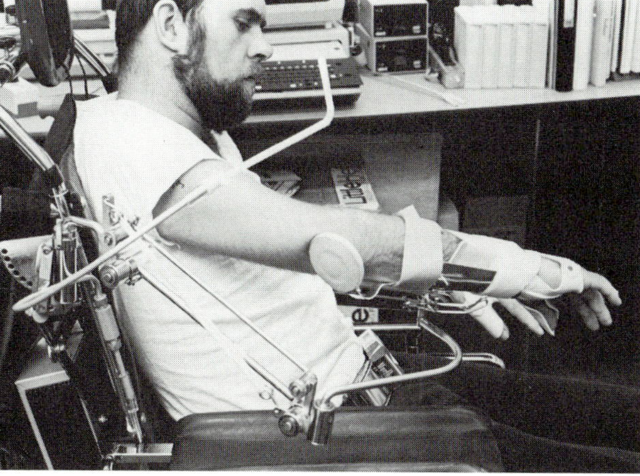

Figure 5–6 Using scapular elevation to depress the hand, extend the elbow and internally rotate with a BFO.

STRENGTHENING SHOULDER GIRDLE AND ELBOW MUSCULATURE

The shoulder girdle and elbow are considered together in this unit because of their close relation in functional arm placement and the action of the biceps in crossing both joints. In approaching the shoulder girdle and elbow in the patient with some C5 innervation, motor skills training options are much broader.

The imbalance in muscle function at this level should be considered:

- Scapular retractors (trapezius) are stronger than protractors (serratus anterior and pectorals).
- Glenohumeral abductors and partial flexors (middle and anterior deltoid) are stronger than full flexors (clavicular pectoralis).
- Glenohumeral horizontal abductors (posterior deltoid) are stronger than adductors (pectorals).
- External rotators must be strong enough to resist gravity to perform their function in scapulohumeral rhythm while the pull into internal rotation is assisted by gravity.
- Elbow flexors and supinators (biceps) are unopposed by triceps and pronators, which are not innervated at this level.

These imbalances necessitate a focus on patterns that will strengthen the weaker musculature needed for functional task performance. The components of the patterns to be stressed are glenohumeral flexion, horizontal adduction, protraction, elbow extension, and pronation. They can be combined in the emphasis on a forward reach pattern (Figure 5–7).

Elbow flexion and supination contractures are a potential problem at this level that can interfere with restoration of extended reach to electric W/C control or W/C projections for mobility (Figure 5–8), forward reach to a table for writing, and pronation to a plate for eating. Biceps strengthening at the C5 level should be monitored closely to ensure that this deformity is not being promoted.

The tendency for the patient to function more in glenohumeral abduction and scapular retraction reinforces the tendency for elbow flexion by stretching the biceps across the glenohumeral joint, interfering with forward reach.

The biceps acts as a shoulder flexor (and abductor in the externally rotated position) as well as an elbow flexor and forearm supinator. When the deltoids are weak, the biceps may be recruited to assist in shoulder flexion, but this will result in elbow flexion as well, again interfering with the forward reach pattern.

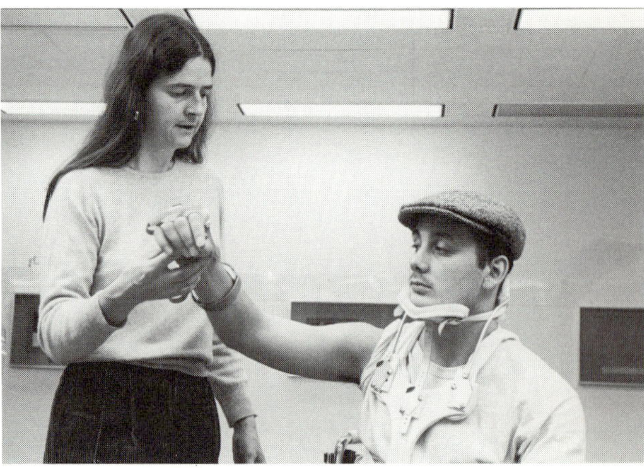

Figure 5–7 Glenohumeral flexion, horizontal adduction, protraction, elbow extension, and pronation are combined in the forward reach pattern.

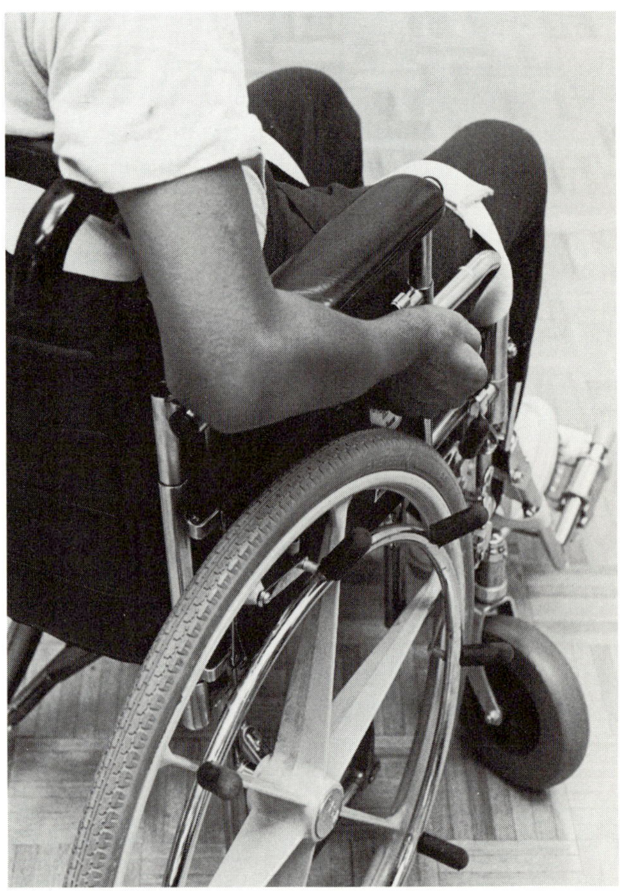

Figure 5–8 At the C5 level, elbow flexion and supination contracture interfere with reach to W/C projections for mobility.

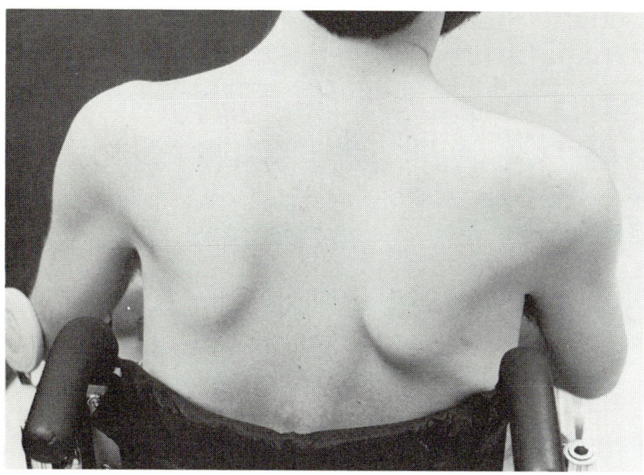

Figure 5–9 Scapulae at rest with serratus anterior weakness. Slight winging is noted.

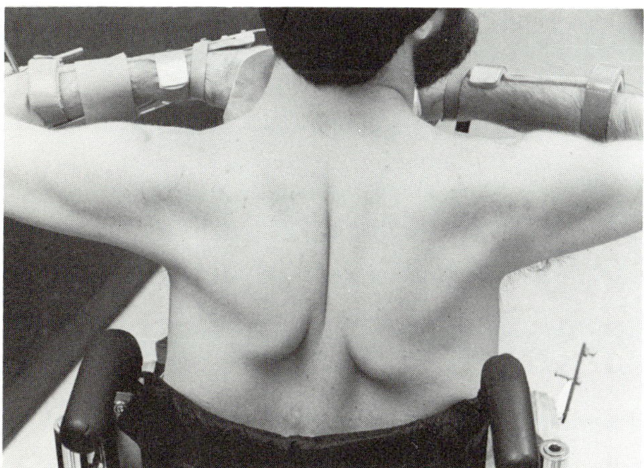

Figure 5–10 With active shoulder abduction, imbalance caused by serratus and pectoral weakness results in severe retraction and winging.

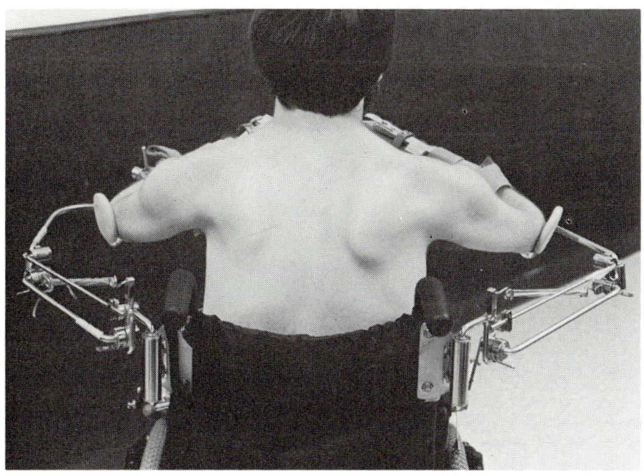

Figure 5–11 Scapular protraction and seating of the scapulae against the rib cage are improved by BFO use.

Lack of scapular stability and ''winging'' of the scapula when shoulder motion is attempted results largely from weakness of the serratus anterior (Figures 5–9 to 5–11). If allowed to occur early, the serratus can be overstretched, which interferes with strengthening and the building of scapular stability. Protection of the muscle through the use of UE assistive devices and strengthening should be attempted. If adequate strength cannot be built and assistive devices become impractical, then it may be consolatory that patients have functioned in spite of this winging. An attempt at strengthening while preventing overstretching is important for the prevention of deformity and pain.

Assistive Arm Placement Devices

Weak deltoids, serratus, and clavicular pectoralis muscles can be strengthened by using an elevating proximal arm on a BFO providing rubber band assistance to vertical motions, or with various types of deltoid-assist counterweighted slings (Figure 5–12).

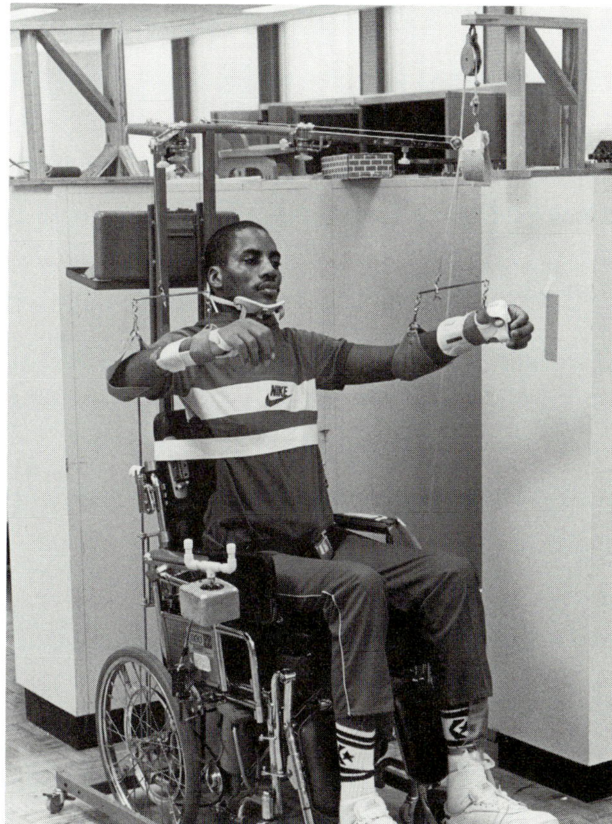

Figure 5–12 The O-B Help Arm, a type of counterweighted, deltoid-assist sling, is used to strengthen deltoids, serratus, and clavicular pectorals.

The amount of rubber band or counterweight assistance provided depends on the strength of the musculature. The assistance can be graded by removing rubber bands or weights until the strength and endurance necessary for shoulder flexion and abduction is present without assistance [usually fair plus strength with good endurance]. Rubber band or counterweight assistance should be enough to allow the patient to actively flex or abduct the shoulder without flexing the elbow and without winging of the scapula.

Generally it is better to instruct the patient on only one device, because motor patterns used vary with the systems and alternating them may be confusing. It is desirable to have BFOs, LSEOs, and deltoid-assist slings in the OT department for patient use in strengthening and functional tasks (Table 5–1). If needed at discharge, the most appropriate equipment can be ordered to take home (usually a BFO).

Functional activities are incorporated into the program by using the assistive arm placement devices. Activities are set up to promote successful task completion and reinforce desirable motor patterns.

Typing with the BFO is set up to assist forward flexion and horizontal adduction. Adequate rubber band assistance is provided to allow the patient to reach forward to the typewriter placed well out in front of him (Figure 5–13). Gradually rubber bands can be removed and adjustments made to provide less assistance or even slight resistance to the desired motions of forward flexion and horizontal adduction at the shoulder.

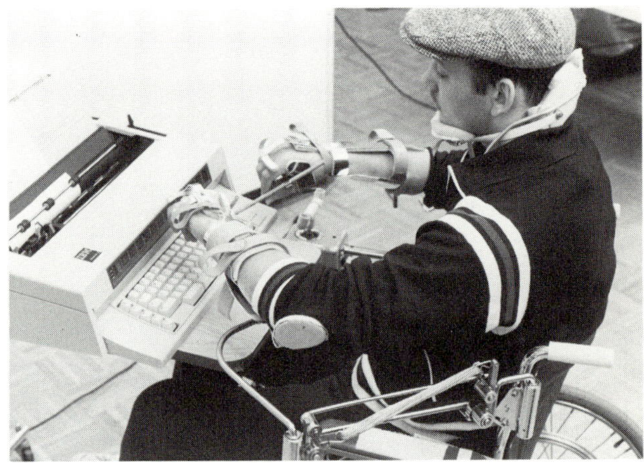

Figure 5–13 Typing with a BFO is set up to encourage forward reach.

Feeding with the BFO with an elevating proximal arm is used to strengthen weak deltoids rather than encourage eating with elbows resting on the table,

Table 5–1 Comparison of BFO, LSEO, and Deltoid-Assist Slings for Shoulder Girdle and Elbow Strengthening

Balanced Forearm Orthosis	*Linear Shoulder Elbow Orthosis*	*Deltoid-Assist Slings*
Portable; easily set up on W/C (or tabletop) in any setting	Portable; easily set up on W/C in any setting	Limited portability; primary use in single setting
Mobile; can use while mobile in chair. Adds width to W/C, making navigating doorways difficult. Balance will be offset when chair is on uneven surfaces	Mobile; can use while mobile in chair. Little lateral width added but extends posteriorly. Balance is offset when W/C is on uneven surface	Stationary
Practical for home use. Three-step setup; insert proximal arm into bracket, distal arm into proximal, swivel into distal arm	Practical for issuing and home use. One-step setup; insert bar into bracket	More for institutional use. Three-step setup; place arm in cuffs, hook cuffs to suspension bar, hook suspension bar to pulley
Many "fine-tuning" adjustment options that can be adapted to specific needs of patient	Many fine-tuning options from bracket and spring loaded trough attachment components. Difficult to maintain adjustments	Limited fine adjustments but may be less complex for patient with motor learning problems to learn to use
Vertical shoulder motion assist through elevating proximal arm for deltoid strengthening advantage for those with weak deltoids (C4-C5)	No vertical shoulder motion assist. More advantageous for weaker patients (C4)	Vertical shoulder motion assist through counterweights
Cost, with elevating proximal arm, less than $200	Cost, more than $500	Cost, $800-$1000

Figure 5–14 Feeding with a BFO utilizing an elevating proximal arm is used to strengthen weak deltoids.

which relies primarily on biceps function (Figures 5–14 and 5–15).

The patient can become involved in an early "volleyballoon" game using BFOs or slings. Tabletop games and avocational activities such as painting can offer a combination of strengthening, coordination, and endurance training.

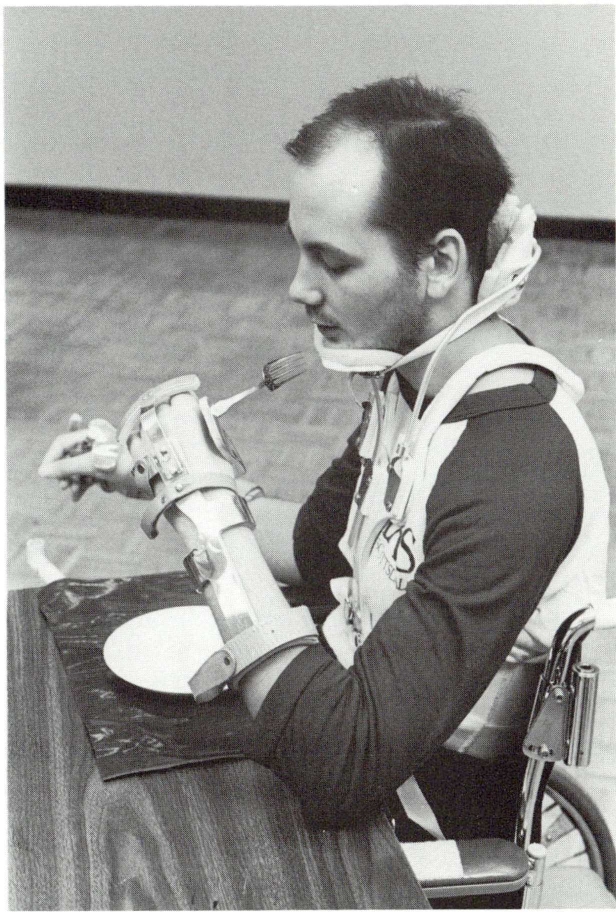

Figure 5–15 Feeding with elbow stabilized on the table does not encourage deltoid use.

Alternating Resistance and Stabilization

Alternating resistance and stabilization can be used to strengthen and increase stability at the shoulder. Placing the shoulder between 90° of flexion and abduction, the therapist instructs the patient, "Hold; don't let me push down, pull out, push in, or pull up," while providing resistance in those directions. The patient is then asked to hold the arm in this position for 5 seconds and then relax. The sequence is repeated three to five times. This can be a good warm-up before functional activity. The amount of resistance applied is graded according to the patient's strength. Resistance should not require strong biceps contraction (Figure 5–16).

This technique can also be used for humeral rotators. Since external rotation against gravity is required for many activities, resistance to that muscle group is accented. The abducted shoulder (elbow flexed to 90°) is placed in approximately 70° of external rotation and instructions to hold and not let the therapist twist the arm up or down are given. The patient is then asked to hold in external rotation (Figure 5–17).

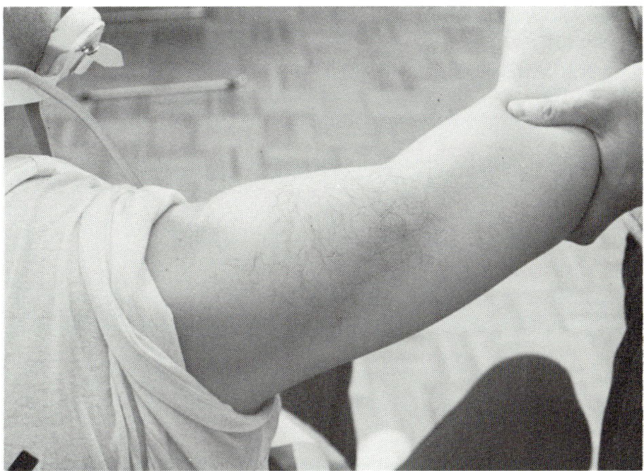

Figure 5–16 Alternating resistance and stabilization is used to strengthen deltoids.

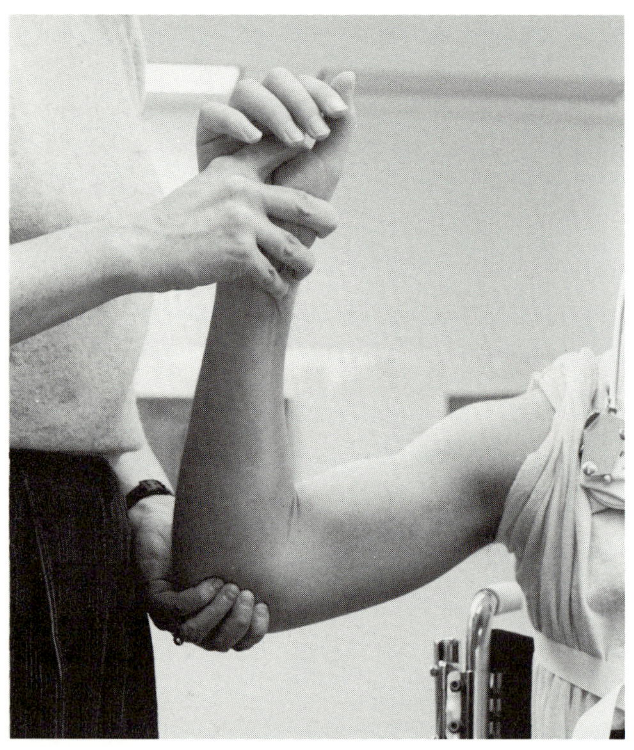

Figure 5–17 Alternating resistance and stabilization is used to strengthen external rotators.

External rotation is important not only for activities but also in allowing the greater tuberosity of the humerus to clear the acromion process during flexion and abduction. Inability to perform this motion can result in shoulder pain and interruption of activity.

Alternating resistance and stabilization is similar to the proprioceptive neuromuscular facilitation (PNF) technique of rhythmic stabilization, but does not include the same degree of constant co-contraction.

Apparatus for Strengthening

Several types of apparatus can be used to strengthen shoulder girdle and elbow musculature. Table 5–2 lists the type of apparatus, the muscles it provides resistance to, and the muscles it assists.

A patient's hands are attached to these devices with flexion mitts (for any of the devices), wrist cuffs (pulleys), tenodesis hand function (biceps assist, dowel ladder, bilateral sander), or natural hand function, if present (any of the devices).

Table 5–2 Strengthening Apparatus

Type	*Resists*	*Assists*
Biceps assist (Gulbrandsen) (Figures 5–18 and 5–19)	Scapular protactors, upward rotators Shoulder flexors Elbow extensors	Shoulder extensors, adductors Elbow flexors
Triceps assist (Gulbrandsen) (Figures 5–20 and 5–21)	Scapular depressors, downward rotators Shoulder extensors, adductors Elbow flexors	Scapular protractors, upward rotators Shoulder flexors Elbow extensors
Dowel ladder (Gulbrandsen) (Figure 5–22)	Scapular protractors, upward rotators Shoulder flexors Elbow extensors	
Dowel ladder—one extremity "levering," the other up (Figure 5–23)	Scapular depressors, downward rotators Shoulder extensors Elbow flexors on one side	Scapular protractors, upward rotators Shoulder flexors Elbow extensors on the other side
Pulley (type 1) (Figure 5–24)	UE extension, internal rotation, depression Horizontal abduction or adduction (depending on placement) Elbow flexion or extension	UE flexion, elevation, external rotation Horizontal abduction or adduction (depending on placement)
Pulley (type 2) (Figure 5–25)	Shoulder flexion, external rotation Horizontal abduction or adduction Elbow flexion or extension	Shoulder extension, adduction, internal rotation
Bilateral sander (Figures 5–26 and 5–27)	On flat surfaces, pushing out resists scapular protractors, elbow extensors Pulling back resists scapular retractors, shoulder extensors, elbow flexors On incline, shoulder flexors, scapular upward rotators	On incline, scapular retractors, shoulder extensors, elbow flexors

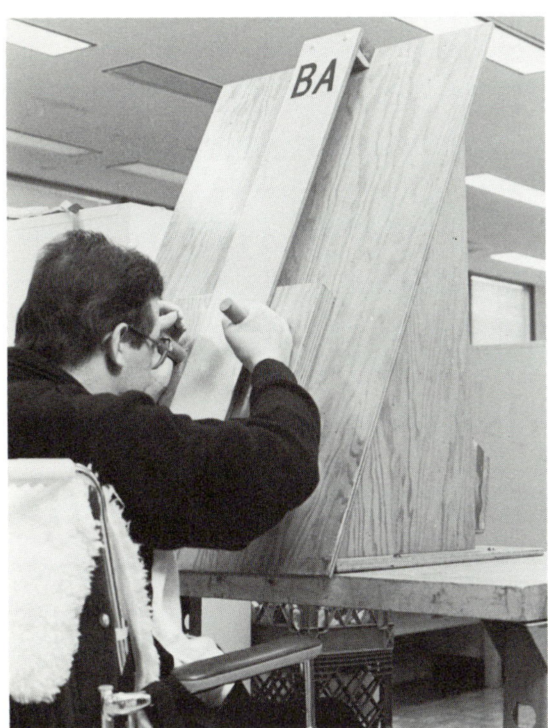

Figure 5–18 Biceps assist (Gulbrandsen) with tenodesis used to hold.

Figure 5–19 Biceps assist pulley mechanism from rear: One pulley is at the top and one is at the bottom of the machine. The weight in the box at the back resists pushing the handles upward.

Figure 5–20 Triceps assist (Gulbrandsen) using flexion mitts.

Figure 5–21 Triceps assist pulley mechanism from rear. With the single pulley set at the top of the machine, the weight in the box assists upward reach and elbow extension while resisting biceps in pulling the handles down.

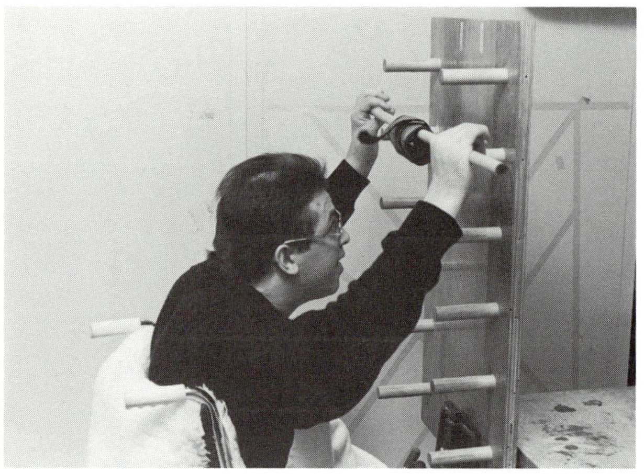

Figure 5–22 Dowel ladder (Gulbrandsen) with tenodesis.

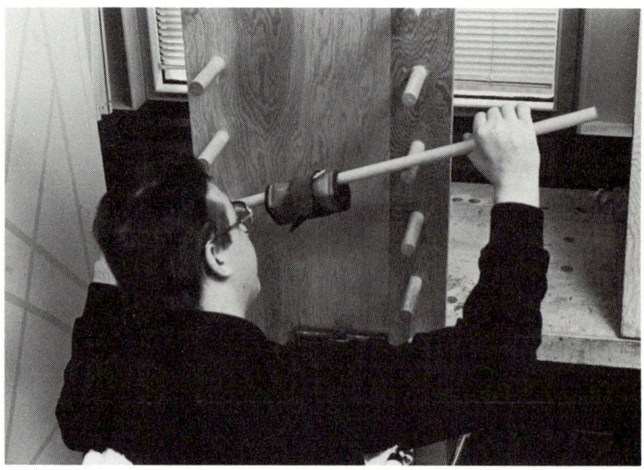

Figure 5–23 Dowel ladder with left UE levering right up a rung.

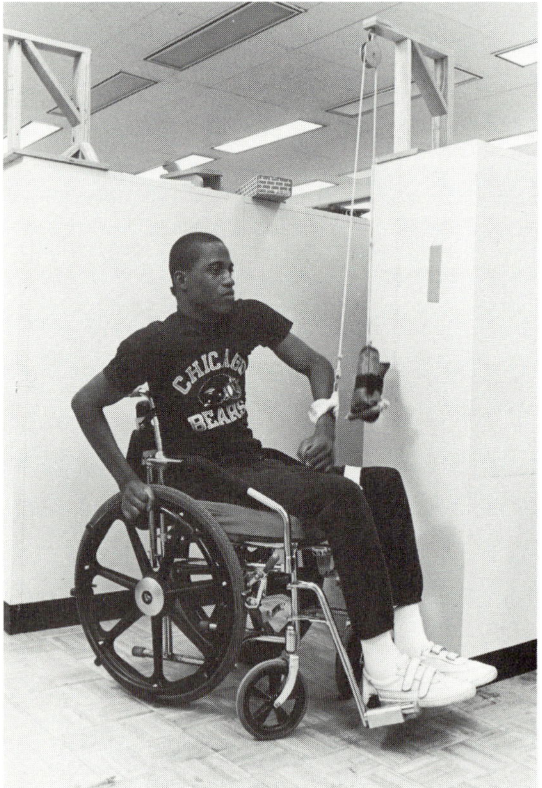

Figure 5–24 Type 1 pulley resists downward motion. A wrist cuff is used to attach the cord to the patient's UE.

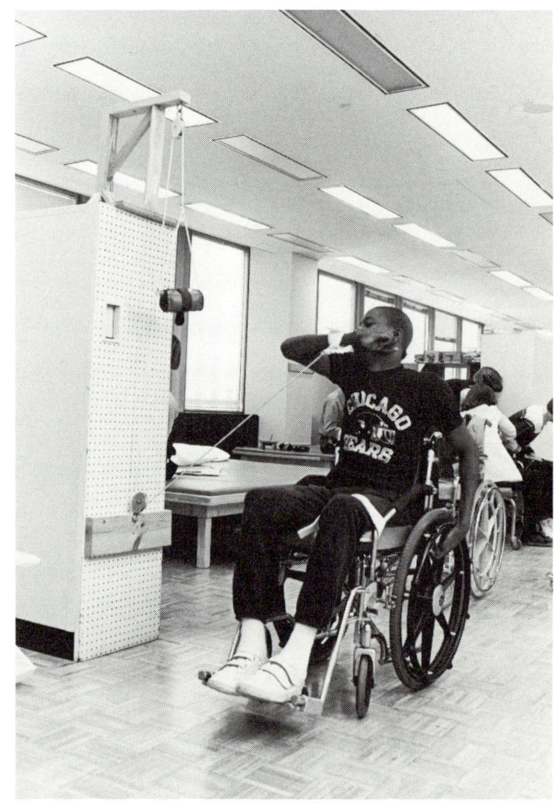

Figure 5–25 Type 2 pulley resists upward motion.

Summary of Shoulder Girdle and Elbow Strengthening

With any of the above techniques, especially the apparatus, the normal scapulohumeral rhythm must be kept in mind at all times. Counterweights providing "assistance" to shoulder flexion may cause damage if the scapular rotation is not occurring in conjunction with humeral flexion. The patient should be thoroughly evaluated and instructed in the proper use of any equipment. If necessary, the therapist may need to provide manual assistance, such as assisting scapular rotation during the activity.

Figure 5–26 Bilateral sander with weight on flat surface, and flexion mitts.

Figure 5–27 Bilateral sander with weight on slant board; involving tenodesis.

WRIST STRENGTHENING

The most frequent strengthening intervention at the wrist is for radial wrist extensors in the trace to fair ranges, which have potential to be built up for tenodesis hand function. Initially, when the wrist extensors are in a trace range, the therapist supports the patient's forearm in neutral and asks him to contract the muscle, while palpating the contraction and asking the patient to hold to the count of five. Biofeedback equipment can also be used in this process. A "quick stretch," vibration, or tapping of the muscle may facilitate contraction. "Place and hold"—placing the wrist in extension, giving some approximation through the wrist joint, and then asking the patient to hold in extension (while still supporting the wrist)—may result in more consistent contraction.

As contraction becomes more consistent and motion is noted in the gravity-eliminated position, active motion is requested of the patient. At this time other, less passive, methods of strengthening can be initiated.

A wrist extension assist can be added to a long opponens wrist-hand orthosis (WHO) to allow active assisted extension throughout the day. A flexion stop is provided to prevent the wrist from dropping into excessive flexion and overstretching the weak extensors. This is an option that is not often utilized because

- Assisted extension status is hoped to be temporary and incorporation of the extension assist into a definitive orthosis is not necessary.
- The extension assist attachment is cumbersome.
- At this stage, endurance is not adequate to utilize the extension assist frequently.

More often, an RIC tenodesis orthosis, with wrist extension assist, is fabricated. This can be used during therapy and at other selected times during the day for both strengthening and incorporation of tenodesis into functional tasks. It cannot replace the long opponens, however, as there is no mechanism for stopping excessive wrist flexion. It is not essential that the finger shell and tenodesis cord be attached at this time because the tenodesis action is relying on the assistance of a rubber band. The force of the rubber band and the wrist extension combined are not sufficient to exert a force capable of making the string taut and forcing the fingers against the thumb. Letting gravity bring the fingers to the thumb when the wrist is extended affords adequate pinch action to pick up light objects such as paper, cards, potato chips, and crackers while beginning tenodesis training and strengthening wrist extensors (Figure 5–28).

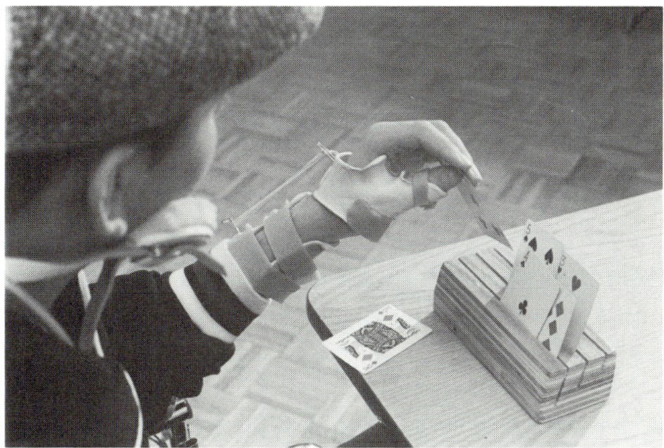

Figure 5–28 RIC tenodesis splint, without finger shell, with wrist extension assist is used to strengthen wrist extensors while playing cards.

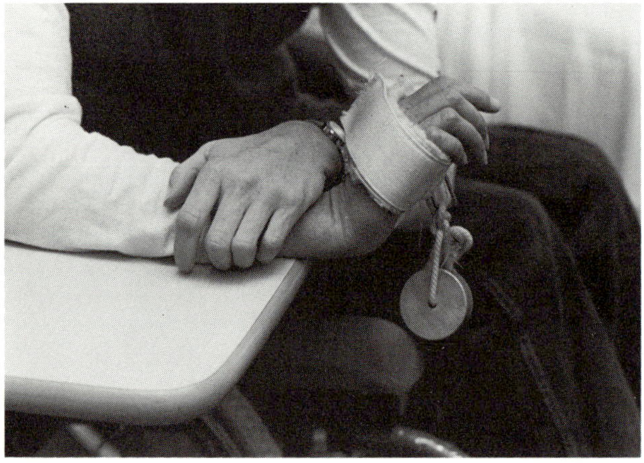

Figure 5–29 A weighted hand cuff is used to resist wrist extension.

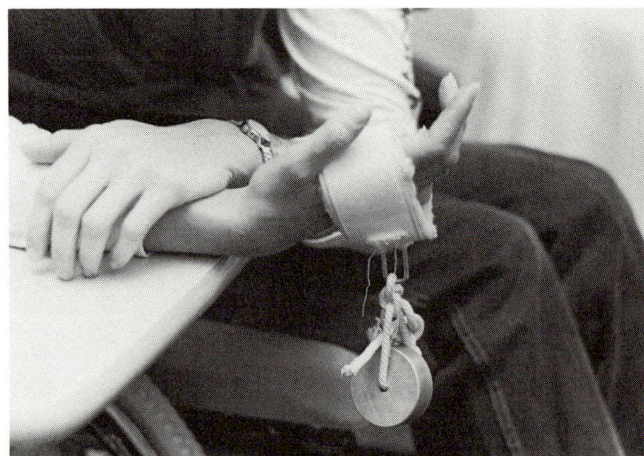

Figure 5–30 The hand cuff is used with the forearm supinated to resist wrist flexors.

A wrist extension assist can also be used on a wrist-driven flexor hinge (WDFH) orthosis. Wrist extensors in the fair range will be needed to operate this orthosis even with the extension assist (because of mechanical friction resistance in the orthosis itself, combined with resistance against the orthosis by the radially deviating wrist). With strength requirements being this great for the WDFH with extension assist, more assisted tenodesis training is done with the RIC orthosis with extension assist. The WDFH orthosis is ordered when good strength is achieved.

Once wrist extensor strength reaches a fair grade, graded resistive exercises can be introduced using the hand cuff and weights (Figure 5–29). These can also be used for weak wrist flexors (Figure 5–30). Strengthening for wrist musculature in the fair to good range can be incorporated into pulley exercises when the flexion mitt is used.

HAND STRENGTHENING

Many of the techniques and devices used in hand strengthening with the SCI patient are the same as those used in strengthening programs designed for other types of hand dysfunction.

With musculature in the poor-grade range, place and hold techniques are used. The therapist places the joint in the desired position, offers some approximation, and asks the patient to maintain the position. This is followed by attempts at active motion by the patient.

With stronger musculature, rubber band grippers and Theraplast are introduced. Functional activities involving built-up handles, as opposed to the cuff-type attachment to the hand, are begun. Fine coordination and manipulation tasks are introduced as the intrinsics develop strength.

The balance between intrinsic and extrinsic hand musculature must always be kept in mind. When intrinsics are not innervated or are too weak to counter the force of the extrinsic flexors and extensors, they should be protected with a metacarpophalangeal joint (MP) extension stop as a component of the orthosis used, to prevent intrinsic-minus hand deformity.

BUILDING TRUNK BALANCE IN SITTING AND STANDING

Getting comfortable with trunk balance (substituting for weakened or denervated trunk musculature) can be a challenge for SCI patients. This becomes a crucial issue in OT when the patient is not able to sit (or stand) without the support of one or both UEs. UEs engaged in stabilizing are not available for use in functional tasks.

Initially, freeing of both UEs for function is practiced with support from the W/C. Dowel rods may be used to hit a balloon or ball. The therapist, in tossing the ball, grades how far away from his center of gravity the patient must reach to return it. Ball tossing or any activity requiring bilateral UE reach, such as suspended macrame, can be substituted (Figure 5–31).

These activities can be upgraded by transferring the patient to the mat table, where no external support is available (Figure 5–32). A spotter should be present until the patient is comfortable sitting unsupported. A rocker board can then be introduced to further challenge balance (Figure 5–33).

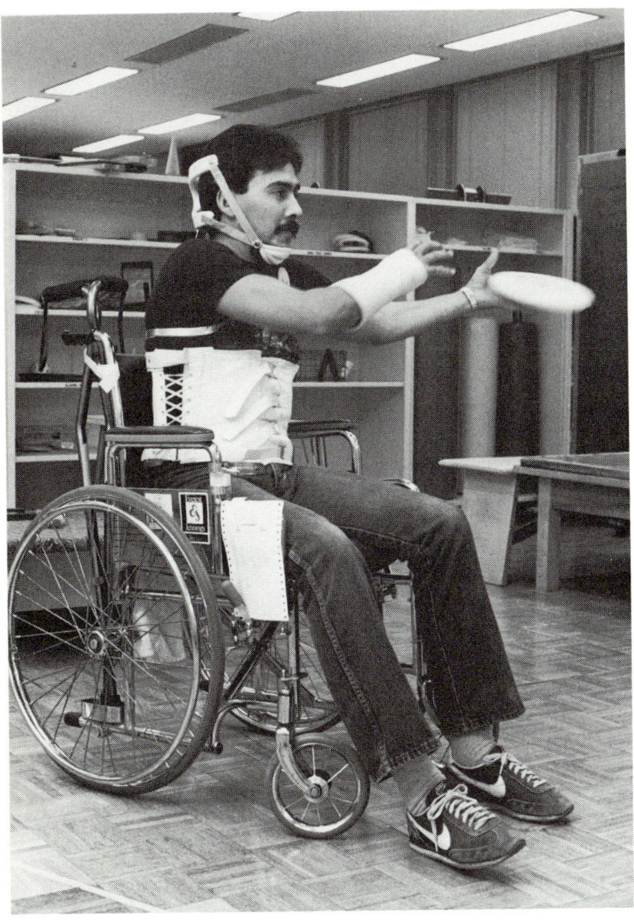

Figure 5–31 Using both UEs for function while stabilized in W/C is required to play Frisbee.

Figure 5–32 Hitting a balloon with a dowel rod while short sitting on a mat challenges balance.

Figure 5–33 Reaching while on a rocker board provides a further challenge to balance.

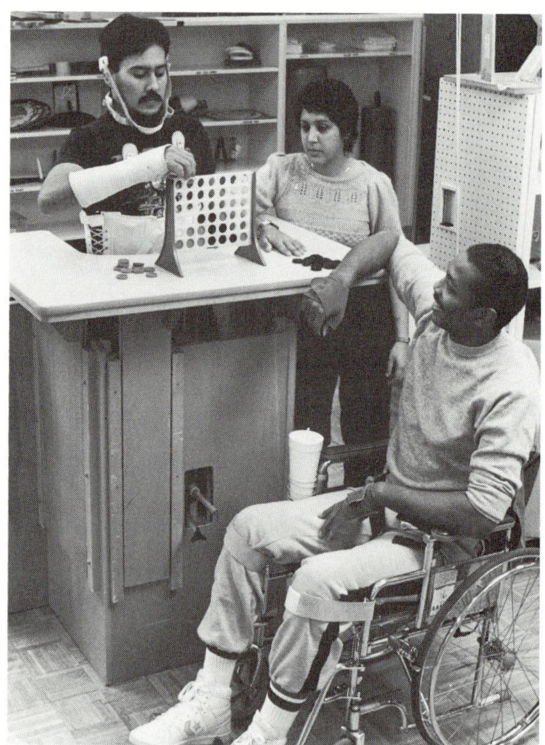

Figure 5–34 Standing table activities begin with one UE used for stabilization.

In standing with LE orthoses, the patient begins functional training in OT in the standing table. Activities requiring the freeing of one, and then both, UEs are introduced, as are activities requiring reaching away from the center of gravity and into increasing degrees of shoulder flexion (Figures 5–34 and 5–35). These activities can be transferred to use in ADL such as standing with support gained by leaning against a cabinet. Free-standing activities usually require that at least one UE remain involved in stabilizing, except in very low injuries (L4 or below) (Figure 5–36).

Any weight added by carrying an object (a back pack, for example) will change the center of gravity slightly and require compensation by the patient, since the muscles of the legs and trunk that would usually provide automatic compensation are not innervated.

Figure 5–35 Standing table activities progress to bilateral tasks.

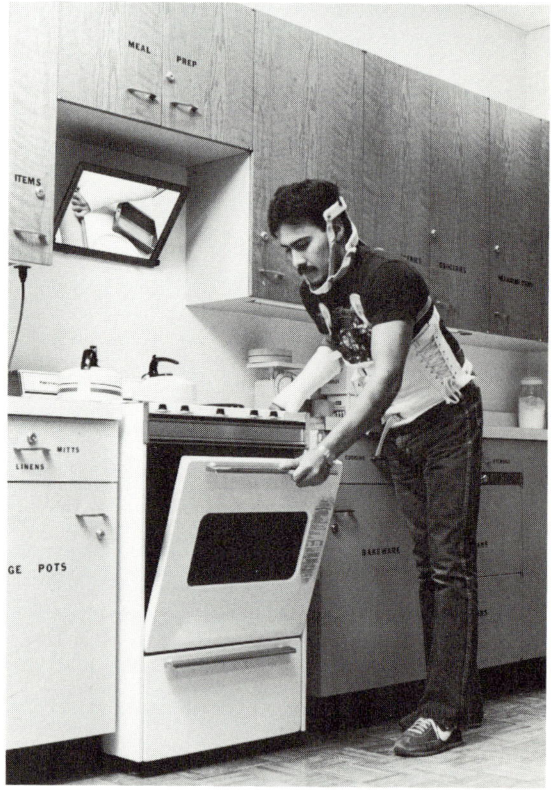

Figure 5–36 When beginning standing activities out of standing table, one UE is used to stabilize.

SUMMARY

Motor skills retraining requires continual monitoring of muscle strength and endurance. As soon as a trace contraction is palpable, strengthening through functional tasks and exercise can begin. It is crucial that OT and PT collaborate in treatment planning to avoid redundancy in one area and oversight of another. Provision for continued strengthening after discharge through daily task performance or a structured exercise program should be made. At any point in the patient's life it can become necessary to institute a specific strengthening program in order to achieve a newly identified goal.

SUMMARY CHART: Strengthening

Goal	*Indicator*	*Recommended Intervention*
1. Limited head control in gravity-eliminated position	1. C2-C3 or incomplete C1 injury 2. Functional head and neck ROM 3. T to P neck musculature	1. Mouthstick activities in reclined position 2. Headrest 3. Activities set up on slant board 4. Magnetic games
2. Limited head control	1. C3-C4 injury 2. Functional head and neck ROM 3. P to G neck musculature strength	1. Mouthstick activities in upright position 2. Activities set up on flat surface 3. Gradual increase in resistance and control requirements
3. Limited scapular control	1. C4 injury 2. Functional ROM 3. Zero to T deltoid, biceps, brachioradialis; F to N trapezius 4. Moderate spasticity	1. Mouthstick activities in upright position 2. BFO, LSEO for very light activities, limited typing, may feed self soft foods
4. Assisted limited arm placement	1. C4-C5 injury 2. T to P deltoid, biceps, brachioradialis and clavicular pectoralis 3. Functional UE ROM 4. Limited endurance 5. Mild spasticity 6. Motor learning abilities and motivation promote use of BFO, sling, or LSEO to enhance function	1. BFO, LSEO, or deltoid-assist sling 2. Forward reach pattern encouragement 3. Alternating resistance and stabilization
5. Unassisted limited arm placement	1. C5-C6 injury 2. Functional ROM 3. P to F deltoids, biceps, brachioradialis, clavicular pectoralis 4. Zero to moderate spasticity in scapular shoulder and elbow musculature 5. F to G endurance in available musculature	1. BFO or deltoid-assist sling initially 2. Alternating resistance and stabilization 3. Biceps assist 4. Triceps assist 5. Pulleys 6. Bilateral sander 7. Dowel ladder

SUMMARY CHART continued

Goal	*Indicator*	*Recommended Intervention*
6. Full arm placement	1. C7 or incomplete higher injury 2. All shoulder, scapular, and elbow musculature in F to N ranges 3. Normal UE ROM 4. Zero to minimal spasticity in above muscles	1. Biceps assist 2. Triceps assist 3. Pulleys 4. Bilateral sander 5. Dowel ladder 6. Overhead reach activities 7. Resistive ADL, craft, and leisure activities
7. Tenodesis hand function	1. C5-C7 injury 2. P to F wrist extension 3. Minimal spasticity in wrist and hand 4. Limited assisted or better arm placement 5. Motor learning abilities and motivation promote use of orthosis	1. RIC tenodesis orthosis (with extension assist initially) 2. Long opponens WHO with extension assist 3. WDFH orthosis with extension assist 4. Place and hold 5. Contraction, manual palpation, and feedback 6. Biofeedback 7. Quick stretch 8. Hand cuff and weights
8. Limited (natural) hand function	1. C8 or incomplete higher injury 2. P to F extrinsic finger musculature; zero to P intrinsics 3. Zero to moderate spasticity in wrist and hand 4. Limited assisted or better arm placement 5. Functional to normal sensation	1. Intrinsic minus deformity prevention with MP stop 2. Place and hold 3. Approximation 4. Hand grippers 5. Theraplast 6. Built-up utensils 7. Peg boards and fine coordination games (Hi-Q, Connect 4)
9. Normal hand function	1. T1 or lower injury 2. Wrist, intrinsic, and extrinsic hand musculature; F to N strength 3. Zero to mild spasticity in wrist and hand musculature 4. Normal sensation	1. Grippers 2. Theraplast 3. Resistive prevocational, ADL, and craft activities 4. Graded-size peg boards

SUMMARY CHART continued

Goal	*Indicator*	*Recommended Intervention*
10. Limited trunk stability	1. C5-C6 injury 2. Limited unassisted arm placement	1. One UE hooked on chair handle or through McCormick Loop to stabilize (ability developed on both sides so asymmetry is not encouraged) 2. The other UE used in tasks beginning with table-height tasks near midline and progressing to reach to feet and overhead 3. Both UEs used for function by keeping weight (trunk) behind center of gravity (pelvis)
11. Trunk stability	1. C8 or lower injury	1. Bilateral UE tasks 2. Dowel rod activities 3. Ball toss 4. Suspended macrame • from W/C • from mat table • rocker board
12. Limited trunk control	2. T6 or lower injury	1. Standing table activities with LE braces • free one UE • free both UEs 2. Standing activities, leaning against stable surface with LE braces • free one UE • apply to functional tasks • carry items in back pack
13. Full trunk control	1. T12 or lower injury	1. Standing table activities with or without LE braces • free one UE • free both UEs • resistive activities (Playbuoy) 2. Standing activities leaning against stable surface with or without LE braces • free one UE • free both UEs • resistive activities 3. Standing activities unsupported with or without LE braces • free one UE • attempt all household ADL from standing • free both UEs for function (L4 or lower injury) • Community ADL from standing (usually L4 or lower injury)

Unit 6

Deformity Control

Judy Hill, OTR/L
Jessica Presperin, OTR/L

When muscle function is lost, deforming forces that may damage muscles, joint structures, and soft tissues become active. These deforming forces include gravity, muscle weakness, and immobility that can result in

- muscle overstretching
- muscle contractures
- joint stiffness
- joint misalignment
- soft tissue tightening
- joint instability

Deformity control should begin as soon after injury as possible. Deformity control includes

- preventing unwanted deformity that will interfere with function (elbow flexion supination contracture may interfere with self-feeding)
- promoting deformity that can support function (tenodesis)
- preserving appearance
- maintaining integrity of UE joints and arches and spinal joints and curvatures

Methods of controlling deformity include ROM, orthotics, casting, and positioning.

RANGE OF MOTION

In the quadriplegic UE where active motion does not exist, ROM must be provided. Self-ROM techniques for the shoulder girdle and elbow of the C4-C5 quadriplegic are limited to the movement that can be attained with LSEOs, BFOs, or deltoid-assist slings. This will not preserve adequate range, particularly at the shoulder girdle. Passive ROM must be provided. Wrist and hand self-ROM can be performed by the patient with C6 function.

Passive ROM

During passive ROM, the therapist moves the UE through the normal arc of joint motion. (See Table 6–1 for motions provided at each joint.)

Several areas require special consideration in passive ROM:

- Shoulder flexion and abduction. The humerus must be externally rotated to achieve full flexion and abduction. External rotation is necessary for the greater tuberosity of the humerus to clear the

Table 6–1 Passive ROM Checklist

Joint	Movement	Joint	Movement
Shoulder	Protraction	Wrist	Flexion
	Flexion		Extension
	Abduction		
	Horizontal adduction	Finger	Flexion
	Horizontal abduction		Extension
	External rotation		
	Internal rotation	Thumb	Flexion
			Extension
Elbow	Flexion		Abduction
	Extension		Adduction
	Supination		Opposition
	Pronation		

acromion process. Assistance to scapular rotation may also be needed during passive shoulder flexion and abduction. For every 20° of glenohumeral flexion, the scapula should rotate 10°. Weak serratus anterior muscles may necessitate manual assistance for scapular rotation (Figure 6–1). Range into horizontal adduction is crucial for ADL. When the pectoralis muscles are not innervated the scapula often becomes fixed or tight in an adducted position, preventing the scapular abduction needed for cross-body reach.

- Elbow. When biceps are in the trace to poor range, positioning the elbow in slight flexion and not ranging into full extension may promote slight contracture, which can give a mechanical advantage to the muscle in exerting its pull on the forearm. In all other cases, full elbow extension should be the goal. The elbow is ranged into extension with the forearm pronated and into flexion with the forearm in neutral.
- Wrist and hand. When performing passive ROM to the wrist, the patient's hand should be held at the metacarpals, leaving the fingers free (Figures 6–2 and 6–3).

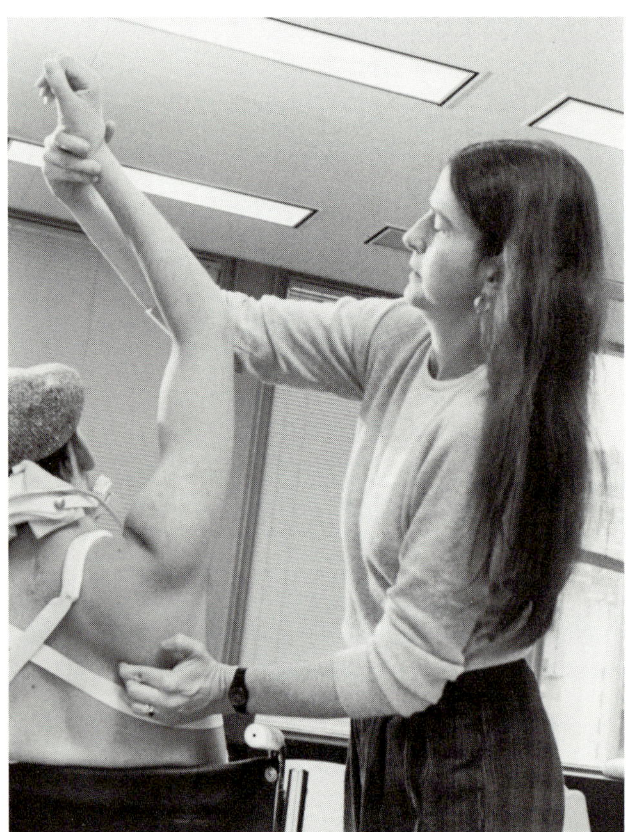

Figure 6–1 Scapular rotation and external rotation are assisted during passive ROM into shoulder flexion.

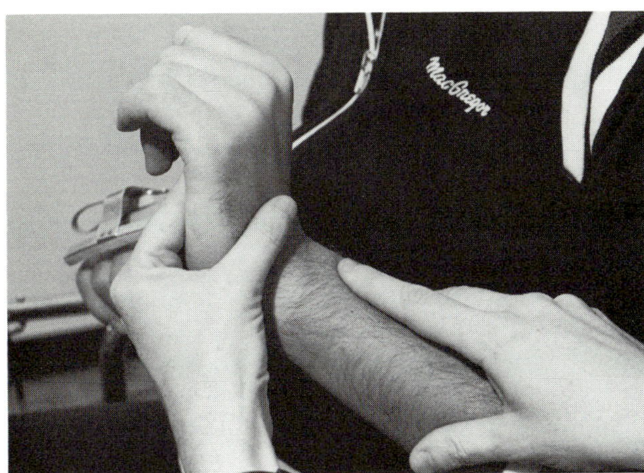

Figure 6–2 The fingers are allowed to flex when ranging into wrist extension.

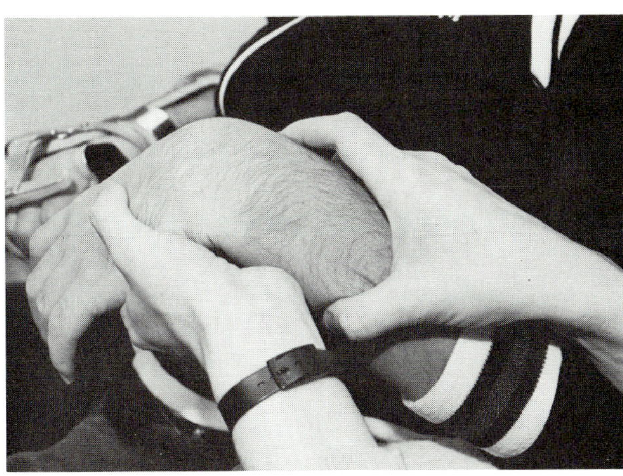

Figure 6–3 The fingers are allowed to extend when ranging the wrist into flexion.

- Finger and thumb extension is performed with the wrist flexed (Figure 6–4). Finger and thumb flexion is performed with the wrist extended (Figure 6–5). This enhances tenodesis hand function by promoting shortening of the finger flexors for grip with the wrist extended and tightening of the finger extensors for improved release with the wrist flexed.

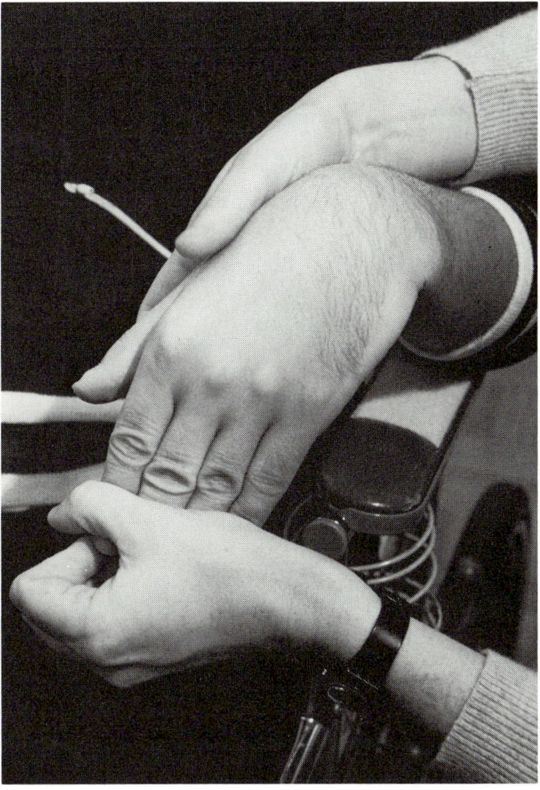

Figure 6–4 The fingers are ranged into extension with the wrist flexed.

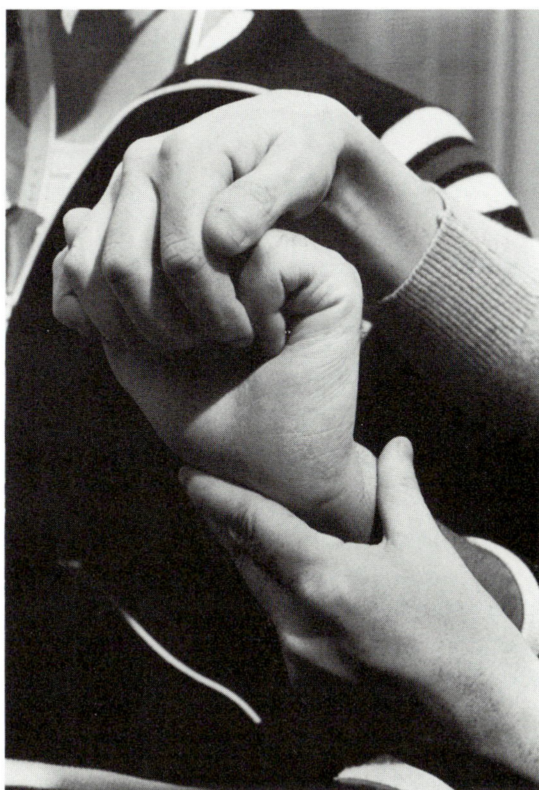

Figure 6–5 The fingers are ranged into flexion with the wrist extended.

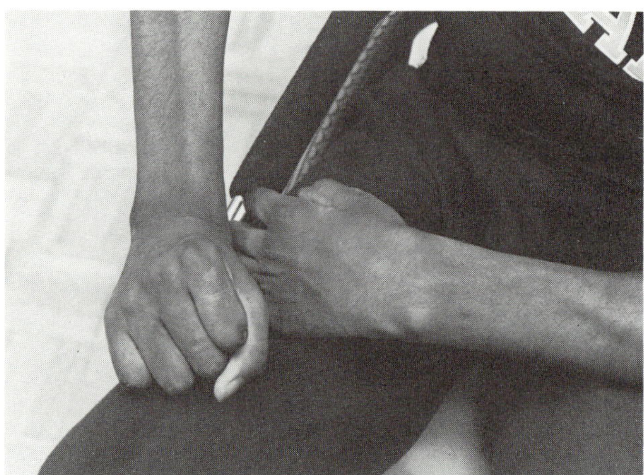

Figure 6–6 Self-ROM of finger extension.

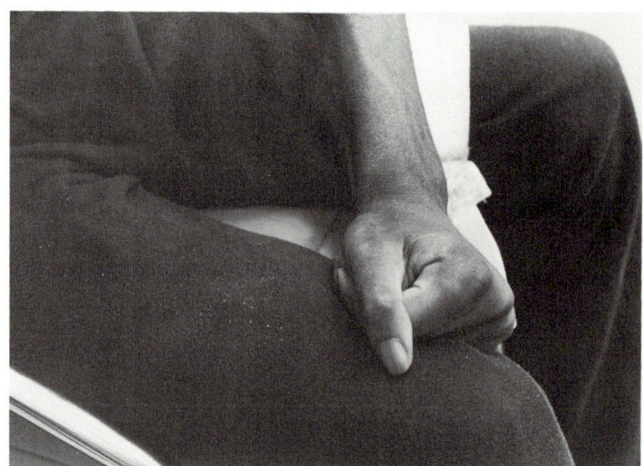

Figure 6–7 Self-ROM of finger flexion.

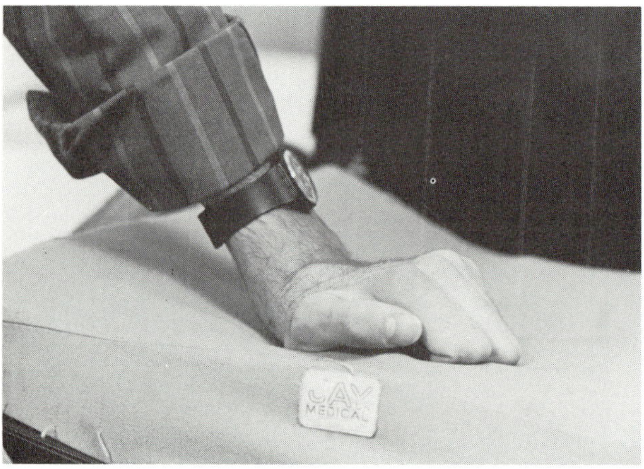

Figure 6–8 UE weight bearing with hand fisted.

Wrist and Hand Self-ROM

For finger extension, the fingers are draped over the thigh with wrist flexed (Figure 6–6). The opposite hand exerts slight pressure over the interphalangeal joints (IPs). The opposite hand is used to bring the thumb into extension with the wrist flexed.

For finger flexion, the dorsum of the hand is placed on the thigh. The elbow is lifted and the forearm pronated to bring the hand into a fist with wrist extended (Figure 6–7).

The hand should remain fisted during UE weight-bearing activities (Figure 6–8). This prevents overstretching of the finger flexors, which will interfere with tenodesis hand function. It also protects the intrinsic hand musculature from overstretching, thus preventing intrinsic-minus (claw hand) deformity.

UPPER EXTREMITY ORTHOTICS

Upper extremity orthoses are used to control deformity by protecting weak muscles, protecting joint structures whose muscular support has been lost or weakened, and providing functional positioning of the hand and wrist. Orthotic devices prescribed for positioning should be incorporated into functional activities. This can be done by adding utensil slots to the orthoses (Figure 6–9).

Shoulder

Deformities that limit function, interfere with dressing and hygiene, or potentially cause pain at the shoulder include subluxation, limited passive flexion and abduction due to dependent positioning, and scapulae fixed in elevation because of unopposed elevators and difficulty relaxing. These problems occur in high SCIs (C4 and above). Orthotic systems to address potential deformities in the shoulder are limited. Passive ROM and positioning are the most effective interventions. The BFO, deltoid-assist sling, or LSEO can be used to achieve limited active shoulder and scapular range at the C4 level while supporting the UEs (see Figures 5–4 to 5–6).

Elbow

Elbow extension contractures may develop in patients with high SCI and when extensor spasticity is present. The most common interventions are positioning in elbow flexion and ROM. In severe cases, when

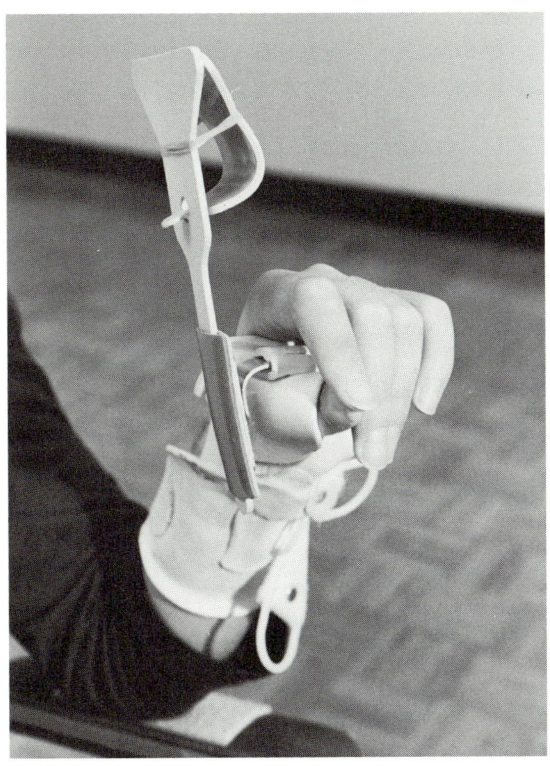

Figure 6–9 A utensil slot on a temporary long opponens allows its incorporation into feeding.

positioning cannot be maintained because of spasm, an elbow orthosis may be fabricated. The BFO or LSEO can be used to assist the patient in achieving elbow motion through scapular elevation and leverage.

Elbow flexion contracture, usually combined with supination contracture, most frequently poses a problem in C5 to C6 SCI in which innervated, sometimes spastic, biceps are unopposed. This tendency is increased when the patient is supine. In the supine position, once the elbow is flexed, either actively by the patient or by spasms, the patient cannot extend it without assistance. Several orthotic options are available to prevent this deformity. If the supination component is not significant, that is, if the elbow can be maintained in extension without pulling into supination, an elbow extension orthosis (Yasukawa-Kozole) (Figure 6–10) can be fabricated. Occasionally, when the pull into flexion is not strong, the Plastizote liner is enough to maintain extension (Figure 6–11).

When the supination component must be controlled as well, an orthosis that crosses the wrist is necessary to provide leverage into pronation. A bivalved, full-circumference, fiberglass orthosis can be fabricated in the OT clinic (Figure 6–12).

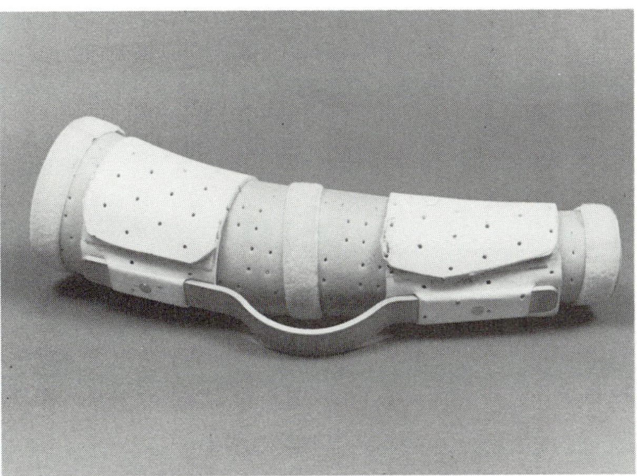

Figure 6–10 The elbow extension orthosis (Yasukawa-Kozole).

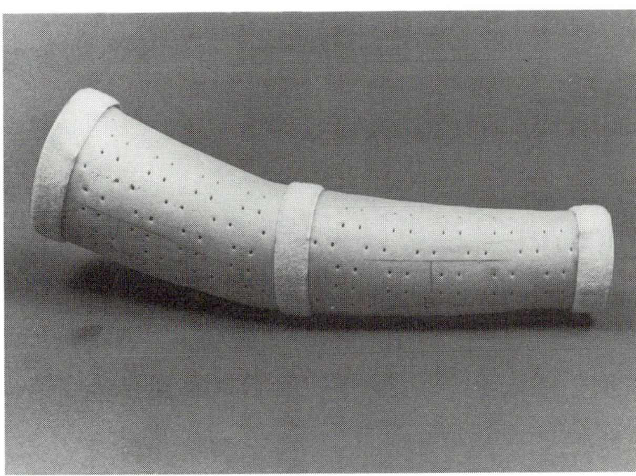

Figure 6–11 The elbow extension orthosis liner may be adequate to position.

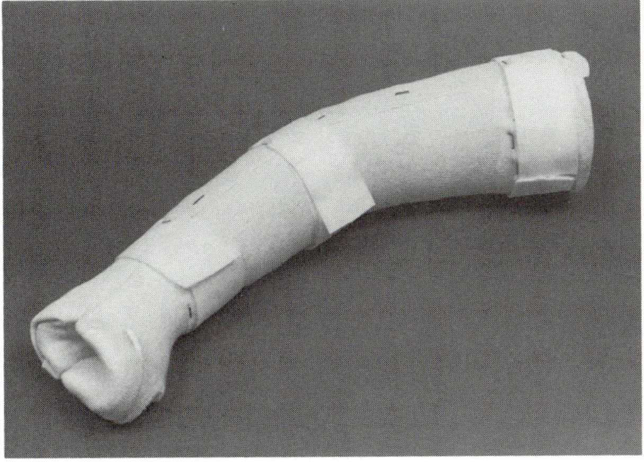

Figure 6–12 Bivalved fiberglass long arm cast is used to position in elbow extension and pronation.

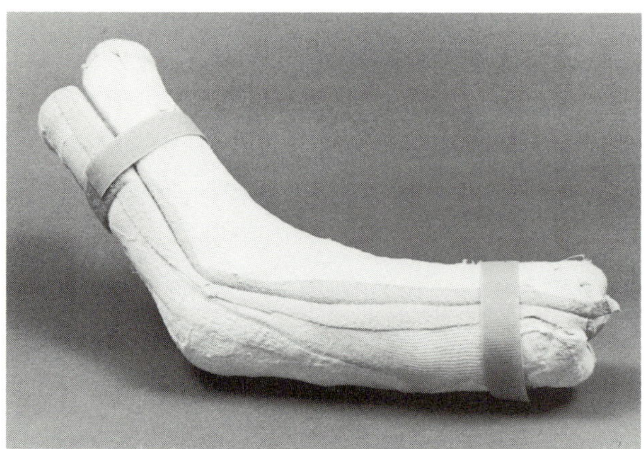

Figure 6–13 Bivalved plaster rigid circular elbow cast.

A third, more definitive and durable option, is the fabrication of an elbow, wrist, and hand orthosis by an orthotist. Elbow extension, forearm pronation, and wrist and hand positioning are provided and the amount of elbow extension is adjustable. This orthosis is made from a plaster model of the patient's extremity. Fabrication is time-consuming and temporary positioning may need to be provided in the meantime. A bivalved plaster cast can provide quick and inexpensive temporary positioning (Figure 6–13).

Wearing Schedule for Elbow Extension Orthoses

Ideally, night use alone will be adequate to prevent elbow and forearm deformity, allowing the UEs to be engaged in functional tasks during the day.

If it becomes very difficult to get the orthoses on each night and the arms are maintained in elbow flexion and supination most of the day, night use alone may not be sufficient. Adding use during rest periods two times a day is the next step. If this schedule is not sufficient to maintain ROM, the orthoses are left on at all times except during therapies, hygiene, and functional task performance. This continuous use can result in considerable joint stiffness and is not considered a long-term solution. It can be used temporarily while other options are being explored (nerve block or surgery). The BFO can also be used to assist in preventing elbow flexion and supination deformity by placing the arm in the trough in pronation and balancing the support toward forward flexion at the shoulder with extended elbow.

Considerations in BFO Adjustment and Use

Two comprehensive resources on BFO adjustment are available and are listed in Appendix C [Wilson, McKenzie, Barber, & Watson, 1984 (General); Thenn, 1975 (Orthotics)]. Therefore, this unit will focus on methods of facilitating various UE motions through special parts and adjustments. Considerations for mounting the BFO on various types of chairs will also be discussed.

Mounting the bracket is straightforward on standard Everest and Jennings chairs. Mounting on electric reclining chairs and Rolls chairs requires modifications.

On electric reclining chairs, the reclining mechanism placement on the uprights prevents mounting at the standard height. Two options are available:

1. Mount the bracket higher, above the reclining mechanism, and use an elevating proximal arm (Figure 6–14).
2. Use an accessory mount to attach the bracket to the W/C upright (Figure 6–15).

Since the elevating proximal arm is frequently used for functional reasons, the first option is the most common.

On many Rolls chairs both the upholstery and the upholstery screws interfere with bracket mounting. If BFOs are to be mounted on these chairs, non-wraparound upholstery can be ordered and the screws moved to above and below the bracket mounting area. A rehabilitation engineer can also be consulted to modify the bracket for mounting (Figure 6–16).

Table 6–2 lists BFO components, the motions they can be adjusted to facilitate, the mechanism for facilitating the movement, and functional implications. General principles of BFO adjustment include

- Balancing the BFO initially in neutral, then making minor adjustments to facilitate functional movement patterns.
- Making adjustments distally first, as a proximal adjustment (at the bracket, for example), which will influence all components and may result in making unnecessary compensatory adjustments distally.
- Providing trunk stability through lateral trunk supports if the patient is unable to maintain himself in an upright position through proper seating and compensation with head, neck, and trunk musculature. Lack of trunk stability will interfere with BFO balance and use, especially bilateral use.

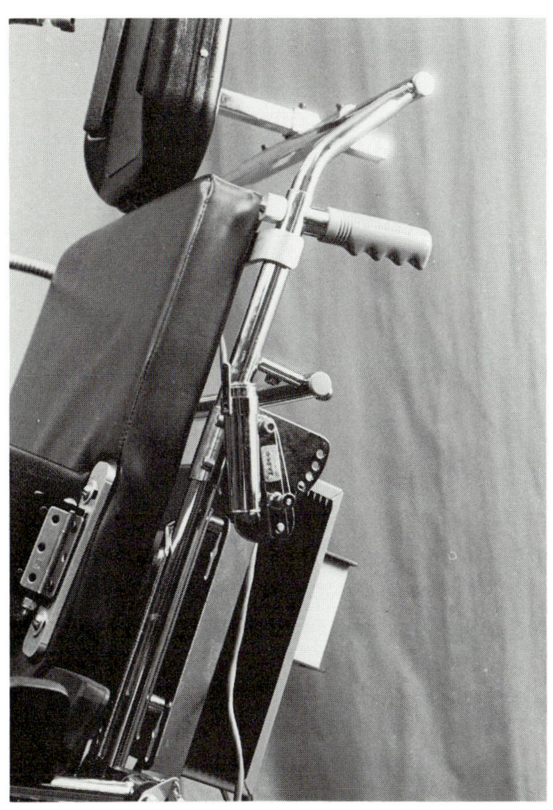

Figure 6–14 BFO bracket mounted above reclining mechanism on electric reclining chair.

Figure 6–15 BFO bracket mounted on accessory mount on electric reclining chair.

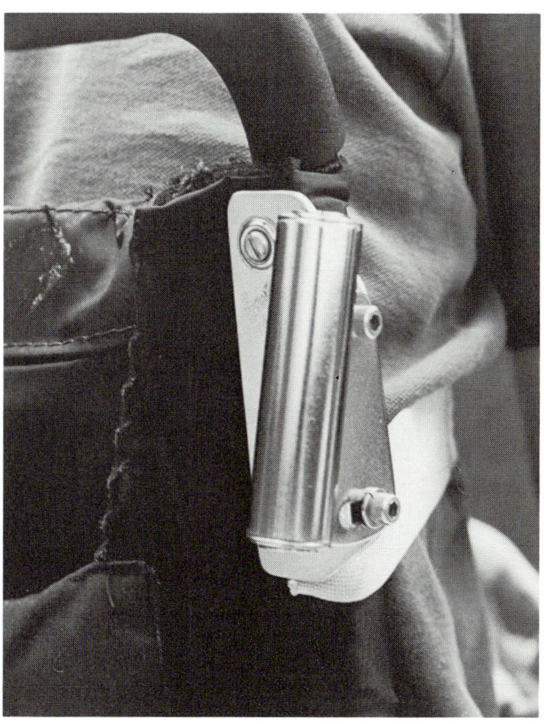

Figure 6–16 Hedman (RIC RE) BFO bracket adapted to mount with upholstery screws on Rolls chair.

TABLE 6–2 BFO Components

Component	*Motion Facilitated*	*Mechanism*	*Functional Task Implications*
Brackets (Figure 6–17)	1. Forward reach with shoulder flexion, protraction, elbow extension	Tilt bracket anteriorly	Assists reach to tabletop for tasks
	2. Hand to mouth, shoulder extension retraction, elbow flexion	Tilt bracket posteriorly	Assists flexion pattern for hand to mouth
	3. Horizontal adduction	Rotate bracket inward	Assists cross-body reach; may be useful in tabletop games, access to typewriter keyboard, reaching mouth
	4. Horizontal abduction	Rotate bracket outward	Assists reach to side; may be useful in reaching electric W/C control; may interfere with cross-body reach, especially where pectoralis not innervated; can be used to strengthen weak pectoralis
Elevating proximal arm (Figure 6–18)	1. Vertical motion; shoulder flexion, abduction	Rubber bands	Strengthens weak deltoids, upward reach for feeding
	2. Elbow extension, internal rotation	Tilt distal bearing housing anteriorly	Assists forward reach; may assist in getting downward pressure for typing and reach to electric W/C control
	3. Elbow flexion, external rotation	Tilt distal bearing housing posteriorly	Assists hand to mouth; resists forward reach
Standard proximal arm (Figure 6–18)	1. Elbow flexion; extension; internal, external rotation same as for elevating proximal arm	Works in horizontal plane. Vertical hand placement (to table, to mouth) achieved through internal and external rotation	

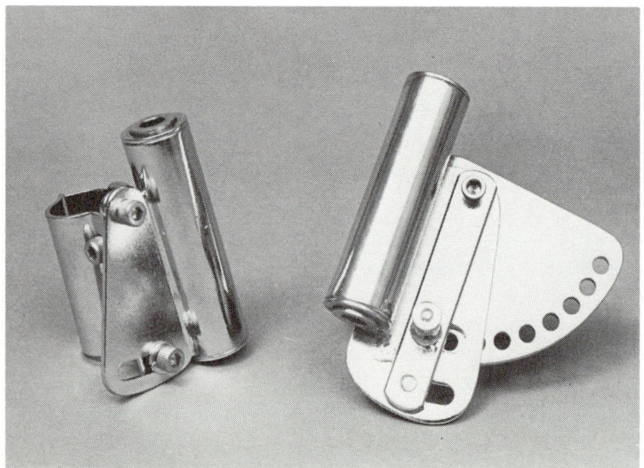

Figure 6–17 Left adjustable BFO bracket (left) and left reclining BFO bracket (right).

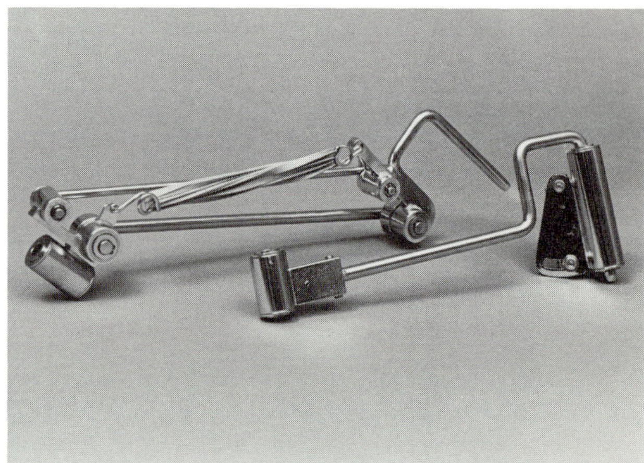

Figure 6–18 Left BFO elevating proximal arm (top and left) and BFO standard adjustable proximal arm (bottom and right).

Table 6–2 continued

Component	Motion Facilitated	Mechanism	Functional Task Implications
Distal arms (standard and extra long) (Figure 6–19)	1. Forward reach	Extra long arm use	
Rocker arm assemblies (swivels)	1. Elbow extension, internal rotation	Mount more proximally (toward elbow) on trough	Assists forward reach to plate, table; downward pressure for typing
	2. Elbow flexion, external rotation	Mount more distally (toward hand) on trough	Assists hand to mouth
Standard swivel (Figure 6–20)	1. Extremes of internal and external rotation, elbow flexion and extension	Simple leverage—once weight shifted to elbow side of pivot (swivel), gravity pulls into full elbow flexion and external rotation and vice versa	May be difficult for the patient with weak rotators or limited scapular mobility to control and reverse the motions
Supinator assist (Figure 6–21)	1. Supination as elbow flexes	Rotation component of swivel	As for standard swivel; assists in bringing food to mouth in self-feeding
	2. Pronation as elbow extends	Rotation component of swivel	Assists in getting food on utensil at plate but may interfere in writing and typing

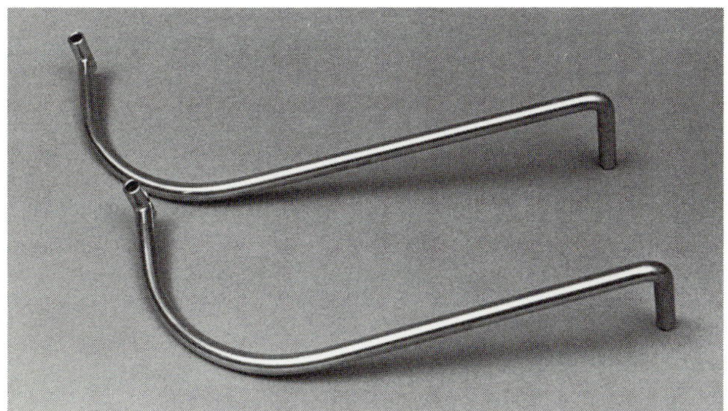

Figure 6–19 Left BFO extra-long distal arm (top) and left BFO distal arm (bottom).

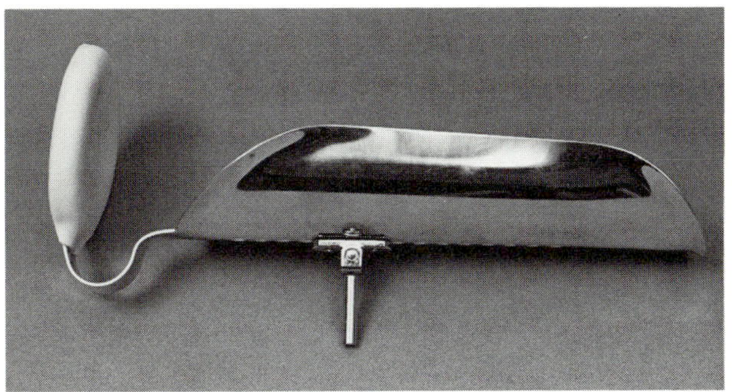

Figure 6–20 Left BFO trough with standard swivel.

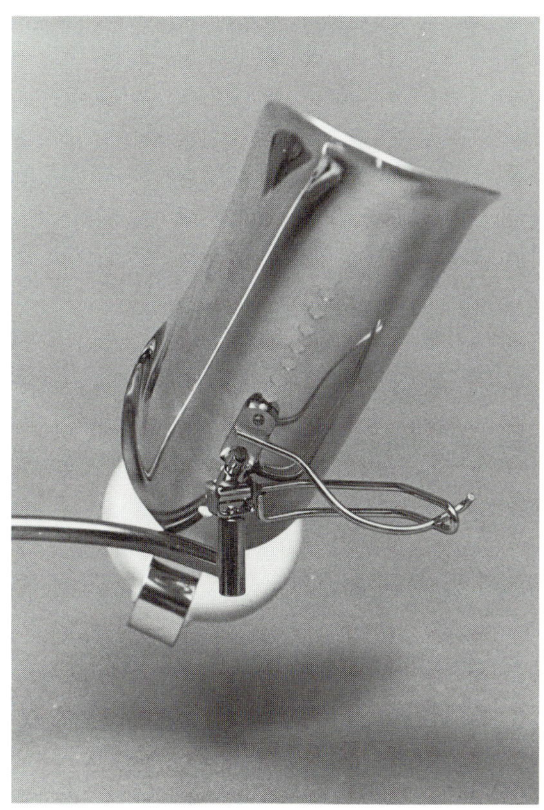

Figure 6–21 Left BFO trough with supinator assist.

TABLE 6–2 continued

Component	Motion Facilitated	Mechanism	Functional Task Implications
Rocker stop (Figure 6–22)	1. Controls extremes of motion on standard and supinator assist swivels	Stops rotation when trough hits screw	1. Allows adjustment of simple leverage to varying muscle pictures 2. Can be graded as rotators, scapular elevators increase in strength
Riser (Figure 6–23)	1. Lifts trough approximately 1.5 inches higher	Inserts onto swivel and extends it	1. Can provide extra height to reach mouth 2. Exacerbates extremes of motion problem 3. Can help to prevent elbow dial from running into distal arm
Offset swivel (Figure 6–24)	1. Graded dampening of extremes of internal and external rotation	Adjusting for highest trough position, dampens motion least—approximating most closely the simple leverage system	Aids in control of horizontal and rotary motions for smoother movement in writing, typing, feeding
	2. Can lift trough higher	Adjusting trough lowest provides most dampening of rotary motion	Offsets trough medially, helping to prevent elbow dial from running into distal arm
Table-mounted BFO			Utilized primarily with ambulatory patients with incomplete injuries (often central cord, where UE return lags behind LE return). Multiple clamps can be mounted at various work stations at home and on the job. Trough and arm components can be carried from one setting to another or provided at each setting

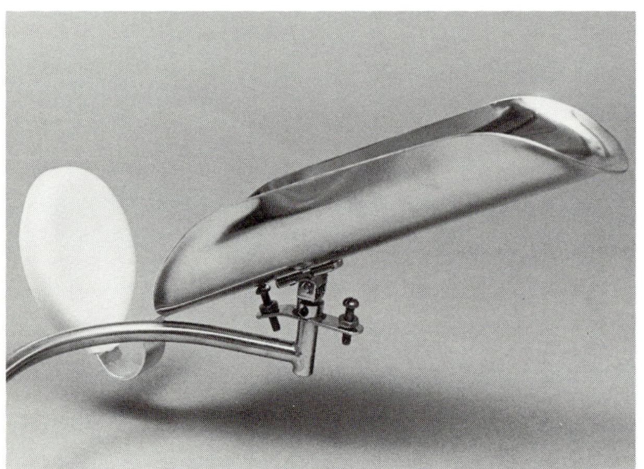

Figure 6–22 Left BFO trough with rocker stop and standard swivel.

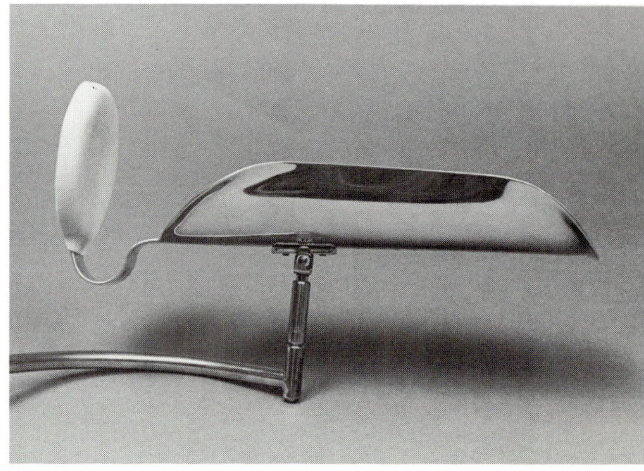

Figure 6–23 Left BFO trough with riser and standard swivel.

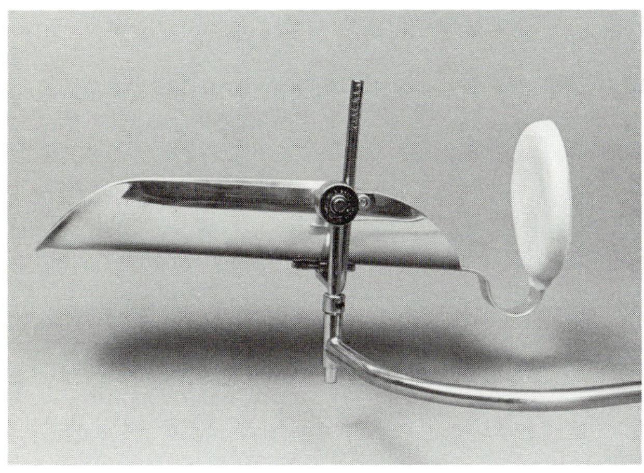

Figure 6–24 Left BFO trough with offset swivel.

The LSEO (see Figure 5–4) is a mobile arm support system alternative to the BFO. Its application and adjustability are described by Burt and Guilford (1982). For two reasons the LSEO is considered for use with higher level injuries, primarily C4. First, since it does not have an assisted shoulder flexion component, which is desirable when deltoids are innervated but weak, it is not used with the weak C5 or C4 to C5. Second, the LSEO may be more easily operated by some patients with scapular musculature only in the fair plus range or above.

The bracket adjustments offer motion assistance similar to that of the BFO. Two spring-assisted adjustment components for the trough are offered. The horizontal-assist spring influences horizontal abduction and adduction. The vertical spring assists vertical motion (through humeral rotation and elbow flexion and extension). In the patient population in which the LSEO is used, few muscles are strong enough to take resistance. For this reason the spring adjustments must be made in small increments. If one motion is assisted by the spring, enough strength is required from antagonistic muscles to oppose the spring.

Once adjusted, the only setup required for the LSEO is placement of the linear support link in the bracket. Another advantage of the LSEO is that it does not extend laterally, adding width that interferes with getting through doorways, as the BFO does.

Wrist and Hand

Deformity control and orthotic intervention goals for the wrist and hand are to

- maintain the integrity of joints and arches
- prevent muscle overstretching
- provide a functional position for natural tenodesis, natural hand function in the event of muscle return, fitting of externally powered or other mechanical grasp-release orthoses, possible future surgical options for hand function, cosmesis, and hygiene

The functional position of the hand includes

- wrist supported in neutral to 30° extension (when wrist extensors are fair plus or below)
- palmar arch supported with fourth and fifth metacarpals slightly anterior to second and third
- finger flexors and extensors positioned to allow moderate shortening for tenodesis
- MP flexion unimpeded
- MP hyperextension prevented
- thumb web space preserved
- thumb opposed to index and ring fingers, with MP and IP joints extended and first metacarpal anterior to second

Lateral prehension, as opposed to three-jaw chuck, is often more functional for a variety of tasks. Early positioning of the thumb in opposition, allowing some shortening of its flexors, actually trains a natural lateral prehension. The tightness in the thumb flexors provides some force against the index finger as the wrist is extended.

This functional position counteracts the following potential deformities in the wrist and hand:

- Wrist extension contracture. Occurs secondary to elbow flexion supination contracture at the C5 to C6 level. If the forearm rests in a supinated position and the wrist flexors are not innervated, gravity pulls the wrist into extension.
- Wrist drop. With wrist extensors fair plus or below, the wrist is not supported against gravity when the forearm is pronated.
- Extended flat hand. At C5 and above, the hand, if left to lie on a flat surface, will lose palmar curvature, passive flexion, and web space. Slight MP hyperextension may occur. At C7 with finger extensors but not flexors innervated, the same pattern may occur.

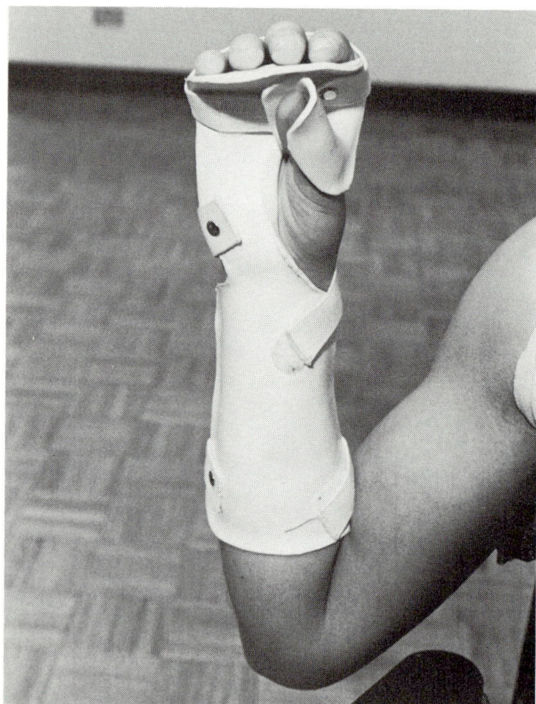

Figure 6–25 Resting hand orthosis, volar view.

- Intrinsic minus hand. Occurs secondary to wrist drop at C5 from pull on finger extensors across the wrist and MPs and from intrinsic overstretch in C6 to C8. This deformity is exaggerated at C8 with lack of intrinsic function to counteract active extrinsics.
- Tight web space. Occurs because of lack of active thumb extension and abduction and flat resting position.

Several UE orthoses provide the components of the functional position while also serving as functional splints in ADL. If properly fitted, all the orthoses described in the following pages provide MP flexion, palmar arch support, thumb abduction, web space preservation, and function through a utensil slot or mechanical grasp and release. The long opponens, resting hand, electric and cable-driven flexor hinge, and ratchet orthoses also provide wrist support. The long and short opponens with MP stops prevent MP hyperextension. All orthoses that cross the wrist control extrinsic length to some degree, although the resting hand orthosis is most effective for this. Level of lesion and wrist extensor strength indicators are listed for each orthosis.

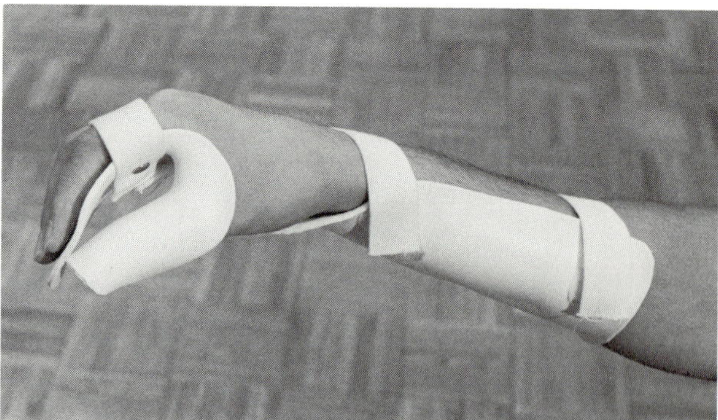

Figure 6–26 Resting hand orthosis, radial view.

Most commercial splints do not provide adequately for all necessary components of deformity control. For example, the wrist support with Palmar clip (BeOK!, Fred Sammons, Inc.) provides wrist support, allows function, and may not impede MP flexion but does not provide palmar arch support or thumb positioning or prevent MP hyperextension. Orthoses provided to SCI patients should be examined to ascertain whether they provide all the necessary components of deformity control.

Temporary Wrist and Hand Orthoses

The resting hand orthosis (Figures 6–25 and 6–26):

- used for night positioning in C7 or higher injury
- controls full length of finger flexors and extensors
- wrist position determined by desired muscle tightness (if more tightness in finger flexors is needed, wrist is positioned in neutral; if finger flexors become too tight, wrist is positioned in 30° extension)
- by design, prevents finger flexion; may not want to use if hand tight in extension
- may discard in C6 and C7 after hand has stabilized (spasticity and muscle length are stable), and the hand is used in functional tasks. This usually occurs 3 to 6 months after injury. Monitor closely after discontinuance of orthosis.

Fabrication tips include the following:

- Fabricate with patient's arm pronated, as fabrication in supination will reinforce supination contracture.
- Use Ace wrap to hold trough while forming hand and thumb.

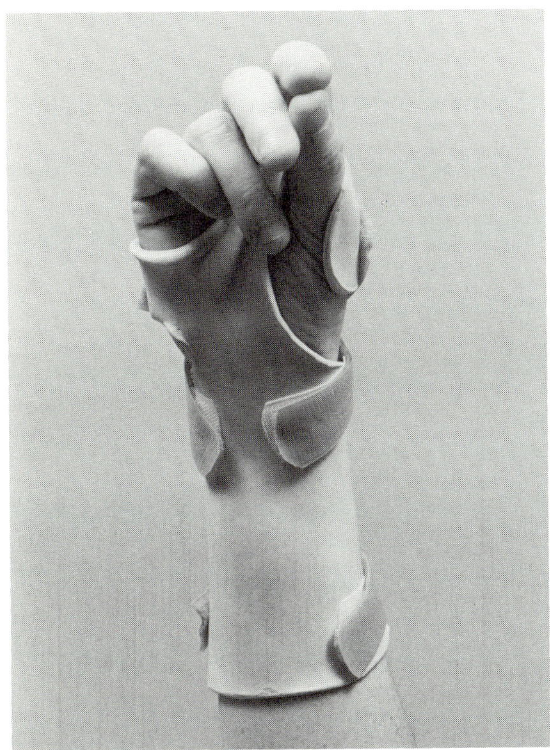

Figure 6–27 Plastic long opponens, volar view.

- Make impression in palmar arch proximal to distal palmar crease.
- Position MPs in flexion (45°).
- Remember, the distal palmar crease angles and the splint must show a corresponding angle to allow all MPs to flex.
- Position IPs in slight flexion.
- Pull palmar material away from thenar eminence to allow the first metacarpal to be aligned with the radius.
- Thumb opposition is achieved through metacarpal abduction with MP and IP extended, not metacarpal extension, combined with thumb MP and IP flexion.
- Place one strap proximal to the proximal interphalangeal joints (PIPs), one at proximal end of orthosis and one diagonally across wrist to prevent slippage across the wrist for stabililty of orthosis.

The long opponens with utensil slot (MP stop) (Figures 6–27 and 6–28):

- C5 to C6 or higher injury; wrist extensors fair plus or below

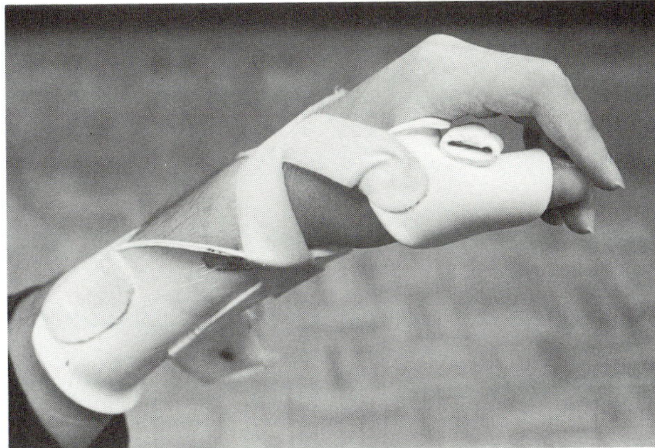

Figure 6–28 Plastic long opponens with utensil slot, radial view.

- used until metal definitive orthoses can be ordered and fitted
- durability, 6 months to 1 year
- used when muscle picture changing rapidly, delaying the ordering of definitive orthoses
- MP stop incorporated if MPs tending to rest in extension; not routinely used as this is seen as a temporary splint
- utensil slot to accommodate vertical holder so that several utensils can be used (Figure 6–29).

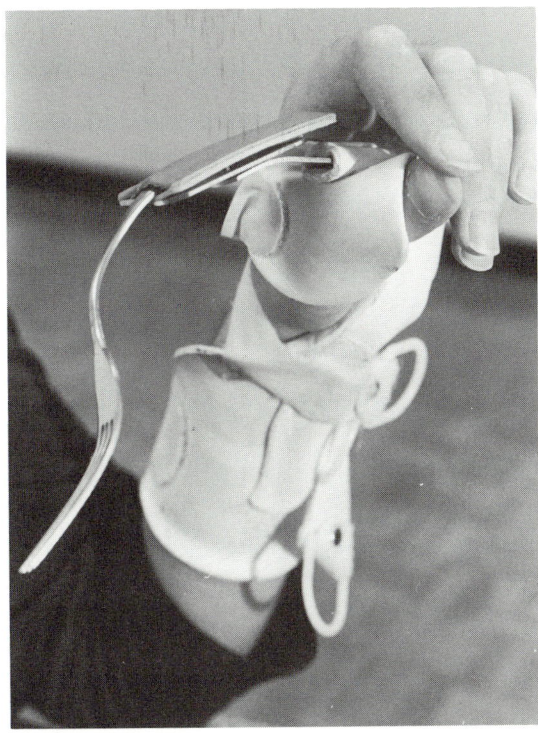

Figure 6–29 Utensil slot on plastic long opponens is made to fit a vertical holder.

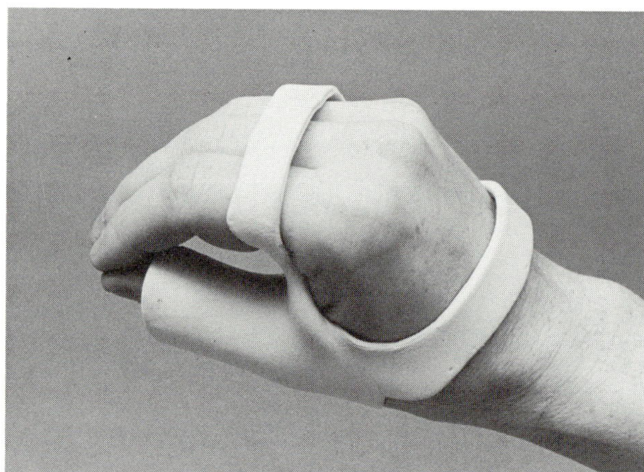

Figure 6–30 Plastic short opponens with MP stop.

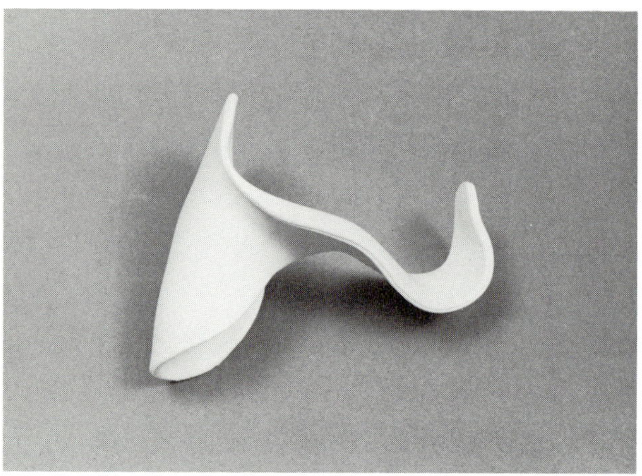

Figure 6–31 Plastic short opponens.

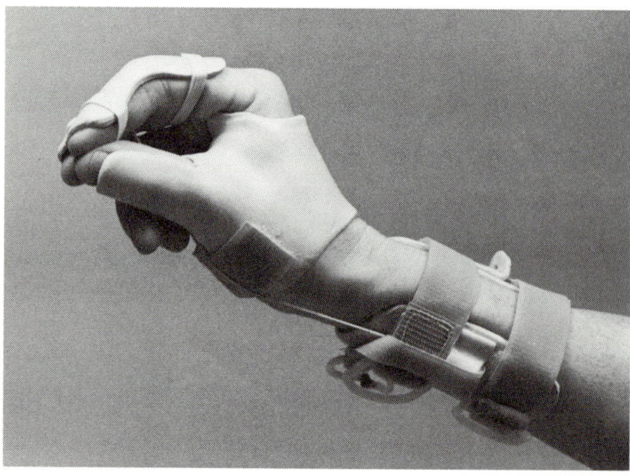

Figure 6–32 RIC tenodesis orthosis.

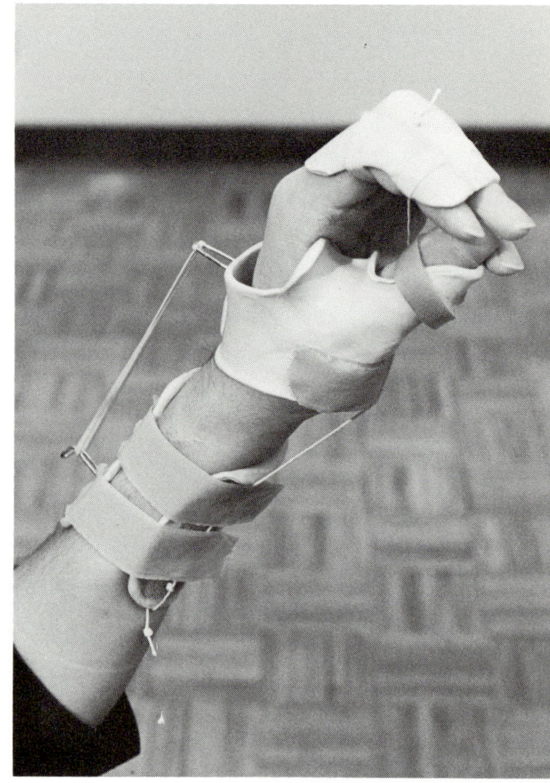

Figure 6–33 RIC tenodesis orthosis with wrist extension assist.

Fabrication tips include the following:

- Fabricate in pronation.
- Slip fingers through slot and position MPs in slight flexion, when MP extension stop is used.
- Use Ace wrap for trough.
- Place wrist in 10° to 20° extension.
- Bring center of C-bar to middle of web space.
- Make impression for palmar arch.
- Roll palmar material back proximal to the distal palmar crease, remembering the angle so that the MPs are not supported in extension.
- Pull material away from thenar eminence to allow first metacarpal abduction and alignment with radius.
- Position opponens bar to hold thumb in abduction from metacarpal.
- Provide three straps, two criss-crossed at the wrist to prevent slippage and reinforce wrist support and the third at the proximal end of the orthosis.
- Attach utensil slot to C-bar.

The short opponens (MP stop recommended for C7 to C8) (Figures 6–30 and 6–31):

- C6 to C8; wrist extensors good to normal
- When active finger flexion and extension present, MP stop assists in achieving full IP extension by stabilizing MPs in slight flexion and substituting for nonfunctional lumbricals.
- Fabricate as long opponens but without trough.

The RIC tenodesis orthosis (optional wrist extension assist) (Figures 6–32 and 6–33):

- C6 to C7; wrist extensors good to normal
- C5 to C6; wrist extensors poor to fair requires wrist extension assist
- easily and quickly fabricated for early tenodesis training
- should be incorporated into functional self-care tasks immediately after brief grasp and release training with objects of various sizes

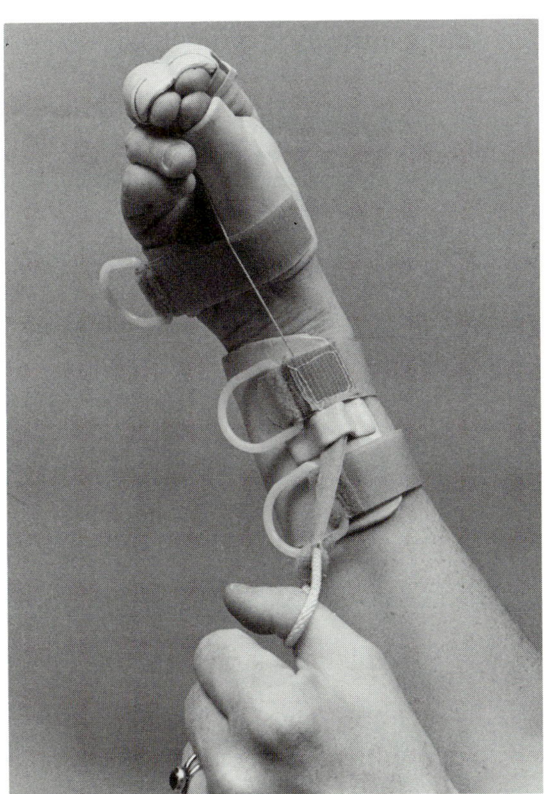

Figure 6–34 Adjustable tenodesis cord on RIC orthosis.

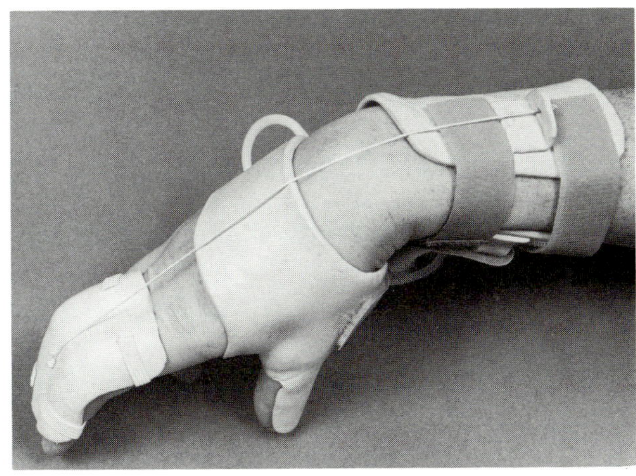

Figure 6–35 Reverse tenodesis cord on RIC orthosis to assist opening.

- tenodesis cord adjustable to allow tight closure in various degrees of wrist extension (Figure 6–34)
- accommodates well when strong radial deviation is present because wrist is free
- free wrist results in some slippage, decreasing efficiency of pinch strength
- if opening for release not adequate, a reverse tenodesis cord can be added (Figure 6–35).

Fabrication tips include the following:

- Fabricate thumb post first; strap is fixed on radial side and fastens on ulnar side to allow pulling the thumb into various degrees of opposition.
- Drape finger shell over fingers, placing index and ring fingers on top of thumb, with thumb post in place; note that in order to evenly align the finger tips, slightly less MP and more IP flexion in the middle finger are needed because of its length.
- Make small hole between fingers just distal to PIP for tenodesis cord.
- Use thin, strong nylon cord—thick cord can leave pressure between fingers.
- In making wrist cuff, remember the opening is radial.
- Flare wrist cuff over ulnar styloid to avoid pressure; the ulnar styloid provides a "stop," preventing the cuff from slipping distally.

- Determine the most effective line of pull for the tenodesis cord with the finger shell, thumb post, and forearm cuff in place.
- Add a D-ring and Velcro attachment if an adjustable length tenodesis cord is desired.
- Add reverse tenodesis cord to achieve adequate opening if necessary (usually where wrist flexors not innervated); the cord is knotted on the inside of the finger shell and attached to the dorsum of the wrist cuff.
- Fabricate wrist extension assist using hanger or heavy paper clip wire for outriggers attached to dorsum of wrist cuff and thumb post; rubber bands are added to assist extension while allowing slight gravity-assisted flexion. Often the finger shell and tenodesis cord are not used when beginning training with the extension assist.

Newly injured patients are fitted with resting and long or short opponens orthoses. As soon as wrist extension reaches P to F, an RIC orthosis with wrist extension assist is fabricated for initial tenodesis training.

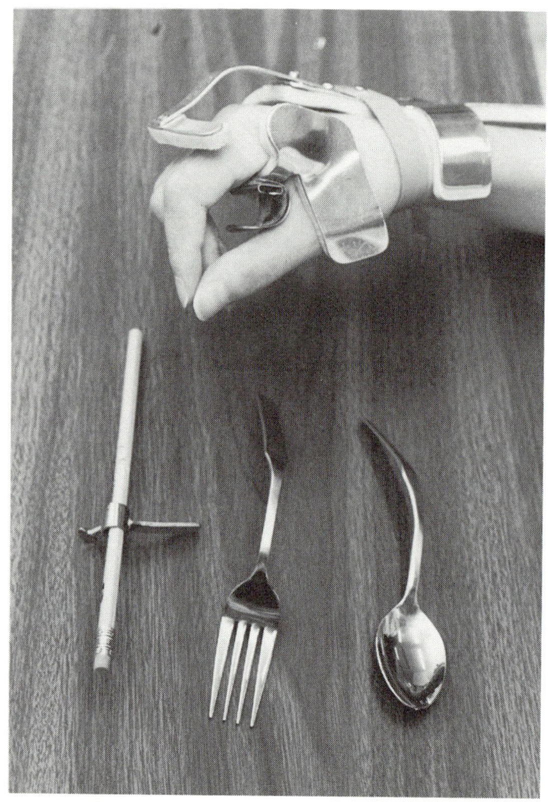

Figure 6–36 Long opponens WHO with MP stop, utensil slot, utensils, and pencil holder.

Definitive Wrist and Hand Orthoses

The need for more durable definitive metal or high-temperature plastic orthoses is considered during initial UE evaluation. Before any definitive orthosis is ordered, the patient is shown a sample and the reason for ordering it is discussed. Ordering is delayed in rapidly changing muscle pictures, usually when the injury is incomplete. All the definitive orthoses listed are fabricated by orthotists at RIC.

The long opponens WHO with MP stop (Figure 6–36):

- C5 or higher injury; wrist extensors zero to trace
- can be cut down to short opponens if wrist extensor strength increases
- very durable, lasting years (lining replacement may be needed)
- utensil slot holds feeding utensils ground to fit, pen holder
- vertical holders also ground to fit utensil slot to accommodate other utensils, paint brushes, standard spoon, fork, or knife
- extension assist an option (Figure 6–37)

The short opponens HO with MP stop (Figure 6–38):

- C6 to C8 injury; wrist extensors good to normal
- shown as option but not routinely ordered because use will most likely be temporary, until hand musculature stabilizes and tenodesis function is utilized—usually 3 to 6 months—during which a temporary plastic type can suffice

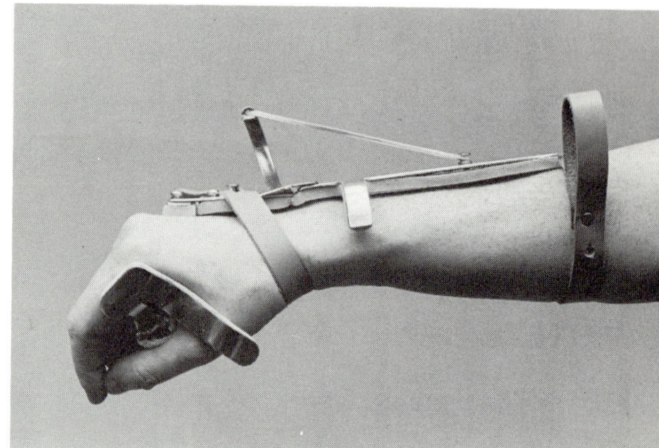

Figure 6–37 Long opponens WHO with wrist extension assist.

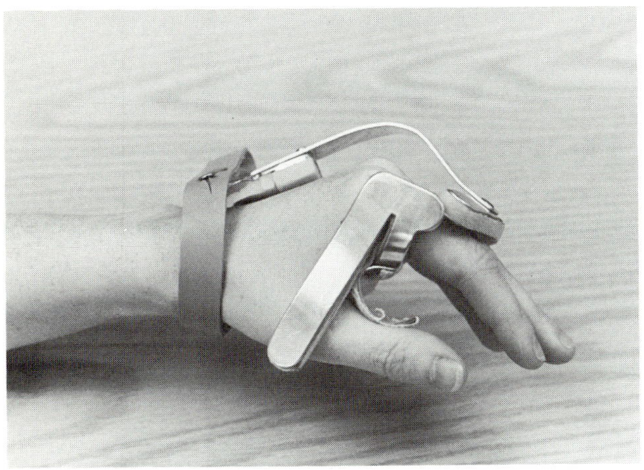

Figure 6–38 Short opponens HO with MP stop.

The electrically driven orthosis (Figure 6–39):

- C5 injury; occasionally considered at C4 to C5; wrist extensors zero to trace
- arm placement adequate to use hand function present
- patient highly motivated and has high gadget tolerance
- patient involved in activities (work, school, ADL) that can be performed more independently with active grasp and release
- patient lives in location where repairs will be available
- patient demonstrates high degree of initiation, coping skills and future planning abilities

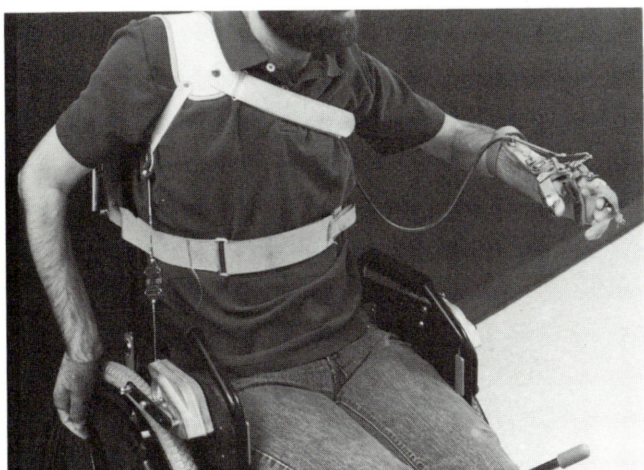

Figure 6–40 Cable-driven flexor hinge orthosis.

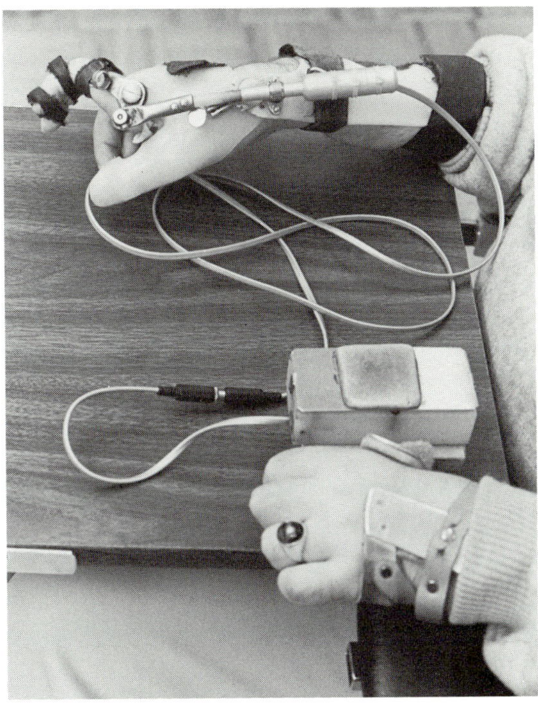

Figure 6–39 Electrically driven orthosis operated by a table switch.

- assistance required for donning and doffing, so full-day tolerance should be the goal
- WHO made of plastic or metal
- proportional grasp and release; patient can "stop" the orthosis in any degree of opening or closure
- reduces adaptation needed for individual items
- therapist, patient, and orthotist consult on best switch option for patient; shoulder elevation switch, table, or W/C-mounted switch, operated by opposite UE or even head, are most common
- funding must be available (cost, over $2,000)
- infrequently prescribed but should always be considered as an option

The cable-driven flexor hinge orthosis (Figure 6–40):

- C5 injury; wrist extensors zero to trace
- mechanically operated by scapular elevation of opposite shoulder
- harnessing similar to prosthesis
- cable attached to chair
- considered for the motivated patient demonstrating initiative in activities who has specific tasks to perform which require mechanical grasp release

- WHO made of plastic or metal
- voluntary opening; maintaining opening so as to not crush objects or develop pressure areas on fingers requires control and endurance in scapular elevators as well as visual compensation for sensory loss in hand
- spring closing—amount of force generated depends on strength of spring and amount of resistance patient can overcome to open the orthosis
- mechanically simpler than electric, more dependable
- assistance required for donning and doffing, so full-day tolerance should be the goal
- funding must be available (cost, about $1,500)

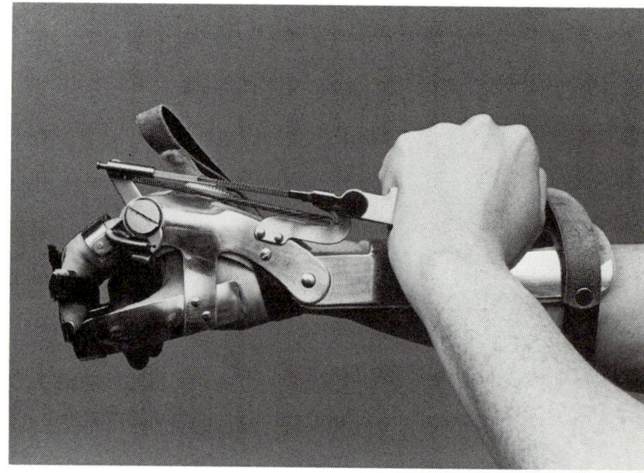

Figure 6–41 Ratchet orthosis.

The ratchet orthosis (Figure 6–41):

- C5; wrist extensors zero to trace
- unassisted tabletop arm placement with opposite UE required
- passively opened by pressing ratchet bar release with opposite UE or by pressing it against a stable surface
- passively closed using the opposite UE to press on the ratchet bar or fingers
- because of all the motions necessary for opening and closing, is most effective for static activities, such as holding a pen, phone, or razor for relatively long periods rather than frequent grasp-release operations
- has been most effectively used by patients with incomplete lesions who have tenodesis or natural hand function on one side and who are able to use the ratchet orthosis on the other to stabilize objects
- independent donning and doffing by the patient possible

Figure 6–42 Wrist-driven flexor hinge orthosis.

The wrist-driven flexor hinge orthosis (Figure 6–42):

- C6 to C7; wrist extensors good to normal
- made of plastic or metal
- adjustable wrist component (Figure 6–43) allows range of opening and closing distances for picking up objects of various sizes; patient instruction in the use of this adjustment is important

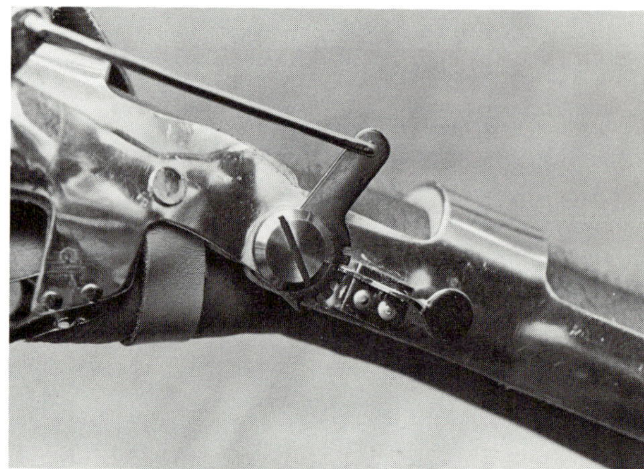

Figure 6–43 Adjustable wrist component on wrist-driven flexor hinge orthosis.

- rigid wrist prevents slippage and results in increased pinch force of up to 12 pounds
- should be ordered only if necessary for functional tasks requiring prehensile strength (homemaking, job tasks, self-catheterization)
- extension assist option available
- strong radial deviation caused by radial but not ulnar extensor innervation at C6 may interfere with effective operation; some accommodation can be made by the orthotist but an RIC tenodesis orthosis may be more effective in this situation

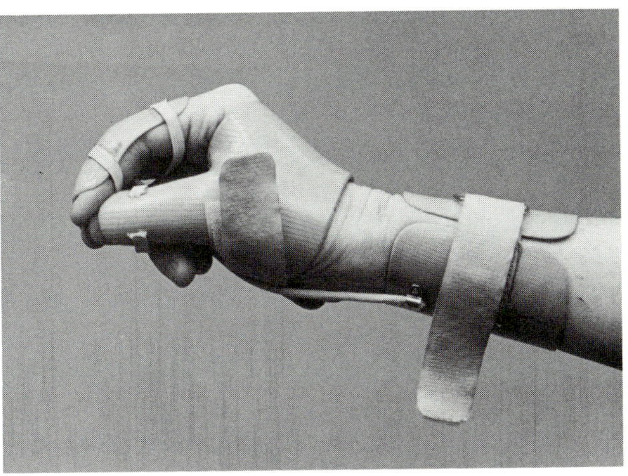

Figure 6–44 Laminated plastic RIC tenodesis orthosis.

The RIC tenodesis orthosis (Figure 6–44)

- C6 to C7; wrist extensors good to normal
- made of laminated plastic
- same characteristics as the temporary RIC orthosis described earlier in this unit
- frequently ordered for patient who continues to use temporary RIC orthoses in functional tasks

Compromises

The preceding material represents a standard approach toward deformity control. Each patient, however, requires individual attention to arrive at the best option. There are times when standard orthotic options seem to interfere with function.

Combining W/C propulsion with deformity control in C6 to C7 quadriplegia is an example. Patients find that short opponens and tenodesis orthoses get in the way during W/C propulsion and do not offer adequate protection to the hands. Available W/C gloves promote deformity, supporting the MPs in extension, providing no support to the palmar arch, and extending the thumb (Figure 6–45).

A compromise solution of a short opponens insert into a modified W/C glove has satisfied both functional and deformity control needs (Figures 6–46 and 6–47).

When working with a patient having an incomplete injury, a problem-solving approach is required to assess wrist and hand function components that require orthotic support. For example, a patient may exhibit finger and thumb motions of fair strength combined with poor wrist extensors, resulting in wrist drop. A full long opponens is not needed. Instead, a simple wrist cockup can provide the necessary support.

Problem solving is also required when patients are initially seen by OT years after injury with deformity already present. Questions to be asked here include the following:

- Does the deformity interfere with function, preventing the patient from accomplishing desired tasks?

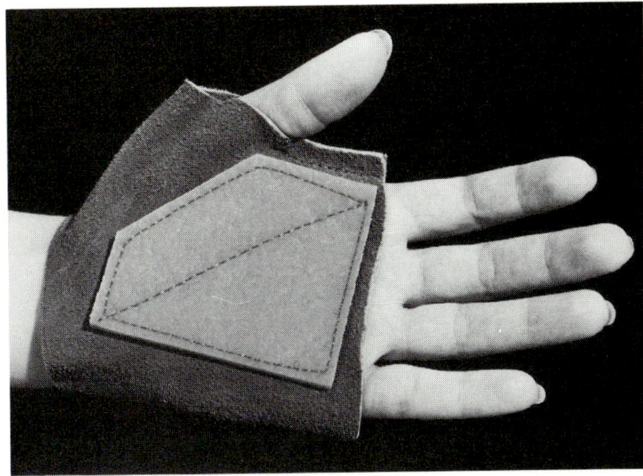

Figure 6–45 Wheelchair glove pushing thumb and MPs into extension.

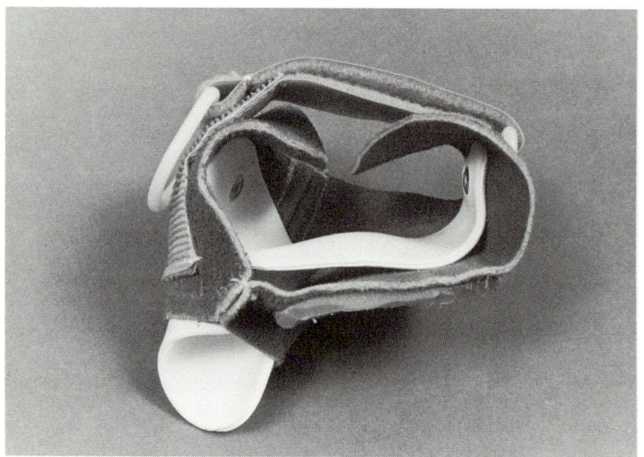

Figure 6–46 Modified W/C glove (Mason).

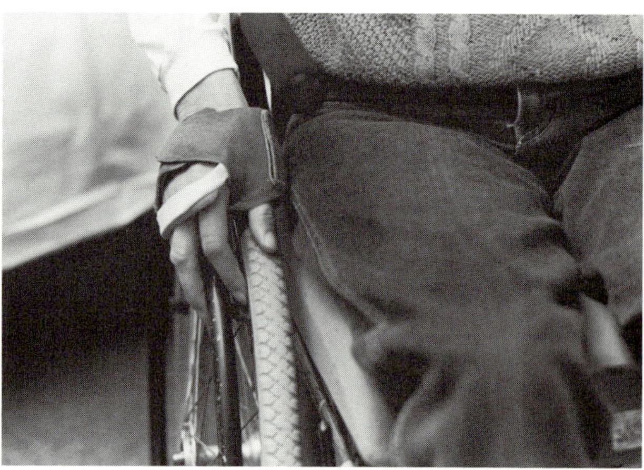

Figure 6–47 Modified W/C glove with MP extension stop in use.

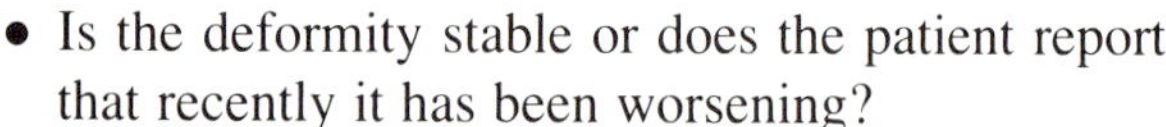

- Is the deformity stable or does the patient report that recently it has been worsening?
- Has the patient incorporated the deformity into function so that correcting it would actually decrease function?
- Is the patient concerned about the deformity?

Based on answers to these questions and a thorough evaluation, recommendations and options can be offered to the patient, including

- no action if there is nothing to be gained functionally or cosmetically
- functional alternatives such as a thumb loop attached to a wrist cuff to provide lateral pinch when thumb flexors have been overstretched (Figure 6–48)
- corrective measures—casting or possible surgery if deformity greatly interferes with function

Wearing Schedules

It is important to combine orthosis use with passive ROM to prevent stiffness.

- Monitor the orthosis for 30 minutes initially.
- If no pressure areas are noted, begin a 2-hour wearing schedule followed by 1 hour off.
- Schedules for night orthoses can correspond to turning schedule to ease the burden on care givers and minimize interruptions to sleep.
- Build up to full night use and full day use as soon as skin tolerance allows.
- Remove at least two times per day for passive ROM and hygiene.
- If tenodesis hand function is expected but the wrist still requires support in extension, make sure passive wrist ROM is maintained.

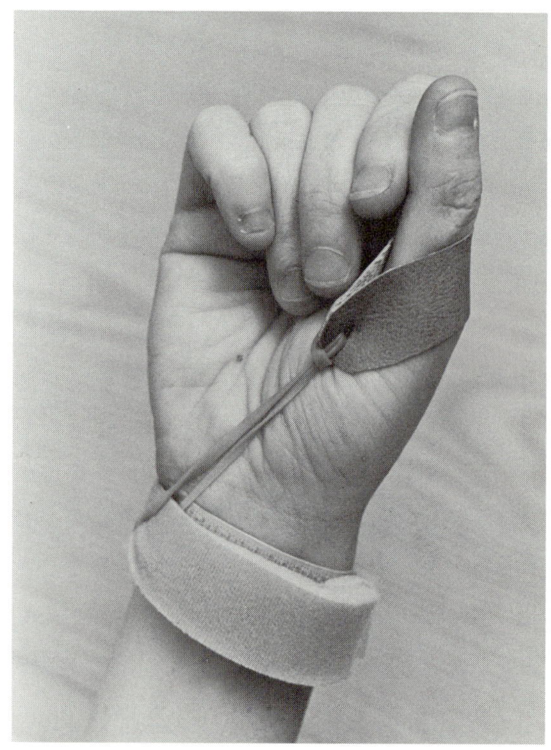

Figure 6–48 A thumb loop can be used to promote lateral tenodesis.

Orthotic Care

Plastic orthoses and Plastizote liners on metal orthoses can be washed with warm soapy water. Plastizote lining may need replacement annually or whenever breakdown occurs.

Summary of UE Orthotic Intervention

Early intervention is the key to promoting a functional hand position as well as preventing deformity. Psychologically, early intervention is necessary to help the patient accept the importance of an orthosis by explaining its purpose and incorporating it in functional tasks. The effects of SCI on the UE should be explained. This education can be aided by photographs and books on muscle testing so that the reasons for wearing the orthosis are clear.

Orthotic programs require monitoring. Muscle pictures change and this may necessitate changing an orthosis. A long opponens may be cut down to a short opponens if wrist extensor strength increases. Pressure sores can develop at any time. Patients should be taught to monitor their own skin by checking for red areas that do not blanch when touched each time the splint is removed. Orthoses can be pulled out of alignment by heavy use, necessitating readjustment or replacement.

Deformity control through orthotics should be combined with function. This is why orthotic systems are not divided into "positioning" and "functional" categories in this unit.

It is desirable to have samples of all the orthoses in the OT clinic for patients to see and try before ordering. When samples are not available, pictures or audiovisual materials and an explanation of purpose and function are helpful.

Most commercially prefabricated orthoses do not adequately provide for both deformity control and functional needs and should be used only temporarily. A poorly fitting orthosis that does not maintain the components of the functional position may promote deformity that may interfere with function. It is better for a patient to go without an orthosis rather than to wear one that promotes deformity and may interfere with function.

Independence in donning and doffing orthoses is always desirable. It is often a decisive factor in incorporation of the orthosis into function.

CASTING

If deformity has already occurred, serial casting is often more effective in reversing it than an orthosis. The most common deformity for which casting is used with SCI patients is the elbow flexion, supination, and secondary wrist extension contracture in the C5 to C6 quadriplegic (Figure 6–49). Three basic types of casts are used to gradually stretch out the contractures.

A drop-out cast (Figure 6–50) is used when

- supination contracture is not present
- the severity of the contracture necessitates gaining elbow extension before managing supination

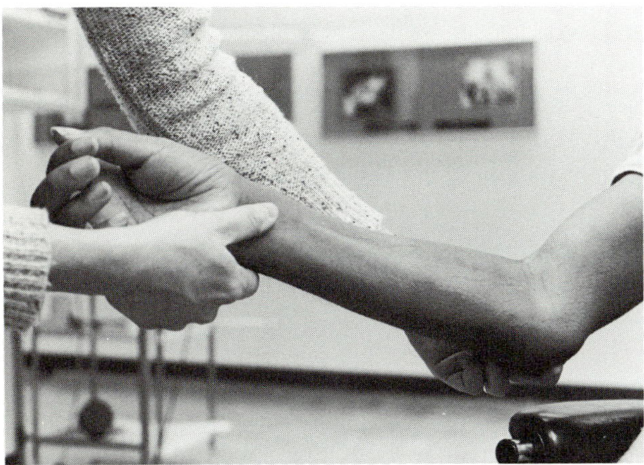

Figure 6–49 Elbow flexion supination contracture.

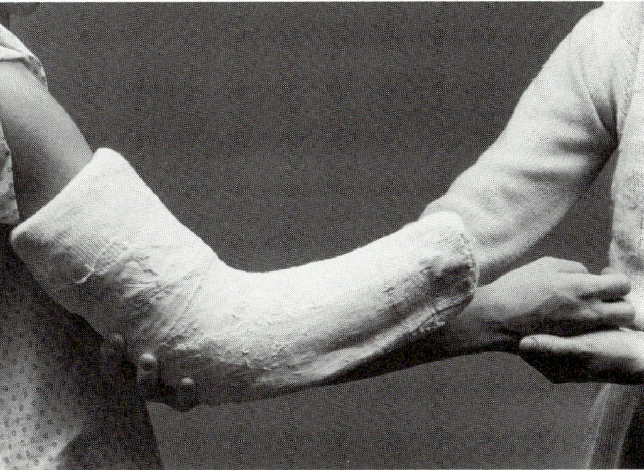

Figure 6–50 Drop-out cast.

Figure 6–51 Rigid circular elbow cast.

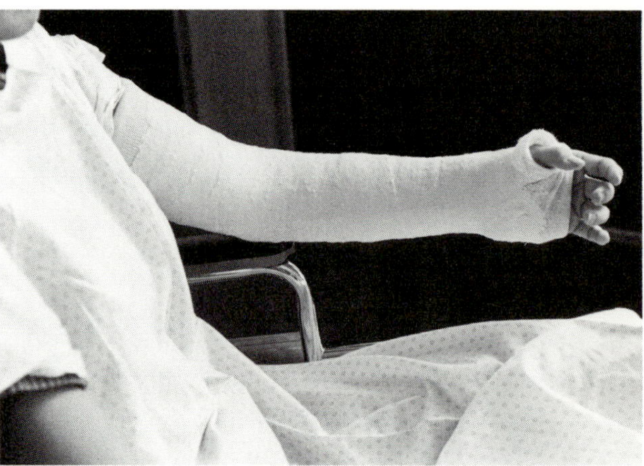

Figure 6–52 Long arm cast.

- the patient is able to be upright for most of the day, allowing gravity to assist the forearm in "dropping out" of the cast

A rigid circular elbow cast (Figure 6–51) can be used when

- supination contracture is not present
- there is strong spasticity
- the severity of contracture necessitates gaining elbow extension before a long arm cast incorporating pronation can be applied
- the patient is recumbant for long periods, interfering with use of a drop-out cast
- minimal contracture is present, allowing a drop-out cast to slide distally (full elbow extension is needed for a patient to achieve elbow locking for a transfer)

The long arm cast (Figure 6–52) is used

- to manage supination contracture (elbow flexion contracture can be managed simultaneously)
- to control forearm supination or pronation

A series of three to five casts, gradually bringing the arm into more elbow extension and pronation, is applied. Cast intervention is stopped when full ROM is achieved, functional ROM for patient goals is achieved (e.g., reach to wheel projections or reach to table for feeding), or no increase in ROM is seen after two casts.

At this level, triceps and pronators are often not innervated, and orthotic follow-up with one of the elbow extension orthoses will be required at least temporarily until the patient can learn relaxation and substitution patterns to compensate for these muscles. A bivalved cast can be used temporarily as a night splint.

Wrist and finger casts are infrequently used with the SCI population. Resources on these casts are listed in Appendix C (Rancho los Amigos Hospital's Rehabilitation of the Head-Injured Adult).

WHEELCHAIR POSITIONING

Individuals with SCIs spend most of their time in W/Cs. To gain optimal function when sitting in the chair, proper support as well as comfort should be provided. Recently, greater attention has been paid to providing W/C modifications needed to position optimally for function and comfort.

Goals in W/C Positioning

- Prevent deformity. By providing a symmetrical base of support, proper skeletal alignment will be preserved, discouraging spinal curvature and other bony deformities.
- Prevent pressure sores. A problem for people confined to a W/C is the susceptibility to pressure sores. Proper positioning and cushioning can help to prevent these sores.
- Promote function. Trunk or pelvic stabilization frees the UEs for participation in functional activities, including W/C propulsion.
- Upgrade sitting tolerance. W/C sitting tolerance may increase as support, comfort, and symmetrical weight-bearing are provided.
- Enhance respiratory function. Support in an erect, well-aligned position can decrease compression on the diaphragm and thus contribute to an increase in vital capacity.

Advancements in technology have provided the W/C user with a wide variety of chairs to choose from. The therapist should become familiar with the pros and cons of those currently available. W/Cs should be chosen on the basis of the patient's functional ability and life-style. A lightweight W/C may be appropriate for one person with a C6 lesion but may not provide adequate support for another. Funding resources are also important in W/C prescriptions.

It is imperative that the therapist involved in W/C ordering keep abreast of the latest additions to the field and be creative with available adaptations. The occupational and physical therapists should work closely with the durable medical equipment specialist to determine the optimal chair and modifications for each patient. A rehabilitation engineer can be an integral part of the team. If possible, the desired W/C and positioning equipment should be used on a trial basis before final purchase. W/C prescription and ordering is a PT rather than an OT function at RIC. Therefore, W/Cs currently on the market will not be compared here. Resources for W/C prescription and a comparison of different products are given in Appendix C [Positioning; Nixon (1985), General].

Evaluation

A thorough evaluation will assist in determining the optimal type of W/C and positioning intervention. Factors contributing to the choice of W/C, cushion, and modifications are

- sensation
- motor function
- ROM/contractures
- flexible curvature
- mobility
- transfers
- activities done in the W/C and positions used when doing them
- tone
- pressure sores
- resting posture
- method of transportation
- home and work setting
- equipment interfacing with the chair, e.g., oxygen, ECU
- patient acceptance
- patient life-style

Once the above information is gathered, a more detailed evaluation of the person's posture is made.

Pelvis

The pelvis is critical in posture and seating. Posterior pelvic tilt commonly contributes to poor posture. This is a backward rotation of the proximal pelvis, with the iliac crest positioned posteriorly. This leads to kyphosis of the lumbar spine with a forward leaning of the head and neck. The chest cavity can become compressed, decreasing vital capacity. The UEs are pulled down by gravity into a position of decreased function. Most noted is the increase in pressure directly over or posterior to the ischial tuberosities (Figure 6–53). Lateral leaning and pelvic obliquity are common because of the decreased stability of the pelvic alignment and spinal vertebrae in this position (Figure 6–54).

The desirable position places the pelvis in a slight anterior tilt, achieving a normal lordosis in the lumbar spine and kyphosis in the thoracic spine. Pressure changes as the iliac crest is pointed anteriorly downward and the ischial tuberosities are slid posterior and rotated superiorly or upwardly in the seat. Direct weight bearing is not present on the ischial tuberosities but moves anterior with increased loading over the

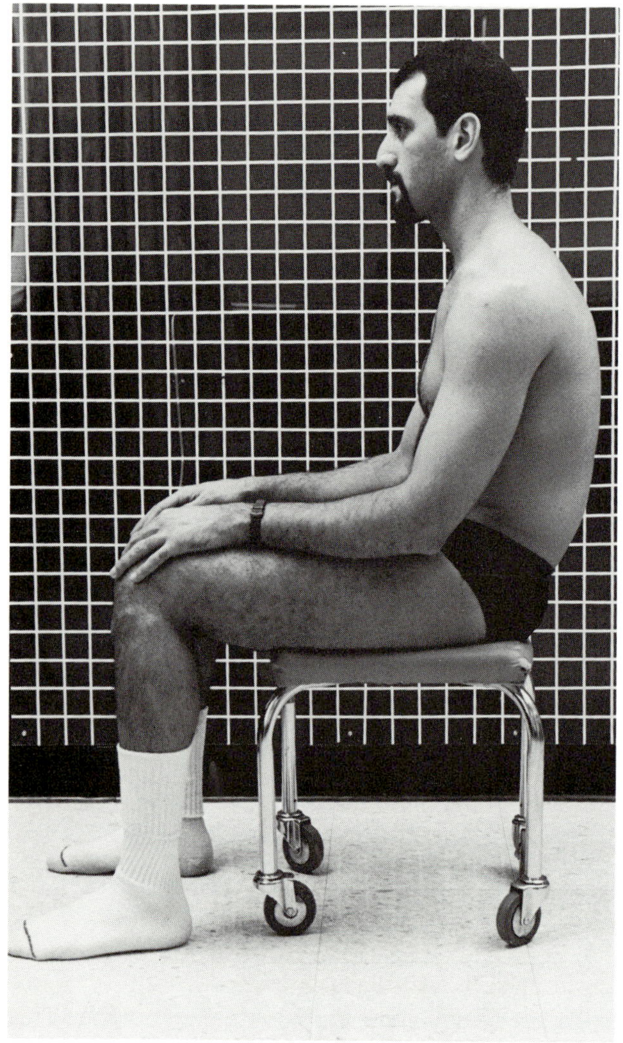

Figure 6–53 Kyphosis of the lumbar spine, anterior head displacement, and compressed chest cavity are characteristic of posterior pelvic tilt.

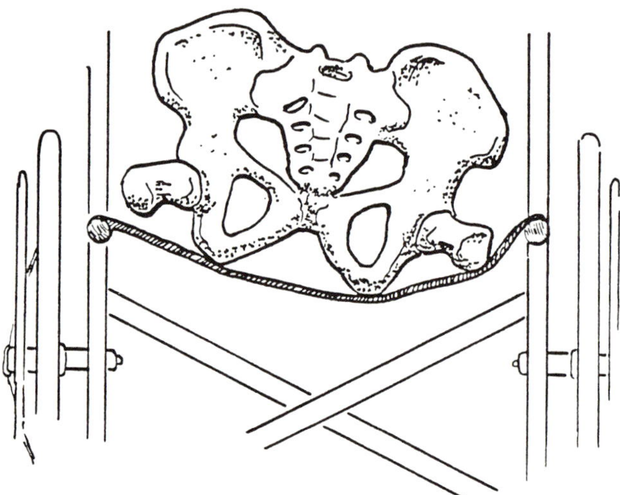

Figure 6–54 Pelvic obliquity on a hammock seat.

femoral shafts, which are better equipped to bear weight. A decrease in weight bearing is also noted in the coccyx and sacral area (Figure 6–55).

The anterior tilt of the pelvis causes the facet joints of the spine to lock, increasing trunk stability. Lateral bending of the spine, possibly leading to fixed curvature, is decreased. The head, neck, and arms are in a more functional, upright position.

It is difficult for a person with normal trunk musculature to dynamically hold the pelvis in an anterior tilt. The spine must be supported. Likewise, an individual with decreased or absent trunk musculature must have external support for that area.

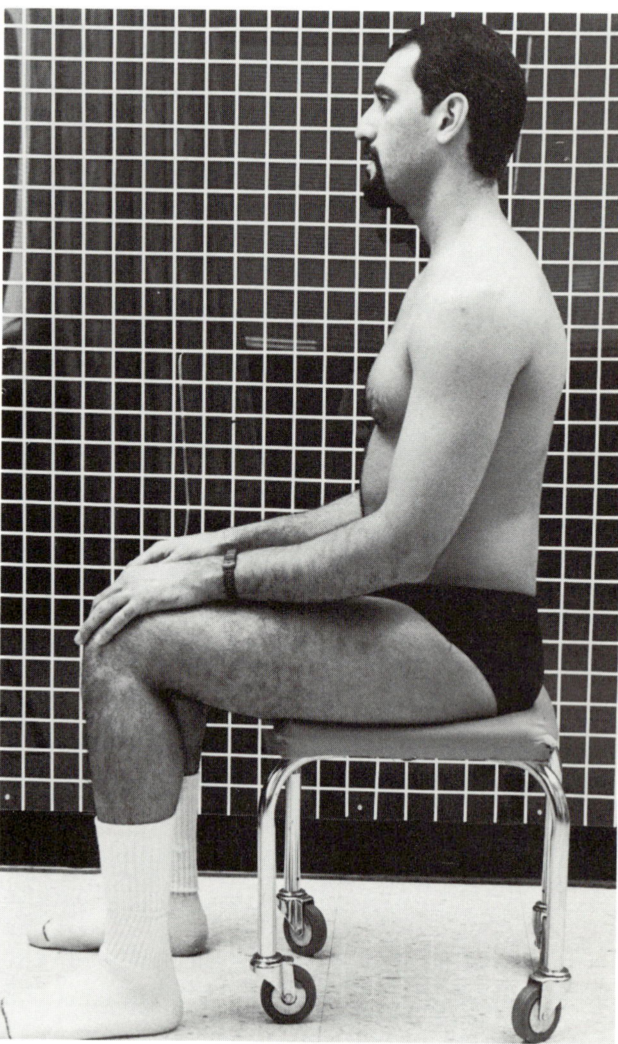

Figure 6–55 With the pelvis in a slight anterior tilt, the spine is more erect, allowing for increased trunk stability. Weight bearing is through the ischial tuberosities and femur.

The vinyl upholstery used on many W/Cs was introduced to allow folding for portability. This vinyl creates a hammocking effect on the seat and back, however, providing an unstable surface area for sitting (Figure 6–56).

Interventions to stabilize the pelvis and provide a symmetrical base of support begin with a firm seat and back, proper seat belt placement, and lumbar support.

Wheelchair cushions help to distribute pressure, provide comfort, and stabilize the pelvis. A firm cushion may be the only intervention needed to provide a stable surface. This is often the choice for paraplegics and individuals with strong trunk musculature. Generally, cushions providing significant pressure relief, such as the ROHO cushion, decrease stability. W/C cushions must be selected on an individual basis, with the user giving feedback about comfort, support, and pressure relief.

A cushion placed on a vinyl seat does not completely alleviate the hammocking effect. The pressure relief components of the cushion are diminished as the cushion conforms to the sling seat. A more stable base for pelvic positioning can be provided by placing a board between the cushion and vinyl. The vinyl, board, and cushion should be joined with Velcro to avoid slippage. A more permanent firm seat can be provided by removing the vinyl W/C upholstery and mounting the plywood onto the horizontal bars of the frame with drop hooks (Figure 6–57). The plywood can be interfaced with T-foam to provide cushioning before upholstering. However, commercially available cushions designed for pressure relief are generally preferred over this T-foam interface and can be attached with Velcro to an upholstered piece of plywood (Figure 6–58).

The seat belt should be placed to allow for a downward and posterior pull. Attaching the belt to the lowest vertical back screw or the rear horizontal seat screw should provide the desired 45° pull across the pelvis below the iliac crest.

Figure 6–56 The hammocking of the vinyl upholstery causes sliding, as depicted by the arrows.

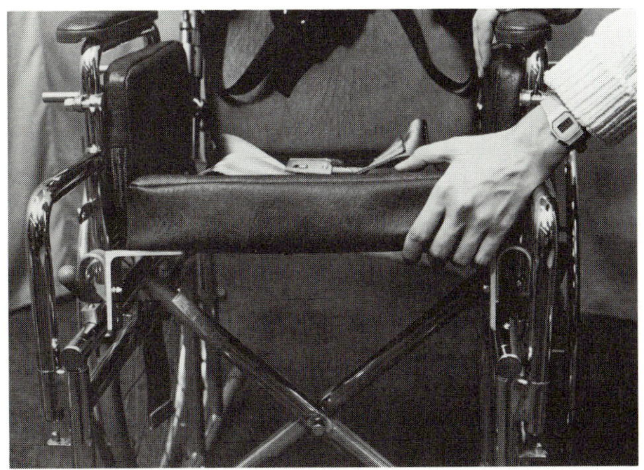

Figure 6–57 Drop hook seat system with an upholstered plywood and T-foam seat.

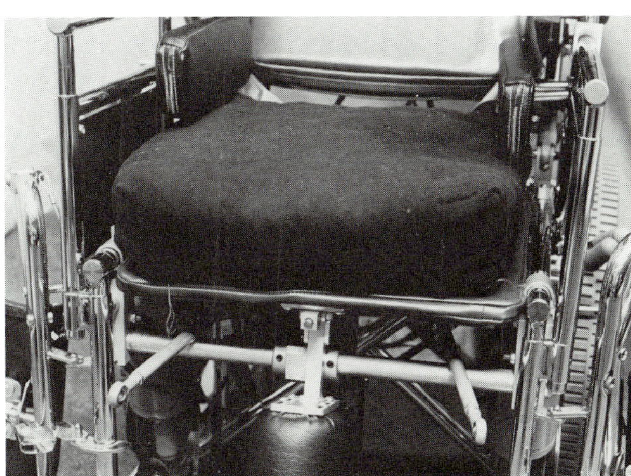

Figure 6–58 Covered ROHO cushion on an upholstered plywood seat drop-hooked onto frame.

Figure 6–59 Upholstered high-density foam fastened onto an extended firm seat in front of the ROHO cushion to add length for leg support.

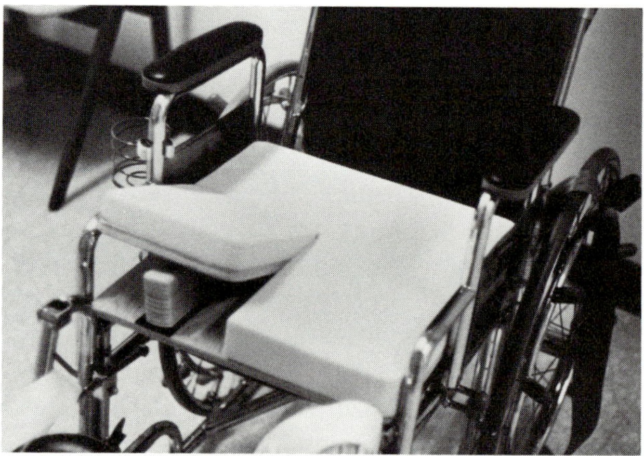

Figure 6–60 Hinged adjustable split seat.

LEs

Leg length is measured to 1.5 inches proximal to the fossa at the knee. If the cushion is too short, a piece of T-foam can be placed on the upholstered plywood extension. The cushion is placed behind this (Figure 6–59). By providing adequate support under the thighs, pressure is dissipated over a greater area.

Discrepancy in leg length greater than 1.5 inches should be compensated for by making one side of the seat board longer than the other. Hip flexor contractures and changes in range at the hip should also be compensated for. This is done by fabricating a split seat. Split seats can be designed to allow for potential increase in hip extension or be fixed (Figure 6–60).

The legs should be maintained in good alignment coming straight out at the hips. Hip blocks help to keep the pelvis symmetrical and align the LEs. The length of the hip block is determined by the amount of lateral support required for the LEs. A short hip block stabilizes the pelvis, while the longer ones also prevent excessive abduction. It is suggested that these be attached to the armrests, allowing for removal for transfers.

To prevent adduction of the LEs, two interventions may be considered. The first is leg straps, fabricated of 2-inch webbing with Velcro at each end. Loops or a D-ring attachment may be added for ease of donning and doffing. Some individuals prefer bandana handkerchiefs or other fabric in place of webbing. In the case of severe tone, where the straps may not be adequate, a pommel is used. The pommel should be removable to allow for catheter care, use of a urinal, and transfers (Figure 6–61). Sometimes a solid seat is all that is needed to prevent rotation and adduction promoted by the hammocking of the upholstery.

The optimal position for the knee is 90° flexion. If the range is less than 90°, it must be compensated for. A person will be forced to slide into a posterior pelvic tilt if compensation is not made for the knee angle. Commercially available legrests with an adjustable knee angle can be attached to the W/C. The vertical bar of the legrest may be bent to the required angle in some cases.

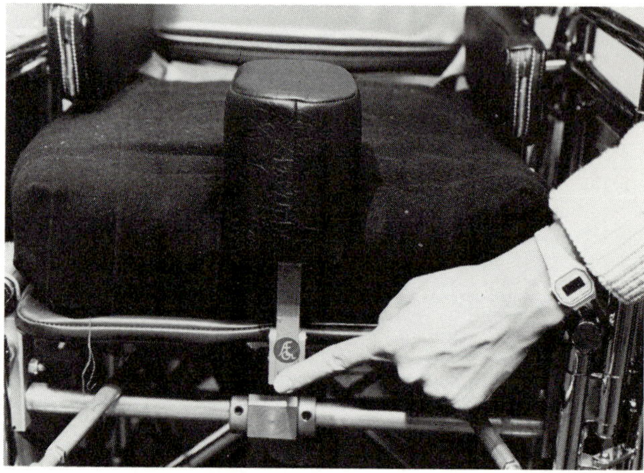

Figure 6–61 The AEL abductor pommel drops down under the chair at the push of a button.

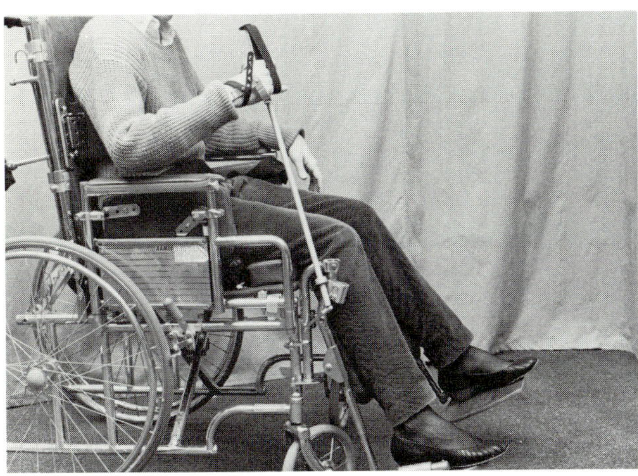

Figure 6–62 Pushing the release button on adapted elevating legrest (RIC RE).

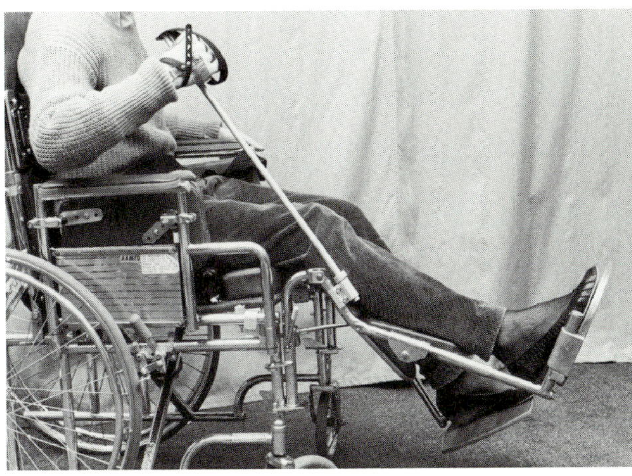

Figure 6–63 Inserting extended shaft into cue on adapted elevating legrest to pull the leg into elevation.

When a chair is reclined, the legrests should provide proper support. Electric reclining W/Cs incorporate the leg rests as the chair reclines. Manual recliners generally have manual elevating legrests. An adaptation can be fabricated to allow independence in the manipulation of elevating legrests (Figures 6–62 and 6–63).

Legrests support the calf and prevent the leg from falling behind the footplate. Pressure on the calves should be avoided. Webbing or latex material may be used instead of calf pads.

Footplates come in different sizes and should support the foot as much as possible, with weight bearing achieved through the heel and total contact to the sole of the foot. Height of the footrest determines ankle, knee, and hip position. The femur should be parallel to the cushion, maintaining hip angle at 96°. Adjustable angle footrests (E&J) are available for those unable to achieve 90° at the ankle. Footstraps, when used, should be placed at a 45° angle to the ankle, providing a downward, backward pull.

Trunk and Back

A firm back is recommended to decrease the hammocking effect of the vinyl back. Several firm backs are commercially available; some include a lumbar roll. These should be individualized for each patient, noting posture, comfort, and effect on balance. The lumbar section of the firm back should fit the lordotic curve of the lumbar spine and should not "push" the individual forward. The firm back should attach to the chair with Velcro or straps to prevent movement.

A plywood foam-padded back, attached to the vertical uprights of the W/C frame with drop hooks, provides a stable support for the trunk. Kydex or another durable plastic can be screwed into the frame behind the upholstery for nonfolding W/C models. A removable lumbar roll allows exact placement for optimal support of the pelvis. The lumbar roll is placed between L1 and L5. The iliac crest, located at L4, is a good landmark to use in placing the lumbar roll.

Wheelchair back height is critical and is determined by functional ability. A person manually propelling the W/C should have free movement of the UEs. The back height should be below the inferior angle of the scapula. A person dependent in manual W/C propulsion or using an electric W/C will require back support and possibly a headrest. A person requiring higher support during rest periods may use removable back extensions.

Seat and Back Inclination

Zacharkow (1984) suggests that the seat be reclined approximately 10°. This helps to prevent forward sliding in the seat and will help to keep the back in an optimal position. A wedge or adjustable drop hook is used for this. He also suggests reclining the backrest to

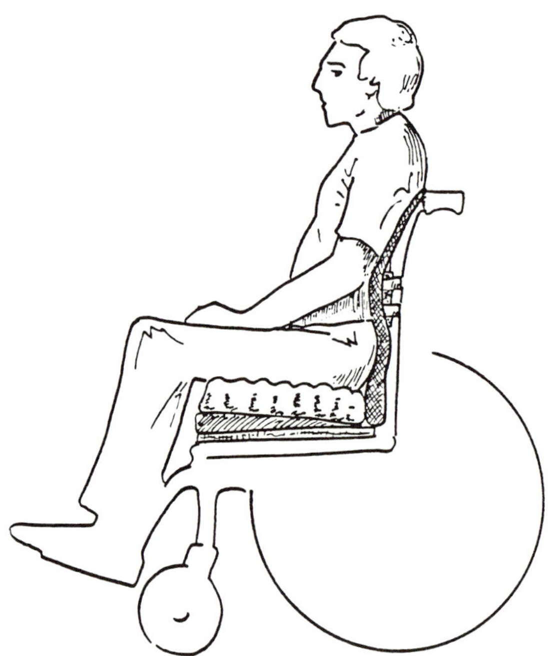

Figure 6–64 Proper sitting posture.

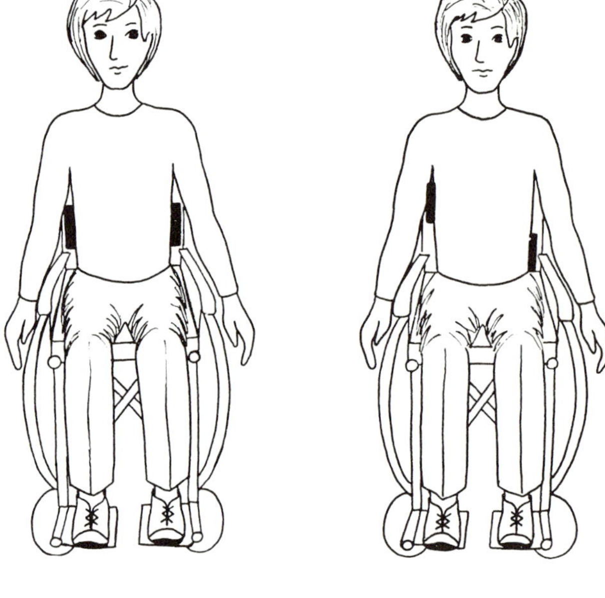

Figure 6–65 Symmetrical trunk supports (left) and oblique trunk supports (right).

15° from the vertical to reduce lumbar disc pressure and help stabilize the trunk. These changes result in a trunk-to-thigh angle of 95° (Figure 6–64). Greater recline will result in the person sliding into a posterior pelvic tilt. A less than 90° hip angle decreases the desired lordosis of the lumbar spine, but may be necessary for individuals with increased tone.

Trunk Supports

Trunk supports are used to provide stability to the trunk, prevent excessive lateral flexion, and promote UE function. Placement of trunk supports is crucial and should be determined with the patient sitting in the W/C with definitive seat and back. At this point, trunk stabilization needs can best be determined. Trunk supports can be placed bilaterally in a symmetrical or oblique manner.

Bilateral symmetrical supports can be used when the patient leans either way and has no established flexible curve. The higher the trunk supports, the greater the stability. The axillary area must be carefully considered in trunk support placement to avoid undue pressure and potential for nerve compression. A general guide is approximately 1.5 inches below the axilla. Closeness of supports to the trunk must also be evaluated. The closer the lateral supports are to the chest, the greater the external stability. When fitting lateral supports it is important to allow for chest expansion and clothing. Some patients may prefer to have the trunk supports farther apart, allowing for dynamic trunk movement while still preventing excessive lateral flexion. Trunk supports should not interfere with UE function.

Oblique alignment of the supports may help to diminish lateral flexion to one side or align a flexible spinal curve. The higher support is placed on the flexed side of the trunk, aligned to the rib cage. The lower trunk support is placed on the opposite side of the trunk, providing a counterbalance to the curvature (Figure 6–65).

Several types of trunk supports are available. Plastic trunk supports made of padded Kydex and webbing (BeOK!) provide the least amount of support. They can be used as temporary support until strength is gained. Modifications can be made with the webbing straps to provide greater stability.

Other commercially available trunk supports are manufactured by Otto Bock, Everest and Jennings, and several other W/C companies. Factors to consider are the amount of support provided, adjustability, and removability for transfers.

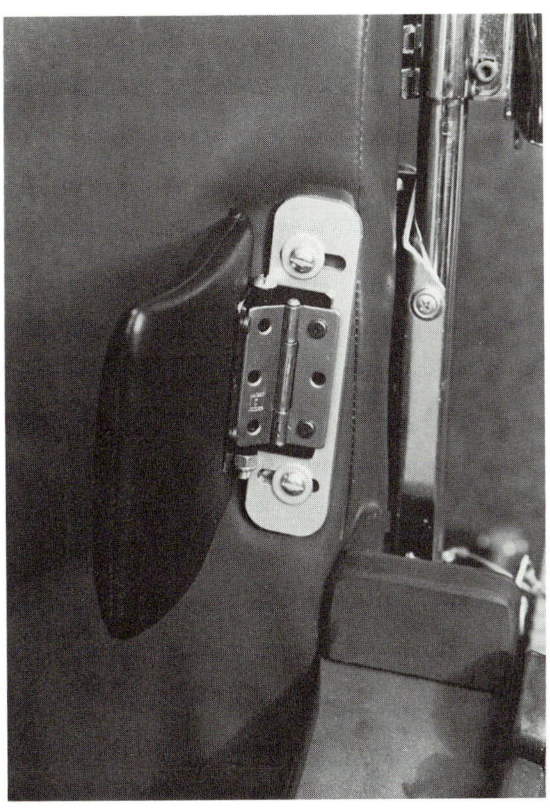

Figure 6–66 RIC RE lateral trunk support hinged in closed position. Allen screws catch hinge to hold support in place.

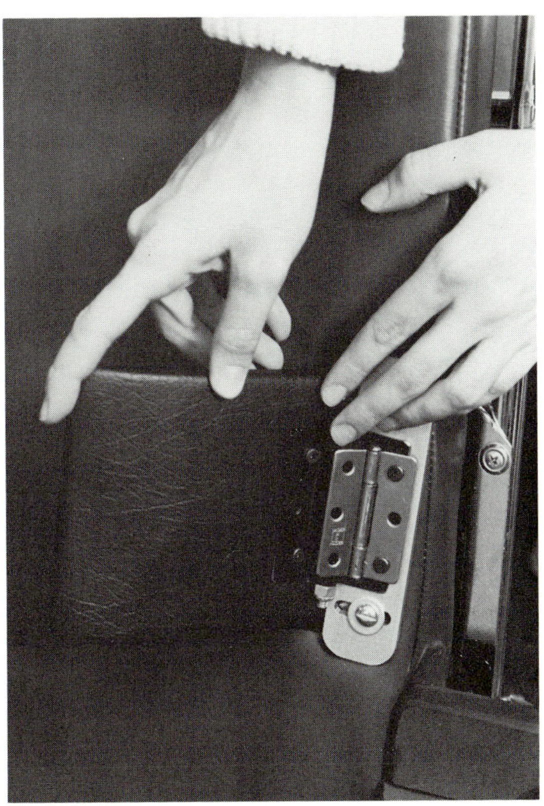

Figure 6–67 Slight inward pressure releases the hinge to open the trunk support.

A hinged trunk support was designed at RIC [Hedman, RIC rehabilitation engineering (RE)]. The pad is commercially available and is fabricated of Kydex, padding, and upholstery fabric. The hinged mechanism, which allows a patient or care giver to pull the support medially to release it, can be placed at the desired area of the trunk and is screwed into the backrest. It opens laterally for ease in transfers. It is generally the preferred trunk support because of its appearance, hinged feature, and durability (Figures 6–66 and 6–67).

If there is no room on the backrest for placement of the hinged hardware, a pushbutton release hardware system (Creative Rehab Engineering) is used with the commercially available trunk support pad. This is attached on the side of the backrest. The Otto Bock trunk support with swing-away hardware attached to the uprights of the chair is another option (Figures 6–68 and 6–69).

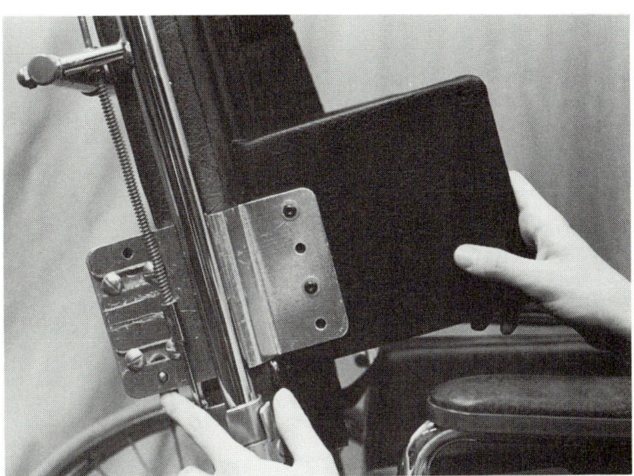

Figure 6–68 Creative Rehab Engineering trunk supports can be removed when pushing the release pin.

Figure 6–69 The Otto Bock trunk support hardware allows the pad to swing away after it is lifted up.

H-Straps and Vests

Vests, H-straps, or webbing across the lateral supports are commonly used to prevent excessive forward flexion. Reclining the W/C backrest decreases the pull of gravity; however, it also hinders UE, head, and neck function. A patient may prefer an upright position for performance of functional activities. An H-Strap or vest may provide the posterior pull and stabilization necessary to allow a person to be upright in a chair without falling forward.

Armrests

Adjustable armrests are recommended to provide optimal arm and shoulder support. The armrests should be placed at elbow height to keep the shoulder in a neutral position. Arm troughs are recommended for individuals who do not manually self-propel their W/Cs. Elevating or flat wooden arm boards (Gulbrandsen) slip easily onto W/C armrests (Figure 6–70). The arm may be secured onto the padded board with Velcro and webbing. Commercial arm troughs are available. Rims along the medial aspect of the trough may be modified to prevent pressure.

Arm troughs are generally provided on electric W/Cs. The style should be considered with care, as some may conform better to an orthosis than others (Figure 6–71). Ethafoam blocks may be placed at the elbow to keep the UE forward in the trough for using hand controls. A padded Kydex armrest can be fabricated for optimal positioning (Figure 6–72).

Lapboards can provide anterior support for the arms as well as provide an accessible working surface for feeding, typing, or tabletop activities. Several types of lapboards are commercially available, with options of rims, elevating bookrests, contours for controls, stor-

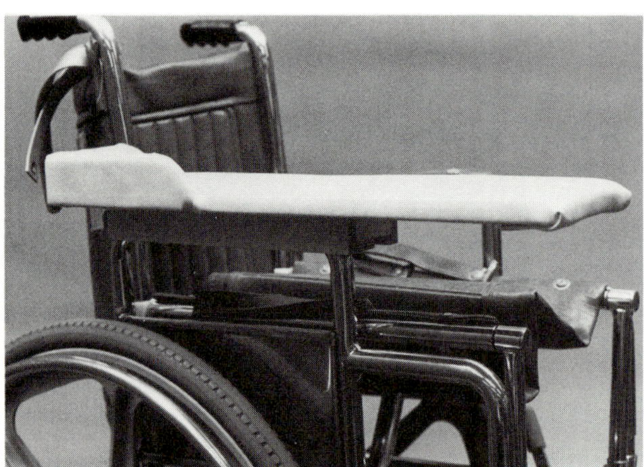

Figure 6–70 Upholstered wooden armrest (Gulbrandsen) slides on standard W/C armrest.

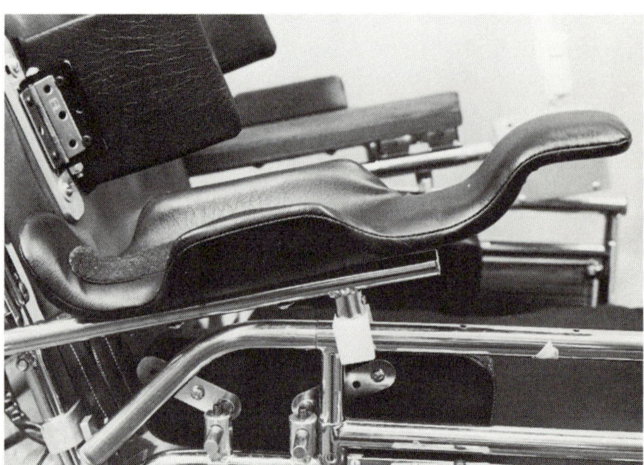

Figure 6–71 Contoured armrest available through W/C vendors.

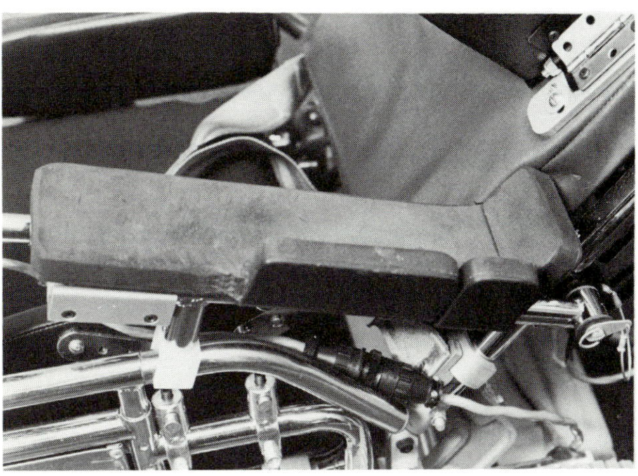

Figure 6–72 Padded Kydex arm trough custom fabricated with lateral and posterior blocks to prevent UE slippage.

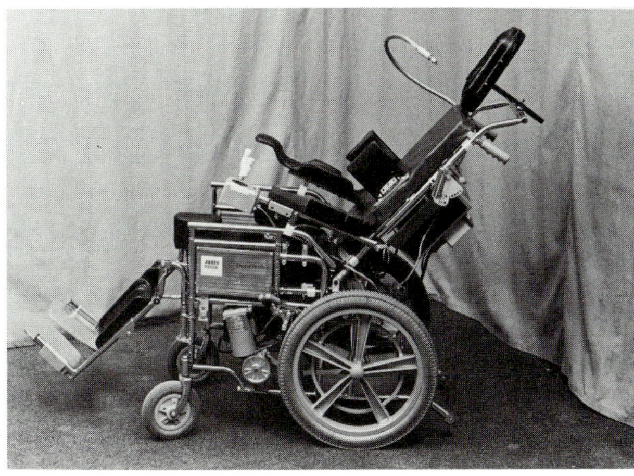

Figure 6–73 An evaluation chair used for assessing positioning and W/C control needs.

age boxes, and clamps for having arm troughs and a lapboard at the same time. Lapboard attachments should be considered if a patient is to be independent in donning and doffing the lapboard. In most cases, however, cam locks or clamps are used for a more secure fit and durability, at the expense of independence in donning and doffing.

Headrests

Head supports are considered for patients with decreased head control. Headpieces on electric W/Cs provide posterior stabilization and are often adequate support. They are generally flat, touching only the occipital region. The reclining mechanism is activated by two lateral strips requiring slight rotation of the head. An individual may require more surface area supporting the head, especially under the occiput. Commercially available headrests (Otto Bock, Miller) may provide the necessary support. The reclining mechanism may be modified to be incorporated into the pneumatic control straw if head rotation is not possible.

Shear versus Antishear

A patient with a high lesion (C1 to C4) may initially have difficulty maintaining an upright position due to respiratory complications and hypotension that results when the body is vertical. A reclining W/C is required for these reasons as well as the need for pressure relief. When providing positioning components for an electric reclining W/C, the shearing factor must be considered. This means that the placement of the trunk supports and lumbar roll will change as the back reclines. Positioning pieces must be placed to provide support in various positions of incline and to avoid pressure as the incline is changed. Antishear W/Cs are now available for placement of positioning devices to remain the same.

Contoured Systems

For patients with fixed curvatures, a linear system may not provide enough surface area for support. Custom-contoured systems follow the curvatures for optimal positioning. Several methods are available for providing a contoured system, ranging from carving and hand upholstering Ethafoam to using advanced technology to mold inserts. The therapist should be aware of the systems available.

Summary of Positioning

Positioning may be the key to functional independence and constitutes an intervention against pressure sores and deformity. An understanding of the anatomical position desired as well as an awareness of technological advances and trial equipment to meet these needs will assist the therapist in providing the most optimal system (Figure 6–73). Positioning systems should provide necessary support without interfering with function or mobility.

Several resources were used to complete this section. References are listed in Appendix C. Special acknowledgment is given to Adrienne Bergen, RPT; Michael Hage, MS, RPT; Glenn Hedman, BSBE, MEME; Denise McCoy, RPT; and Dennis Zacharkow, RPT.

SUMMARY CHART: Deformity Control

Goal	*Indicator*	*Intervention*
1. Prevent neck deformity	1. C1-C4 injury 2. Disease process complications (arthritis) 3. Zero to P neck musculature	1. Headrest on W/C 2. Cervical collar or other neck support 3. Mouthstick use for activities
2. Prevent, support, or reduce subluxation of the shoulder	1. C1-C5 injury 2. Rotator cuff musculature, deltoids below F	1. Armrest or lapboard 2. BFO or LSEO (overhead suspension slings considered in unusual cases) 3. Subluxation slings considered in unusual circumstances such as incomplete injuries with LE function
3. Promote proper spinal (trunk) alignment (for stability to free UEs for function)	1. C4-C5 injury (C6 injury initially) 2. Unable to use both UEs in function, while maintaining trunk stability 3. Zero to G scapular and shoulder musculature 4. Unable to shift weight to relieve pressure	1. Firm cushion 2. Proper W/C positioning 3. Hard back and seat 4. Lateral trunk supports
4. Prevent UE extension contractures	1. C4 or higher incomplete injury 2. Extensor spasticity or spasm 3. Zero to F flexor musculature	1. Armrest or lapboard 2. Promote minimal elbow flexion contracture by night positioning or orthosis 3. BFO and other techniques to promote flexion 4. Long opponens WHO with MP extension stop 5. Flexion loops added to WHO 6. Casting to correct elbow extension contracture
5. Prevent elbow flexion, forearm supination contracture	1. C5-C6 injury 2. Biceps spasticity 3. Recumbent positioning 4. Zero to P triceps	1. Night elbow extension orthosis, elbow extension orthosis liner, bivalved cast, or elbow, forearm, wrist, hand orthosis (definitive) 2. Casting to correct existing deformity 3. BFO balanced to assist weak extensors and deltoids 4. Muscle reeducation to isolate biceps from shoulder flexion 5. Armrest positioned to encourage elbow extension 6. Long opponens WHO to prevent wrist extension contracture 7. Proper W/C positioning to encourage shoulder flexion, elbow extension in forward reach pattern
6. Prevent wrist drop	1. C5-C6 or higher injury 2. Zero to F wrist extensors	1. Long opponens WHO or long opponens WHO with wrist extension assist 2. Tenodesis orthosis with extension assist 3. Ratchet, electric, or cable-driven flexor hinge orthosis 4. In incomplete injuries where hand musculature is innervated, a cockup splint 5. Casting to correct existing deformity

SUMMARY CHART continued

Goal	*Indicator*	*Intervention*
7. Prevent intrinsic-minus hand (MP hyperextension, PIP flexion)	1. C8 or higher injury 2. Zero to P intrinsics 3. May be more severe when extrinsic extensors and in some cases flexors innervated (C7-C8) 4. May be exaggerated in higher injuries (C4-C5) if wrist not supported, secondary to increased pull on extrinsic extensors	1. Long opponens WHO or short opponens HO (MP extension stop) 2. Resting hand orthosis (MPs in at least 45° flexion) 3. Ratchet, electric, or cable-driven flexor hinge, tenodesis orthosis 4. Teach self-ranging of hands with MPs flexed
8. Provide assisted hand function while preventing deformity	1. C5-C6 injury 2. Zero to P wrist extensors 3. Limited assisted or better arm placement 4. Patient motivated to use orthosis functionally	1. Electric or cable-driven flexor hinge orthosis, ratchet orthosis
9. Promote balanced, moderate shortening of finger flexors and extensors for tenodesis hand function	1. C5-C7 injury 2. P to N wrist extensors 3. Zero to T finger musculature	1. WHO (initially), WHO with wrist extension assist or short opponens HO 2. Resting hand orthosis 3. Tenodesis orthosis (WDFH or RIC); initially extension assist may be needed 4. Range fingers into extension only with wrist flexed and in flexion only with wrist extended 5. If inadequate flexor tightness present in fingers, night flexion mitt or flexion loops on splint; decrease amount of wrist extension in night resting splint to maintain flexors in more shortened position
10. Maintain thumb abduction, opposition (at least 45° carpal-metacarpal abduction)	1. C8 or higher injury 2. Zero to F thumb abduction, opposition	1. WHO or HO, long or short opponens type, with C-bar 2. Resting hand orthosis 3. Ratchet, electric orthosis, or wrist-driven tenodesis orthosis

Appendix 6A

RECONSTRUCTIVE SURGERY

Upper extremity surgery to provide substitute motor function for muscles denervated as a result of SCI has developed significantly over the past 20 years. Tendon transfer surgery can offer active elbow extension to persons with denervated triceps and active forceful lateral prehension to the tenodesis hand. Two basic types of surgeries are performed. The first involves the transfer of a portion of the tendon of a functioning muscle (good to normal strength) to the muscle bulk of a nonfunctional muscle, as in the posterior deltoid to triceps transfer. The second is the reattachment of the tendon of a nonfunctional muscle to bone to create a mechanical pull as the joint is moved by other muscles. An example is the insertion of the flexor digitorum profundus tendons into the radius to create gross grasp as the wrist is extended. These procedures, developed by Dr. E. Moberg, Dr. E. Zancolli, and others, offer a reliable, cosmetic, and functional alternative to mechanical grasp-release orthoses and other adaptive equipment.

The surgery does not result in normal UE or hand function, but provides more functional prehension and arm placement. For example, restored elbow extension as the result of posterior deltoid to triceps transfer affords increased ability in reaching to retrieve objects and in self-care, but usually not the ability to do a lateral transfer. This is partly because other musculature needed for this type of transfer may not be strong enough at the level of injury where the triceps is denervated.

Spinal cord injury patients with involvement at T1 or above can be considered for UE surgery. Occupational therapists, in consultation with the attending physician, are involved in an initial screening process to determine whether a patient might benefit. Information gathered in the screening process covers the following areas:

- muscle strength
- sensation
- adjustment to disability
- therapist goals for surgery
- patient goals for surgery
- motivation and follow-through demonstrated by patient in self-care and therapy
- discharge plan and living situation
- financial resources

Generally, the patient should maximize ADL skills using current abilities and equipment before surgery is considered. In addition, it is important that psychological adjustment be evident before surgery. For these reasons, as well as allowance for stabilizing of the

TABLE 6A–1 General Guidelines for UE Surgeries in Quadriplegia by Functional Level

Functional Level	*Function Provided*	*Surgical Procedures*
C5	Elbow extension	Posterior deltoid to triceps tendon transfer
	Key (lateral) prehension	Brachioradialis to wrist extensor and flexor pollicis longus to volar radius with thumb IP arthrodesis
C6	Elbow extension	Posterior deltoid to triceps tendon transfer
	Key (lateral) prehension	Flexor pollicis longus to radius with thumb IP stabilization
	Gross grasp	Extensor carpi radialis longus to finger flexors
C7	Gross grasp	Pronator teres to flexor digitorum profundus
	Gross release	Extensor carpi radialis longus to extensor digitorum communis and extensor pollicis longus *or* Half extensor carpi radialis and half extensor carpi ulnaris to extensor aponeurosis
	Thumb flexion	Brachioradialis to flexor pollicis longus
	Thumb opposition	Flexor carpi radialis to thumb
Hand position during depression-type transfers has been observed to overstretch and reverse the benefits of the above surgeries. Alternative surgical combinations at the C7 level include the following:		
C7	Gross grasp with wrist extension	Flexor digitorum profundus to radius tenodesis
	Gross release with wrist flexion	Extensor digitorum communis and extensor pollicis longus to radius
	Thumb opposition *or*	Opponensplasty with sublimis in ulna
	Gross grasp	Extensor carpi radialis longus to flexor digitorum profundus
	Thumb flexion	Pronator teres to flexor pollicis longus
	Thumb opposition	Brachioradialis to thumb opposition
C8	Thumb opposition	Extensor carpi ulnaris to flexor carpi ulnaris to thumb using sublimis tendon
	MP flexion with PIP extension	Sublimis tendon to lumbrical canal to lateral band *or* Extensor carpi radialis longus to lumbrical insertion using palmaris longus

physical recovery process, surgery is usually not performed until 1 year after injury. The patient will then be better able to realistically consider the pros and cons of such a procedure. Although surgery will usually not be performed until then, initial assessment by the orthopedic surgeon may occur earlier.

Some of the surgical procedures commonly considered for SCI patients are listed in Table 6A–1.

Treatment after tendon transfer surgery generally includes a period of immobilization followed by gradual active mobilization of the tendon transfer within a protected or shortened range. There is some variance in this time, and the orthopedic surgeon determines the rate of progression of postoperative treatment.

In summary, the occupational therapist's role in the reconstructive surgery process includes

- maintaining awareness of current surgical options
- considering each patient for possible benefit from surgical procedures
- consulting with the patient, physiatrist, and surgeon regarding potential benefit from surgeries
- assisting the patient through the consultation and surgical process and planning for postsurgical self-care needs
- pre- and postoperative therapy prescribed by the surgeon

Appendix 6B

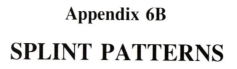

SPLINT PATTERNS

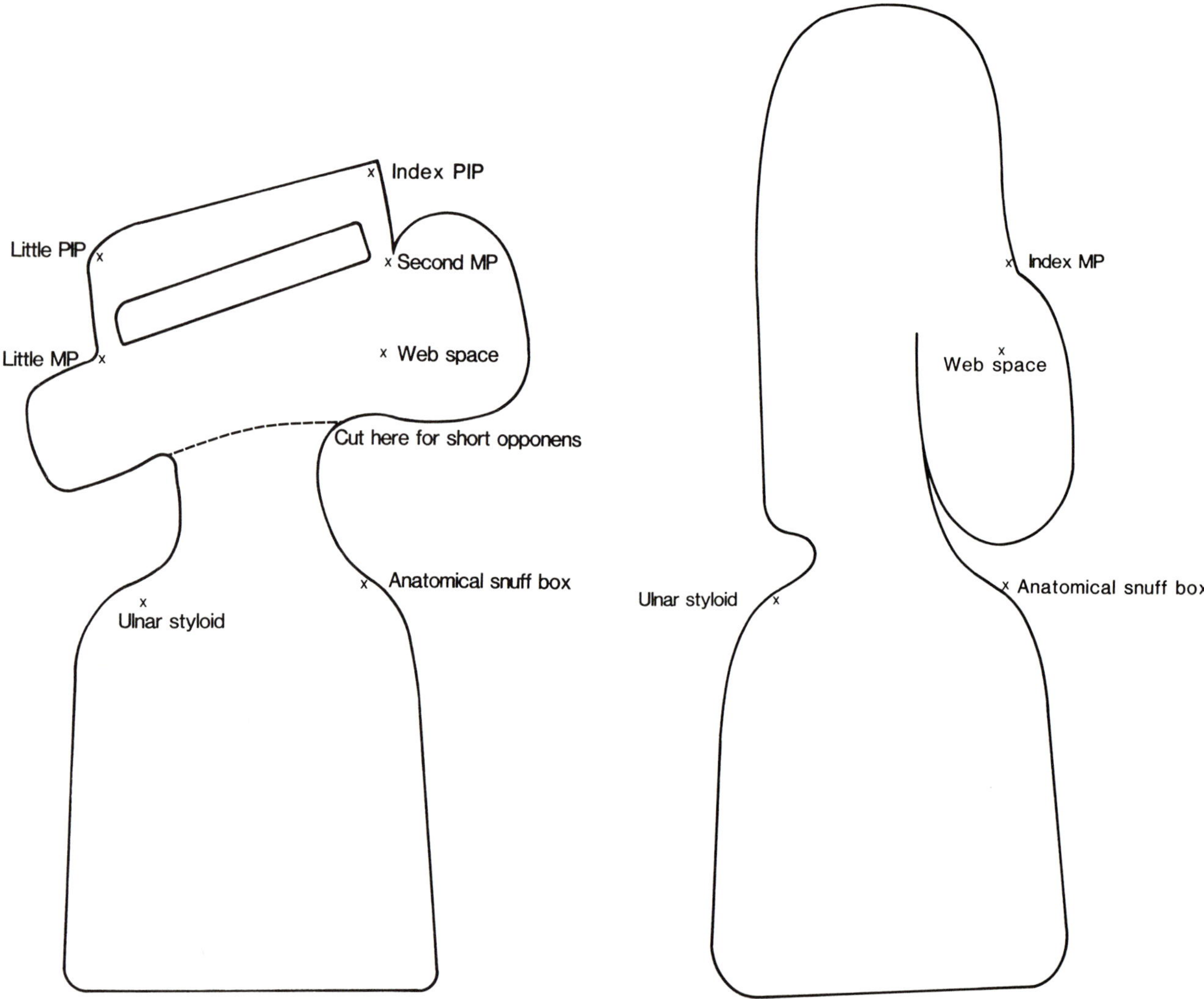

Figure 6B–1 Volar long and short opponens orthosis.

Figure 6B–2 Resting hand orthosis.

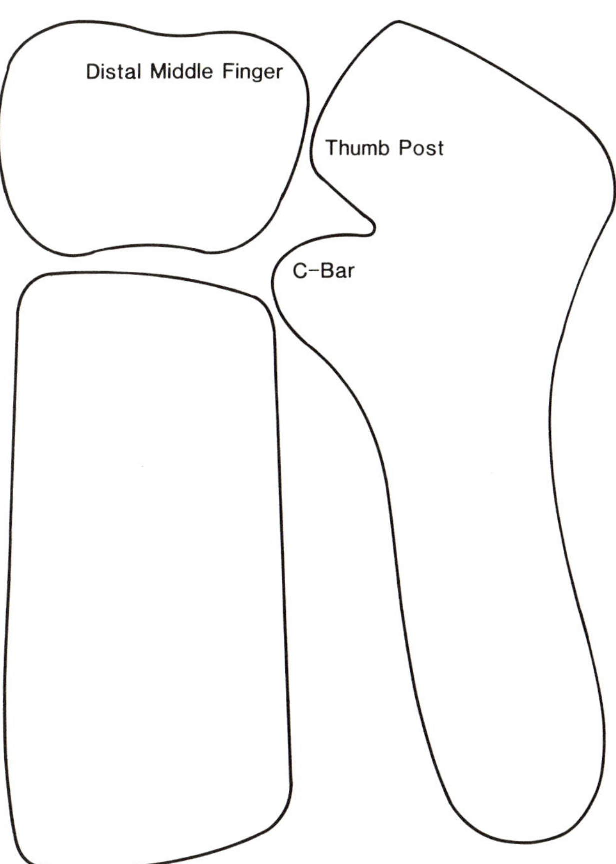

Figure 6B–3 RIC tenodesis orthosis.

Unit 7

Self-Feeding

Karen Kovich, OTR/L

Feeding is often one of the first functional tasks attempted by the SCI patient, since there is often a high level of motivation to learn to eat independently as well as a sense of achievement gained in doing so.

The task of feeding oneself includes

- drinking from a cup or straw
- finger feeding
- utensil feeding
- the setup required to eat a meal, such as cutting food and opening containers

Independence may be gained in one or all components of the task, depending on available muscle strength and the use of adaptive equipment.

DRINKING

Drinking from a straw or cup can be done independently with equipment and setup, even with minimal head and neck control. This can be achieved by mounting commercially available cup holders or bicycle water bottles to the W/C or bed. The straw should be secured in a position that can be accessed by a slight movement of the head. The closer the cup is mounted to the patient, the less effort will be required to drink, which may be an important consideration for patients with decreased vital capacity.

In bed, the cup holder can be mounted to the side rail, but should be lower than the patient so that the straw is inclined upward. Larger containers of liquid may be desirable for bed use. In the W/C, the cup holder is most often mounted to the armrest or upright portion of the backrest. When the holder is mounted on the armrest, a commercially available 18-inch plastic straw and straw holder are placed so that it can be reached by forward flexion or rotation of the head. If additional length is necessary, clear plastic Tygon tubing can be used to connect two straws. This provides additional length and enables the straw to be angled for greater variability in positioning. The weight of Tygon tubing will cause the straw to fall, so the joint should be placed as close to the cup as possible for stability.

When the cup holder is mounted on the backrest, the long straws can be secured to the upright pole with wire ties or small Velcro straps. If a sip-and-puff mechanism is used to control the chair, the straw tubing can be attached to it. The drinking straw is secured below the pneumatic control straw. A regular jointed plastic straw can be placed in the end, allowing it to be changed often. A cup with a tight-fitting lid will be necessary to prevent spills when the chair is reclined.

A patient with table-to-mouth arm placement with or without assistive devices, yet no tenodesis hand func-

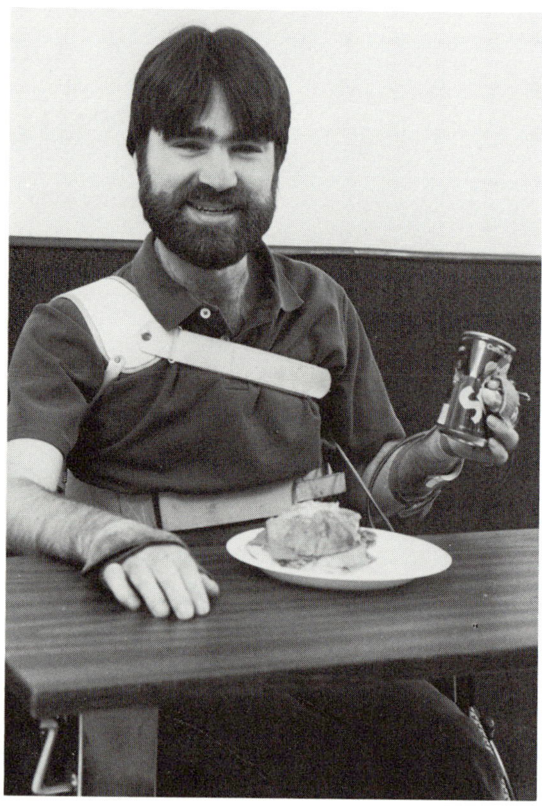

Figure 7–1 A cable-driven flexor hinge can be used to hold a can or cup.

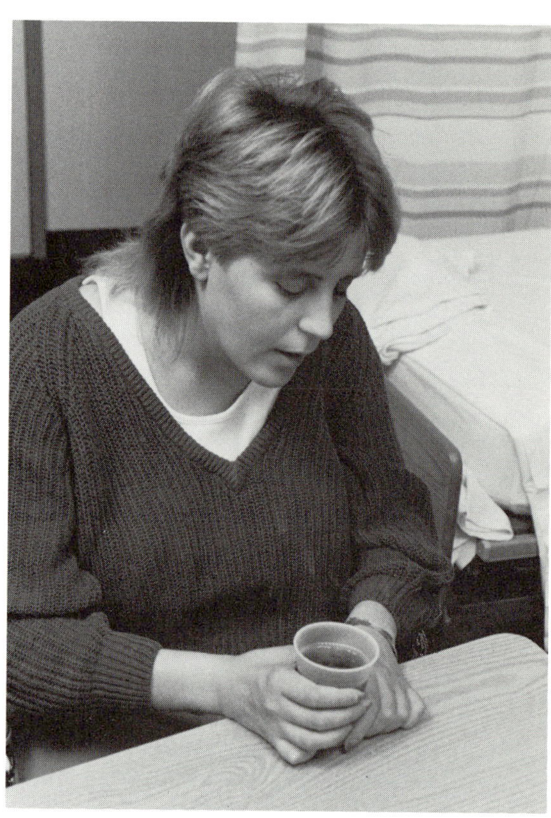

Figure 7–2 A cup is stabilized with one hand while the other is placed around it.

tion, will be able to drink independently with equipment after setup. If the patient prefers, a stabilized cup with straw may still be used; however, other alternatives are available.

Equipment for this task usually consists of various cup holders and cups—preferably thin, nonbreakable, and lightweight. Cups usually have or require an adaptation to secure them to the hand while moving from tabletop to mouth. When a long opponens orthosis is worn to stabilize the wrist joint, cups can be adapted to fit into the utensil slot or over the orthosis. A cable-driven flexor hinge, ratchet, or electric flexor hinge orthosis can also be used to hold the cup (Figure 7–1).

When a patient first practices bringing a full cup to the mouth, strength and control may not be sufficient to lift the cup. Practice should begin with small portions of liquid until enough control is gained to use the skill functionally. To pick up or release the cup, the free hand is placed on top of the cup for stabilization and the other hand is placed into or taken out of the handle.

A patient with tenodesis function will be able to lift a cup or can using wrist extension (Figures 7–2 and 7–3). Initially, bilateral use of the hands may be

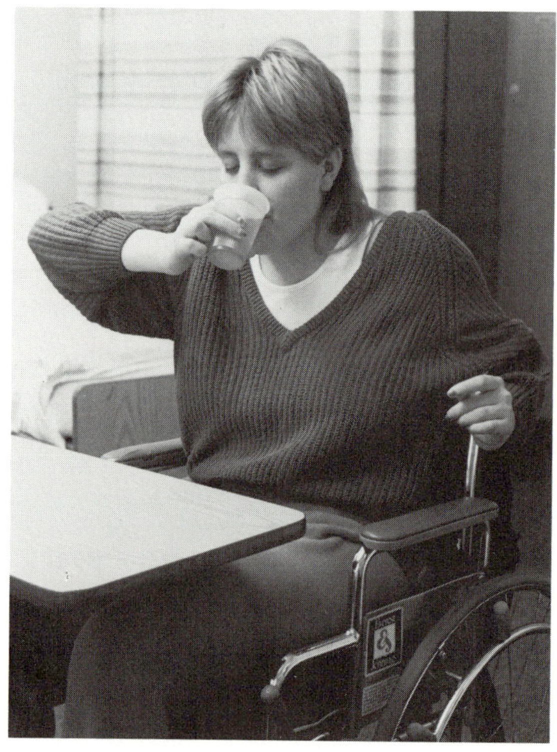

Figure 7–3 Natural tenodesis is often sufficient to lift a can or cup.

required to stabilize the cup while moving to or from the mouth. With practice, the patient should be able to lift a moderate-sized cup with one hand. A wrist-driven flexor hinge (WDFH) can also be used to hold the cup, and is especially useful with wider or heavier cups or cans.

UTENSIL FEEDING

Feeding with utensils can be accomplished with a variety of equipment. Patients with no functional arm placement but functional head and neck control can learn to feed themselves independently when set up with a quad feeder (Figure 7–4). Use of the feeder requires motivation and determination. (The therapist's attitudes toward the equipment may also affect acceptance or rejection by the patient.) Use of the feeder depends primarily on neck rotation, protraction, and flexion, and requires the patient to be upright. Training cannot begin until spine stabilizers are removed.

The feeder is set up on an elevating bedside table approximately at shoulder height. It contains a plate, bowl, cup and straw, sandwich holder, and rotating utensil stabilizer. The utensils have a clip on them so that they attach easily onto the stabilizer.

The patient takes the fork or spoon in his teeth and stabs or scoops the food onto the utensil. Protracting the head, he clips the utensil back onto the stabilizer and rotates it 180° with his chin. The utensil is then facing the patient, so that the food can be taken from it with the mouth. When ready for another bite, he rotates the utensil back in the same manner. The process is repeated throughout the meal. Sandwiches, cookies, and so forth are placed in the sandwich holder and, as a bite is taken, the rest of the sandwich is pulled out toward the patient. The straw is placed in a position where it can be reached by rotation of the head but does not interfere with eating.

Although eating a meal with a quad feeder can take up to 1 hour, it is invaluable to those patients who wish to independently control the rate and sequence of their meal. Patients who require assistance for arm placement can begin training with the use of BFO, WHO, utensils, and a plate guard (Figure 7–5).

The hand-to-mouth pattern requires a combination of shoulder flexion, horizontal adduction, external rotation, and elbow flexion. Scooping food requires shoulder extension, abduction, internal rotation, and elbow extension and then horizontal adduction to move the arm across the plate. The BFO can be adjusted to maximize any of the above-mentioned motions and to compensate for weakness in those areas. The supinator assist, a BFO component described in unit 6, is often useful in providing the forearm rotation necessary for scooping food off the plate.

Unless wrist musculature is fair plus, a WHO with a utensil slot is necessary to stabilize the wrist and hold the utensil. When ordering definitive orthoses a utensil slot should be requested. If working with temporary orthoses, a utensil slot can be made of orthotic material and bonded to the thumbpost of the long opponens. Utensils often have to be bent downward to compensate

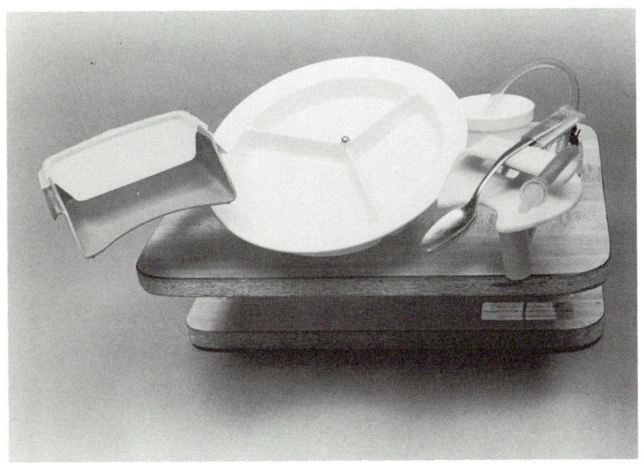

Figure 7–4 The quad feeder, with sandwich holder and rotating utensil stabilizer.

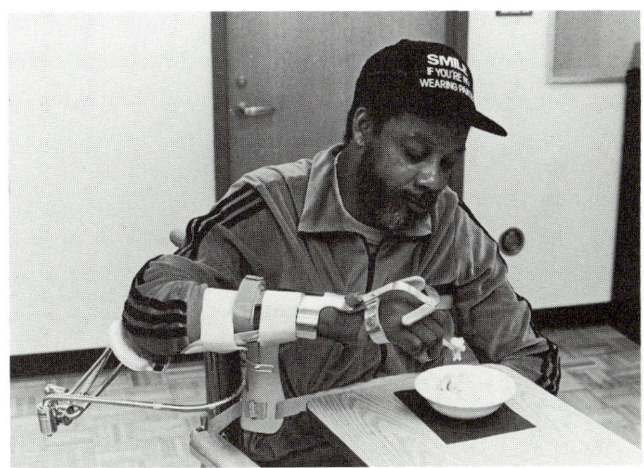

Figure 7–5 A BFO provides arm placement sufficient for self-feeding.

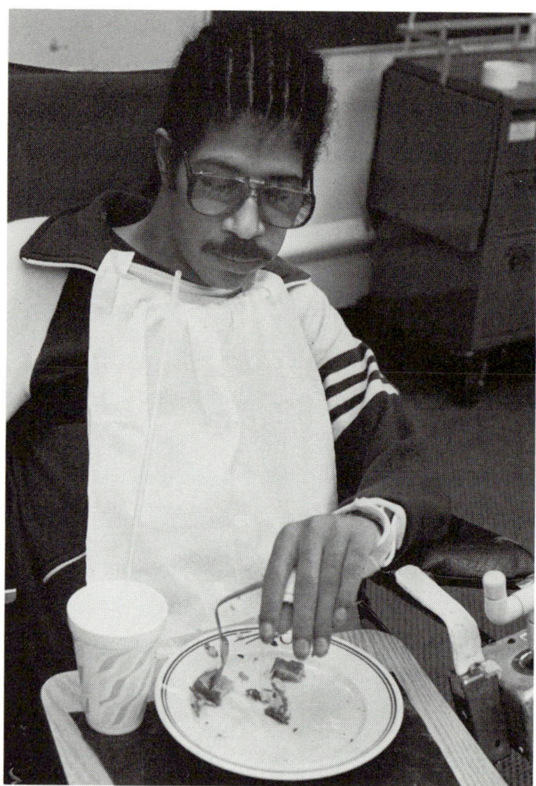

Figure 7–6 Adapted utensils can compensate for lack of forearm rotation.

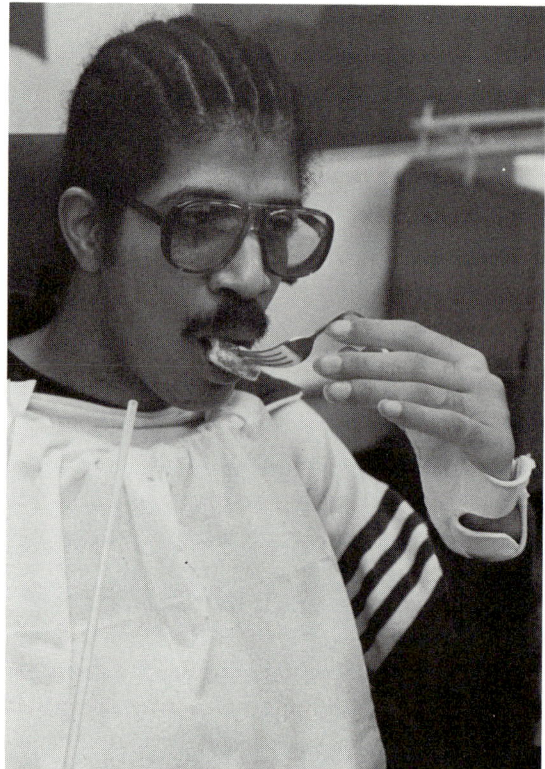

Figure 7–7 Utensils must be bent at an angle that allows ease in stabbing food as well as moving it to the mouth.

for the lack of forearm rotation. Swivel utensils are also available; however, the swivel mechanism may make scooping difficult. Locking swivels should be used, adjusted to allow only enough movement to maintain a level utensil when bringing the hand to the mouth.

Arm placement in a BFO is limited and may necessitate an adjustable table to position the plate. Other equipment often used includes plate guards, sandwich holders, Dycem, and trunk supports to maintain proper alignment and to free the UEs for functional use. Patients with bilateral BFOs may find it beneficial to use both for a meal. A spoon can be placed in the nondominant hand, angled downward, and used as an assist to position the food and scoop it up. Individuals may wish to use a fork with one UE and a spoon or sandwich holder in the other.

Initially, a patient may lack the endurance to feed himself an entire meal. With daily practice, however, the necessary strength and control can be developed. Strengthening activities can also be used (unit 5). When unassisted arm placement is achieved, feeding can be done independently with equipment but without a BFO (Figures 7–6 to 7–8).

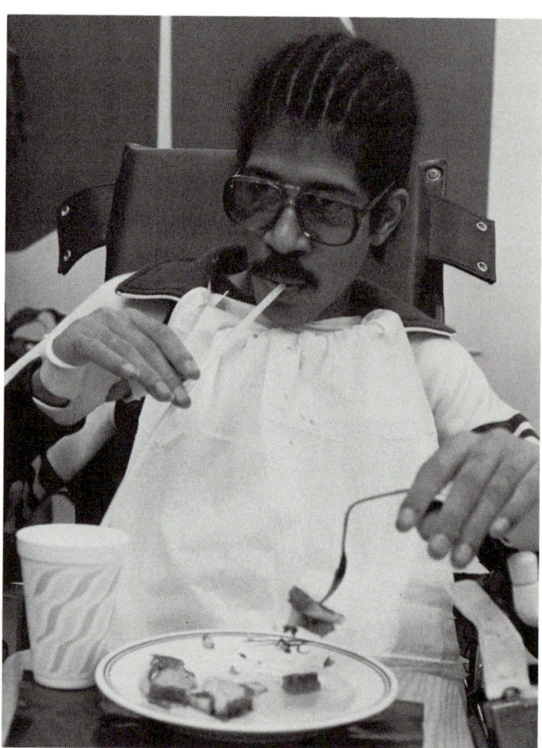

Figure 7–8 Eighteen-inch plastic straws allow for independence in drinking.

Figure 7–9 Utensils can be adapted with thumb rings to compensate for lack of hand function.

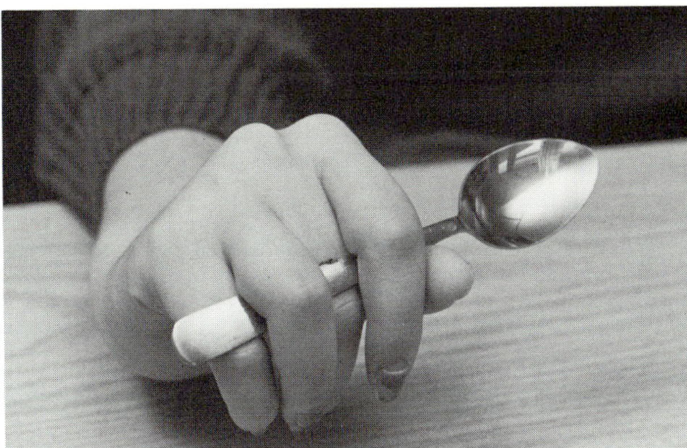

Figure 7–10 Utensils can be laced through the fingers to allow independence without equipment.

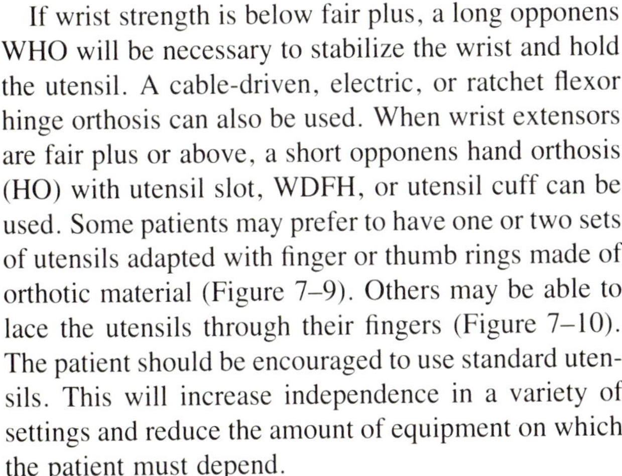

If wrist strength is below fair plus, a long opponens WHO will be necessary to stabilize the wrist and hold the utensil. A cable-driven, electric, or ratchet flexor hinge orthosis can also be used. When wrist extensors are fair plus or above, a short opponens hand orthosis (HO) with utensil slot, WDFH, or utensil cuff can be used. Some patients may prefer to have one or two sets of utensils adapted with finger or thumb rings made of orthotic material (Figure 7–9). Others may be able to lace the utensils through their fingers (Figure 7–10). The patient should be encouraged to use standard utensils. This will increase independence in a variety of settings and reduce the amount of equipment on which the patient must depend.

A WDFH can also be used to hold a utensil. Before ordering a cable-driven, ratchet, or electric orthosis, specific uses should be determined by the patient and therapist to ensure that it is the most cost-effective way of meeting the patient's needs. For example, a WDFH would not be ordered to be used only in feeding, when a short opponens HO may meet the same need. When finger flexors and extensors are innervated, no equipment is necessary for feeding.

FINGER FEEDING

Finger feeding is done through the use of tenodesis hand function or a mechanical grasp and release orthosis (Figure 7–11). At the C6 injury level and below, finger feeding is done with no equipment, as natural tenodesis is sufficient for "finger foods." Some finger foods, such as sandwiches, can be cut up and eaten with utensils.

CUTTING FOOD

In order to cut food, one must have unassisted arm placement, fair plus wrist strength for adequate distal control and pressure, and a secure means of holding a knife.

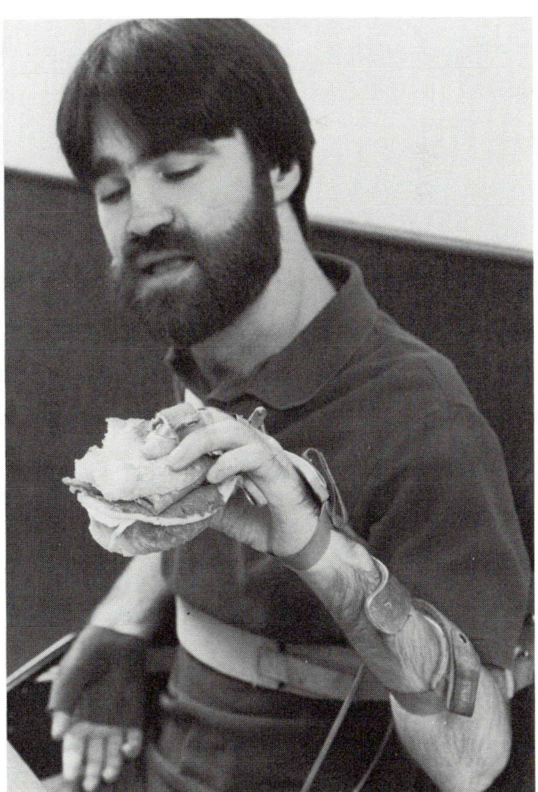

Figure 7–11 A cable-driven flexor hinge provides grip and release for finger feeding.

Knives can be easily adapted with orthotic material if those commercially available do not prove adequate (unit 14) (Figure 7–12). A high-temperature orthotic material such as Kydex will provide a more durable adaptation.

A serrated knife is the most versatile. Care should be taken to cover any sharp edges that could come into contact with the skin.

In determining the type of adaptation, the patient should help define which forearm position is most comfortable and provides the most leverage. With the forearm in pronation, a forward and backward stroke can be used with the knife extending between the third and fourth finger, or a side-to-side stroke can be used with the knife pointing radially between the thumb and index finger. If the patient is more comfortable or has more control with the forearm in the neutral position, a forward and backward stroke can be used with the knife extending between the third and fourth fingers. Unless wrist flexors are innervated to stabilize against resistance in pronation, the knife may have to be slanted downward to allow for cutting in full wrist extension.

Blade covers, or sheaths, are fabricated of orthotic material or webbing so that the knife can be safely handled. The covers should fit snugly. A loop or D-ring can be attached to the covers for easy removal.

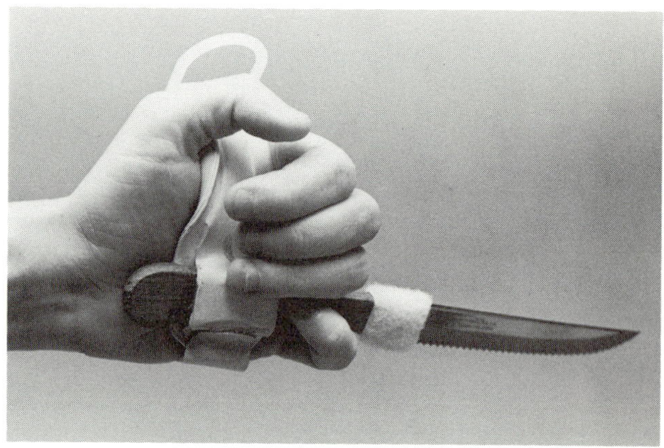

Figure 7–12 Knives can be adapted to allow independence in cutting despite lack of finger or thumb movement.

Patients who are unable or choose not to cut their own food may ask to have their food cut in the kitchen when dining out. Some prefer to pick up large pieces of food with their fork and take bites rather than cutting.

Eating is not only a daily task, but often an important social activity as well. Independence in eating is of primary importance to most persons with SCI, not only with the minimum amount of equipment but in a manner that can be done neatly. Practice should begin in a comfortable environment and then, as the individual gains control, progress to social situations.

SUMMARY CHART: Feeding

Goal	*Indicator*	*Equipment*
Drinking		
1. Independent with equipment and setup	1. C1-C5 injury 2. Absent, limited, or functional head control 3. Assisted limited arm placement	1. Cup holders, cups, bicycle water bottles, Tygon tubing, Velcro straps, wire ties, long straws
2. Independent with equipment	1. C5-C6 injury 2. Unassisted limited arm placement 3. Assisted hand function	1. Adapted cups 2. WHO; cable-driven, ratchet, electric, or WDFH orthosis
3. Independent	1. C6 or lower injury 2. Unassisted limited arm placement 3. Tenodesis hand function to normal hand function	None
Utensil Feeding		
1. Independent with equipment and setup	1. C3-C4 injury 2. Functional head control 3. Ability to sit upright	1. Quad feeder 2. Adjustable height table
	1. C4-C5 injury 2. Assisted limited arm placement	1. BFO 2. Trunk supports 3. Adjustable height table 4. WHO 5. Adapted utensils, Dycem, plate guard, sandwich holder
2. Independent with equipment	1. C5-C7 injury 2. Unassisted limited arm placement 3. Assisted or tenodesis hand function	1. WHO; HO; utensil cuff, wrist-driven, cable, ratchet, or electric orthosis 2. Adapted utensils, sandwich holder
3. Independent	1. C6 or lower injury 2. Tenodesis or limited natural hand function	None
Finger Feeding		
1. Independent with equipment	1. C5-C6 injury 2. Unassisted limited arm placement 3. Assisted hand function	1. Cable-driven, wrist-driven, electric, or ratchet orthosis
2. Independent	1. C6 or lower injury 2. Tenodesis hand function to normal hand function	None
Cutting Food		
1. Independent with equipment	1. C5-C8 injury 2. Unassisted limited arm placement 3. Tenodesis or limited natural hand function	1. Adapted knives
2. Independent	1. C8 or lower injury 2. Limited natural to normal hand function	None

Unit 8
Communication

Karen Kovich, OTR/L
Jessica Presperin, OTR/L

For most people, hardly a day goes by without picking up the telephone, jotting down an address or message, or paging through a magazine, book, or newspaper. Access to these communication functions can be limited for SCI individuals if UE function is impaired or absent. Resuming independent use of written communication, telephone, and reading functions is a goal at all levels of injury. Independence in these skills offers renewed interaction and privacy of interaction with family and friends as well as preparation for resuming or initiating vocational or educational pursuits.

This unit describes adaptive methods and equipment used to achieve independent communication functions with various degrees of motor involvement.

TURNING PAGES

Turning pages is often the first communication task attempted because it requires minimal arm placement and control. An SCI patient with minimal to no head control can operate electronic page turners via various input switches (unit 17). Page turners can be set up to be used from the W/C or bed and often require the use of an elevating table and prism glasses.

If functional head and neck control is present, a mouthstick can be used for turning pages (Figure 8–1). An eraser or rubber tip is used to provide the necessary friction. Additional equipment often includes an elevating table and bookrest. Bookrests are commercially available that not only support the book at various angles but hold the pages open as well. Adjustable bookrests can be fabricated with hinged plexiglass strips that rest against the book to hold the pages open (Figure 8–2).

The book or magazine is placed in the bookrest and, if necessary, secured to the table with a clamp or stabilized with Dycem. The mouthstick tip holder is clamped to the table or W/C. The position of the bookrest and tip holder is determined through problem solving and trial and error. The tip is placed on the top right corner, followed by a downward diagonal stroke of the mouthstick to turn the page. Practice should involve turning pages forward and backward.

When limited assisted arm placement is present, a BFO setup with a WHO, vertical holder, and pencil is used to achieve independence in turning pages. A bookrest may be indicated for those patients still in spine stabilizers or for patients who prefer it. The BFO should be adjusted in slight extension for tabletop placement. Bilateral use of BFOs may be indicated initially to compensate for lack of control.

The pencil is inverted so that the eraser is pointing downward. Therefore, it has to be placed into a vertical

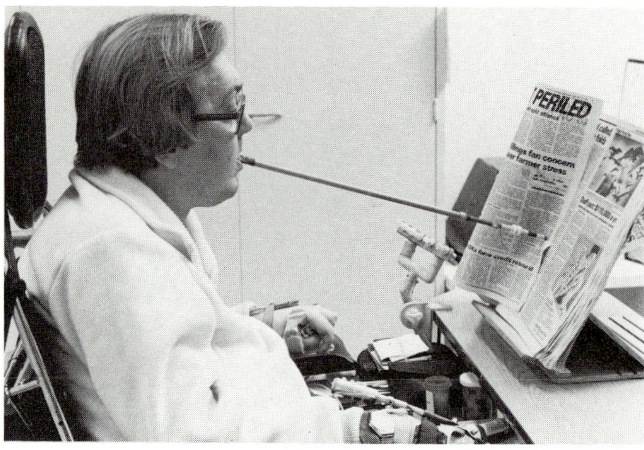

Figure 8–1 A mouthstick with an eraser tip is used to turn pages.

Figure 8–2 (Right) The Pagemate book holder keeps pages in place with sponge tabs. (Left) The hinged plexiglass book holder (RIC RE).

holder or pen holder that is then placed in the utensil slot of a WHO.

As with the mouthstick, the eraser tip is placed on the top right of the page to be turned; then, using a combination of shoulder extension, horizontal adduction, and internal rotation, the patient brings the eraser across the page (Figure 8–3).

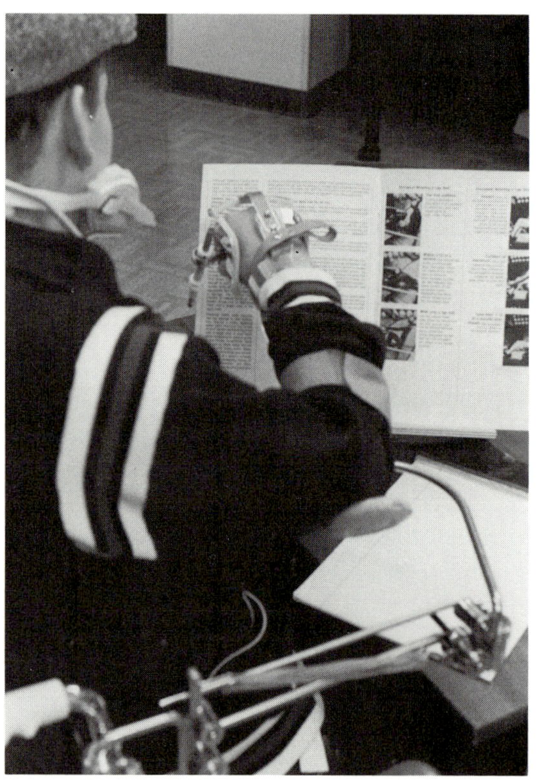

Figure 8–3 A BFO assists to provide sufficient arm placement for turning pages.

When unassisted arm placement is present with no tenodesis, the same methods are used for turning pages without the BFO. Equipment includes an eraser, vertical holder, and WHO. As an alternative method, Dycem can be placed on the ulnar portion of the WHO palmar bar or MP stop to catch the page.

When tenodesis is present, page turning should be independent after practice. If a book is lying flat, the ulnar portion of the hand may be used to turn pages. When the book is on a bookrest, the thumb or fingers may be used to catch the edge of the page and turn it. The use of a bookrest will be based on patient preference rather than functional necessity. Patients are encouraged to turn pages without a bookstand to avoid dependence on that equipment.

TYPING

A conventional typewriter may not be operable by a patient with motor involvement limiting his function to minimal head control and decreased neck rotation (C1–C2). This is because of the need to press individual keys for printing. Accessing the keyboard can be accomplished by using a computer operated via input switches. Printing is accomplished by a scanning method, Morse code, or voice input (unit 17).

A quadriplegic with limited or functional head control (C3–C4) may opt to use a mouthstick for typing. The mouthstick provides direct selection of the various keys. An eraser or rubber tip is used for pushing down the keys. A key guard, used to guide the mouthstick to the designated key and prevent it from slipping onto another, may be available commercially through the typewriter company. A plexiglass key guard can also be fabricated by drilling holes above the keys. The key guards may be screwed into the typewriter or attached with Velcro to provide stability (Figure 8–4). The keys should not protrude above the plexiglass, as this defeats the purpose of the key guard. Key guards can be fabricated for calculators, adding machines, pushbutton games, and computer keyboards.

Many portable and super-portable typewriter models are convenient for use in the classroom or if work stations are frequently changed. Daily use and goals for the typewriter should be considered before ordering one. Is the individual going back to school or a work setting where he will use a typewriter more frequently? The expense must be justifiable, and greater independence, at school or on the job, is a criterion that will often carry weight. Features such as a continuous paper roll, a key guard, light touch control, an automatic feeder, and correction keys should be considered when choosing a typewriter. Correction memory is almost a necessity for functional typing by quadriplegics.

If a continuous roll of paper is not available, computer paper is recommended. This acts as a continuous roll because it is inserted once and continues for as many sheets as are perforated together. A mouthstick user may learn to use a pincer mouthstick to insert paper into the typewriter. This is useful when letterhead and special forms are required.

Typewriting setups may be necessary to provide a consistent work area from which the individual can type independently. Typewriter holders allow the typewriter to be placed at a comfortable and accessible angle for the mouthstick user. The holes of the key guard must be angled to allow the mouthstick to freely press the keys without becoming caught.

Safe stabilization is necessary to ensure that the typewriter will not slip or fall during use. Two typewriter holders are presently used at RIC. One resembles an elevating book holder. The slotted bottom piece allows for various degrees of angulation. A hinged piece in front of the angled board folds out to a 90° angle; this supports the typewriter on the holder (Figure 8–5). The typewriter holder is clamped to the table to ensure stability. Another typewriter holder is a four-sided elongated block of plywood. It is covered on each end with a piece of rubber foam to prevent slippage. The block is trapezoidal in shape, allowing for various angles (Figure 8–6).

Figure 8–4 Typewriter key guard.

Figure 8–5 Elevating typewriter holder (Gulbrandsen); slots on base allow for changes in angulation.

Figure 8–6 Trapezoidal typewriter holder (Gulbrandsen); angulation is adjusted by moving the typewriter forward or backward on the holder.

An adjustable hospital table may also be used instead of a permanent work station. The advantage of a wheeled table is its portability. The typewriting setup can be pushed away when not in use.

Balanced forearm orthoses or deltoid-assist slings assist the C4 to C5 patient with unilateral or bilateral typing. The BFO setup is explained in unit 5. Generally, a unilateral approach is taken initially, allowing the other arm to rest or provide stabilization during the activity. Bilateral BFOs are incorporated as strength, coordination, and trunk stability increase. Typing speed can thus be increased, as each BFO covers half of the keyboard.

Orthoses are used to stabilize the wrist and keep the hand in a functional position during BFO use. The orthoses provide an attachment point for typing sticks, pencils, and pens. Many of the orthoses listed in unit 6 may be used with the BFO in typing. The most commonly used orthosis is the long opponens WHO with pen holder (Figure 8–7). Electric, cable-driven, or RIC orthoses may also be used. A pen holder, fabricated for the definitive long opponens, fits into the utensil slot. It is set at a fixed angle and holds the pencil or pen with a screw, allowing for adjustability of length.

An adjustable writing orthosis that can be used for typing was developed at RIC (Yasukawa/Hedman). It was designed to allow for independence in changing tips (eraser, pen, pencil, paintbrush) and for adjustability of the writing angle. The angle can be adjusted with an Allen wrench into the set screw. The setup is similar to that developed for the mouthstick (described later in this unit) with an arrow shaft, coupling device, and appliance holder clamp (Figures 8–8 and 8–9). The components are commercially available as a kit or can be fabricated. The adjustable writing device may insert into the utensil slot on any definitive orthosis.

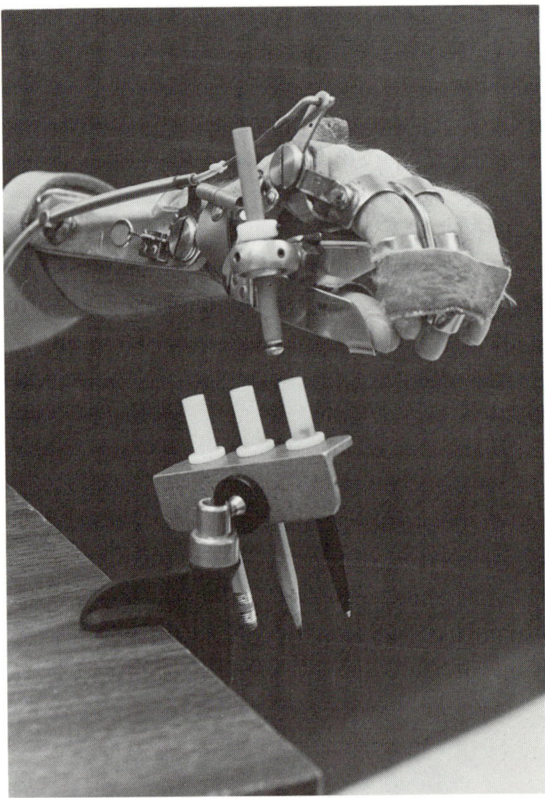

Figures 8–8 and 8–9 The adjustable writing orthosis is used for typing by inserting an eraser tip in the holder.

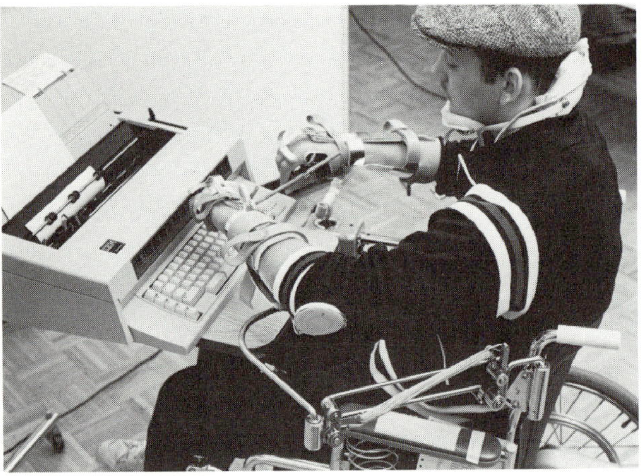

Figure 8–7 Long opponens WHO setup with pen holder and inverted pencil for typing.

Insertion of paper into the typewriter is difficult with BFOs, but can be accomplished when using an electric or cable-driven flexor hinge orthosis or bilateral BFOs. An automatic feeder is essential to assist with loading the paper. A continuous roll or computer paper is generally recommended.

The person with unassisted arm placement but no hand function may type using a long opponens WHO with typing attachments. A cable-driven, electric, or ratchet orthosis can be used with a built-up pencil eraser or typing sticks. The user can pick up the paper and insert it with the assistance of an automatic feeder.

Tenodesis at the C6–C7 level enables use of

- WDFH hinge orthoses holding an inverted pencil
- short opponens with pen holder
- typing sticks
- utensil cuff with pencil inserted
- Wanchick Writer and Decker writing splint
- pencil threaded through the fingers

A key guard is generally no longer necessary.

Insertion of the typing paper is done with a WDFH or tenodesis pinch, or bilaterally using the palms of the hands for holding the paper. Automatic feeders are recommended but not necessary.

The C7 to C8 quadriplegic may be able to isolate a finger, thread a pencil through his fingers, or use a built-up pencil with eraser to type. Insertion of the paper is done with tenodesis or, as finger flexors are innervated, natural hand function.

WRITING

Learning to write with a mouthstick requires significant coordination of the head, neck, and eyes, as well as perseverance and practice (Figure 8–10). For the C4 quadriplegic, equipment includes a mouthstick, elevating table, and adjustable bookrest. There are many considerations other than equipment that need to be taken into account in order to make writing with a mouthstick a successful experience.

Pads of paper should be used rather than individual sheets and can be secured by taping the last several pages to the bookrest or by using Dycem. This enables the patient to turn the page by switching to an eraser tip. The bookrest should be adjusted so that the paper is sitting nearly upright, placing the top and bottom of the page an equal distance from the patient.

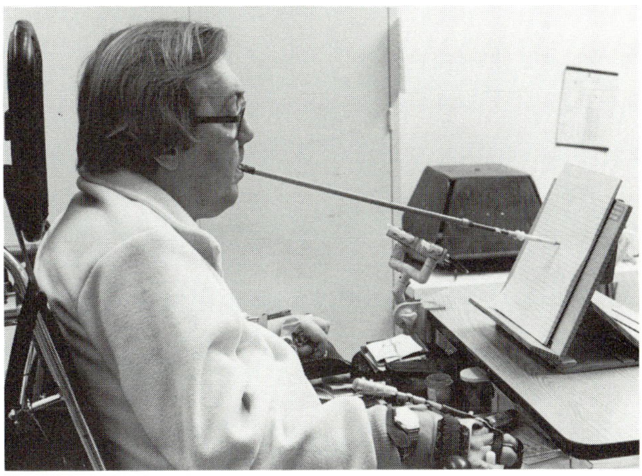

Figure 8–10 Writing with a mouthstick requires coordination of head, neck, and eyes.

Felt-tip or antigravity pens are recommended for even writing at all angles. A ballpoint pen can be used only in a position where gravity is able to assist the ink flow. Shortening the mouthstick shaft will increase control.

Writing practice should begin with large rather than small strokes. Making circles and side to side and up and down lines enables the individual to get the feel of the pressure and movement necessary to control the pen. Practice can then progress to printing the alphabet or numbers in large script. As control increases, attempts can be made to make smaller letters within the lines on a page, while still maintaining the same legibility.

First attempts at writing with a mouthstick can create a mixture of feelings, ranging from frustration and anger to a sense of accomplishment. Although this activity is a step in improving functional independence, it often indicates to the individual the severity of his disability and the extent of his dependency. Much encouragement should be provided by the therapist.

A BFO can be used for writing if there is sufficient controlled arm placement for a tabletop task. Equipment includes a WHO with utensil slot, pen, and a vertical or pen holder.

If a definitive orthosis is to be used for writing, a metal pen holder that fits into the utensil slot can be fabricated by the orthotist. The holder will be at a fixed

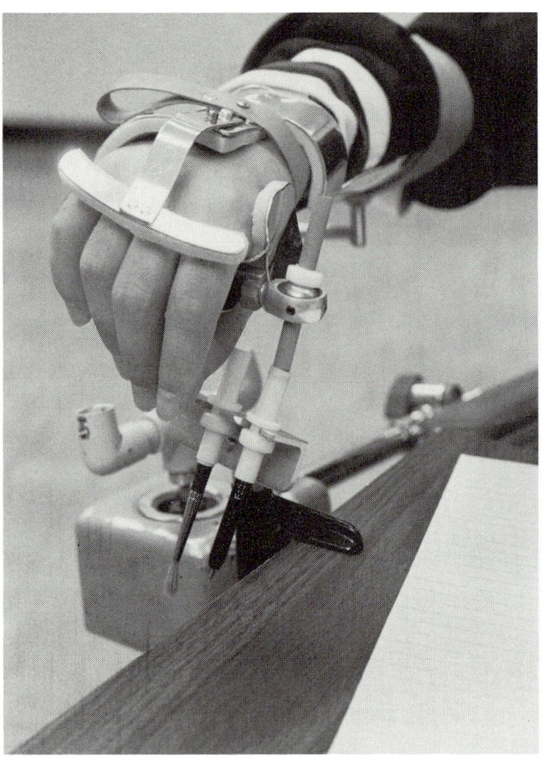

Figure 8–11 The adjustable writing orthosis used with a long opponens WHO for writing.

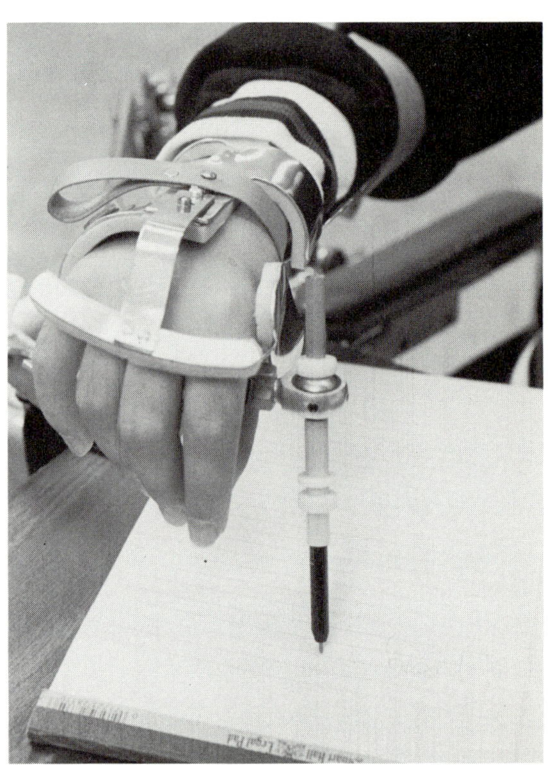

Figure 8–12 The angle of the pen can be changed to meet individual needs.

angle and holds the pen with a screw, thus allowing for adjustability of pen length.

The adjustable writing orthosis (Yasukawa/Hedman) described above is also used for writing (Figures 8–11 and 8–12). The angle of the pen is determined and then secured by tightening a set screw. The pen angle cannot be adjusted independently by the patient.

If preferred, a vertical holder placed into the utensil slot of a temporary or definitive WHO can be used to hold a pencil or pen. The vertical holder can be moved to change the writing angle; however, there is no means of securing this rotary adjustment and it often becomes loose over time.

When writing with a BFO, Dycem is usually required to stabilize the pad of paper. Bilateral BFOs may be used, with the nondominant arm set up for turning the pages as they are filled.

When unassisted arm placement is present without tenodesis, the same adaptations are used for writing as with a BFO. A cable-driven, electric, or ratchet orthosis can also be used to hold a pen.

If tenodesis is present, a variety of hand orthoses and adaptations can be used for writing. A definitive short opponens HO can be ordered with a utensil slot and pen holder. A WDFH can be used to hold a pen or pencil.

The Decker writing splint consists of a thin strip of low-temperature plastic fitting into the palm, through the thumb web space, and onto the dorsal aspect of the hand, with a portion supporting the index finger in a functional position (Figures 8–13 and 8–14). A pen holder is fabricated of the same material and bonded to the bottom of the finger portion at the desired angle for writing. A strap with a D-ring crosses the ulnar portion of the hand, and a thin strip of elastic stabilizes the distal phalanx of the index finger. A similar splint, the Wanchik Writer, is now commercially available in lightweight metal; however, the angle of the pen is fixed (Figure 8–15).

A thin cuff of orthotic material that crosses the dorsal aspect of the hand, through the web space, and onto the volar aspect can be used to write. The pen is held by a thin ring of material bonded to the cuff in the web space (Figures 8–16 and 8–17).

A figure-eight writing splint covers the thumb, index, and middle fingers only, supporting the pen and holding the fingers in three-point prehension (Figure 8–18).

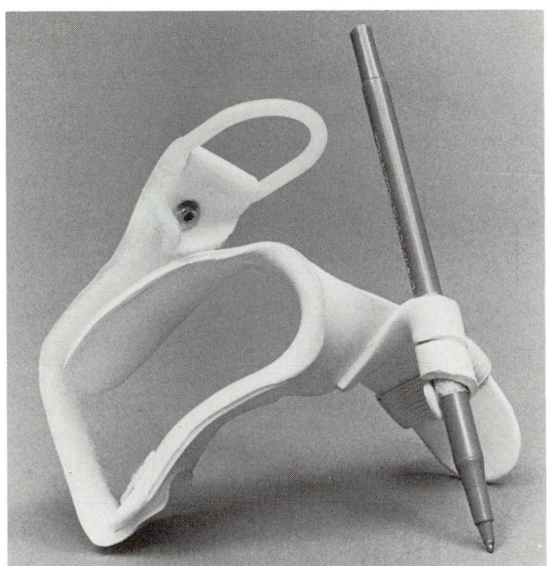

Figure 8–13 The Decker writing splint.

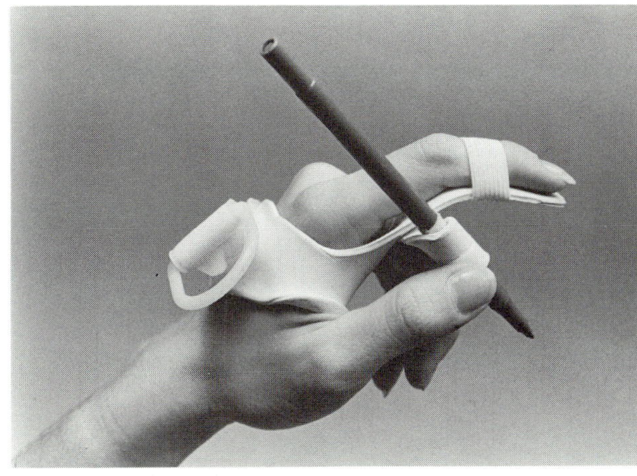

Figure 8–14 The Decker writing splint supports the index finger and stabilizes the pen.

Figure 8–15 The commercially available Wanchik Writer.

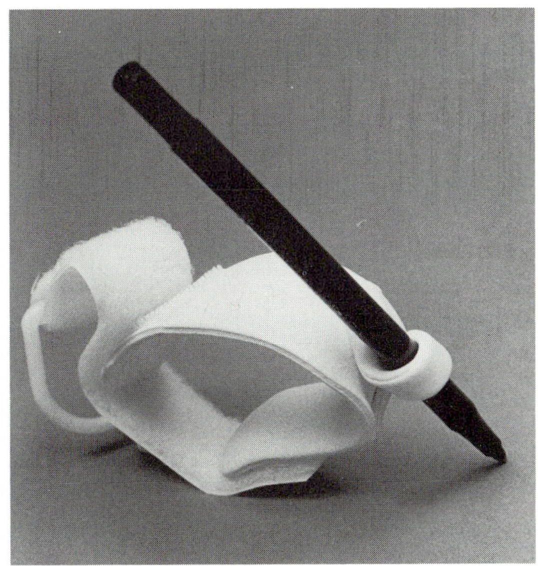

Figure 8–16 The palmar writing cuff.

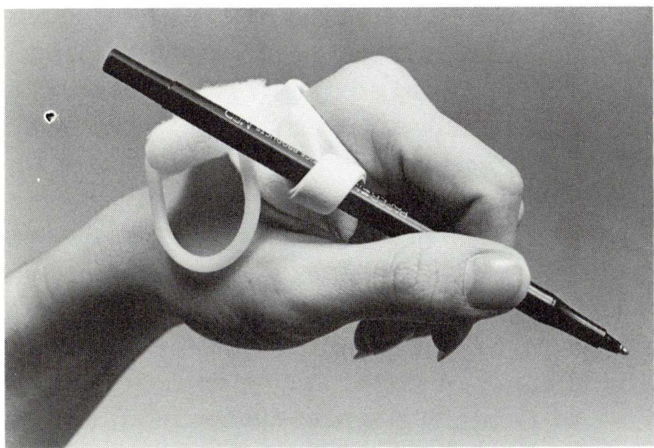

Figure 8–17 The palmar writing cuff stabilizes the pen in the web space.

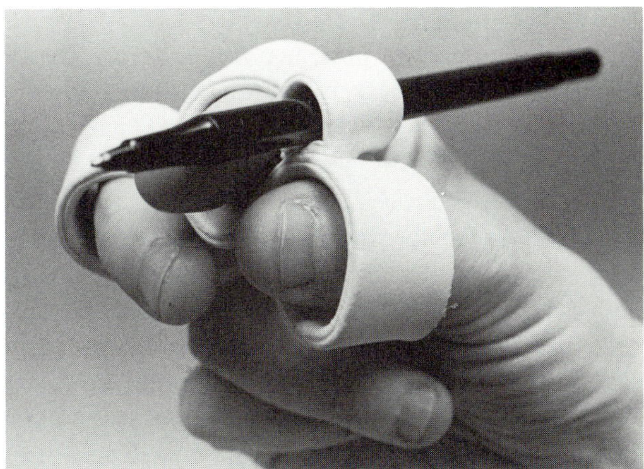

Figure 8–18 The figure-eight writing splint.

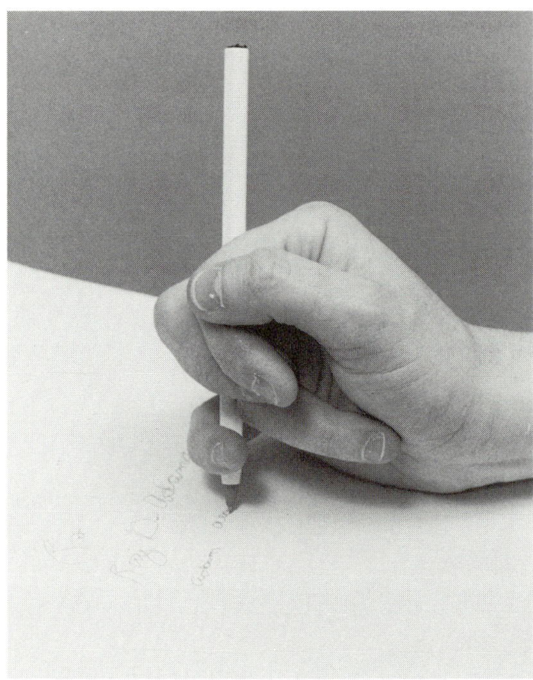

Figure 8–19 A pen can be laced through the fingers for independence in writing without equipment.

A pen holder can also be fabricated of 0.5-inch elastic. One large loop is sewn together and then divided into three smaller loops: one to fit the index finger, the middle to hold the pen, and the third to fit the thumb. Although small and lightweight, this holder can be difficult to put on independently. For individuals wishing to use no equipment, a pen can be laced through the fingers, extending from the ulnar side of the hand (Figure 8–19), or secured to the hand with a rubber band.

TAPE RECORDER OPERATION

Tape recorders are now available with one-button recording. For buttons that are difficult to press down or for two-button recorders, tabs can be mounted on the buttons to improve the leverage. For depressing two buttons simultaneously, a cross-strip is fabricated that attaches to one button and angles to overlap the extension on the other button (Figure 8–20).

A pincer mouthstick may be used to insert the cassette tape. A BFO user can insert a pencil into one of the holes of the cassette. After the ejection button is pressed, the cassette is dropped into place. A tenodesis orthosis or natural tenodesis may be used to hold a cassette for placement.

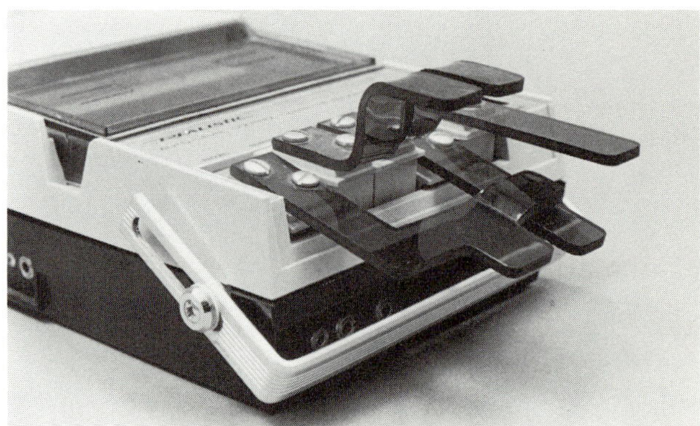

Figure 8–20 A tape recorder adapted to allow simultaneous pressure on two buttons for recording.

TELEPHONE USE

To activate a telephone, a quadriplegic with minimal head and neck control uses an environmental control unit (ECU). Eyebrow, eye blink, head, voice control, and sip and puff switches are some of the input options enabling the user to dial specific numbers or allow for operator-assisted calls. ECUs are described in detail in unit 17.

Phonation and respiratory function must be evaluated when considering phone use. Paralysis of the vocal cords will, of course, prevent talking into the phone. A speech pathologist should be consulted. Voice amplifiers are an option for those with weak phonation.

The phone system can be set up using a speakerphone that allows the user to communicate from across the room but does not allow privacy. The receiver can also be mounted with a metal gooseneck to enable private calls. The setup of the gooseneck is critical to allow consistent access to the receiver (Figure 8–21).

A patient who can use a mouthstick has direct access to the phone. On/off toggle switches replace the switchhook mechanism, allowing the phone to be off the hook and mounted on a gooseneck. By pressing the toggle, one can access a dial tone and dial out (Figure 8–22). Pressing the toggle again disconnects the call. A key guard can be used to guide the mouthstick to the buttons. Enlarged pushbutton systems for easier access are commercially available. Another system, developed by AT&T, is a faceplate that is positioned over the operator button. By lightly touching this faceplate, the user is immediately connected with the operator.

Besides pushbutton or rotary dialing, one can choose a phone with automatic dialing, memory, or redial options. BFO users can use the orthoses and typing

Figure 8–21 A gooseneck phone setup must allow easy access to the receiver and phone base.

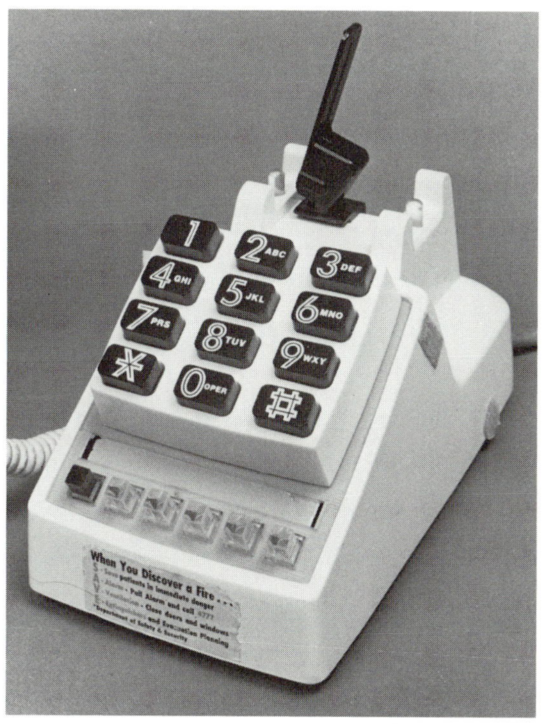

Figure 8–22 Toggle switch and enlarged pushbutton phone system.

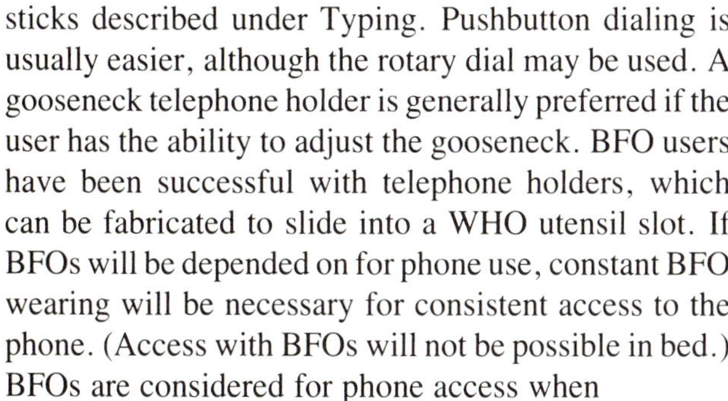

sticks described under Typing. Pushbutton dialing is usually easier, although the rotary dial may be used. A gooseneck telephone holder is generally preferred if the user has the ability to adjust the gooseneck. BFO users have been successful with telephone holders, which can be fabricated to slide into a WHO utensil slot. If BFOs will be depended on for phone use, constant BFO wearing will be necessary for consistent access to the phone. (Access with BFOs will not be possible in bed.) BFOs are considered for phone access when

- unassisted limited arm placement is expected
- the patient expects to use BFOs for multiple activities (typing, page turning) as well as phone use so that they will be in place during most of the time he is in the chair
- a backup to ECU or mouthstick setup is required

An individual with unassisted arm placement may use a WHO with pen holder and inverted pencil, a cable-driven flexor hinge, or an electric or ratchet orthosis to dial the phone. The user can opt for a gooseneck setup or hold the receiver himself (Figure 8–23). A shoulder rest or headset may be used. A phone with the dialing mechanism on the receiver is not recommended.

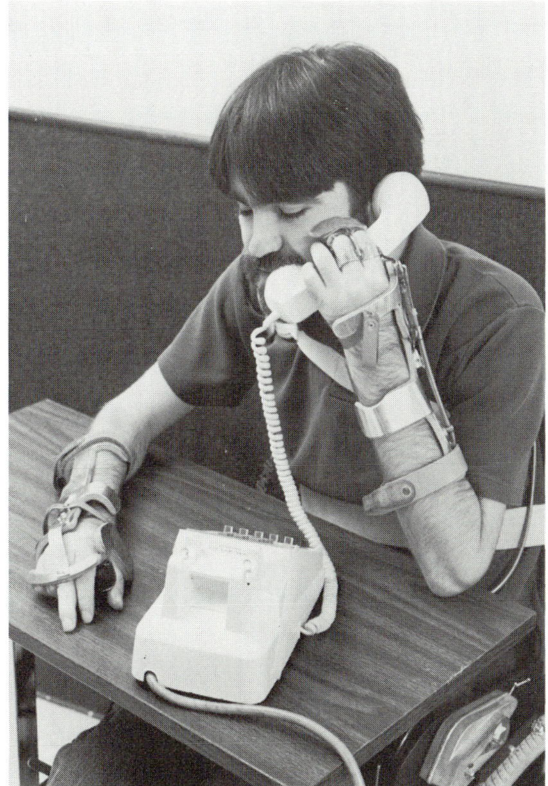

Figure 8–23 Cable-driven orthosis allows this C5 quadriplegic to pick up the receiver.

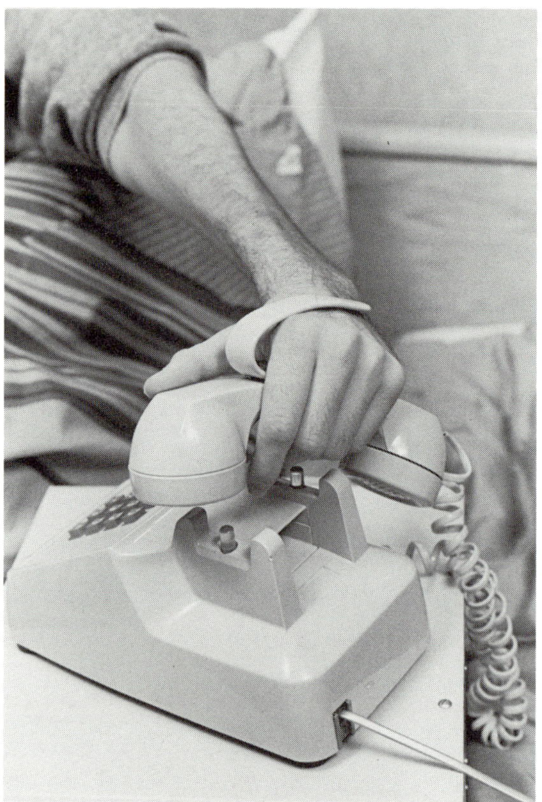

Figure 8–24 Commercial phone holder assists in picking up the receiver with tenodesis.

The C6 quadriplegic often uses the thumb or knuckle to depress the buttons. Typing and writing devices can also be used such as typing sticks, T-sticks, and built-up pencils. Any equipment used for dialing should be kept readily accessible, either near the phone or on the W/C. A phone holder is often used, although the phone can be picked up bilaterally and held between the neck and shoulder. Even when equipment is used at home or office for convenience, training without equipment offers use of unadapted phones when necessary (traveling, pay phones, etc.). A gooseneck or headset may be used in a work setting if it is necessary to write during phone conversations. Tenodesis orthoses can also be used to hold the receiver. An adapted U-shaped holder that can be used to pick up the phone is commercially available or can be fabricated from low-temperature plastic (Figure 8–24).

Quadriplegics with C7 to C8 injury are generally independent in phone use, with most using their thumb or a pencil threaded through their fingers for depressing the buttons. A shoulder rest may be used for holding the phone during long conversations. Portable cordless phones provide easy and safe access to the phone.

Some telephone and electronics companies offer the disabled person a variety of telephone adaptations. Company personnel may come into the home or work setting to assist with modifications. Centers have opened in larger cities that are specifically designed for displaying and assisting with telephone aides for the disabled. Free operator-assisted calls are available through many telephone companies if a form is returned to the company with a physician's verification. The therapist can assist the patient by identifying these services.

MOUTHSTICK OPTIONS

The C3 to C4 quadriplegic with limited or functional head control may use a mouthstick for typing, turning pages, and telephoning, allowing greater control and efficiency through direct selection than with an ECU scanning input system. It also provides a means for writing and further involvement in tabletop leisure activities. Training in mouthstick use is limited until the cervical spine–stabilizing brace is removed because of decreased available head and neck range.

Commercially available mouthsticks are used at RIC

- for training purposes until a definitive custom mouthpiece is fabricated
- for specific functions
- for patients who have the potential to use a BFO at a later date
- for patients with limited funding
- for patients with low motivation to accept a mouthstick

The page turner and pincer mouthstick are the most frequently issued commercial mouthsticks. The page turner is used for turning pages, typing, activating switches, and tabletop games. A writing device may be temporarily attached with tape or Velcro. The pincer mouthstick is used for inserting paper into the typewriter, and has been successful with insertion of cassette tapes (Figure 8–25). Another temporary mouthstick is a football mouthguard with a small dowel inserted into it and a rubber tip placed on the end.

Mouthsticks are potentially harmful to the patient's teeth and gums. A dentist should be consulted before a mouthstick is used to ensure stability of the teeth and to perform any necessary dental work. All mouthpieces should be made from materials approved for oral use.

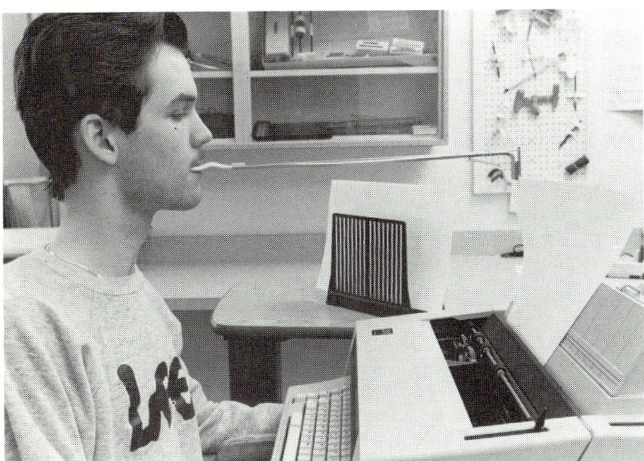

Figure 8–25 Pincer mouthstick (AliMed) can be used to insert paper into the typewriter.

A modular mouthstick system with a custom-fabricated mouthpiece was designed and developed jointly by the Northwestern University RE Program, the RIC OT department, and the Northwestern University Dental School (Kozole, Gordon, Hurst). The mouthstick offers the following features:

1. user-changeable tips
    - eraser
    - pen
    - pencil
    - paintbrush
2. telescoping shaft allowing adjustable lengths
    - shorter for writing, painting
    - longer for typing, game playing, turning pages
3. custom-fitted mouthpiece for protection and maintenance of the integrity of the teeth during mouthstick use
4. appliance holder with mounting bracket and adjustable clamp assembly

The patient can independently change tips by placing the plastic coupling into the slots of the holder and retracting his head back. The tip will release from the mouthstick and stay in the slot. He can then line up the arrow shaft with the desired tip and coupling. By inserting the arrow shaft and pushing forward, the coupling will connect and the mouthstick is ready for use (Figure 8–26).

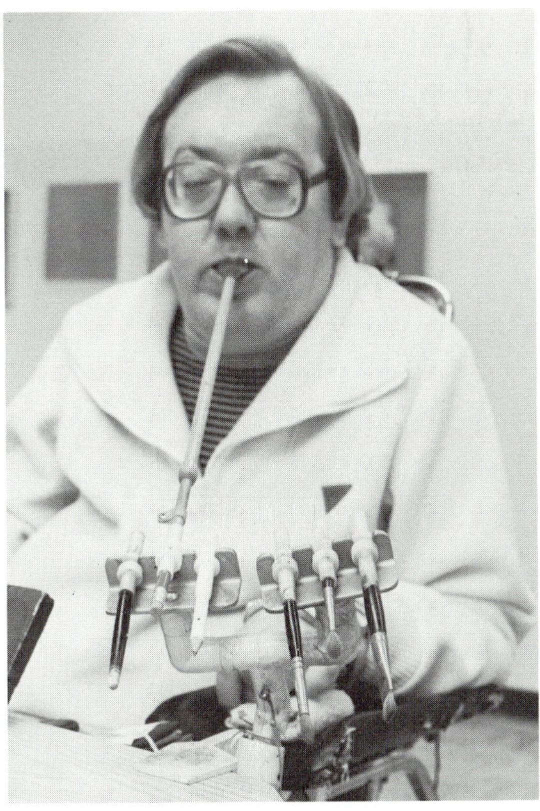

Figure 8–26 Coupling the appliance tip to the modular mouthstick system shaft.

To lengthen the shaft, the user catches the anchor tab on a stationary object and pulls back (Figure 8–27). Shortening is done by pressing the end of the mouthstick against a fixed object. A mouthstick kit, excluding the mouthpiece and telescoping mechanism, is commercially available through BeOK! (Fred Sammons, Inc.). The telescoping mechanism is available through RIC RE.

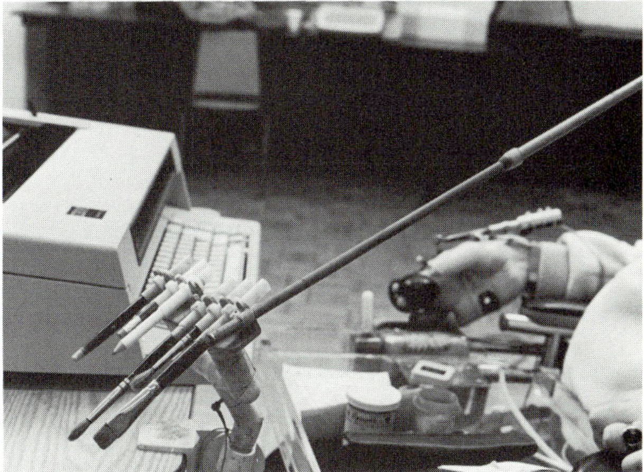

Figure 8–27 Lengthening the telescoping mouthstick shaft.

SUMMARY CHART: Communication Skills

Goal	*Indicator*	*Equipment*
Writing		
1. Independence with equipment and setup	1. C3-C4 injury 2. Limited or functional head control	1. Mouthstick, mouthstick holder, book-rest, elevating table
	1. C4-C5 injury 2. Assisted limited arm placement	1. BFO, WHO writing adaptation • metal pen holder • vertical holder • adjustable writing splint
	1. C5-C6 injury 2. Unassisted limited arm placement 3. No hand function to assisted hand function	1. WHO, writing adaptations • metal pen holder • vertical holder • adjustable writing orthosis 2. Electric, cable-driven, or ratchet orthosis
2. Independence with equipment	1. C6-C7 injury 2. Tenodesis hand function 3. Unassisted limited placement or full arm placement	1. Writing splints • Decker writing splint • Wanchik Writer • palmar cuff • figure-eight pen holder • elastic pen holder 2. WDFH or RIC tenodesis orthosis
3. Independence	1. C6-C8 or lower injury 2. Full arm placement 3. Tenodesis to limited natural hand function	None—may lace pen through fingers
Typing		
1. Independence with setup and equipment	1. C1-C2 injury 2. Zero to minimal head and neck control	1. ECU 2. Switches 3. Computer with printer
	1. C3-C4 injury 2. Functional head and neck control	1. Mouthstick 2. Key guard 3. Pincer mouthstick 4. Continuous roll or computer paper 5. Electric typewriter 6. Typewriter holder
	1. C4-C5 injury 2. Assisted limited arm placement 3. No hand function	1. BFO 2. WHO, pen holder, and inverted pencil 3. Continuous roll or computer paper 4. Key guard 5. Typewriter holder

SUMMARY CHART continued

Goal	*Indicator*	*Equipment*
	1. C5 injury 2. Unassisted limited arm placement 3. No hand function to assisted hand function	1. Long opponens WHO; electric, cable-driven, or ratchet orthosis 2. Key guard 3. Continuous paper roll or computer paper
2. Independence with equipment	1. C6 injury 2. Unassisted limited arm placement 3. Tenodesis hand function	1. WDFH holding inverted pencil 2. Short opponens with pen holder 3. Typing stick or writing splints
3. Independence	1. C7-C8 or lower injury 2. Full arm placement 3. Limited natural hand function	None—may use inverted pencil laced through fingers
Page Turning		
1. Independence with setup and equipment	1. C1-C4 injury 2. No head control to functional head control	1. Elevating table, electronic page turner, prism glasses, bookrest
	1. C3-C4 injury 2. Limited or functional head control	1. Elevating table, mouthstick, bookholder
	1. C4-C5 injury 2. Assisted limited arm placement	1. BFO, elevating table, WHO with adaptation
2. Independence with equipment	1. C5-C6 injury 2. Unassisted limited arm placement	1. WHO or HO with pen holder and inverted pencil or Dycem on MP stop
3. Independence	1. C6 or lower injury 2. Unassisted limited arm placement 3. Tenodesis or natural hand function	None
Tape Recorder Use		
1. Independence with equipment and setup	1. C3-C4 injury 2. Functional head and neck control	1. Mouthstick with eraser tip 2. Adapted tabs on tape recorder 3. Pincer mouthstick
	1. C4-C5 injury 2. Assisted limited arm placement	1. BFO 2. WHO with eraser tip attachment
	1. C5-C6 injury 2. Unassisted limited arm placement 3. No hand function	1. WHO, pen holder, and inverted pencil
2. Independence with equipment	1. C5-C6 injury 2. Unassisted limited arm placement 3. Assisted to tenodesis hand function	1. Electric, cable-driven, ratchet, or RIC or WDFH tenodesis orthosis 2. Built-up pencil
3. Independence	1. C7-C8 injury 2. Limited hand function	None

SUMMARY CHART continued

Goal	*Indicator*	*Equipment*
Telephone Use		
1. Independence with equipment and setup	1. C1-C3 injury	1. Switches
	2. Minimal to no head and neck control	2. Voice amplifier
		3. Speakerphone
		4. Gooseneck
	1. C3-C4 injury	1. Mouthstick
	2. Functional head and neck control	2. Toggle phone flipper
		3. Key guard
		4. Enlarged pushbutton system
		5. Operator faceplate
		6. Gooseneck
		7. Speakerphone
	1. C4-C5 injury	1. BFO
	2. Assisted limited arm placement	2. Gooseneck
	3. No hand function	3. Telephone holder
		4. WHO with pen holder and inverted pencil
	1. C5-C6 injury	1. Long opponens WHO; electric, cable-driven, or ratchet orthosis
	2. Unassisted limited arm placement	2. Gooseneck
	3. No hand function to assisted hand function	3. Phone holder
		4. Shoulder rest
		5. Headsets
2. Independence with equipment	1. C1-C5 injury	1. ECU
	1. C5-C6 injury	1. Phone holder
	2. Unassisted limited arm placement	2. WDFH or RIC tenodesis orthosis
	3. Tenodesis hand function	
3. Independence	1. C6-C7 or lower injury	None—may lace pencil through fingers to dial

Unit 9

Oral and Facial Hygiene and Grooming

Karen Kovich, OTR/L

Throughout the rehabilitation process, many patients, either independently or with the assistance of the therapist, come to identify daily tasks that they would like to perform as independently as possible. Initially, these often center on self-care tasks, such as oral and facial hygiene, makeup, and hair care. For most levels of SCI these tasks can be done independently with daily practice, problem solving, and the use of adaptive equipment.

WASHING THE FACE

Learning to wash the face is often simple because it requires limited arm placement and little setup and equipment. Practice begins when the patient has sufficient arm placement with a BFO to reach the face. A terrycloth wash mitt with a D-ring strap at the wrist can be fabricated or purchased, or a standard washcloth can be used. Both can easily fit over temporary or definitive orthoses required to stabilize the wrist. The soap can be stabilized on the sink with a circular suction pad so that the patient can move the wash mitt across it.

To perform the task independently with setup and equipment, the sink must be accessible to a W/C or a washbasin can be set on an accessible table. The patient lightly wets the wash mitt and then applies soap. Excess water is blotted onto a dry towel placed near the basin or sink. Washing the face is done through a combination of UE, head, and neck movement. The mitt and then the face are rinsed and the wash mitt is removed. A towel can be draped over the hand so that the face can be dried.

As independent arm placement to the face is achieved, the BFO is no longer required. The soap remains stabilized on the sink and the wash mitt is put on and removed using the teeth or contralateral thumb to fasten the strap. Many patients who normally require WHOs to support the wrists prefer to perform this task without their orthoses. With the forearm supinated, the washcloth or mitt is placed in the palm and the palm is brought to the face (Figures 9–1 and 9–2). To wring out the excess water from the washcloth, the patient can rest the hand with the cloth against the sink and then use the other hand to apply pressure.

If tenodesis is present, no equipment will be necessary to wash the face. With natural tenodesis, the washcloth is picked up and placed over the hand and soap is applied.

BRUSHING TEETH

Brushing teeth can begin when hand-to-mouth motion can be achieved with a BFO. It is often best to begin practice without toothpaste in order to gain skill in achieving adequate pressure and brush placement.

When using BFOs, the setup requires placing toothpaste on the brush and then inserting the brush into a vertical holder, which is in turn inserted into the utensil

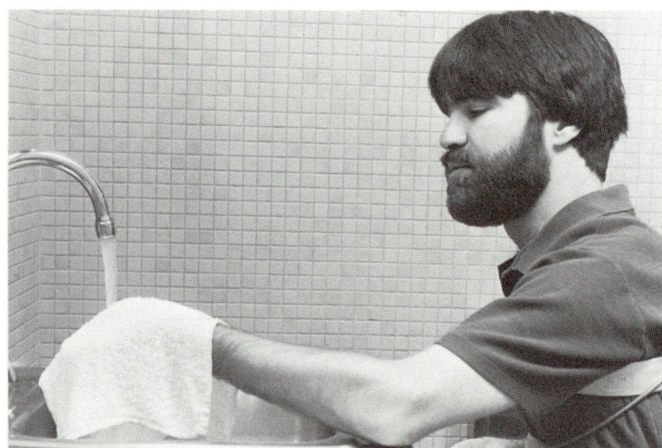

Figure 9–1 The forearm is supinated so that the washcloth can be placed in the palm.

Figure 9–2 The forearm remains supinated to wash the face.

slot of the WHO. Square- or round-handled brushes are the most versatile. Flat-handled brushes can also be used, and may be filed if necessary to fit properly.

The patient begins with the brush facing him. One side of the mouth is brushed and then the brush is turned to reach the other side. The brush is held securely between the teeth and the hand is turned so that the brush faces the opposite direction. If the patient is unable to rotate the hand, the brush can be held between the teeth, pulled out of the utensil slot, and turned with the mouth so that the bristles face in the opposite direction. The hand is brought back up to the mouth and the brush is placed back in the slot.

A cup of water with a straw and an empty cup can be used for rinsing the mouth. Assistance may be needed for stabilizing the cup.

With unassisted arm placement the same techniques will be used, but performance does not require assistance. A cable-driven, electric, or ratchet orthosis or a long opponens WHO can be used to hold the toothbrush.

There are several techniques for managing toothpaste. The easiest is often to pick the tube up between the hands and put the paste directly into the mouth (Figure 9–3). Adaptations to standard toothpaste tubes provide additional leverage. These are made of orthotic material and consist of holders for the standard tube and the newer pump tube (Decker) (Figure 9–4). Adapting the pump has proven most successful, with the adaptation serving to stabilize the tube and increase leverage so that less pressure is required. With the brush placed in the utensil slot, the free arm can be used to apply the toothpaste.

If tenodesis is present, the task requires the same techniques but less time and effort. A universal cuff, a WDFH, or a short opponens with utensil slot can be used to hold the toothbrush (Figure 9–5). The brush is picked up from the table and placed in the mouth. The mouth is then used to place the brush in the splint. At this level it will be possible to lean forward and rinse into the sink.

DENTURE CARE

To adequately clean dentures independently with equipment, unassisted arm placement as well as teno-

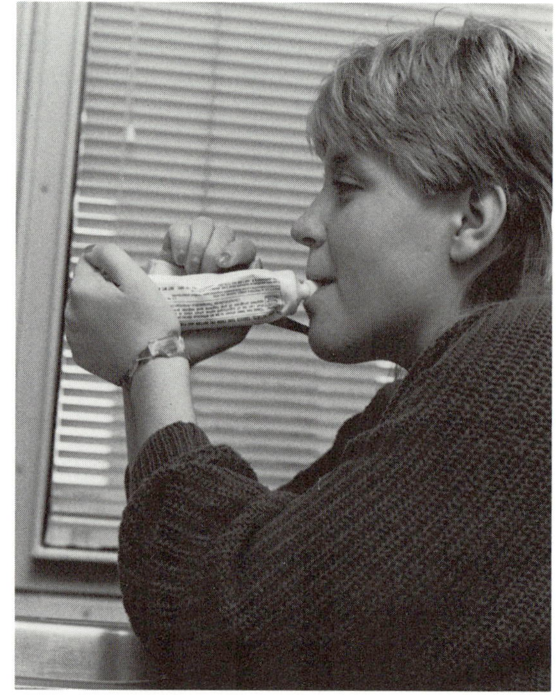

Figure 9–3 Patients may choose to use the mouth to remove the toothpaste cap.

desis hand function are required. Equipment used varies according to patient preference. Commercially available brushes attach to the sink with suction cups, leaving both hands free to manipulate the dentures.

To clean dentures, toothpaste or denture cleaner is applied to the brush and the patient rubs the dentures against the brush using tenodesis. If a toothbrush is preferred, dentures can be held in one hand and the brush in the other. A universal cuff, short opponens, or tenodesis orthosis can be used to hold the brush. Denture cleansing tablets can be used between brushings.

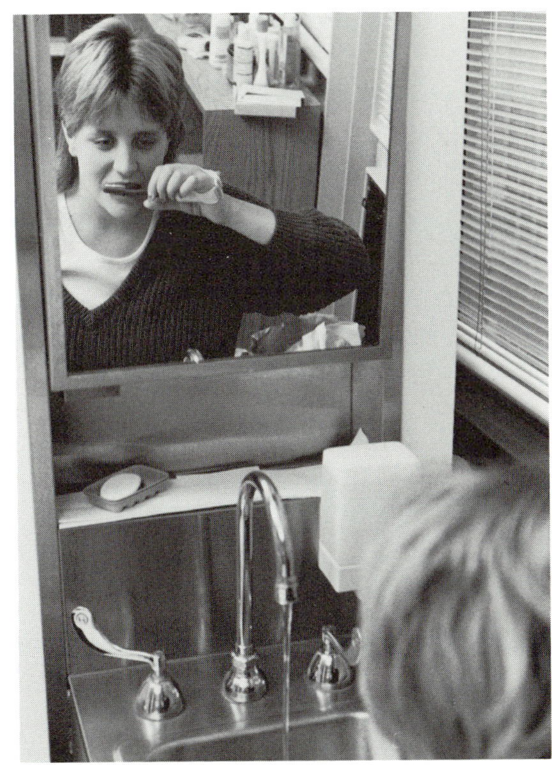

Figure 9–5 A utensil cuff is used to hold a toothbrush.

FLOSSING TEETH

Because of the manipulation necessary for flossing, a commercially available floss holder is recommended. The device is wishbone-shaped and secures the floss tightly between the two points. Several types can be found; those with a flat handle can be easily filed down to fit into the utensil slot of a WHO. A short opponens, ratchet, electric, or cable-driven orthosis or a tenodesis orthosis can be used to hold the device (Figure 9–6).

With active finger flexion and extension, no equipment is necessary. However, the floss can be stabilized by wrapping each end around the index fingers and pulling tightly.

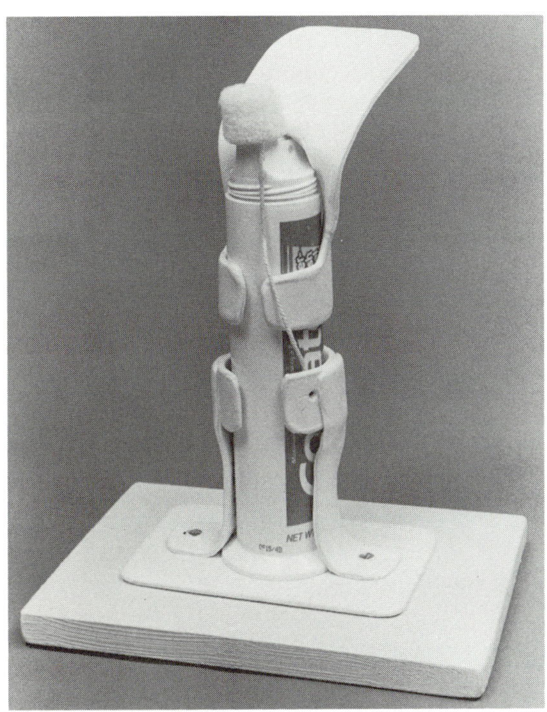

Figure 9–4 Adaptation to stabilize the toothpaste pump (Decker).

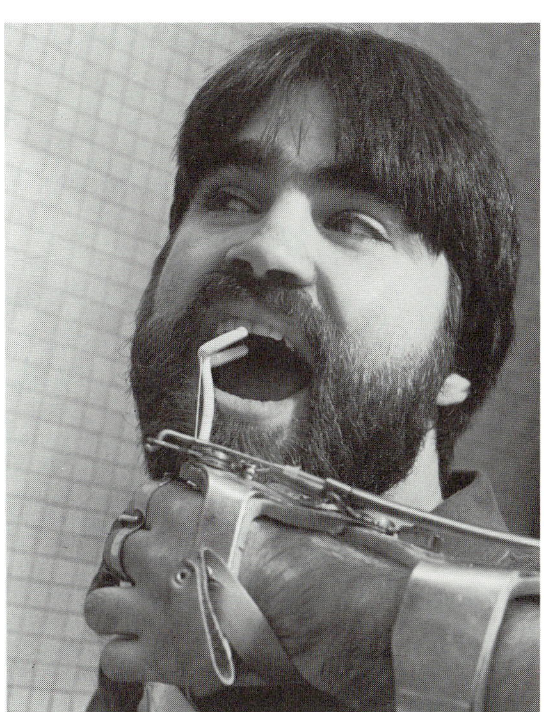

Figure 9–6 A cable-driven orthosis is used with a commercially available dental floss holder.

SHAVING THE FACE

Shaving the face can be done with an electric or safety razor, depending on personal preference. If unassisted limited arm placement is available, this task can be done independently with equipment and setup.

An electric razor is often easier to use in that it does not require the application of water and shaving cream to the face. The razor can be held with a cable-driven, ratchet, or electric flexor hinge orthosis or secured in a holder with a handle fabricated of orthotic material. The handle can fit over the hand or attach into the utensil slot on the WHO, depending on the weight of the razor. At this level of function, it is often difficult to manipulate the on/off switch as well as change the razor from one hand to the other. These steps are usually part of the setup required in the task.

When using a safety razor, an adaptation can be made of low-temperature plastics so that it can insert into the WHO. An adaptation created at RIC (Hedman, RIC RE) is a safety razor with a reusable handle and changeable blades (Figure 9–7). The handle has an adjustable collar placed at the top and bottom, between which is a tubular handle. The circumference of the tube is larger than the width of the handle, allowing the razor to rotate 360°. The rotation of the handle compensates for the lack of forearm rotation necessary to move the blade across the contours of the face. The device can be fitted into a WHO or held with an electric, ratchet, or cable-driven flexor hinge orthosis.

The application of shaving cream includes not only placing it on the face but getting it out of the can. Commercially available devices have a longer lever arm attached to the can to create the necessary pressure. Adaptations can be fabricated of low-temperature plastics that perform the same function (Figure 9–8). A 3-inch strip of orthotic material is molded around the top of the can. A 1-inch-wide strip of material is cut and rolled lengthwise to create a circle of material, which is then bonded to the 3-inch strip. The circle of material is placed so that it fits directly over the button area of the can. Both devices are used by placing the ulnar side of the hand on the lever and using the weight of the arm to provide the necessary pressure. If a WHO is used, a washcloth can be placed over the hand. The individual then puts the shaving cream on the cloth and applies it to the face. The razor is placed in the utensil slot. When shaving is completed, a cloth is used to wipe the face.

When tenodesis is present, shaving can be done independently with equipment. The equipment described above is still used; however, the patient uses a tenodesis orthosis or short opponens orthosis with utensil slot or natural tenodesis to hold the razor.

If the electric razor is too heavy, a handle adaptation may be required (Figure 9–7). The on/off button is usually operated with the thumb.

When shaving with a safety razor, the patient places the shaving cream on his face with a washcloth or his hand. Shaving cream can also be placed in a small container and applied with a barber's brush. The adapted rotating razor is then used to shave (Figures 9–8 to 9–11). Some patients can safely and effectively use a standard safety razor with tenodesis hand function. If this is not possible and the adapted rotating razor is not available, an electric razor may provide the safest option.

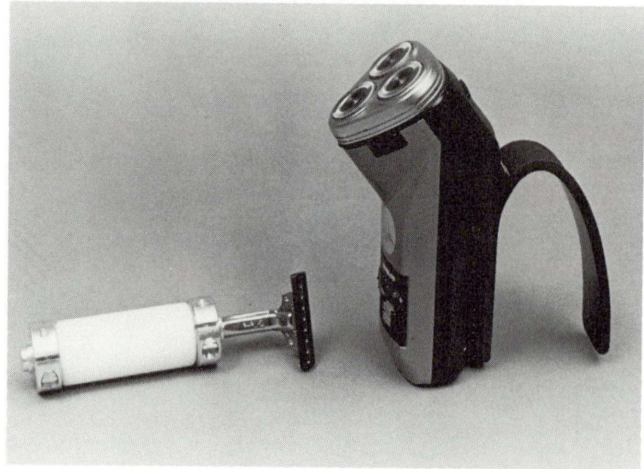

Figure 9–7 The rotating handle blade razor (Hedman, RIC RE) (left) and Kydex handle adaptation for electric razors (right).

Figure 9–8 Shaving cream can adaptation.

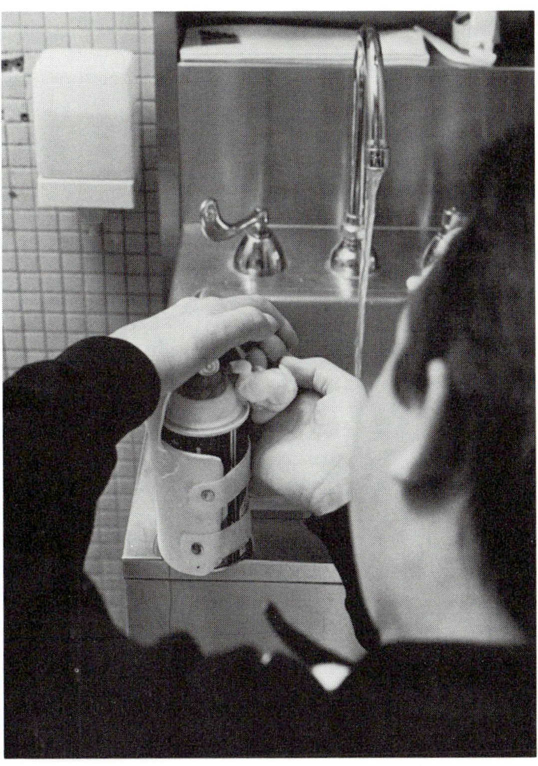

Figure 9–9 The palm of the hand is used to apply pressure to the adaptation.

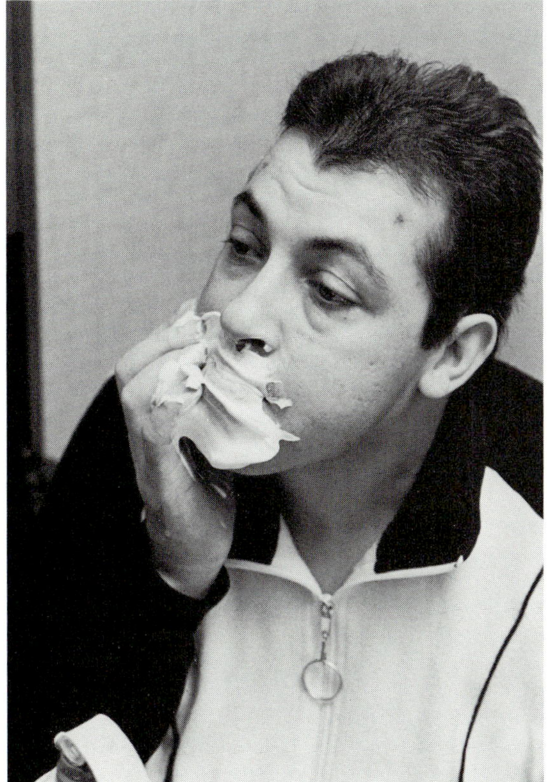

Figure 9–10 Shaving cream is placed in the palm to apply it to the face.

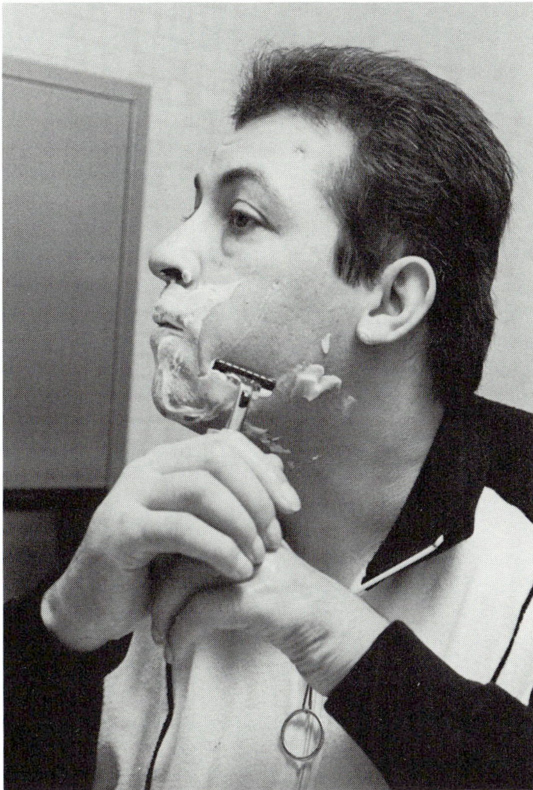

Figure 9–11 Natural tenodesis is used to hold the rotating handle blade razor.

SHAVING THE LEGS AND UNDERARMS

For females, shaving the legs and underarms is often an important aspect of grooming. Leg shaving requires unassisted limited arm placement, tenodesis hand function, trunk control sufficient for leaning forward in the bed or W/C, and UE strength adequate to lift the legs. Underarm shaving requires unassisted limited arm placement and tenodesis hand function. Equipment needed includes a shaving cream dispenser, razor adaptation, and washcloth.

A safety razor can be adapted by securing it to the end of a dowel rod with low-temperature plastics or screws. The dowel rod provides the extended length necessary to reach all parts of the leg. A strap or handle can be placed on the end of the dowel to provide the necessary stabilization. It is often necessary to alternate hands to reach all areas of the leg; therefore, the patient may prefer that a handle be attached on both sides of the dowel in order to easily switch the razor from hand to hand. The razor extends from the ulnar side of the hand, with the blade facing the patient. A washcloth can be manipulated with tenodesis and used to wet the legs. The adapted shaving cream dispenser can be used, requiring only downward pressure of the arm to dispense the cream. After cream has been applied to the legs, the razor is held by the handle or WDFHs, then switched to the other hand when necessary.

An electric razor can be adapted with low-temperature plastics. Handles are fabricated and attached to both sides of the razor with strips of orthotic material, with care taken not to cover the on/off switch. Electric razors offer extra safety when shaving legs and underarms with impaired or absent sensation. When using an electric razor, many patients prefer to shave their legs while in bed in the long sitting position. By placing the hand under the knee the leg is lifted and crossed over the other. One hand is used to shave while the other stabilizes the leg. A tenodesis orthosis can also be used to hold the razor. If the bathroom is W/C-accessible, the patient may prefer to shave by propping the leg up on the toilet or tub. Underarm shaving is usually performed at the sink with safety or electric razor.

APPLYING MAKEUP

Application of makeup can be done independently with equipment and setup when controlled assisted arm placement is present. Whether a BFO or unassisted arm placement is used, makeup has to be adapted and stabilized in a container, such as a basket filled with a piece of dense foam. The foam can be covered with an attractive fabric (Figure 9–12).

Plastic compacts for blush and eye shadow must be adapted. The plastic catch can be filed down, making the compact easier to open (Figure 9–13). A Velcro or plastic finger loop can be fabricated and attached with Velcro to the top of the compact. A strip of orthotic

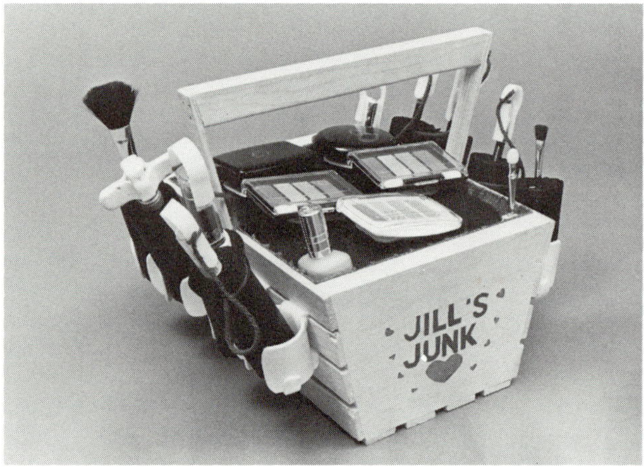

Figure 9–12 A basket filled with dense foam is used to stabilize makeup.

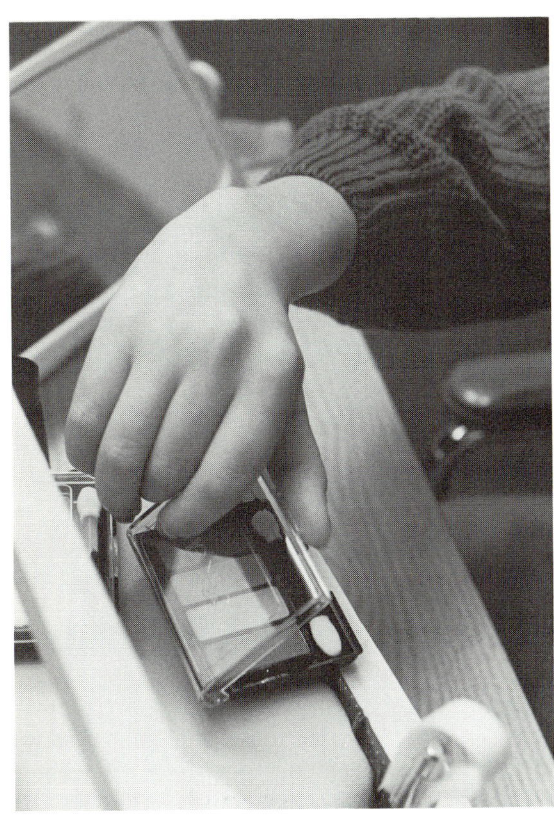

Figure 9–13 Compacts are easily opened after the catch is filed down.

material can be attached to the bottom of the compact with Velcro. This strip will fit snugly into a slit cut in the foam with an X-ACTO knife and will stabilize the compact (Figure 9–14).

Sponge-tipped applicators can be placed in a vertical holder or adapted by extending them with orthotic material that fits into the utensil slot of a WHO. These must be placed in the basket so that they can be picked up and put back independently. Larger brushes for blush should be adapted with orthotic material to fit into the utensil slot or can be placed in a vertical holder.

Mascara, eyeliner, and lip gloss tubes require adaptation to fit into the utensil slot. The adaptations should fit the tube snugly, but not attach permanently, so that they can be transferred to new tubes as needed. Cutting a single slit in the foam will securely hold small tubes, and an "X" can be cut to accommodate larger ones. The tops to these tubes are not screwed down tightly so that they can be opened independently. It is possible to

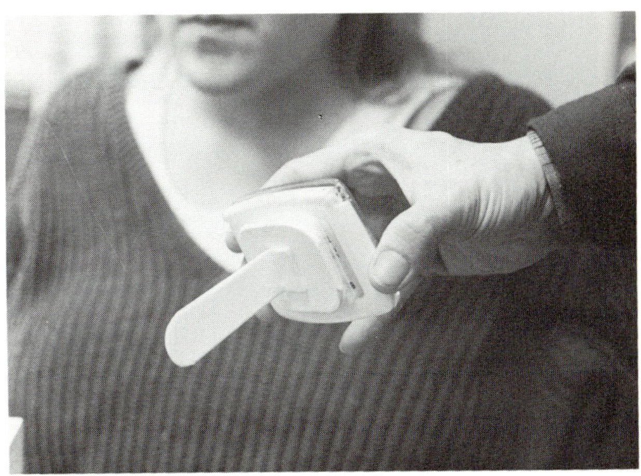

Figure 9–14 Compacts are adapted to be stabilized in the foam.

rotate the basket with one hand while still holding the brush with the other, thereby closing the cap slightly.

If tenodesis is present, makeup can be successfully applied using minimal equipment. A short opponens orthosis, WDFH, RIC tenodesis orthosis, or natural tenodesis can be used, depending on personal preference. It is still often advantageous to stabilize the makeup in a basket for easy access.

Sponge-tipped applicators should be positioned vertically in the basket and can be built up with foam to make them easier to grasp (Figure 9–15).

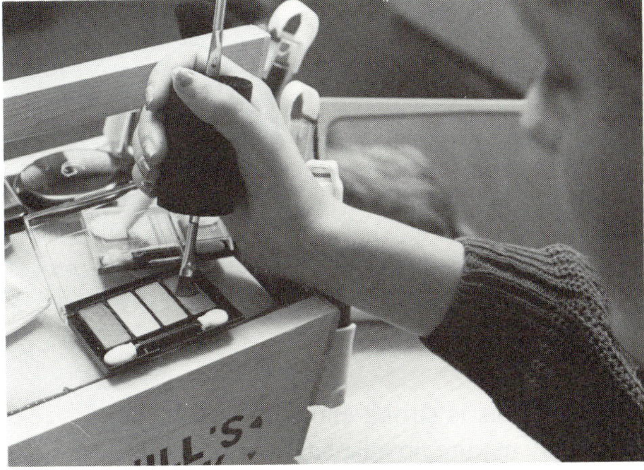

Figure 9–15 Built-up foam and natural tenodesis are often sufficient to manipulate makeup brushes.

Figure 9–20 A cup is used to wet the hair.

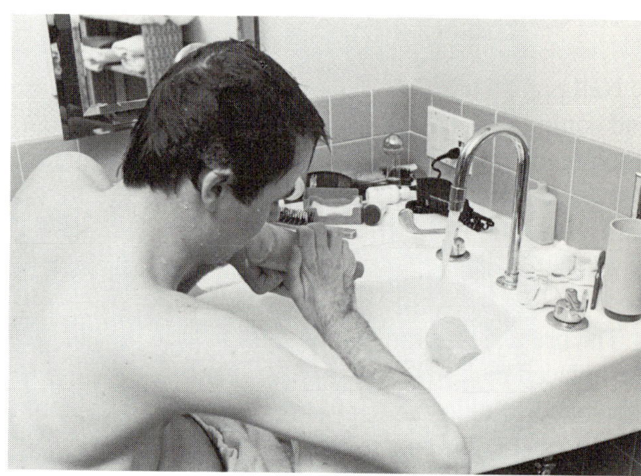

Figure 9–21 Natural tenodesis is often sufficient to manipulate shampoo bottles.

WASHING AND DRYING THE HAIR

Washing the hair is most easily done when in the shower or bath, and techniques for this are described in unit 12. Still, many patients wash their hair daily, while showering only every other day, making it necessary to learn other methods.

To wash hair independently at the sink, unassisted arm placement to the top of the head, neck and trunk mobility, and tenodesis are required. The bathroom and sink must also be W/C-accessible.

The W/C is positioned near the sink and the patient leans forward, stabilizing himself with his elbows on the sink. A cup is used to wet the hair (Figure 9–20). An alternative is a commercially available hose with a small spray nozzle on the end. This can usually be held using natural tenodesis, but may be hard to control if the water pressure is strong.

Shampoo can be poured directly on the hair or placed in a pump bottle used for hand soap or lotion (Figure 9–21). The palm of the hand is used to work the shampoo into the hair. If insufficient pressure is achieved by this method, small plastic brushes are commercially available. The hair is rinsed using the cup or hose method.

Drying the hair can be done independently with equipment and setup by patients with unassisted limited arm placement. Lightweight travel dryers are most often used because they are not as difficult to lift as full-sized dryers.

If arm placement does not reach the top and back of the head, or if endurance is poor, the dryer can be stabilized in a telephone gooseneck and clamped to the table. A longer lever arm is attached to the portion of the gooseneck that holds the dryer to provide leverage sufficient to change the direction of air flow (Figure 9–22). A small piece of plexiglass is glued to the on/off switch to provide easy access. An adapted brush or comb can be used in the dominant extremity to brush the hair while drying. A dryer can also be adapted to fit into the utensil slot of a WHO by attaching a thin strip of metal or orthotic material. Handles of the same material can be made to fit over the WHO. A cable-driven, ratchet, or electric orthosis can also be used to hold the dryer.

Once tenodesis is present, a patient will be able to dry his hair independently with equipment. A tenodesis orthosis can be used to hold the dryer or a phone holder can be attached to the dryer with the bottom strip of material angled up at the end to prevent the hand from slipping out.

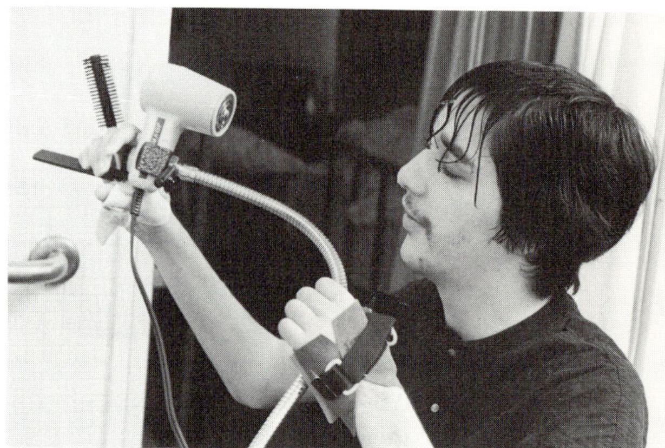

Figure 9–22 A hair dryer is stabilized on a gooseneck to free hands for brushing.

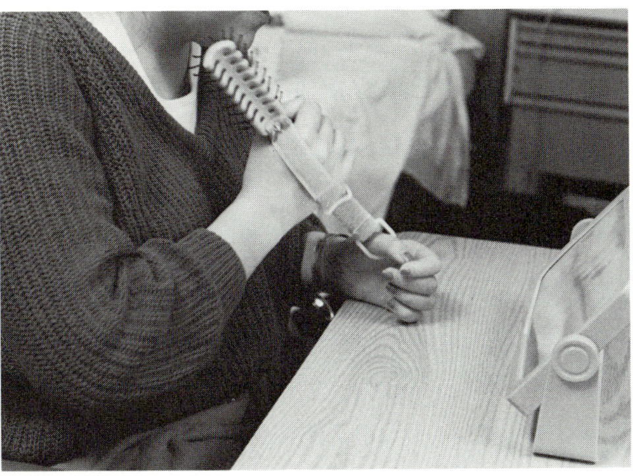

Figure 9–23 Brushes are adapted with D-ring Velcro handles.

Figure 9–24 One arm is used to assist with trunk balance while the other is used to brush the hair.

COMBING, BRUSHING, AND SETTING THE HAIR

Combing or brushing the hair requires unassisted arm placement to the top of the head as well as wrist control. Although natural tenodesis is often enough to pick up a brush or comb, it does not provide the stability needed to pull the brush through the hair. Handles or straps can be added to provide the necessary stability, or a tenodesis orthosis may be used.

A commercially available phone holder can be strapped onto a hairbrush. To provide additional support the bottom strip is angled up to prevent the hand from slipping out. Straps can be fabricated of 1-inch webbing. A D-ring is used to enable the strap to be tightened and attached back on itself with Velcro (Figures 9–23 and 9–24). This handle can be permanently secured by drilling two small holes through the brush handle and securing the strap with screws.

The use of hot curlers requires full arm placement, limited natural hand function, and trunk stability. Curlers with a flock coating that assists in gripping the hair are recommended. Rubber-coated nonelastic wire curlers that are twisted to stay in the hair may be more easily manipulated than standard hot curlers.

To use a curling iron, full arm placement, tenodesis, and trunk stability must be present. Professional curling irons have no spring mechanism in the handle and may be easier to use. An extension of high-temperature plastic can be attached to the handle of a professional or standard curling iron to lengthen the lever arm. The extension may be flat or in the form of a handle.

Hair dryer and styling brush combinations require less manipulation than curlers or an iron. They can be adapted with a handle for increased stability.

A patient performing hair care must have good control of all electric appliances due to the risk of an accident. Endurance with arm placement above the head varies and will have an effect on performance.

FEMININE HYGIENE

Independence in feminine hygiene requires tenodesis hand function, full arm placement, and the ability to move to and from the bed or toilet independently. Adhesive pads are the easiest to use. They can be placed in the underwear before dressing and are most easily changed when lying in bed. Although an individual may be able to change the pad, assistance may be required with the transfer to and from the bed. A WDFH or RIC tenodesis orthosis, or the teeth can be used to peel the backing off a clean pad.

When tenodesis or limited hand function is present, a tampon can be used independently with a mirror and a commercially available tampon inserter. Tampons with looped strings are used. When in bed, the patient sits and positions the mirror to provide a view of the perineal area, compensating for sensory loss. The tampon is inserted with the commercially available device or natural hand function. It can be removed by hooking the thumb into the loop of string attached at the end of the tampon. This procedure can also be done while sitting on a toilet with a mirror that attaches to the seat.

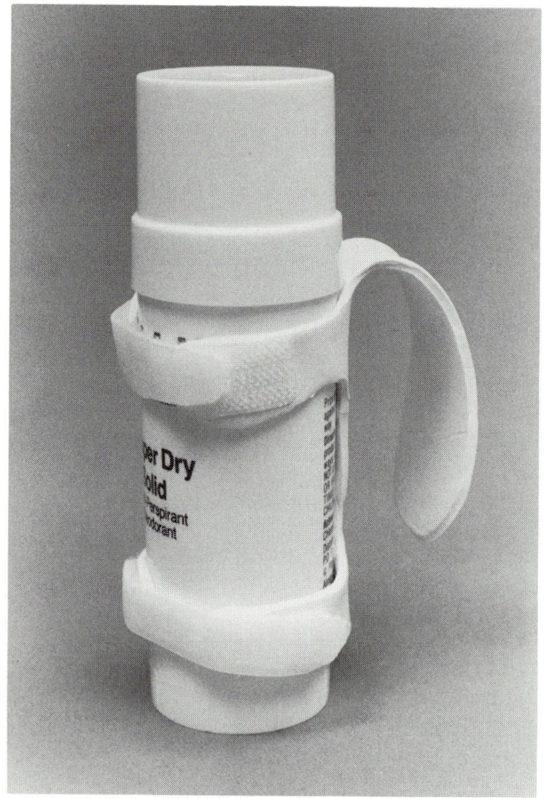

Figure 9–25 Handle adaptations are used for application of deodorant.

APPLYING DEODORANT

Deodorant can be applied independently with equipment and setup by patients having unassisted limited arm placement. Stick and roll-on deodorants can be used at this level of SCI.

Holders for deodorant can be made of low-temperature plastics, either in the form of a handle fitting over the WHO or a strip of material fitting into the utensil slot. A cable-driven, electric, or ratchet orthosis can also be used to hold the deodorant. When wrist extensors are present, natural tenodesis may be sufficient to hold roll-on and stick deodorant. A tenodesis orthosis or a handle adaptation for increased stability (Figure 9–25) may also be used. Aerosol cans can be adapted with commercially available lever arms. With limited natural hand function, the patient should be independent in the application of deodorant.

Figure 9–26 Natural tenodesis is used to put on and remove eyeglasses.

DONNING GLASSES

Glasses can be put on independently by patients with unassisted limited arm placement. Glasses are opened and then lifted by using pressure against both sides of the frame. A cable-driven, electric, or ratchet orthosis can also be used.

When tenodesis is present, the ear pieces of the glasses are hooked between the thumb and index finger and lifted to the face. The glasses are removed in the same manner (Figure 9–26).

Glasses can be cleaned independently if unassisted arm placement and tenodesis are present. Once the glasses are wet, soap can be put on using a washcloth held with tenodesis or by rubbing the pad of the thumb over the soap and then directly onto the lenses. Glasses are dried with a towel, which can be manipulated with tenodesis.

APPLYING CONTACT LENSES

Because of the fine motor control necessary to manipulate soft contact lenses, limited natural hand function is required for independence in their application. Hard lenses can be cleaned, put in, and removed independently with equipment by persons with limited arm placement and tenodesis. Equipment includes adaptations to the contact case and solution bottles. A tenodesis orthosis can be used to manipulate the case and bottles. A finger extension splint can be used to stabilize a finger in order to place the lens on the eye.

Caps to the contact case are adapted with a tab or ring of orthotic material for easier opening. The same material is used to fabricate handles or holders for solution bottles. With the handle the bottle is inverted and pressed against the edge of the sink to obtain solution. Solution can also be placed into pump bottles usually used for hand soap, which require no adaptation.

The contact is removed from the case using the pad of the thumb or finger, and solution is applied with the other hand. By combining the wetting and soaking solutions, the step of solution application can be eliminated. The wet contact is then placed on the first MP joint or extended finger and placed on the eye.

Contacts are removed by using the thumb or MP joint to pull the corner of the eye, letting the lens fall onto the table or into the hand. The pad of the thumb is wetted and used to pick up the lens and place it in the case.

EAR CARE

Q-Tips are manipulated by natural tenodesis or are laced underneath the index finger. Q-Tip cases may have to be adapted for easier opening.

SUMMARY CHART: Oral and Facial Hygiene and Grooming

Goal	*Indicator*	*Equipment*
Washing the Face		
1. Independent with equipment and setup	1. C5 injury 2. Assisted limited arm placement	1. BFO 2. WHO 3. Wash mitt, soap stabilizer
2. Independent with equipment	1. C5 injury 2. Unassisted limited arm placement	1. WHO 2. Soap stabilizer, wash mitt
3. Independent	1. C6 or lower injury 2. Unassisted limited arm placement to full arm placement 3. Tenodesis hand function to normal hand function	None
Oral Care		
1. Independent with setup and equipment in brushing teeth	1. C5 injury 2. Assisted limited arm placement	1. BFO 2. WHO 3. Toothbrush, toothpaste stabilizer
2. Independent with equipment in brushing teeth, flossing teeth, or denture care	1. C5-C7 injury 2. Unassisted limited arm placement 3. Assisted or tenodesis hand function	Brushing: 1. WHO; HO; cable-driven, electric, or ratchet orthosis; WDFH; or RIC tenodesis orthosis 2. Toothpaste stabilizer Dentures: 1. HO, WDFH, or RIC tenodesis orthosis 2. Denture brush Flossing: 1. WHO; HO; cable-driven, ratchet, or electric orthosis; WDFH; or RIC tenodesis orthosis 2. Floss holder
3. Independent in brushing teeth, flossing teeth, or denture care	1. C8 or lower injury 2. Limited natural hand function to normal hand function	None
Shaving		
1. Independent with setup and equipment in shaving the face	1. C5 injury 2. Unassisted limited arm placement	1. WHO or electric, ratchet, or cable-driven orthosis 2. Electric razor, handle adaptation 3. Adapted rotating safety razor 4. Shaving cream can adaptation

SUMMARY CHART continued

Goal	*Indicator*	*Equipment*
2. Independent with equipment in shaving the face, legs, and underarms	1. C6-C7 injury 2. Unassisted limited or full arm placement 3. Tenodesis hand function	1. WDFH or RIC tenodesis orthosis 2. Electric razor with handle adaptation 3. Rotating safety razor 4. Shaving cream can adaptation
3. Independent in shaving the face, legs, and underarms	1. C8 or lower injury 2. Limited natural hand function to normal hand function	None
Makeup/Nail Care		
1. Independent with equipment and setup	1. C5 injury 2. Assisted arm placement	1. BFO 2. WHO 3. Makeup basket 4. Nail polish board
2. Independent with equipment	1. C5-C7 injury 2. Unassisted limited arm placement 3. Assisted or tenodesis hand function	1. WHO, WDFH, RIC, ratchet, or electric orthosis 2. Makeup basket 3. Nail polish board
3. Independent	1. C8 or lower injury 2. Limited natural hand function to normal hand function	None
Hair Care		
1. Independent with equipment in combing and brushing hair, washing hair, drying hair	1. C6-C7 injury 2. Unassisted limited arm placement 3. Tenodesis hand function 4. Trunk stability	1. WDFH or RIC tenodesis orthosis 2. Adapted brush and comb 3. Shampoo dispenser 4. Gooseneck adapted with hair dryer
2. Independent in combing and brushing hair, washing hair, drying hair, setting hair	1. C8 or lower injury 2. Full arm placement 3. Limited natural hand function 4. Trunk stability	None
Feminine Hygiene		
1. Independent with equipment	1. C6-C7 injury 2. Unassisted limited arm placement 3. Tenodesis hand function 4. Independent LE dressing	1. Mirror, tampon inserter 2. WDFH or RIC tenodesis orthosis

SUMMARY CHART continued

Goal	*Indicator*	*Equipment*
2. Independent	1. C8 or lower injury 2. Full arm placement 3. Limited natural hand function 4. Independent in transfers 5. Independent in LE dressing	None
Applying Deodorant		
1. Independent with equipment	1. C5-C6 injury 2. Unassisted limited arm placement 3. Absent, assisted, or tenodesis hand function	1. WHO; cable-driven, electric, or ratchet orthosis; WDFH; or RIC tenodesis orthosis 2. Handle adaptation
2. Independent	1. C6-C8 or lower injury 2. Tenodesis or limited natural hand function	None
Eye Care		
	Contacts	
1. Independent with equipment	1. C6-C7 injury 2. Unassisted limited arm placement 3. Tenodesis hand function	1. Adaptations to solution bottles and contact case 2. Finger extension splint
	Glasses	
	1. C5-C7 injury 2. Unassisted limited arm placement 3. Assisted or tenodesis hand function	1. Electric or cable-driven orthosis, WDFH, or RIC tenodesis orthosis
	Contacts	
2. Independent	1. C8 or lower injury 2. Limited natural hand function	None
	Glasses	
	1. C6 or lower injury 2. Tenodesis hand function	
Ear Care		
1. Independent with equipment	1. C6-C7 injury 2. Unassisted limited arm placement 3. Tenodesis hand function	1. Adaptation to containers 2. WDFH or RIC tenodesis orthosis
2. Independent	1. C8 or lower injury 2. Limited natural hand function or normal hand function	None

Unit 10

Dressing

Annette Russell Farmer, OTR/L

This unit describes dressing techniques, adaptations, and equipment used by SCI patients. In determining which technique to use, several factors should be taken into consideration. The patient's motivation and ability to solve problems will have a direct effect on skill achievement. Physical factors that influence dressing skills include the following:

- bed mobility (rolling, LE positioning)
- body weight
- flexibility
- spasticity
- arm placement
- hand function
- endurance

DRESSING UPPER EXTREMITIES

Two basic techniques for UE dressing are the over-the-head and the around-the-back methods.

Over-the-Head Method

This method can be used for either slipover or front-opening garments. The garment is placed on the patient's lap with the neckline nearest the knees, the bottom at the waist, and the front side down. Arms are placed into the sleeves one at a time and the garment is lifted over the head while the arms are raised. The garment is then pulled down in back. The over-the-head method can be used by the care giver for patients with SCI levels C1 to C4 with slight modifications. The care giver places the garment as mentioned, then puts his or her own arm through the sleeve from the wrist up to the shoulder portion and, by holding the patient's hand in a handshaking position, gently guides it through the sleeve (Figure 10–1). The other arm is guided in the same manner. While raising the patient's arms up, the care giver pulls the garment over the head (Figure 10–2). The care giver then leans the patient forward and pulls the garment down in back (Figure 10–3). The amount of effort needed can be reduced by using the following suggestions and adaptations:

- jackets with removable sleeves [Sleeves that are attached with snaps, buttons, and zippers are available (Figure 10–4). These sleeves can be removed and the remaining garment can be left on while indoors if needed.]
- clothing that slips over the front of the body and fastens in the back
- loose-fitting clothing
- poncho-type garments

The C5 SCI patient is able to assist in donning shirts and jackets in the over-the-head method. The patient

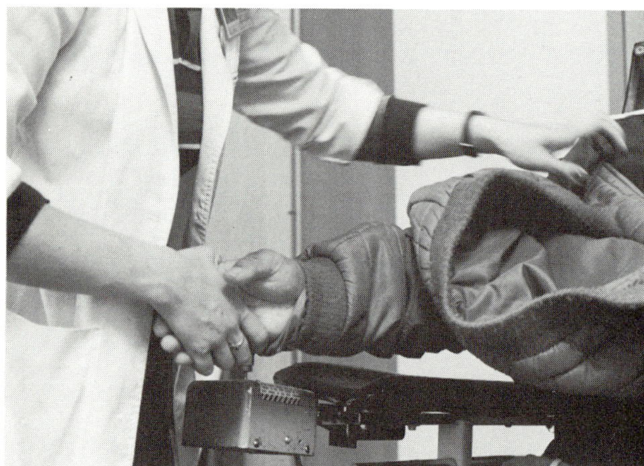

Figure 10–1 Guiding the dependent patient's hand through the sleeve.

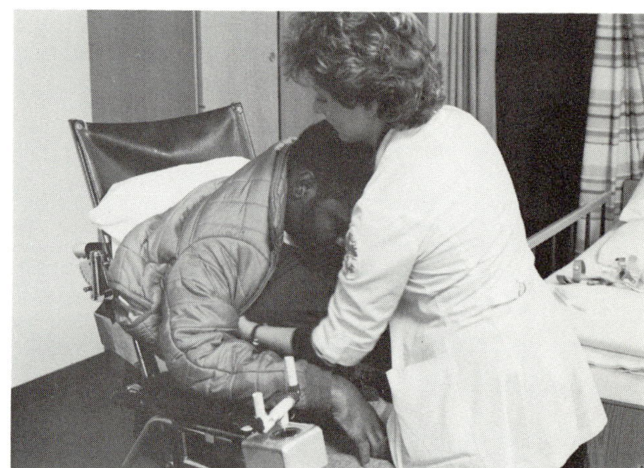

Figure 10–3 The patient is leaned forward to pull the garment down in back.

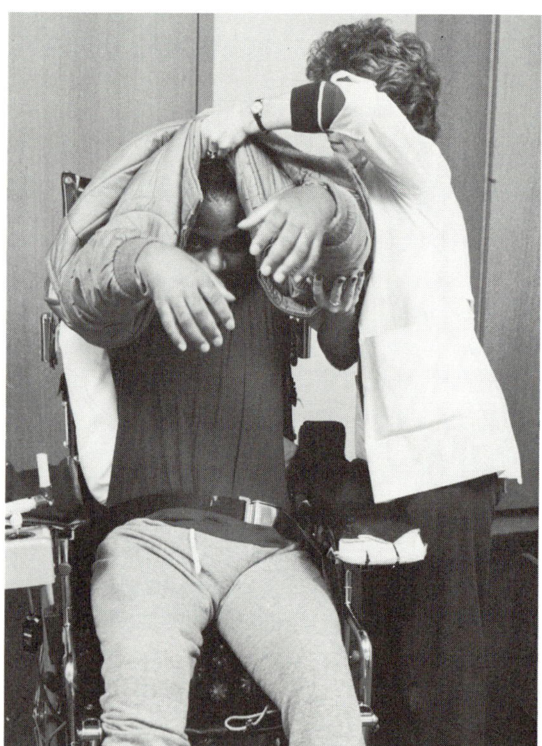

Figure 10–2 Pulling the garment over the patient's head.

Figure 10–4 Zip-off sleeves.

has limited arm placement and requires back support, such as an electric bed in an upright position or sitting in a W/C for balance. He is able to place his UEs into the garment and requires assistance to lift the garment over the head and pull it down in the back.

Patients with C6 or lower injury are able to don UE garments independently by using the over-the-head method. The position chosen to don the garment depends on the patient's balance abilities. Options include

- long sitting in bed without back support
- long sitting in bed with back support
- sitting in the W/C

For those with C6 or C7 function, tenodesis is used to position the garment on the lap. The arms are placed in the sleeves one at a time (Figure 10–5). With garments that have fitted wrists, the patient can pull the garment over his hand with the teeth (Figure 10–6) or use the friction of his hand against the lap for resistance. The

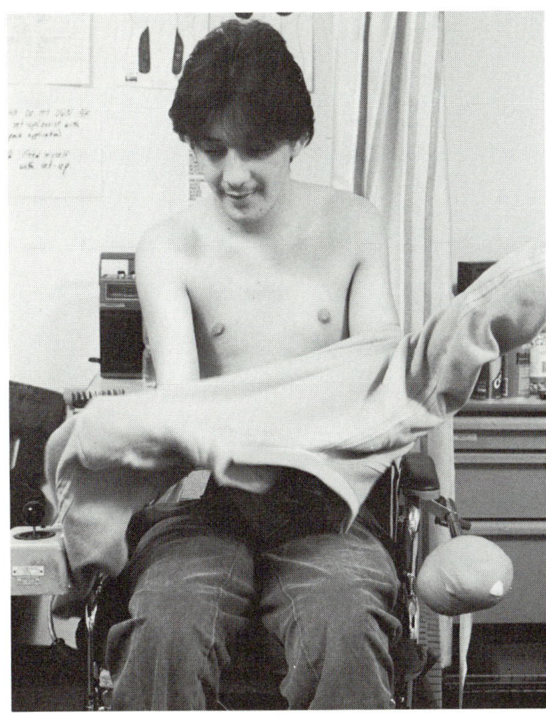

Figure 10–5 C6 patient placing his arms in the sleeves.

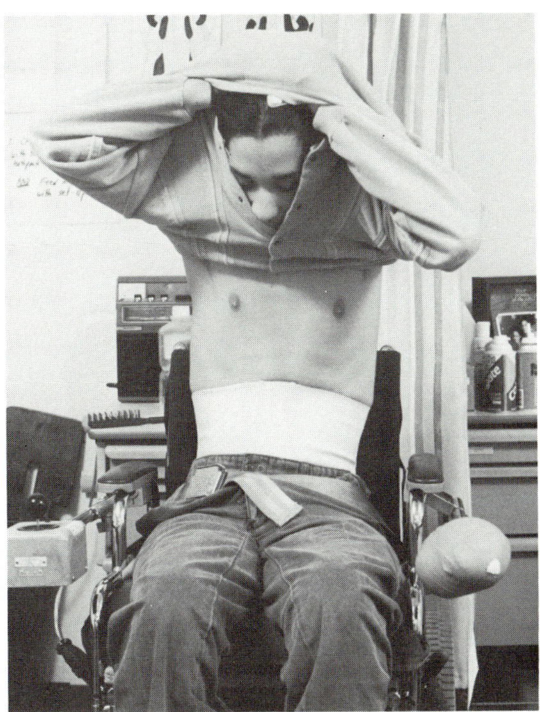

Figure 10–7 Lifting the garment overhead.

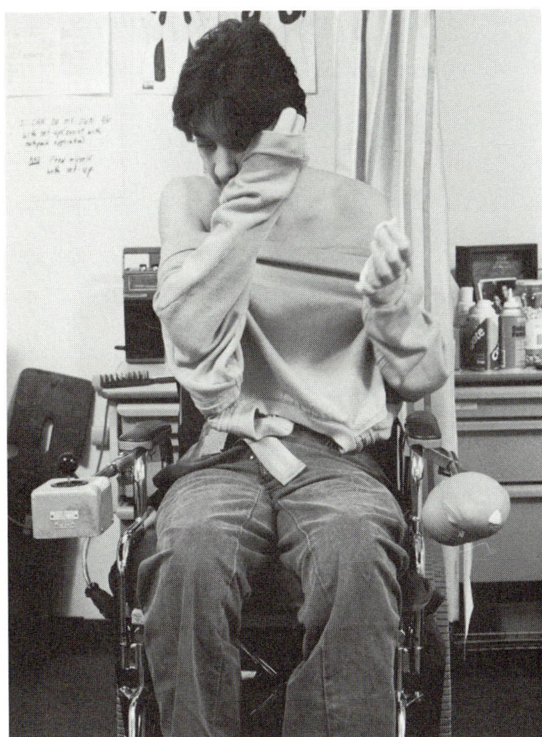

Figure 10–6 Pulling shirt sleeve over the hand with the mouth.

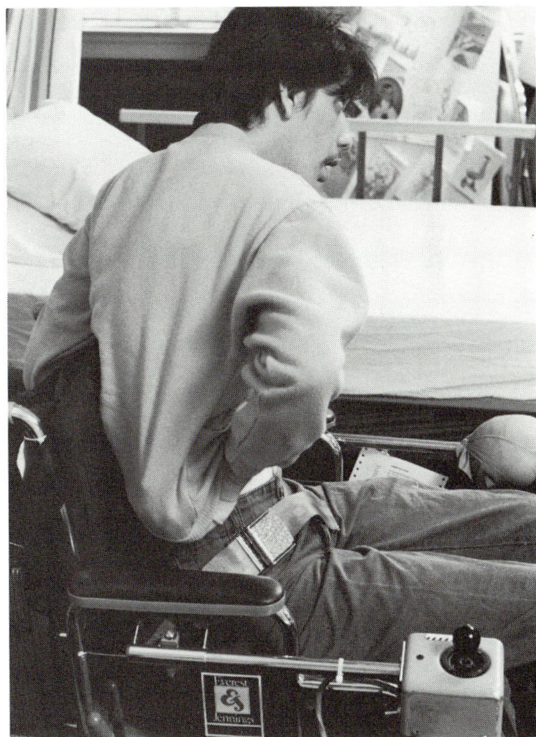

Figure 10–8 Pulling the garment down in back.

patient then lifts his arms up and moves the garment over his head (Figure 10–7). To pull the garment over the back, the patient can lean forward and shake his shoulders, which moves the shirt over the back. Then, by placing one arm over the back handle of the W/C, the other arm is freed to place around the back and get underneath the garment to pull it down (Figure 10–8). The process is repeated for the opposite side.

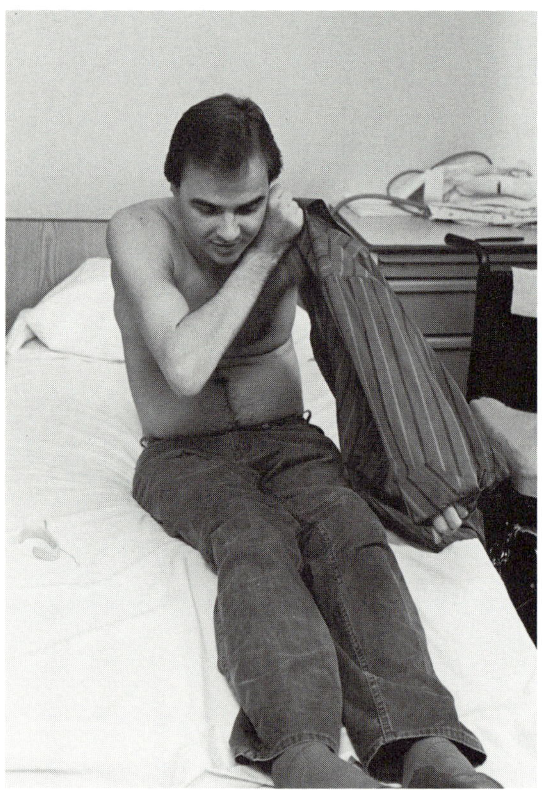

Figures 10–9 to 10–12 C7 SCI patient using around-the-back method to don a button-down shirt.

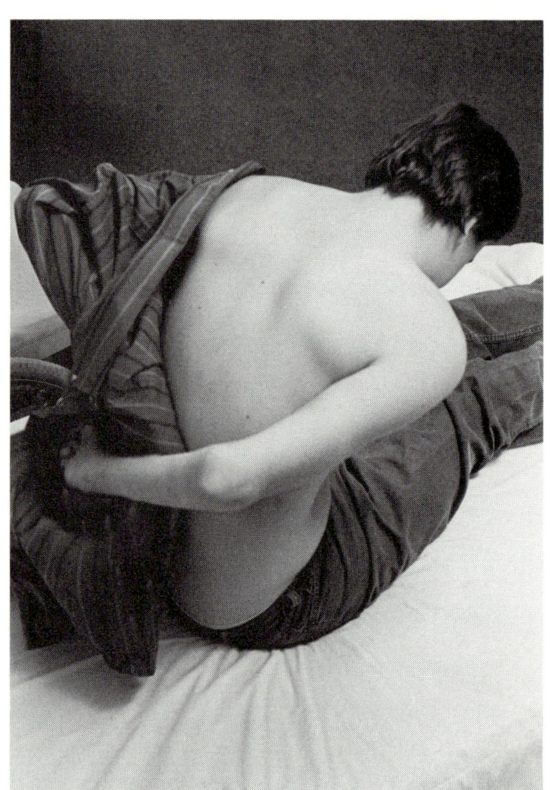

Figure 10–10

Around-the-Back Method

The around-the-back technique can be used for button or zip-front garments. The garment is donned by placing one UE in a sleeve, then pushing the garment around the back. The other UE is then placed into the sleeve. Looser fitting garments may be used to accommodate for limitations in ROM.

This method may be used by the care giver for patients with C1 to C4 SCI. Patients with C5 SCI can use the method with assistance while sitting in a W/C or long sitting in an electric bed for support. Patients with C6 to C7 or lower injury can use the method long sitting unsupported in bed or short sitting on the side of the bed or in the W/C (Figures 10–9 to 10–12). Support binders can be donned by patients with C6 or lower injury by adapting the binder with thumb loops (Figure 10–13).

Bras with front Velcro closures adapted with thumb loops to allow for adequate pull are used by SCI patients with C5 to C7 lesions (Figure 10–14). When using a bra with front closures, one arm is placed through the strap, the bra is pulled around the back, and the other arm is placed through the other strap. The right thumb is placed through the thumb loop on the right side and the left thumb through the thumb loop on the left side. The ends are pulled to overlap, thus fastening the Velcro. Bras with back closures can be fastened first, then donned like an overhead garment, although this technique is difficult for those with limited hand function or obesity. Back-closing bras can also be adapted to convert them to front closure.

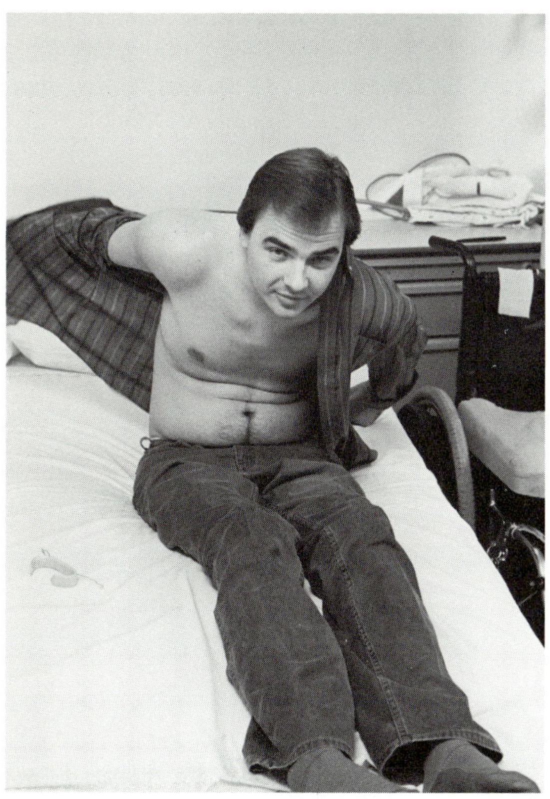

Figure 10–11

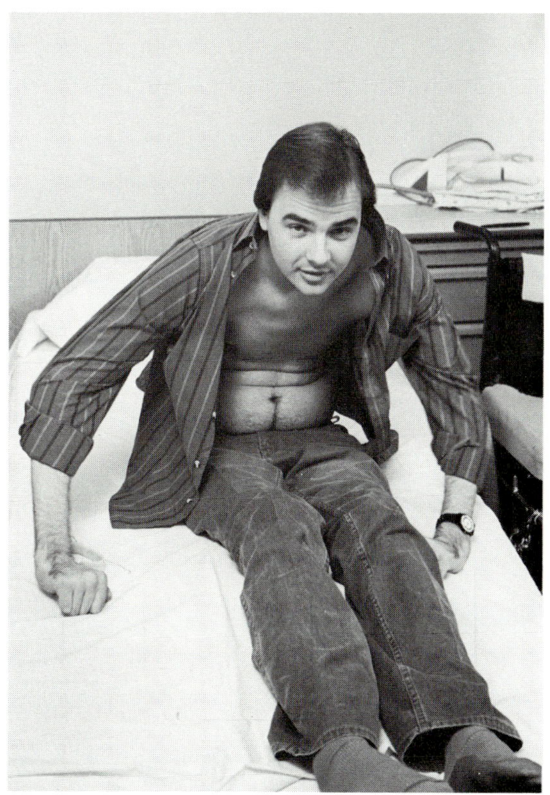

Figure 10–12

Figure 10–13 Abdominal binder adapted with loops.

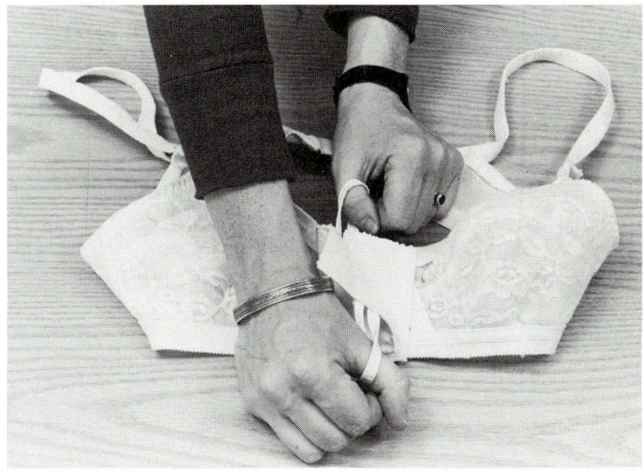

Figure 10–14 Bra adapted with front Velcro closure and loops.

UNDRESSING UPPER EXTREMITIES

In UE undressing, the over-the-head and behind-the-back techniques are reversed. Additional adaptations may be required. SCI patients with C1 to C4 injury are dependent in undressing the UEs and trunk. C5 patients require assistance, with the over-the-head and around-the-back methods being reversed. To doff a garment, the care giver stands in front of the patient and leans him forward. While supporting the patient, the care giver pulls the back of the garment up to the neck (Figure 10–15) and the patient is then repositioned against the back of the W/C. The garment is pulled over the head (Figure 10–16) and the sleeves are removed one at a time (Figure 10–17). An option with this technique is to remove the arms first, then take the shirt off over the head. In reversing the behind-the-back method, one sleeve is removed, the patient is leaned forward to pull the garment from behind the back, and then the second sleeve is removed. C5 patients participate by placing their arms independently in the doffing process.

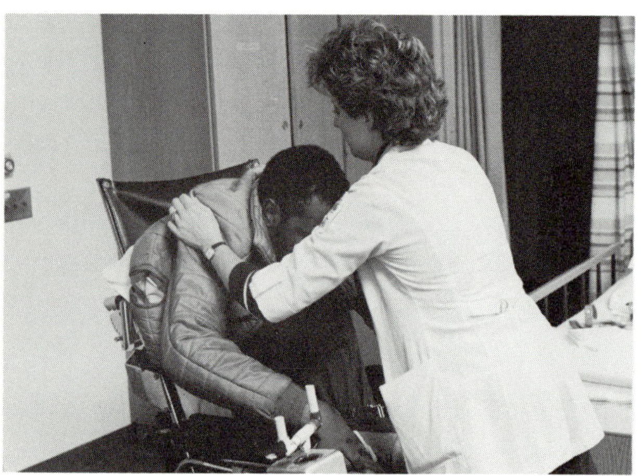

Figures 10–15 to 10–17 Reversing the over-the-head method in removing UE garments.

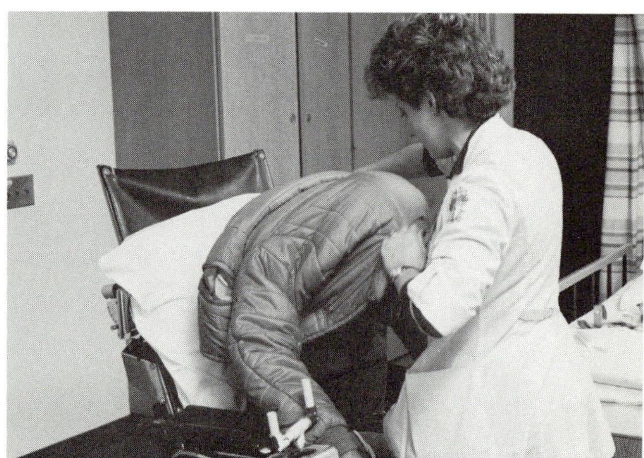

Figure 10–16

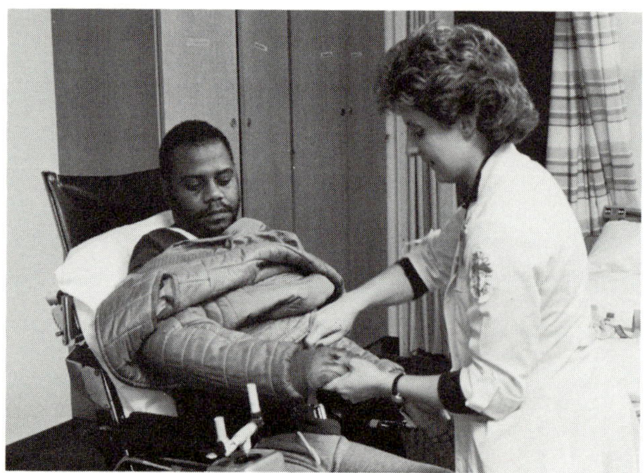

Figure 10–17

Doffing a pullover garment can be accomplished independently by patients with injuries at C6 or below. One arm is placed underneath the garment up to the sleeve portion of the opposite arm and the garment is stretched around the elbow so that the arm can be pulled out of the sleeve (Figure 10–18). The garment is then pulled over the head and the other arm is removed from the sleeve (Figures 10–19 and 10–20). This is a variant of the over-the-head method. A loop can be placed inside the back of the neck of the garment. The patient places his thumb or hand through the loop and pulls the garment over the head. The arms are then removed from the sleeves one at a time. Front-opening garments can be doffed by pulling one side off the shoulder and then pulling that arm from the sleeve (Figures 10–21 and 10–22). Moving the garment around the back, the other arm is removed from the sleeve (Figures 10–23 and 10–24). This is the reversal of the behind-the-back method.

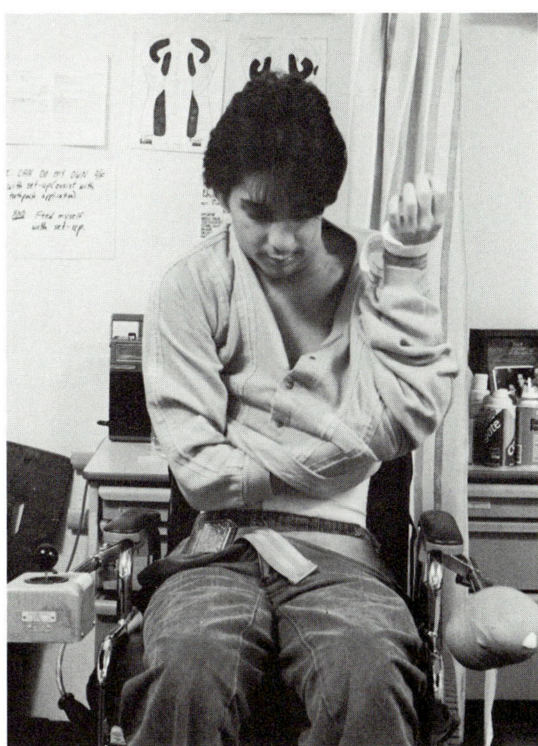

Figure 10–18 C6 patient removing arm from sleeve.

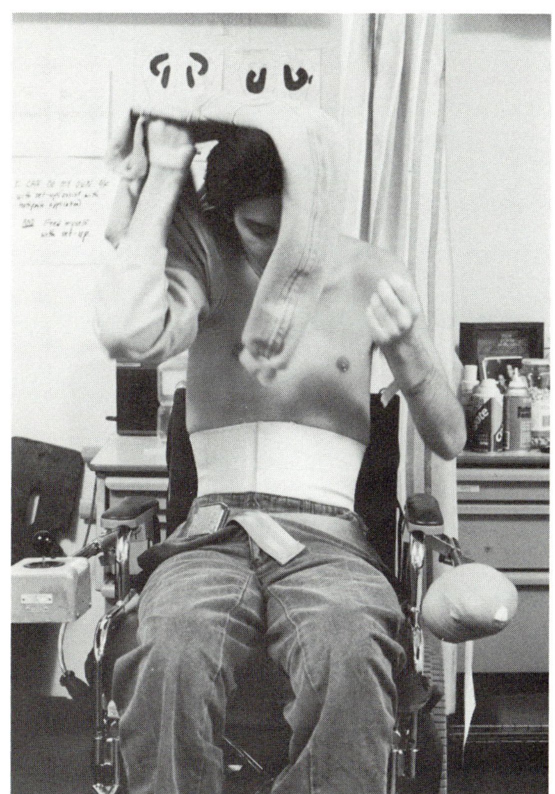

Figure 10–19 Removing the garment over the head.

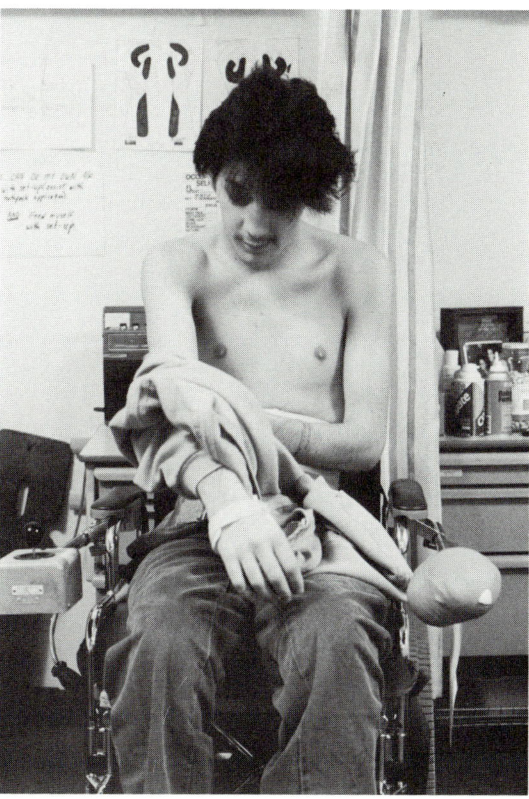

Figure 10–20 Removing arm from second sleeve.

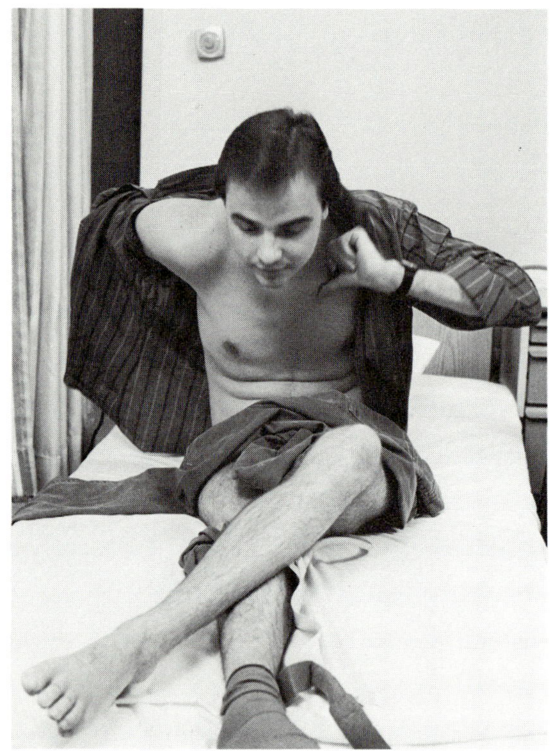

Figures 10–21 to 10–24 C7 patient removing button-down garment by first removing shirt from shoulder, then pulling his arm from the sleeve, pulling the shirt around back, and removing the second sleeve.

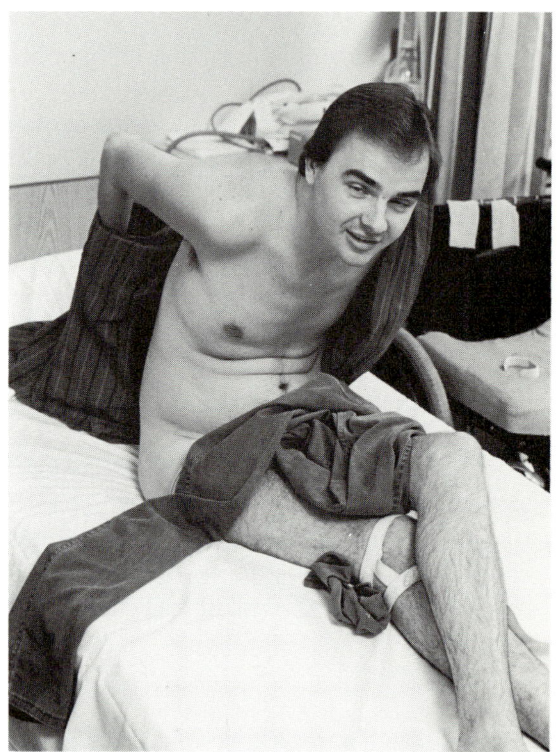

Figure 10–22

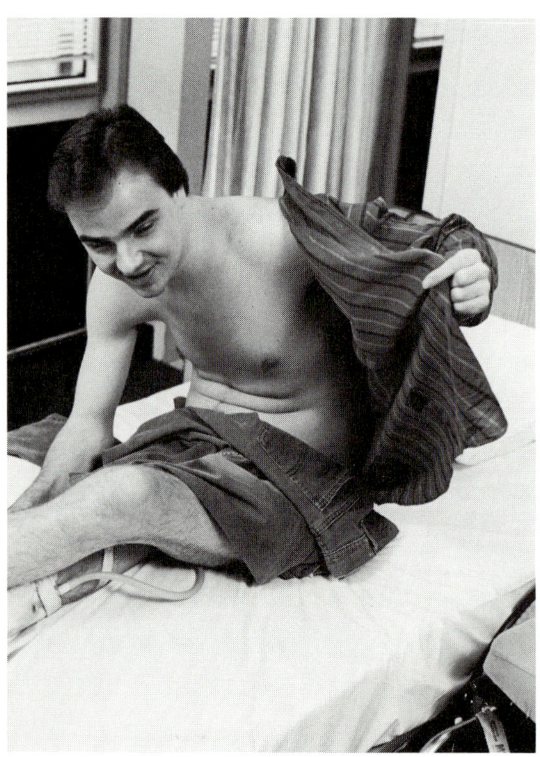

Figure 10–23

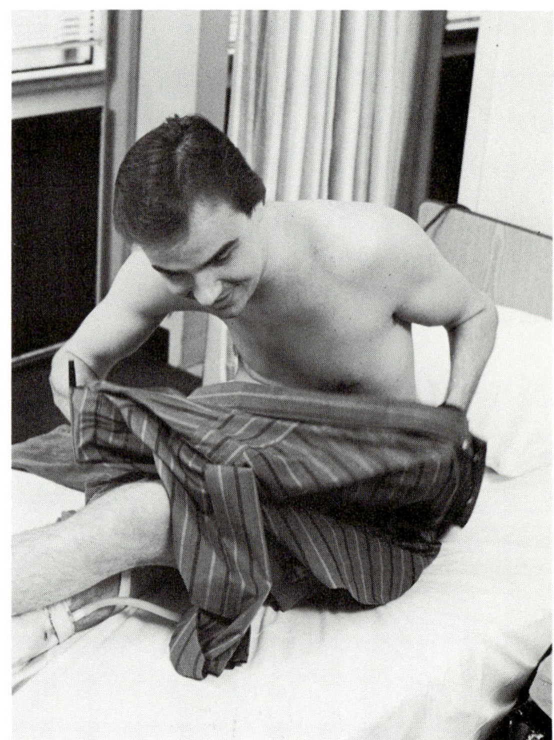

Figure 10–24

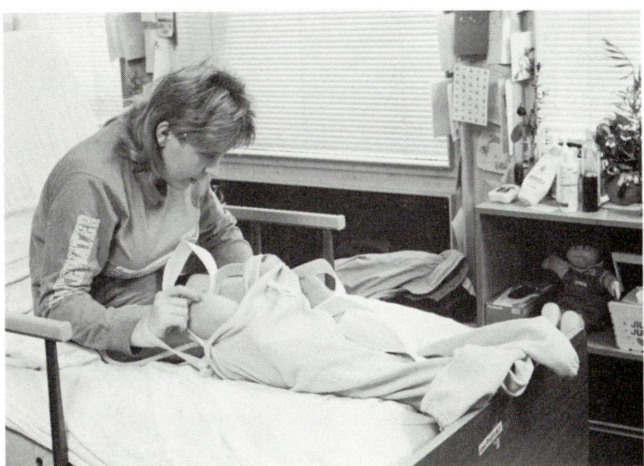

Figure 10–25 C6 patient using loops to pull pants on.

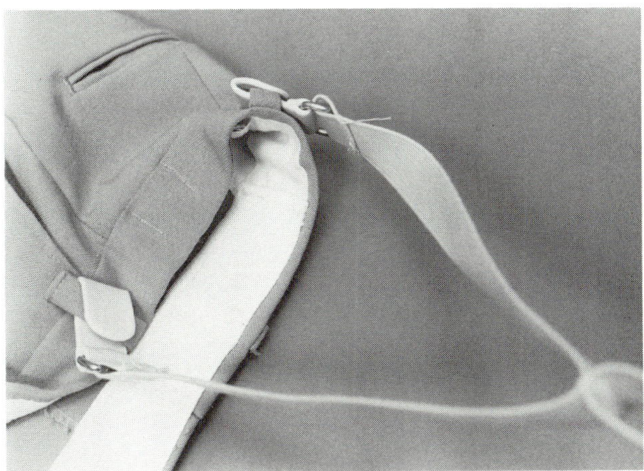

Figure 10–26 Dressing loops attached to belt loops with plastic hooks.

DRESSING LOWER EXTREMITIES

Patients with C1 to C5 injury will be dependent in LE dressing. Adaptations to ease performance include

- pants and slacks with elastic waistbands
- Velcro closures
- fasteners on the sides
- loose-fitting clothes
- slip-on shoes
- shoes with Velcro closures

The common techniques used in each step of LE dressing are described below.

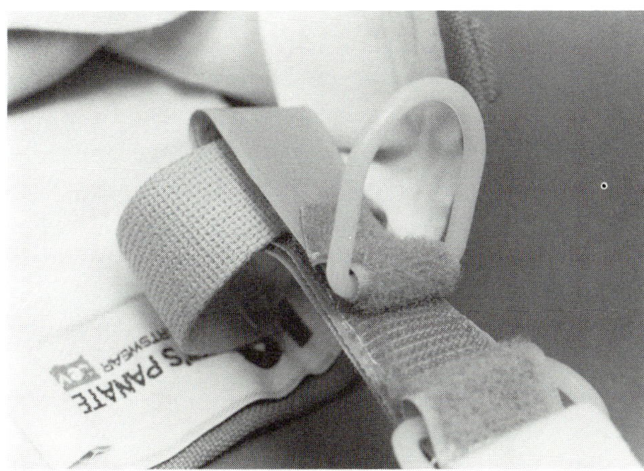

Figure 10–27 Dressing loops attached with Velcro to loops sewn inside pants waist.

Getting Pants Over Feet

The patient assumes the long-sitting position. A loop ladder or an electric bed may be used to assist in achieving long sitting, if necessary. If the patient requires back support to maintain long sitting, the electric bed or a wall may be used.

If the patient is unable to maneuver the LEs, dressing loops can be attached to the pants and thrown distal to the feet so that the pants can be pulled over the feet (Figure 10–25). Dressing loops can be attached to belt loops with Velcro or plastic hooks (Figure 10–26); on garments without belt loops they can be attached to loops sewn inside the pants waist (Figure 10–27). Dressing loops may be sewn directly on the pants, but are then difficult to hide. A dressing stick can also be used to place the pants distal to the feet (Figure 10–28).

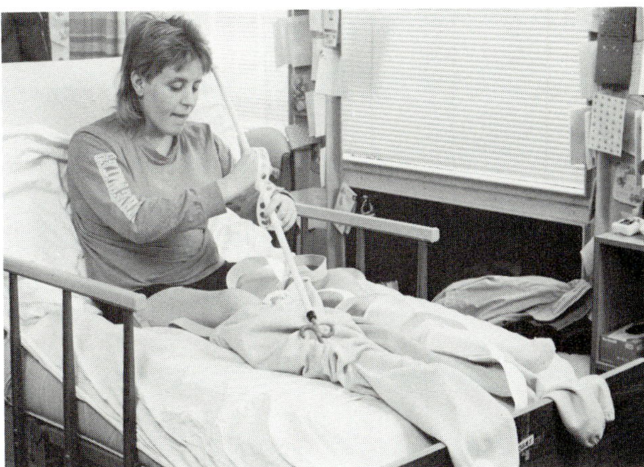

Figure 10–28 Using a dressing stick to place pants on foot.

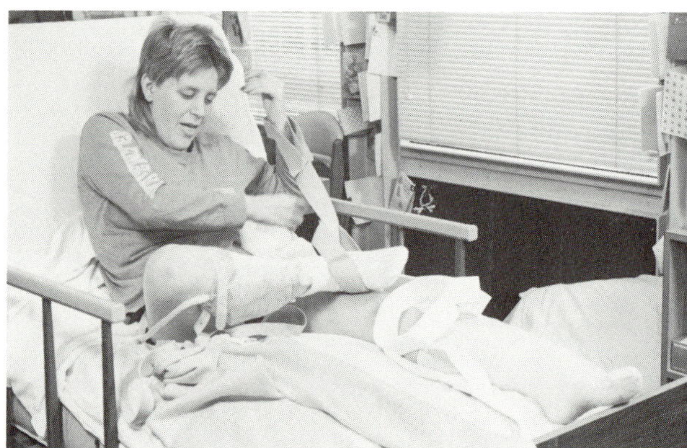

Figure 10–29 Using a loop to cross the right foot over the left knee.

Maneuverability of the LEs may be achieved with a loop placed over the foot to lift and cross the foot over the opposite knee (Figure 10–29). The loop is removed and the pants are pulled over the foot until the foot is through the pants (Figure 10–30). The LE is uncrossed by replacing the loop over the foot and pulling the foot off the knee. The process is repeated with the other LE.

The LEs can also be maneuvered without loops by using the UEs. The LE is crossed over the opposite leg, the pants are placed over the foot, and the leg is uncrossed. The process is repeated with the other LE.

Pants may also be started by placing them face up at the calf or knee level. The UE is used to flex the knee and insert the foot into the pants leg. Pushing above the knee is used to extend the leg, pushing it into the pants (Figures 10–31 and 10–32). An alternative is to lift the leg into flexion, place the pants leg near the hip, insert the foot, and push on the knee to extend the leg.

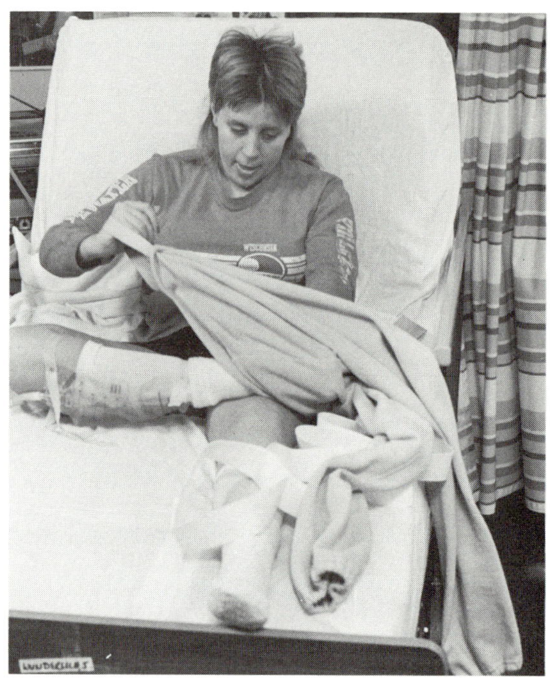

Figure 10–30 Pulling pants leg onto crossed leg.

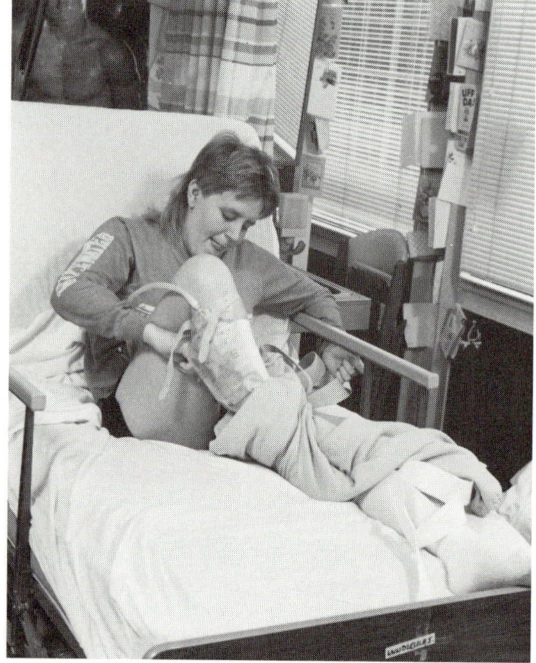

Figure 10–31 Flexing the leg to insert into pants leg.

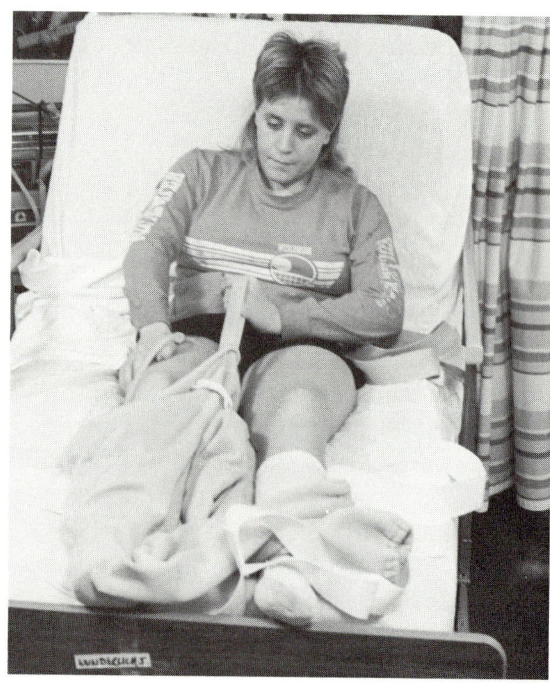

Figure 10–32 Pushing the leg into extension and into pants leg.

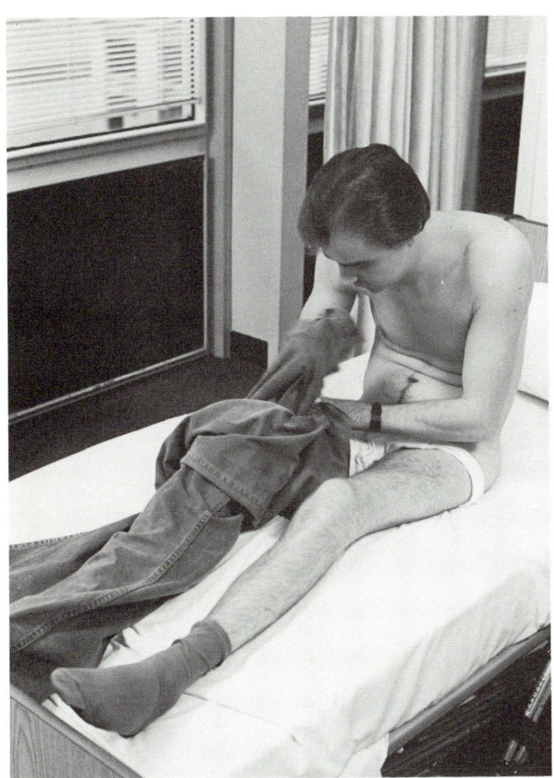

Figures 10–33 and 10–34 Pulling pants leg over knee is accomplished by wrapping hand in pants pocket or by using belt loop.

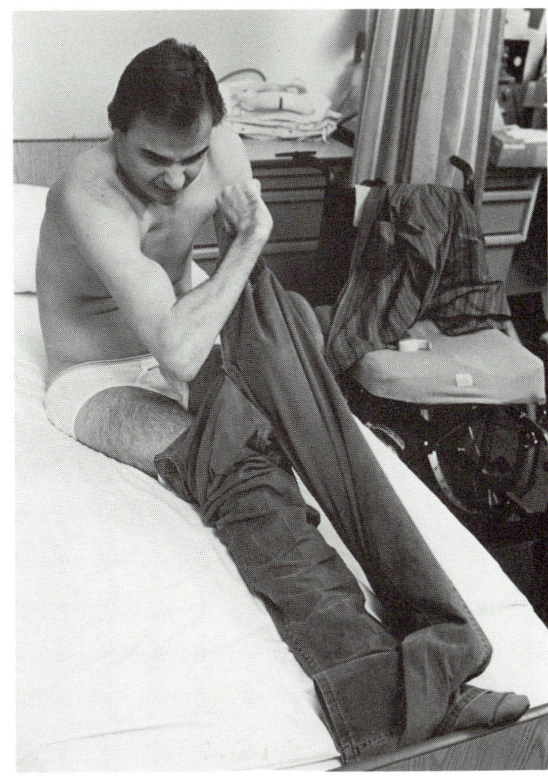

Figure 10–34

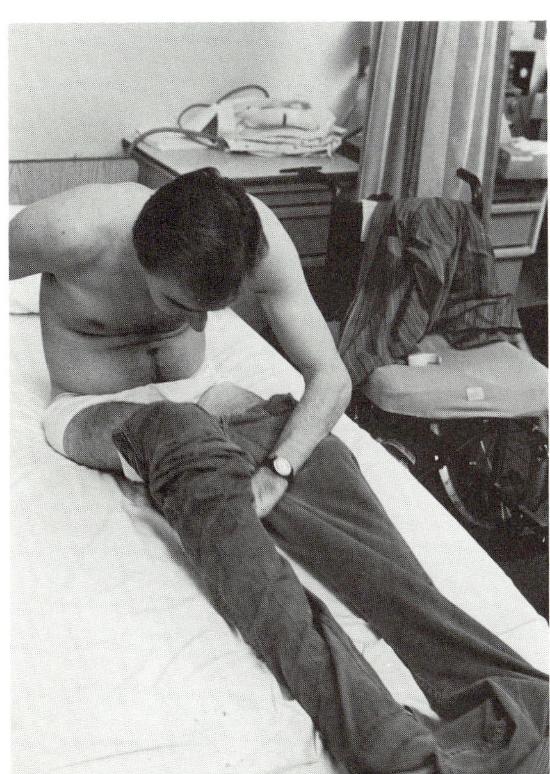

Figure 10–35 Pulling pants up onto both legs.

Pulling Pants Over Legs

Pants are pulled over the knees to the hips by placing the hand inside the pants, putting a hand in the pocket (Figure 10–33), or pulling on the belt loop with the thumb (Figure 10–34). The forearm is placed at the crotch of the pants to pull them up (Figure 10–35). Pant loops or a dressing stick can also be used to pull the pants up to this point (Figure 10–36).

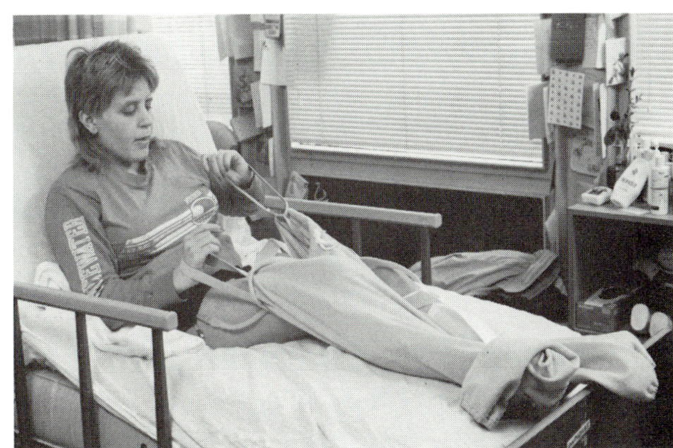

Figure 10–36 Using dressing loops to continue to pull pants up.

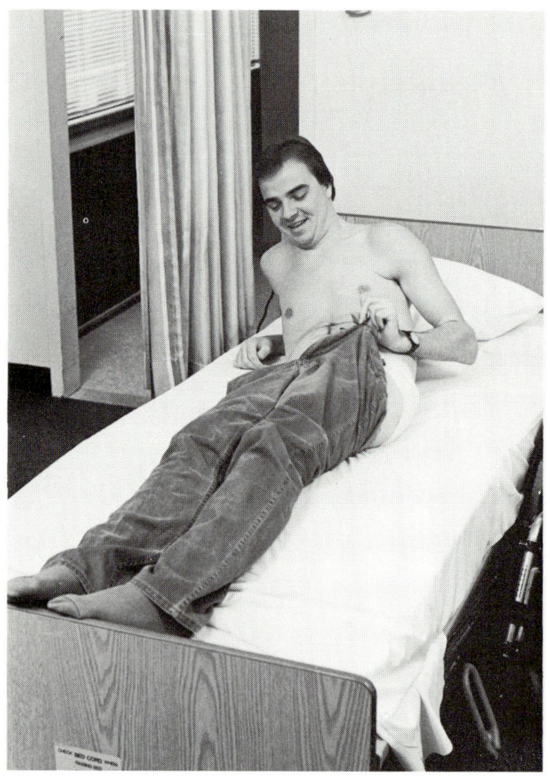

Figures 10–37 to 10–39 Rolling to pull pants over hips.

Pulling Pants Over Hips

Next, the patient assumes a supine position and begins a series of rolls to pull the pants over his hips. Bed railings can be used to assist in the rolling process. The pants are pulled up by placing a hand in the pants, a pocket, belt loops, or dressing loops and pulling them over the hips (Figures 10–37 to 10–39).

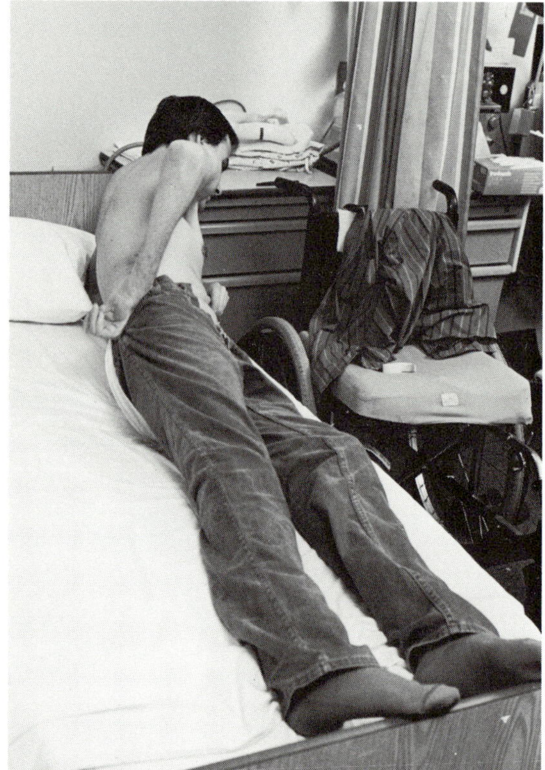

Figure 10–38

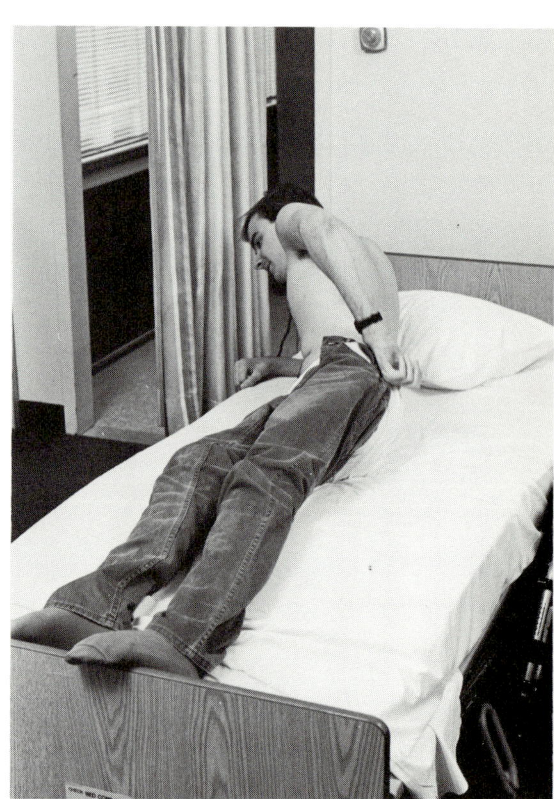

Figure 10–39

Sock Donning

Thumb loops may be sewn on socks or loops can be made with the sock itself by folding over and tacking down the top (Figures 10–40 and 10–41). A sock donner may also be used. It is placed distal to the foot and pulled over the foot. A zipper pull cuff (Figure 10–42) can also be used to pull the sock over the heel. The foot is crossed over the opposite knee. The sock is placed over the toes with a tenodesis grasp (Figure 10–43) and is pulled over the foot with the heel of the hand. Licking the heel of the hand provides friction.

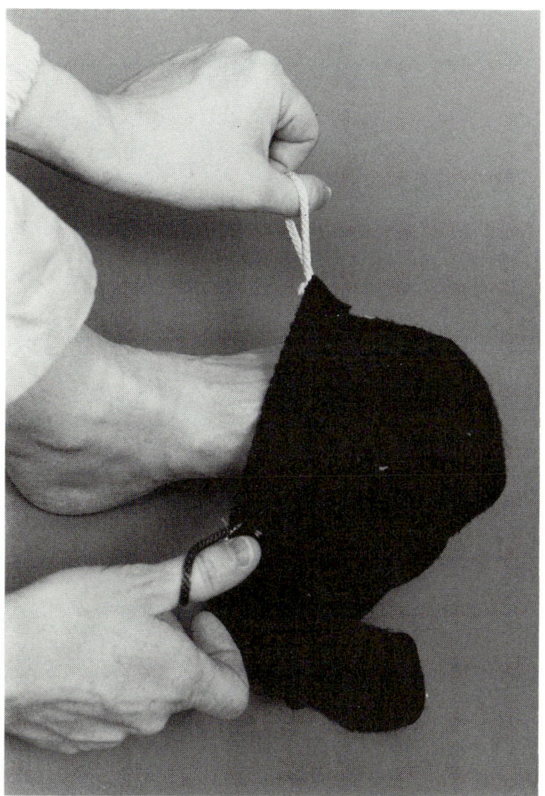

Figure 10–40 Loop on sock.

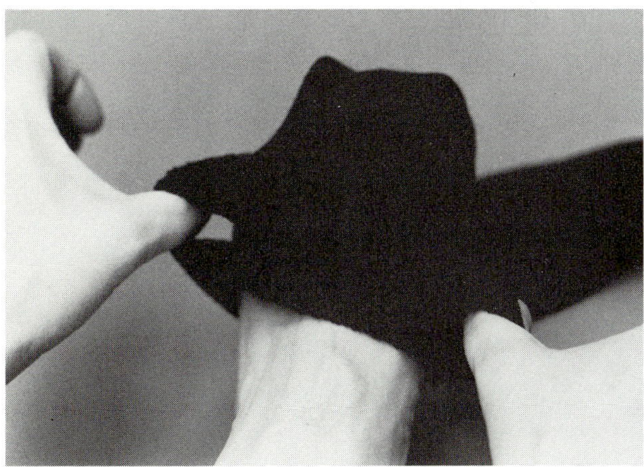

Figure 10–41 Loop made from sock.

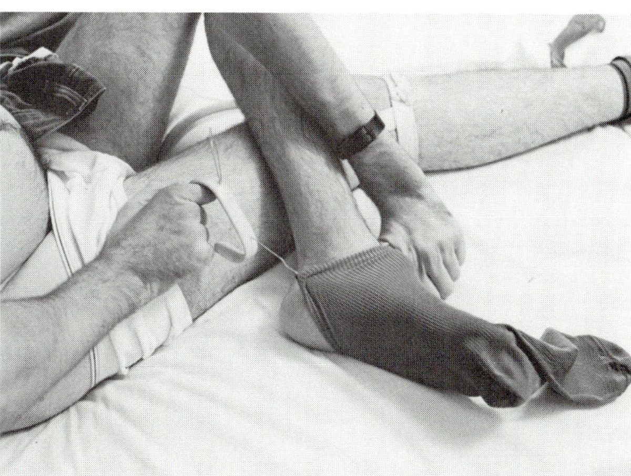

Figure 10–42 Using a zipper pull cuff to pull on socks.

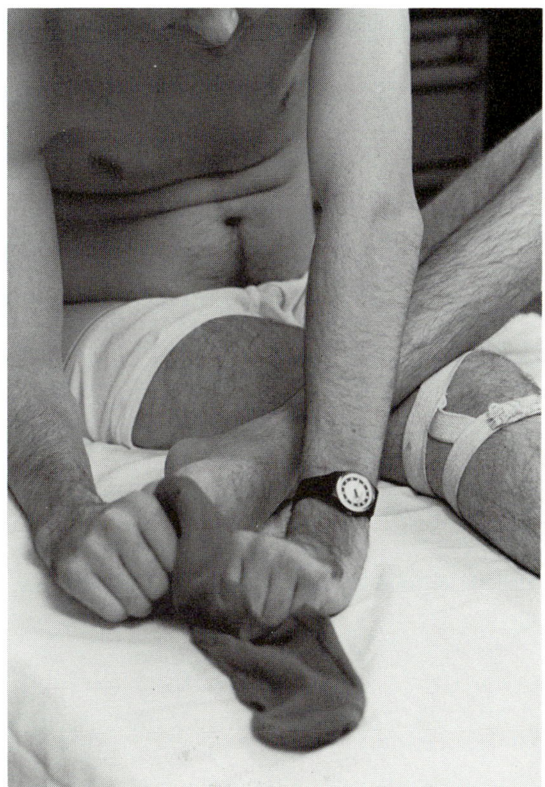

Figure 10–43 Bilateral tenodesis is used to start sock over toes.

Shoe Donning

Shoe donning can be performed either in bed or in the W/C. Slip-on shoes or shoes with Velcro closures are recommended. Thumb loops can be added to the Velcro closures. A thumb loop can be added to the top of the back of the shoe to aid in pulling it over the heel (Figure 10–44). The shoe is donned by crossing the LE over the opposite knee. Tenodesis is used to secure the shoe in the hand and slide it onto the foot (Figure 10–45).

Figure 10–44 Thumb loop attached to gym shoe.

The C6 SCI patient may range from assisted to independent in LE dressing. Initially, performance of LE dressing is time-consuming (30 minutes to well over 1 hour). It takes patience and problem-solving ability to learn this skill. Family members and friends should also be instructed in these techniques.

The C7 quadriplegic may begin learning these dressing techniques with equipment and adaptations; however, as the patient's UE strength and trunk control improve, the equipment and adaptations may be discontinued or limited. The patient with C8 or lower injury will use these techniques to manage the LEs in dressing without equipment and adaptations.

It may be helpful to set out garments the night before and lay them within reach for dressing.

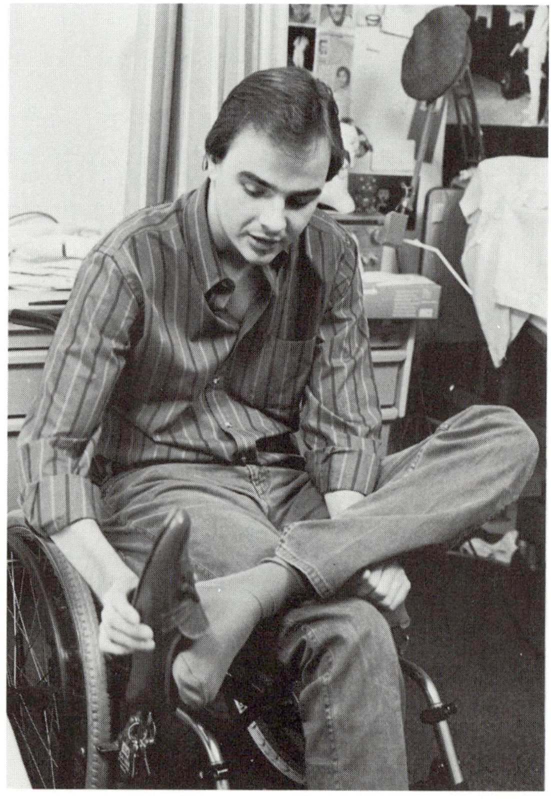

Figure 10–45 Tenodesis can be used to slide a shoe onto the foot while sitting with legs crossed.

UNDRESSING LOWER EXTREMITIES

Removing Pants from Hips

Pants removal can be started in the W/C or when short sitting in bed by doing weight shifts (Figures 10–46, 10–47, and 10–48). The patient leans to one side and uses the opposite arm to pull the pants over the opposite hip. The process is repeated for the other side. The patient transfers into bed to complete the process. Pants removal may also be started supine or supine on elbows in bed, with the patient rolling from side to side to push them down over the hips.

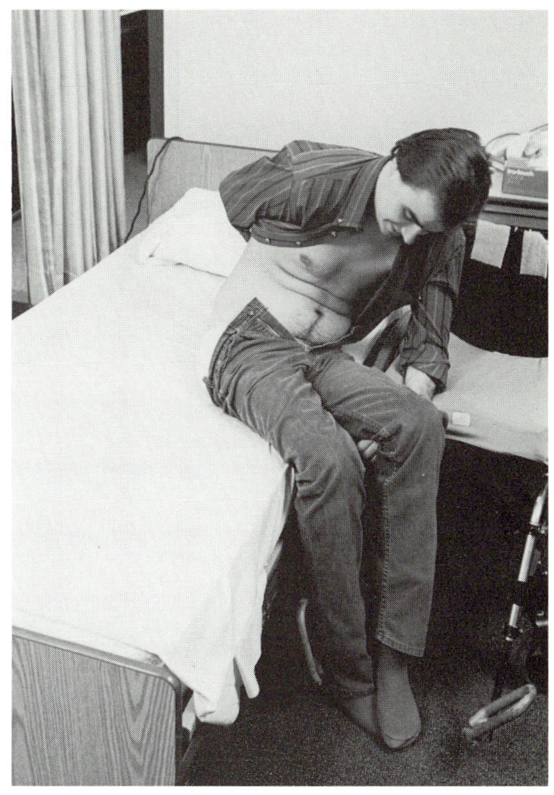

Figures 10–46 to 10–48 Weight shifting while short sitting is used to slide pants down over hips.

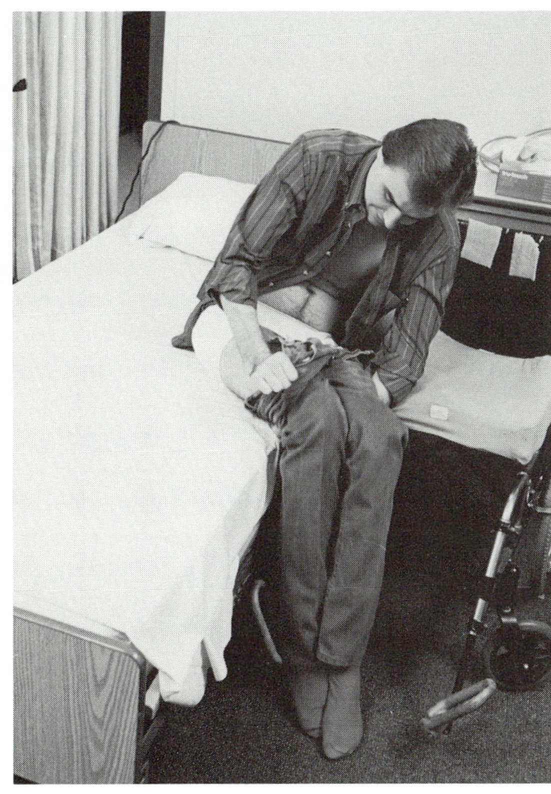

Figure 10–47

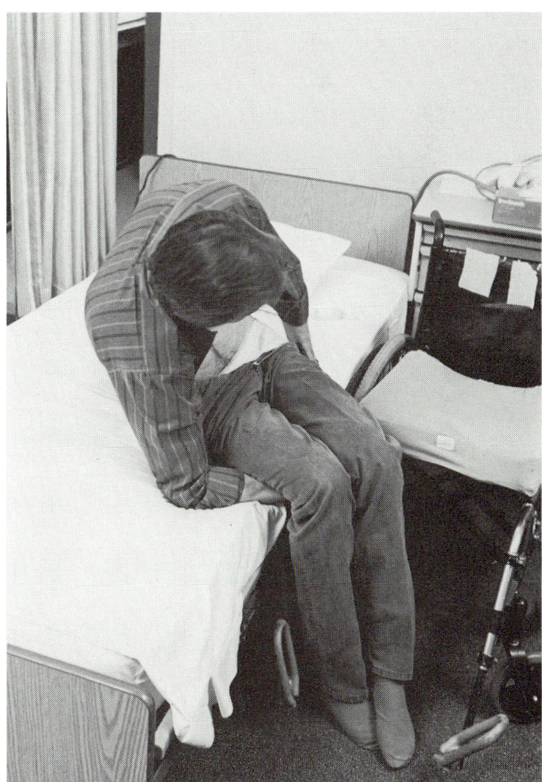

Figure 10–48

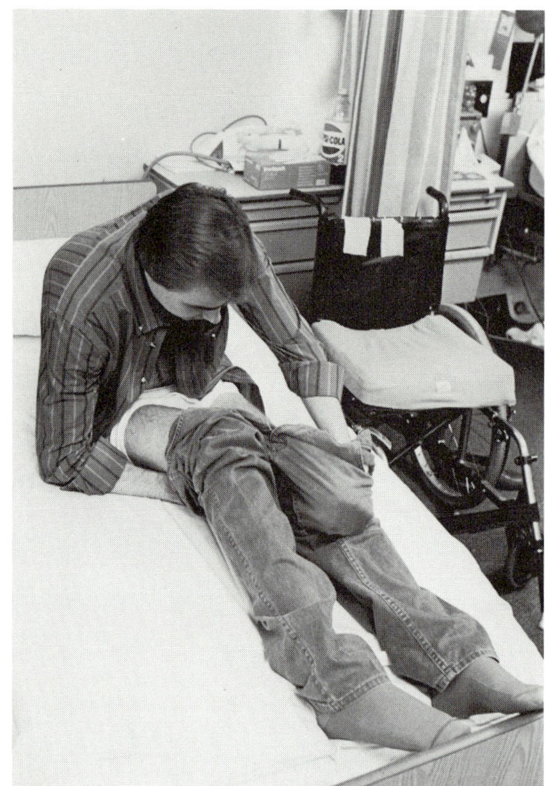

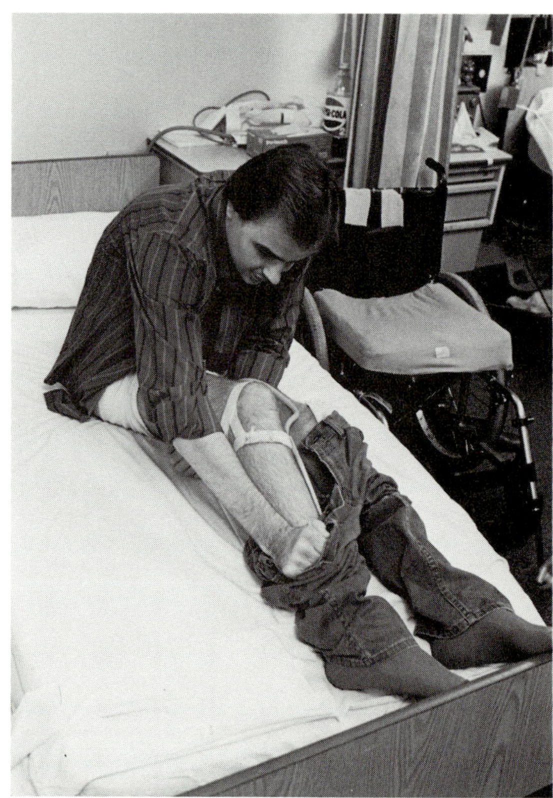

Figures 10–49 and 10–50 Pushing pants down past the knees using a hand in the crotch of the pants in long sitting, then pushing them down from the side.

Figure 10–50

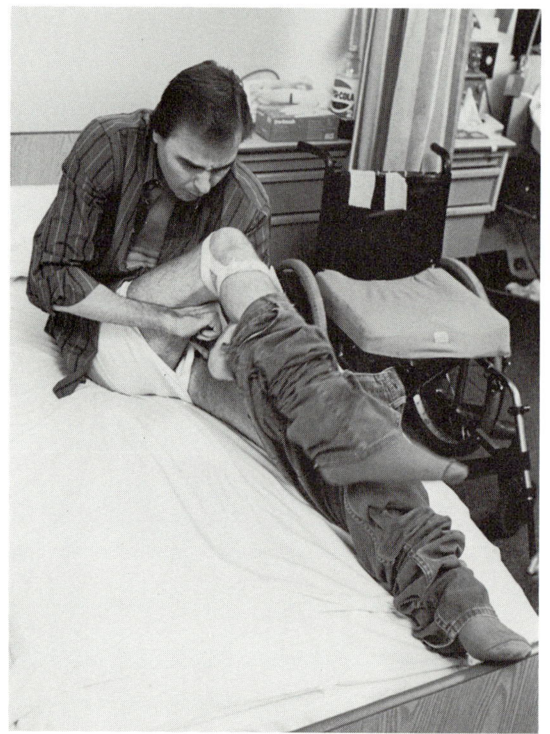

Figure 10–51 One UE is used to flex the knee, while the other pushes the pants leg off the foot.

Removing Legs From Pants

In long sitting in bed the hand is placed inside the pants near the crotch and they are pushed toward the feet (Figure 10–49). The sides of the pants can be moved toward the feet by placing the web space or heel of the hand on the waistband and pushing (Figure 10–50). A dressing stick can also be used to push the pants down. The UEs can be used to flex the knee and pull the foot out of the pants (Figure 10–51).

Doffing Shoes

Doffing shoes may be performed in the W/C or in bed. The LE is lifted and crossed over the opposite leg. The shoe is pushed off the foot by using the heel of the hand, a finger, or a shoe horn (Figure 10–52).

Doffing Socks

The LE is crossed over the opposite leg. The thumb or index finger is placed in the top of the sock and pushes it off (Figure 10–53). A zipper pull is some-

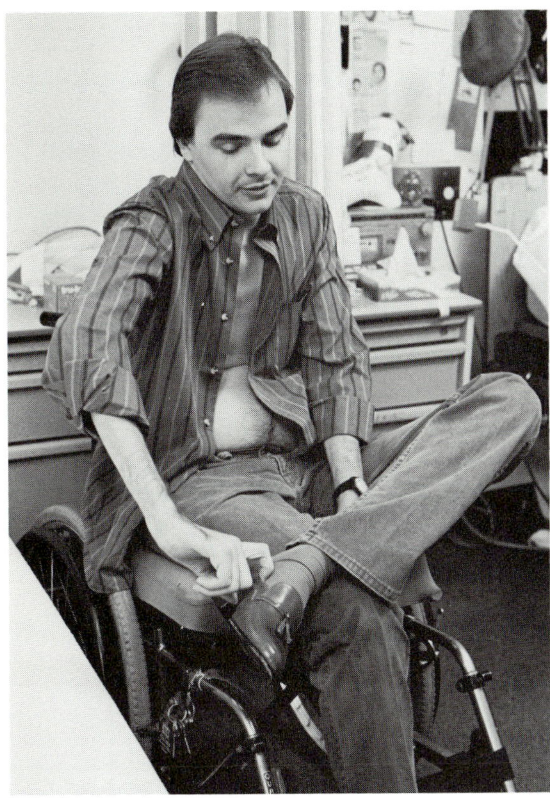

Figure 10–52 Pushing the shoe off the foot using a finger.

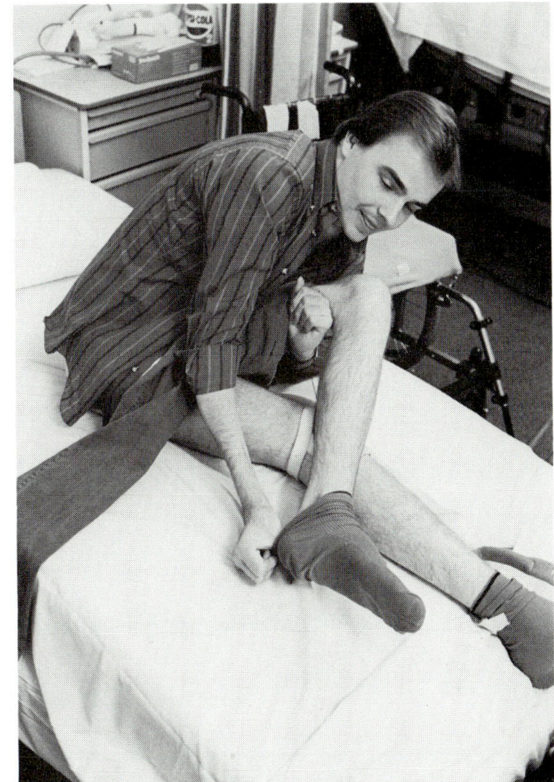

Figure 10–53 Using the thumb to pull off the sock.

times used to pull the sock off. If socks have been adapted with loops, the loops are used to pull the sock off.

Patients with C1 to C5 quadriplegia will be dependent in LE undressing. The skills of the C6 quadriplegic vary from assisted to independent depending on UE control, wrist and hand function, and trunk control. C7 quadriplegics vary from independent with equipment to independent. Patients with C8 or lower injury are usually independent.

MANAGING FASTENERS

Patients with C1 to C5 injury are dependent with fasteners. C6 to C7 and some C8 patients use equipment to manage fasteners.

Zippers

A zipper pull ring may be attached to zippers, allowing opening and closing with the thumb or finger. After donning the garment, the side of the zipper without the pull ring may be stabilized by using the palm of the hand and stabilizing the garment against the abdomen. The other side of the zipper is then slid onto the stabilized side using the pull ring. A zipper pull cuff can also be used (Figure 10–54). A zipper may be started before donning and the garment donned as a pullover.

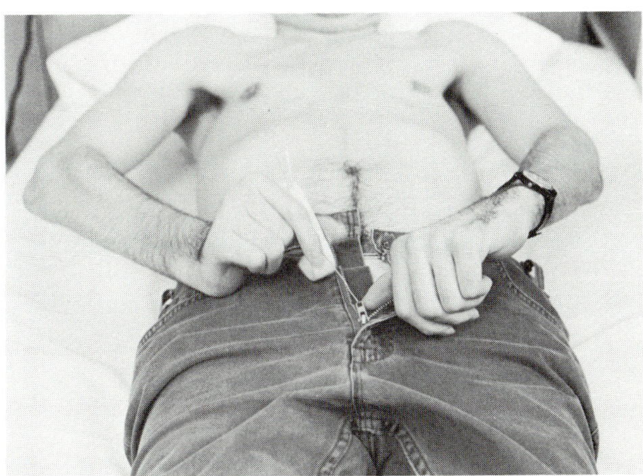

Figure 10–54 Zipping pants with a zipper pull cuff and tenodesis.

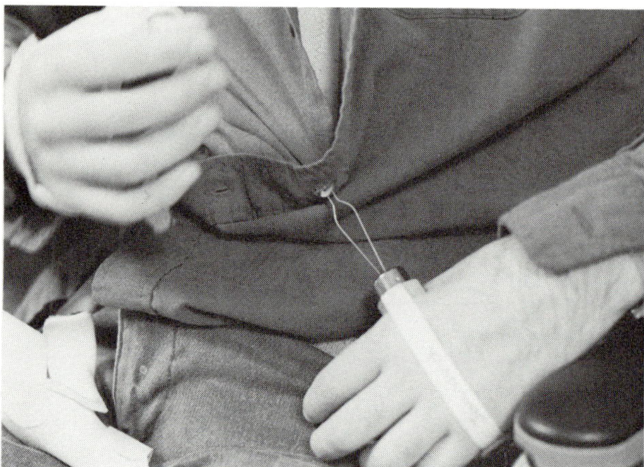

Figure 10–55 A button hook adapted with elastic is used to pull a button through the buttonhole.

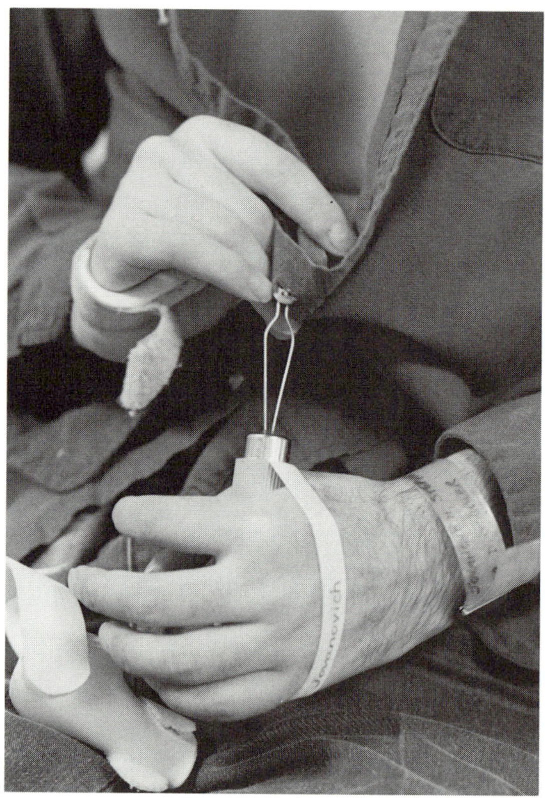

Figure 10–56 The opposite hand can be used to assist in pulling the buttonhole over the button.

Buttons

The patient should practice using the various types of button hooks available in order to choose the best style. The hook is placed on the hand of the side the buttonholes are on and is placed through the buttonhole, hooked over the button, and pulled to bring the button through the hole (Figure 10–55). The opposite hand may be used to pull the material over the button (Figure 10–56).

A zipper pull can be used for unbuttoning. The zipper pull hooks on the buttonhole and pulls the material over the button. To unbutton with a button hook, the hook is placed on the hand of the side the buttons are on and woven through the buttonhole and over the button. The other hand assists to remove the buttonhole from the button (Figure 10–57).

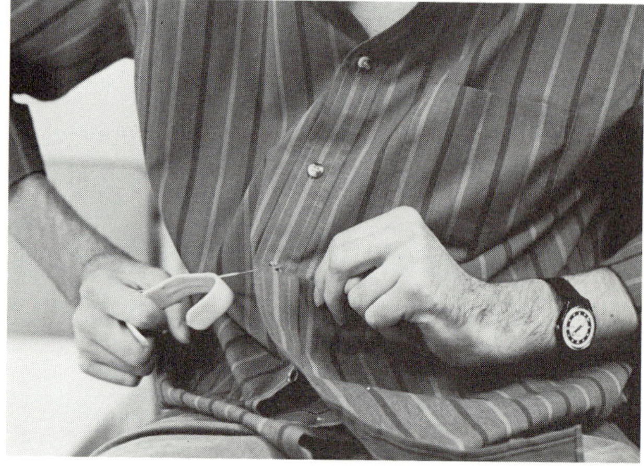

Figure 10–57 Unbuttoning by using a button hook and the opposite hand to push the buttonhole over the button.

Accessories

Watches or bracelets can be slid on with ease by patients with C6 or lower SCI. Watches with elastic wrist bands are recommended. Clip-on earrings may be donned with tenodesis. Hook-type pierced earrings may also be donned with tenodesis; however, this requires fine control and practice.

SUMMARY

The patient's motivation to perform the task of dressing is of the utmost importance. The goal of dressing should be mutually agreed on by patient, therapist, and family members. It should be approached as an acquirable skill for the C6 quadriplegic if it is within the scope of the patient's goals and priorities. It takes many hours of training, problem solving, and adapting to achieve this goal.

The techniques described in this unit are those commonly used at RIC. Developing new techniques and adapting existing techniques for a particular patient—highly motivated to perform his own dressing—is an ongoing challenge to the occupational therapist. The techniques described can be used as the basis for further individualized problem solving.

Whenever physical indicators make independence in dressing an option, patient and family should be offered training. Training in dressing is in itself an excellent strengthening and mobility activity. Patients choosing to remain assisted in dressing on first admission should be told that such training can remain a desirable future option.

Factors that contribute to decisions about dressing goals in the SCI patient are prioritization of time and availability of assistance. In order to reach an educated decision about making independence in dressing a goal, it is necessary to spend several evaluation sessions on the techniques. These sessions give the patient an understanding of the process and the therapist an idea of the patient's skills and potential.

SUMMARY CHART: Dressing

Goal	*Indicator*	*Equipment*
UE Dressing and Undressing		
1. Assisted	1. C5 injury 2. Assisted limited to unassisted limited arm placement 3. No hand function 4. Limited to no trunk stability	1. Loose-fitting garments 2. Zip-off sleeves
2. Independent with equipment	1. C6-C7 injury 2. Unassisted limited to normal arm placement 3. Tenodesis hand function 4. Limited trunk stability	1. Binder adapted with thumb loops 2. Bra with front Velcro closure and thumb loops 3. Loop on back collar of shirt
3. Independent	1. C8 or lower injury 2. Normal arm placement 3. Limited natural to normal hand function 4. Trunk stability	None
LE Dressing and Undressing		
1. Independent with equipment	1. C6-C7 injury 2. Unassisted limited arm placement 3. Tenodesis hand function 4. Limited trunk stability	1. Dressing stick or dressing loops 2. Loops for bed mobility 3. Leg lifter loops 4. Velcro shoe closures 5. Thumb loop on shoe 6. Loops on socks 7. Zipper pull to pull socks up 8. Sock donner
2. Independent	1. C7-C8 or lower injury 2. Normal arm placement 3. Tenodesis to normal hand function 4. Trunk stability	None
Fasteners		
1. Independent with equipment in zipping, buttoning, unzipping, unbuttoning, and managing accessories	1. C6-C7 injury 2. Unassisted limited to normal arm placement 3. Tenodesis hand function	1. Button hook 2. Velcro closures 3. Zipper pull 4. Zipper pull ring or loop 5. Clip earrings 6. Hoop-type earrings

Unit 11

Bladder and Bowel Management

Robin Jones, COTA/L

Even though urological and bowel management are primarily guided by the medical team, the occupational therapist may assist the SCI patient in performing the management techniques with adaptive equipment and technique. A patient's ability to perform all or part of his established program can influence discharge plans and attendant care needs.

The steps and equipment involved in bladder care and bowel management are not always familiar to occupational therapists. Therefore, this unit is more detailed than the units describing skills training in areas more conventional to OT. Bladder care and bowel management procedures differ from facility to facility. Occupational therapists should consult with nurses to adapt the procedures presented in this unit to those of their facilities.

It is essential that the nurse and the occupational therapist work closely to coordinate the patient's program. Nursing can communicate the patient's readiness for training in self-management once bladder and bowel programs are established as well as facilitate carry-over of learned skills on the nursing unit. The occupational therapist's primary responsibility is to determine whether the necessary motor skills are present and to provide the patient with adaptive equipment and train him in its use.

BLADDER FUNCTION AFTER SPINAL CORD INJURY

The detrusor or bladder muscle is innervated at levels S2 to S4. With complete SCI above that level, sensory feedback is absent, voluntary control over contraction of the bladder is lost, and the synergic relaxation of the external sphincter when the bladder contracts does not always occur automatically. When the injury is incomplete, partial or total control may be preserved.

Spinal shock in the acute phase after injury results in flaccidity of the bladder and loss of voluntary control. Later after complete injury, patients may be able to spontaneously void through reflexes or detrusor muscle–sphincter synergy, but voluntary control continues to be absent. Spasticity of the external sphincter muscle usually results in insufficient emptying of the bladder.

The goal of urological management is to maintain a low residual volume of urine in the bladder to decrease the risk of infection and reflux of urine into the kidneys. High urine volumes can cause autonomic hyperreflexia, the symptoms of which are described in the introductory unit. When the bladder is not able to empty effectively, pressure within increases and it overdistends. Overdistention of the bladder may contribute to infection or structural kidney damage.

BLADDER EVACUATION TECHNIQUES

Commonly used techniques for draining the bladder include the following:

- The internal (indwelling) catheter, a tube inserted into the bladder via the urethra which drains the bladder continuously. Its placement is maintained in the bladder with a balloon that is inflated after the catheter is inserted. It is commonly used by females and males who are unable to void spontaneously. A Foley catheter is an example.
- The external catheter, a device primarily used by males. A condom type-device is placed on the penis and attached to drainage tubing and a leg bag to collect urine. It is used by those who void spontaneously or with limited voluntary control. External catheter devices for women tend to be not acceptable because of difficulties with skin breakdown, application, and keeping the device in place.
- The straight urethral catheter, a tube inserted into the bladder on a periodic basis to empty it. It is similar to the internal catheter but has no balloon.
- The suprapubic catheter. This involves a surgical procedure by which an opening in the bladder wall is made above the pubic bone and a catheter is inserted to continuously drain the bladder.

INTERMITTENT CATHETERIZATION

The process of discontinuing the use of an internal catheter is called decatheterization. Patients who are able to void spontaneously but continue to lack voluntary control use an external catheter for collecting urine and a urethral catheter to periodically check and drain residual urine from the bladder. Intermittent catheterization is used by patients who are unable to void spontaneously or effectively. This process involves use of a urethral catheter to empty the bladder, usually every 4 to 6 hours. Fluid intake and output are closely monitored to maintain bladder capacity.

There are three methods of using a urethral catheter to perform intermittent catheterization or for checking residuals:

1. The clean method: a nonsterile technique, most commonly used after discharge from the hospital, that involves the use of soap and water for cleansing and reuse of the same catheter. This is the simplest procedure and the most practical for quadriplegics. It is not recommended for those who catheterize fewer than 4 times a day because of risk of infection.
2. The traditional sterile method: a technique commonly used in the hospital and by those who catheterize fewer than 4 times a day. It requires elaborate sterile measures. It is a difficult method for quadriplegics to perform. The catheter can be sterilized for reuse.
3. The nontouch sterile method: a technique involving a nontouch catheter sheathed in plastic. This method is frequently used in the hospital setting at RIC. The high cost of the nontouch sterile catheter kit makes this method impractical for most patients on a frequent catheterization schedule.

OCCUPATIONAL THERAPY IN URINARY CARE MANAGEMENT

For the occupational therapist, urinary care management training includes the following components:

- evaluation of physical skills necessary for performance
- provision of general and adaptive equipment
- training in use of adaptive equipment and techniques for performance

Evaluation includes assessment of the following:

- Arm placement. Forward and side reach with a minimum of 90° active shoulder flexion are necessary.
- Hand function. Tenodesis or limited natural hand function is necessary for most components of urinary care (leg bag emptying excluded). Wrist extensor strength adequate to result in 5 to 7 pounds of pinch with an orthosis is helpful.
- Mobility. Catheterization in bed requires the assumption and maintenance of long sitting, with hips flexed to 90° with or without back support. An electric bed may be used for back support. The ability to move into and out of bed and stability in

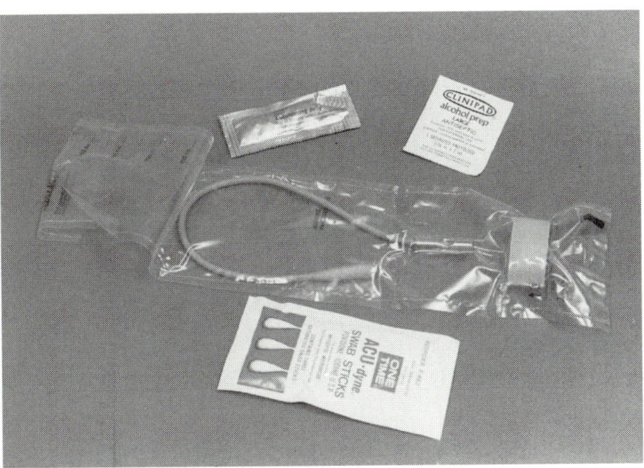

Figure 11–1 Nontouch sterile catheter kit.

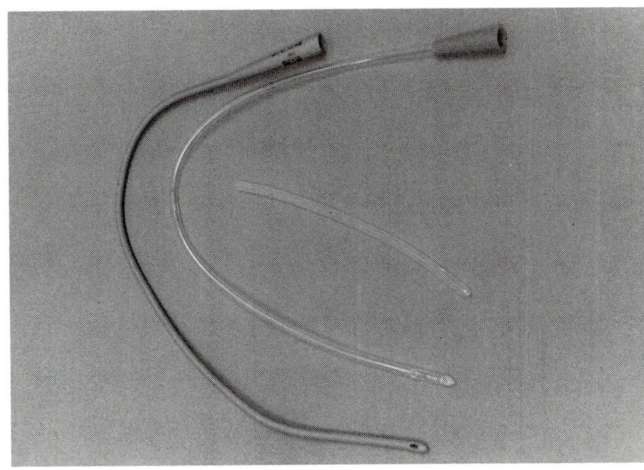

Figure 11–2 Rubber urethral catheter (left), semirigid plastic urethral catheter (middle), and rigid short plastic urethral catheter for females (right).

the W/C will affect whether catheterization is performed in bed or in the chair. Catheterization in bed and chair is the goal for most patients. Catheterization on a toilet may also be a goal for those with good mobility skills.

- Endurance. Forty-five minutes of endurance in long sitting with bilateral UE use is required for self-catheterization in bed.
- Clothing management. The ability to manage clothing in order to expose the urethra for catheterization is required.

Two forms used by OT in the evaluation process are shown in Appendix 11–A.

Equipment

Both general and adaptive equipment are required for independent urinary care management. General urinary care equipment is used regardless of who is to perform the catheterization, and includes the following:

- The nontouch sterile catheter kit (Diamed, Bard), which includes a urethral catheter sheathed in plastic, lubricant packets, Betadine swabs, alcohol pad, and rubber glove (female kit only). The plastic sheath is used for urine collection. Both male and female kits are available (Figure 11–1).
- Urethral catheters (Mentor), which can be purchased separately or in kits and which come in a variety of sizes, lengths, and flexibilities. Rigid catheters may be easier to manipulate with limited hand function. Shorter catheters are often preferred for catheterizing on the toilet (Figure 11–2).
- External catheters of various sizes and types. Some have a self-adhesive interior for a more secure fit (Freedom and Gizmo). Flexibility of the external catheter varies; however, the more rigid catheters are usually easier for quadriplegics to apply (Figure 11–3).

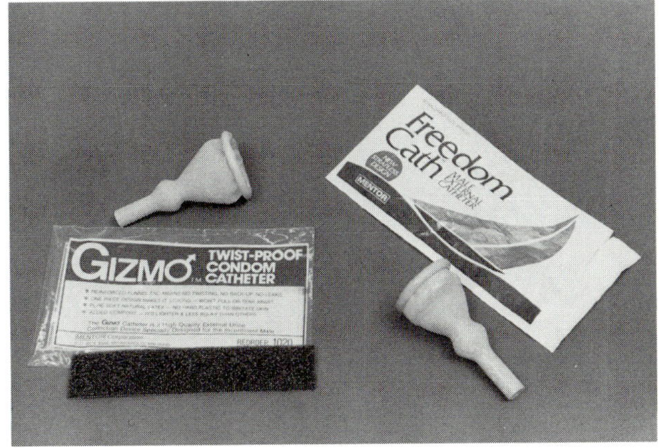

Figure 11–3 Two types of external catheters.

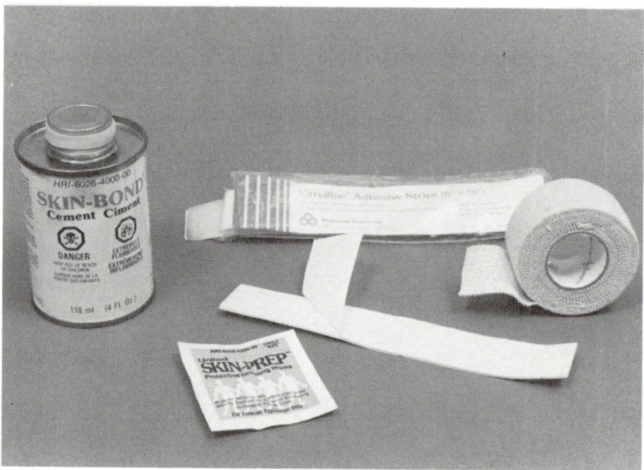

Figure 11–4 Skin-Bond is applied directly onto the penis with the brush applicator. Skin-Prep swabs help to prevent skin irritation caused by adhesives.

- Adhesives, including skin bonds, tapes, and sprays, used to secure the catheter in place (Crixiline tape, Elastikon tape, Skin-Bond, and Skin-Prep) (Figure 11–4).

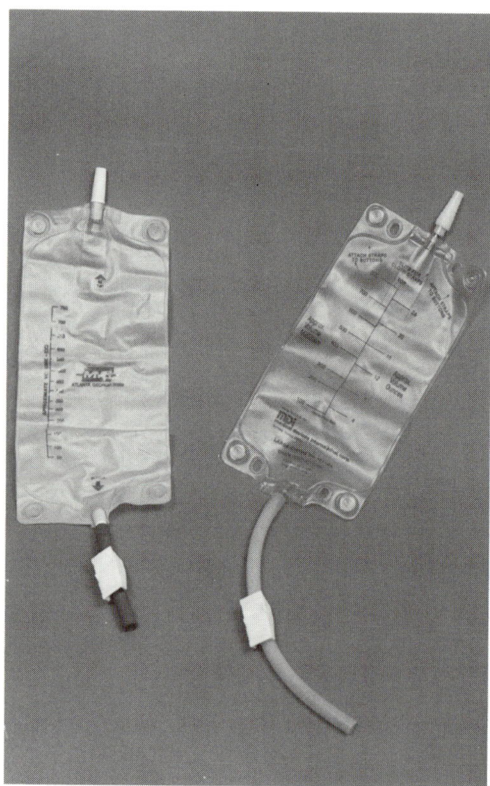

Figure 11–5 Preassembled urinary drainage bags with clamps in place.

- Urinary drainage bags. These vary in size and connector type. Patients with limited hand function require conical connectors for ease in attaching tubing. Bard and Medical Devices, Inc., manufacture such bags. Medical Devices manufactures the bag with drainage tubing and clamp already attached (Figure 11–5). Urinary drainage bags are attached to the leg with latex straps that button onto the bag or are laced through the holes in it.
- Urinary drainage clamps, which are included in most drainage bag kits and may also be purchased as a separate item. Standard clamps, which can also be adapted, include the following:
    - Plastic flip-top catheter clamp. It may be mounted on a base for securing to the leg or thumb loops may be added for easier operation (Figure 11–6).
    - Durable plastic clamp. Operates by a ratchet mechanism. Requires some finger or thumb musculature to operate (Figure 11–7).
    - Deluxe Lever Catheter Clamp. Metal clamp with an extended lever that requires minimal pressure to operate. It is easily adapted with thumb loops or mounted on a base for securing to the leg (Figure 11–8).
    - Double Loop Catheter Clamp. Small metal clamp with two nylon loops for hooking thumb or fingers to operate. It can be easily mounted on a base for securing to the leg (Figure 11–9).

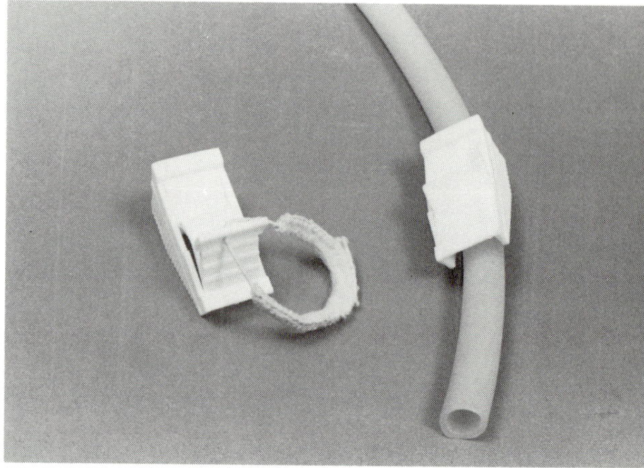

Figure 11–6 Plastic flip-top catheter clamp (right) and clamp adapted with a ring for finger operation (left).

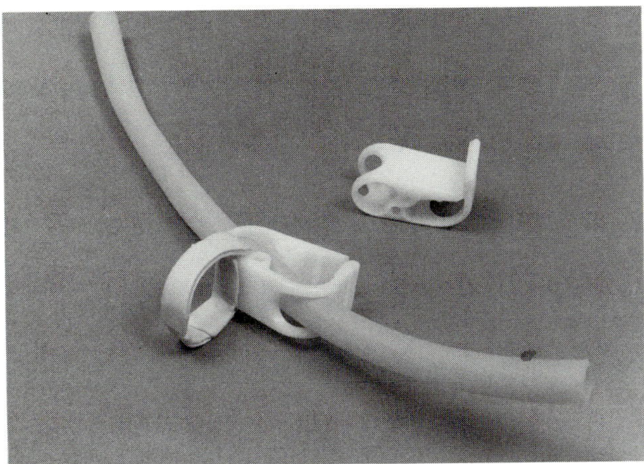

Figure 11–7 The durable plastic catheter clamp (right) is more difficult for individuals wth limited hand function to operate and may be adapted with a finger ring for stabilization (left).

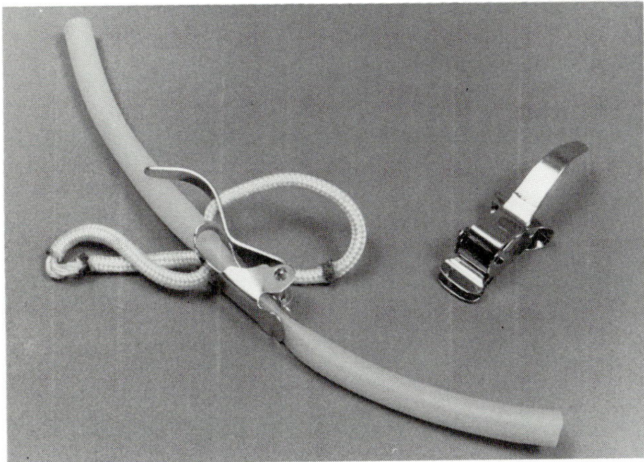

Figure 11–8 Deluxe Lever Catheter Clamp may be operated as is or finger loops can be added for stabilization or two-handed operation.

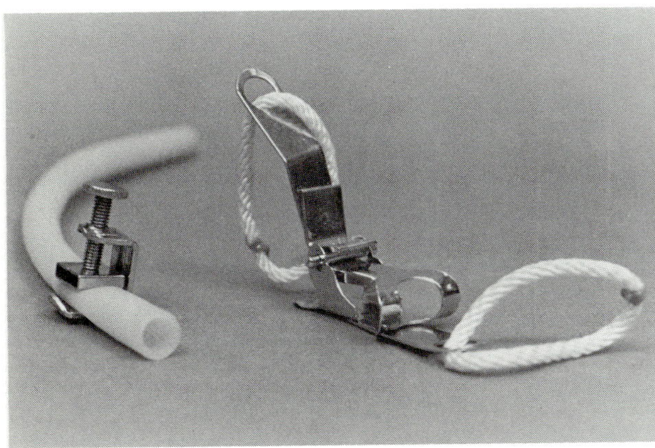

Figure 11–9 Double Loop Catheter Clamp (right) is designed for two-handed operation; screw-down clamp (left).

- E-Z Pull Urinary Drainage Valve (BeOK!). This rubber-sheathed valve is connected to the drainage tubing and operated by a pull ring that requires 2.4 pounds of pressure to release the valve. When the ring is pulled the rubber sheath stretches, resulting in release of urine flow. The device may be operated directly by the user's hand or indirectly through attachment of a cord onto the ring. The valve may then be activated by pulling the cord with the hand or by attaching the cord to the armrest of the W/C and using the reclining motion to pull the cord to open the valve (Figure 11–10). The rubber sheath does deteriorate, causing leakage and necessitating replacement of the clamp.
- Screw-down clamp. Small metal clamp operated by a small thumb screw. It requires good hand function and dexterity to operate and is not recommended for quadriplegics or others with limited hand function (Figure 11–9).

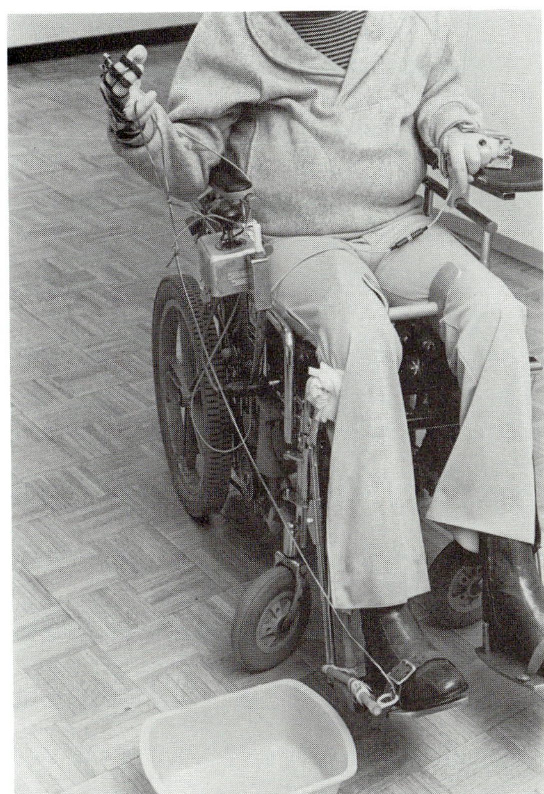

Figure 11–10 The E-Z Pull Drainage Valve mounted with W/C footplate and operated by pulling an attached cord.

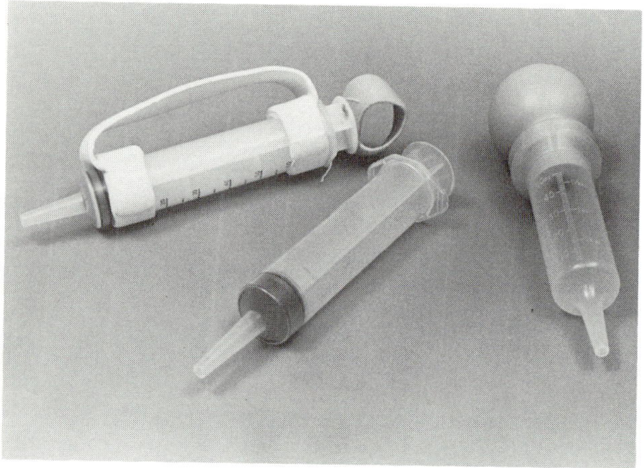

Figure 11–11 Adapted syringes.

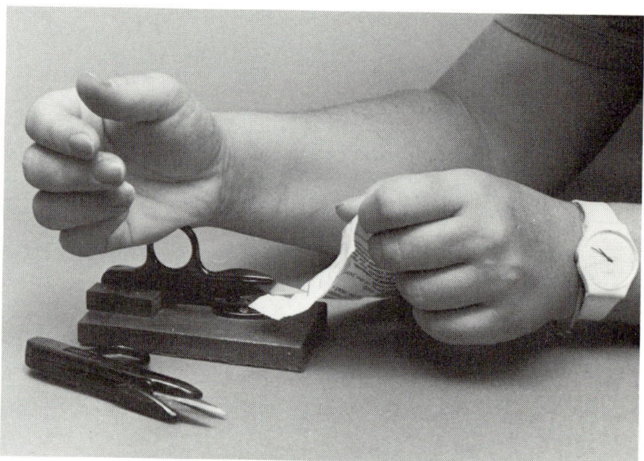

Figure 11–12 Quick-Clip Speed Cutter Scissors are operated with tenodesis or mounted onto a firm surface for operation with the heel or palm of the hand.

- Water-soluble lubricants, available in tubes or individual portion packages.
- Collection devices, such as a urinal or other drainage basin.
- Cleansing materials, such as soap and water or premoistened towelettes, wash cloth, towel, or disposable wipe.
- Syringes. Bulb-type syringes for irrigation are easily operated by patients with C6 or lower injury. Large syringes are commercially available and can be adapted with low-temperature plastic handles and thumb loops (Figure 11–11).

Adaptive equipment includes the following:

- Scissors, used for opening packages and cutting tubing and tape, especially by those with limited hand function. If use of standard scissors is not possible, Quick-Clip Speed Cutter scissors can be used with a tenodesis orthosis or by stabilizing on a firm surface and applying downward pressure (Figure 11–12).
- Adaptive catheter clamps, such as electric and breath-control clamps and adaptations made to the commercial clamps previously described.
- Manual pneumatic clamp [Leg Bag Users Valve (L.U.V.), Dynamic Mobilities, Inc.]. This device is operated by sipping on the tubing, which has a vacuum switch in it and attaches to the clamp. The tubing can run inside the pants leg and shirt to allow easy access or may exit at the waistband and be manually brought up to the mouth when needed (Figure 11–13).
- Puff-Sip automated leg bag emptier (Handi Medi Devices). Receives its power source from the electric W/C and, like the manual pneumatic clamp, is

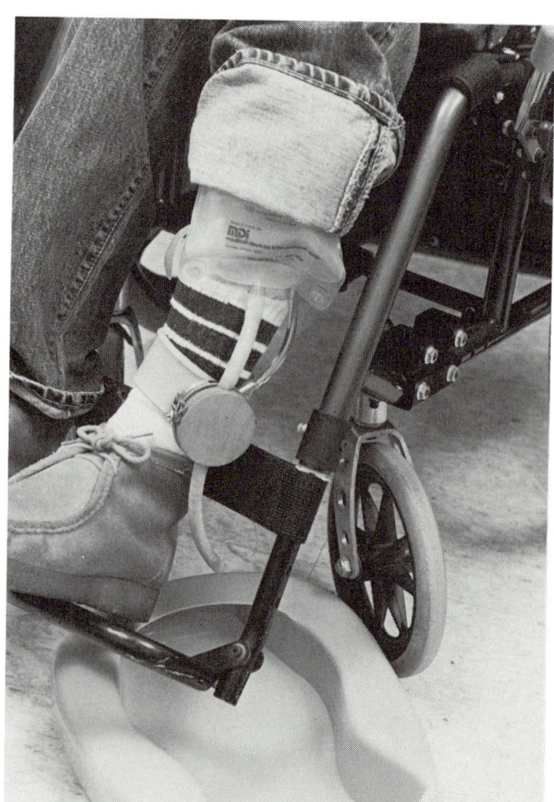

Figure 11–13 The manual pneumatic clamp is secured to the calf and concealed under clothing.

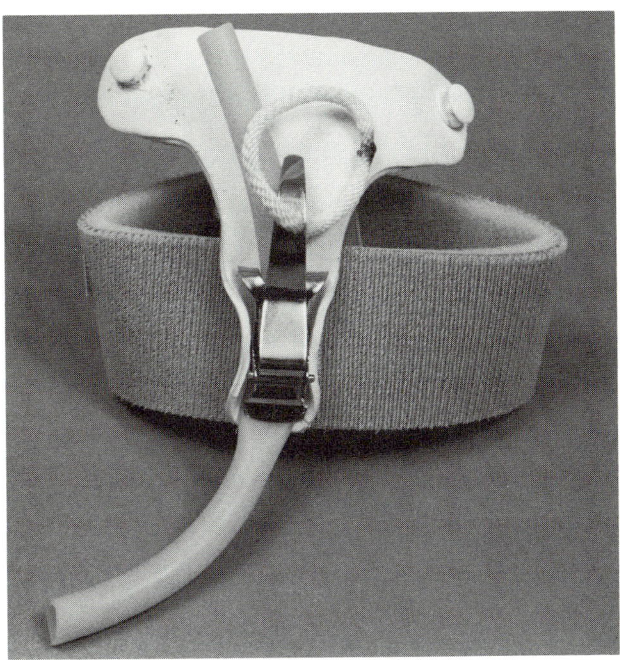

Figure 11–14 The Deluxe Lever Catheter Clamp mounted on low-temperature plastic and attached to the leg with a Velcro strap for more stability.

operated by breath control. Puffing into the tubing turns it on to release the urine and sipping on the same tube turns it off. The tubing can be attached to the straw that controls the W/C or pinned to the clothing near the shoulder within reach of the mouth.

- Electric leg bag emptiers (Handi Medi Devices and R.D. Equipment). These require arm placement to operate an activator switch. Handi Medi Devices offers two models, one using electric W/C power and the other its own external power pack. The R.D. Equipment clamp operates off electric W/C power. Extra care is needed when using these devices to keep the system clean and the wires intact. Both systems are small and lightweight and are easily concealed under the pants leg.
- Clamp adaptations. Thumb loops for unilateral or bilateral use can be added to standard commercial clamps. The loops are made of plastic or nylon cord. Mounting a clamp on a plastic base to stabilize it is recommended for unilateral operation. The base may be secured to the leg with Velcro straps for added stability (Figure 11–14).
- Drainage bag straps. Conventional latex drainage bag straps packaged with the bags are difficult for patients with limited hand function to use. They can be modified by adding thumb loops to the strap ends. Adapted straps are frequently substituted for the latex ones (Figure 11–15). Velcro straps with nylon thumb loops at the ends are easy to fabricate and easily applied. Cotton webbing, elastic, or foam may also be used to fabricate leg bag straps.
- Condom catheter holders are used to secure the condom catheter in place on the penis. The most commonly used is a catheter posey, which can be adapted with loops for easy fastening. It requires two hands to apply. A second type can be fabricated of cotton webbing and nylon cord. This type of condom catheter holder is applied by slipping it onto the tubing before placing the condom onto the penis. It is then slipped over the condom and positioned on the penis. It is fastened by looping back onto itself with Velcro. It is easily operated by a patient with C6 function (Figure 11–16). Condom catheter holders must be carefully monitored for tightness.

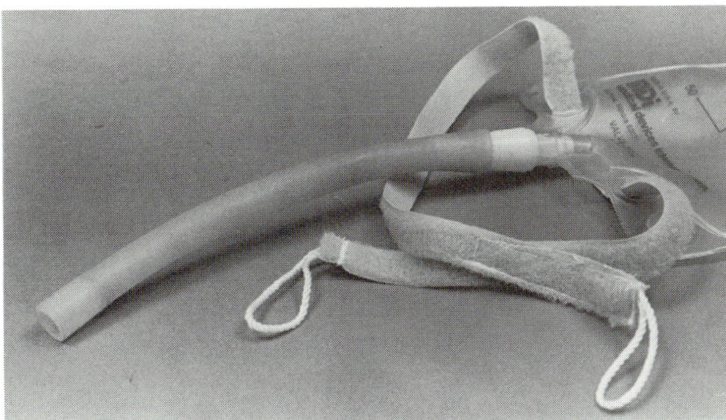

Figure 11–15 Velcro straps with finger loops are often substituted for the traditional latex straps.

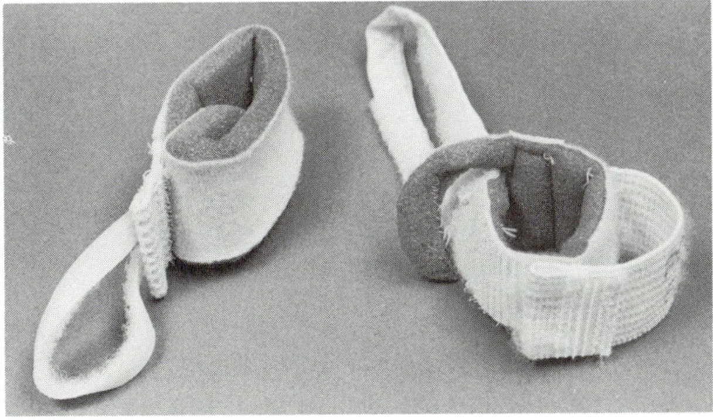

Figure 11–16 A loop added to the condom catheter holder for easier handling (left). A hole is made in the holder and the strap is threaded through and pulled back onto itself for a secure hold (right).

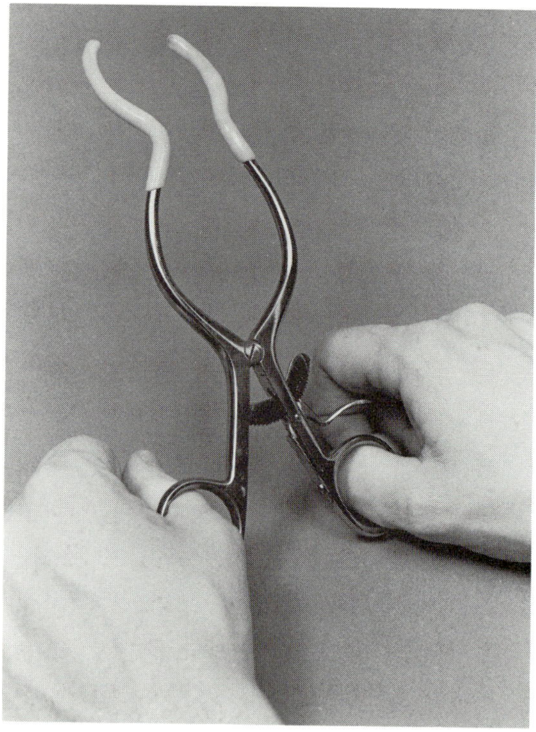

Figure 11–17 A commercially available labia spreader.

- Leg separators. Commercial stainless steel leg separators offer limited adjustments and are often not adequate for use in bed. Low-temperature plastics can be used to fabricate leg separators. The spreader bar should be long enough to allow for adequate abduction of the thighs and knees. A mirror may be mounted directly onto the spreader bar. Thigh abductors may be necessary if the thigh occludes the perineal area. A strap attached to a piece of low-temperature plastic formed to fit around the thigh can be used to pull the thigh and excess skin out of the way. The strap can be attached to the bed rail for leverage.

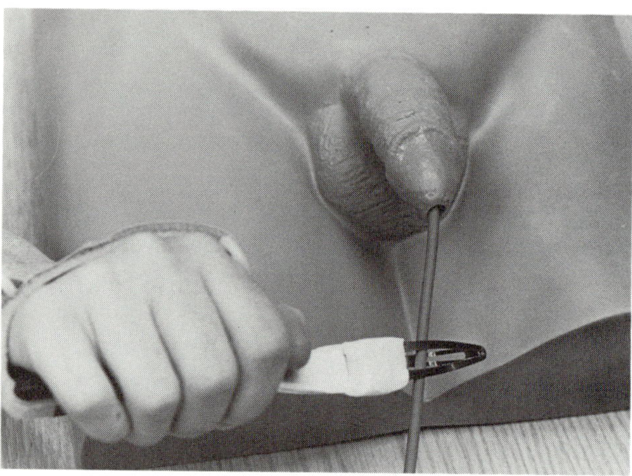

Figure 11–18 The urethral catheter inserter.

- Labia spreaders are commercially available and resemble a surgical clamp that has plastic-coated ends to prevent skin breakdown (Figure 11–17). They are operated by placing the spreader on a flat surface (mattress or W/C cushion) and sliding it forward until the tips are between the labia. The handles are pressed together so that the clamp will spread (see Figure 11–36). A ratchet hook locks the clamp into position at whatever angle the user requires; to release the clamp, the user must apply pressure to the ratchet hook. The main obstacle to using the labia spreader is that it may get in the way of the user's hands when inserting the catheter. It cannot be used when catheterizing on the toilet.
- Mirrors may be necessary for the female to view the perineal area. They are used for training purposes, and may be discarded once the patient feels comfortable with the technique and positioning. A small adjustable mirror is recommended. Often the mirror used for skin inspection will be adequate (see Figure 11–36). The mirror may need to be mounted on a firm surface for use in bed or the W/C. A mirror may be mounted inside the toilet bowl if necessary.
- The urethral catheter inserter may be used in place of a tenodesis orthosis for inserting the catheter. It is fabricated with a hair clip and low-temperature plastic. The device fits into a utensil slot and can be used with an orthosis or utensil cuff. The hair clip is modified to accommodate the circumference of the catheter and secured onto a ⅝ by 4½ inch strip of low-temperature plastic. The plastic strip is then heated and twisted approximately 90°, or to suit individual needs. Minimal effort is needed to open and close the clip, and the device is easily applied by the patient (Figure 11–18).
- The urinary drainage tubing stabilizer may be useful for patients who transfer themselves and perform weight shifts independently. It is designed to secure the tubing to the thigh in order to prevent it from getting pulled by clothing (Figure 11–19).

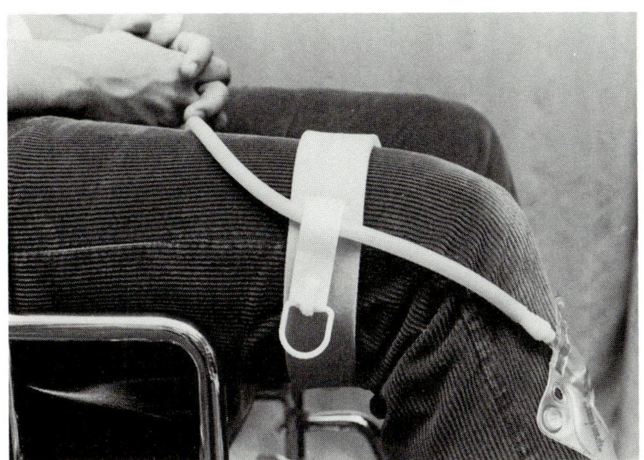

Figure 11–19 The urinary drainage tubing stabilizer.

A urinary evaluation box may be helpful to the therapist when introducing bladder management techniques and equipment to the patient. It includes an assortment of urethral and external catheters, adhesives, clamps, syringes, urinary drainage bags, leg bag straps, and scissors (Figure 11–20).

Emptying the Urinary Drainage Bag

The most basic component of urinary care training, which all SCI patients have the potential to perform independently, is emptying the urinary drainage bag. Training is done from a W/C into a urinal and a toilet and from bed into a urinal if functional abilities allow. Patients with C4 or higher injury and some C5 patients use the pneumatic or electric clamps described under adaptive equipment earlier in this unit. They are limited to emptying their urinary drainage bag into a floor drain, basin, cat litter box, or grass (Figure 11–21). Draining must be performed in the upright position of the W/C for gravity to assist.

Reaching the drainage tubing and clamp is often difficult for C5 and some C6 patients because of poor trunk stability and UE muscle strength. At these SCI levels and below, the clamps described under general urinary care equipment are most often used. The ability to lean forward to reach the drainage tubing and resume the upright position is necessary. This can be accomplished by hooking one arm behind the push handles of the W/C for stability while lowering and pulling back

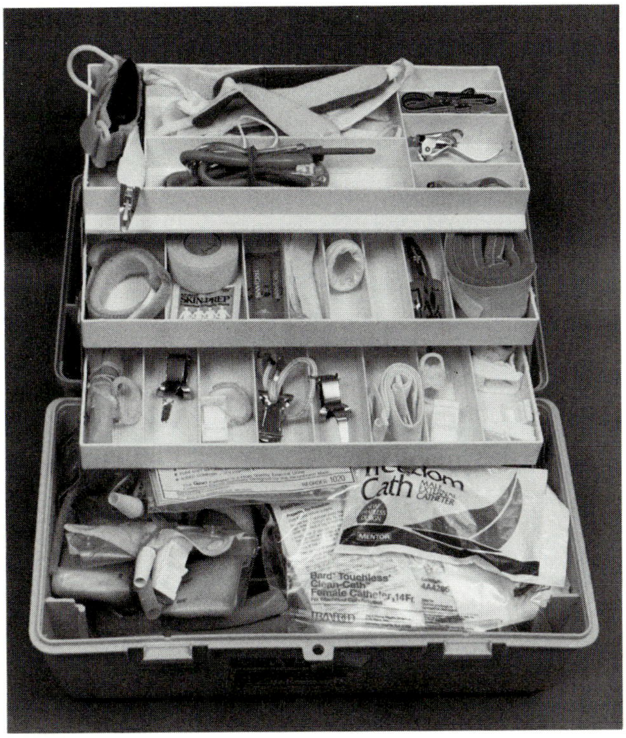

Figure 11–20 The urinary care evaluation box contains adaptive equipment necessary for training.

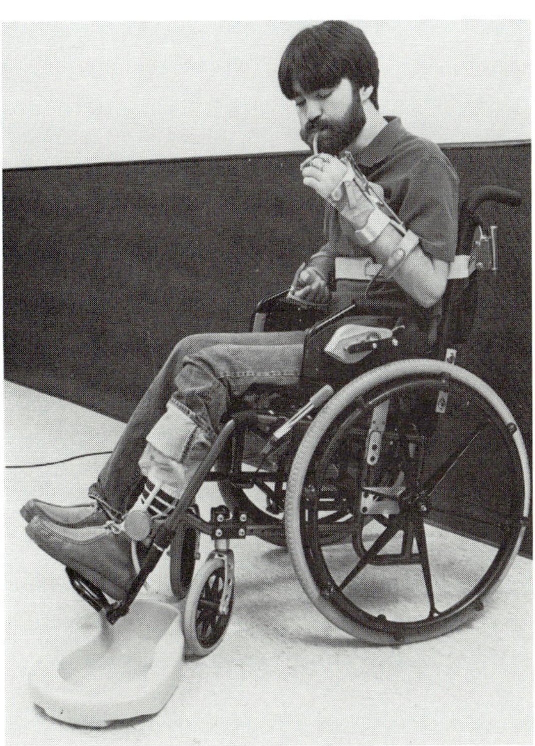

Figure 11–21 The manual pneumatic clamp (LUV valve) user can position himself over a basin or floor drain for drainage.

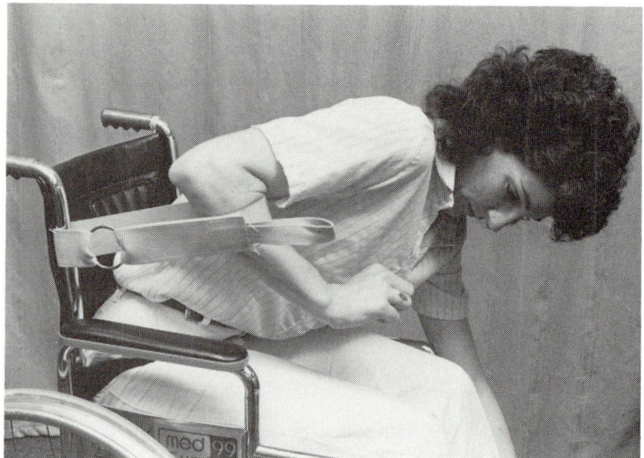

Figure 11–22 The McCormick loop is used to maintain stability while leaning forward to empty the drainage bag and then resume upright sitting.

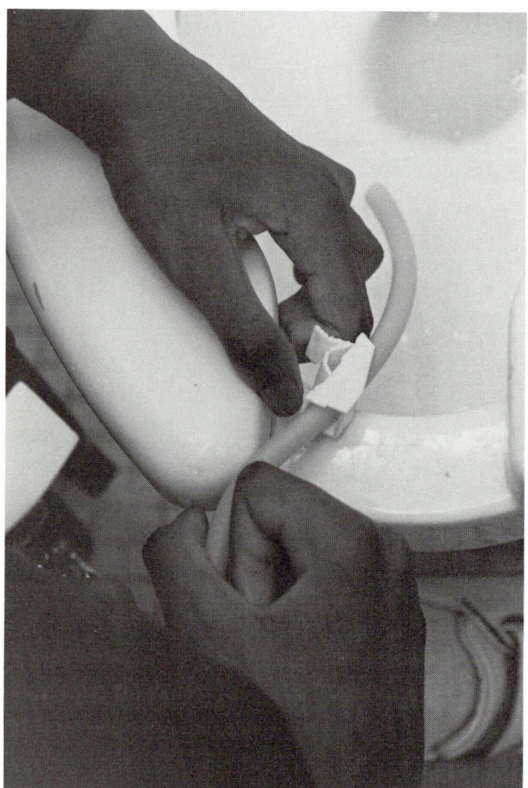

Figure 11–23 Two hands are often used to operate the drainage clamp.

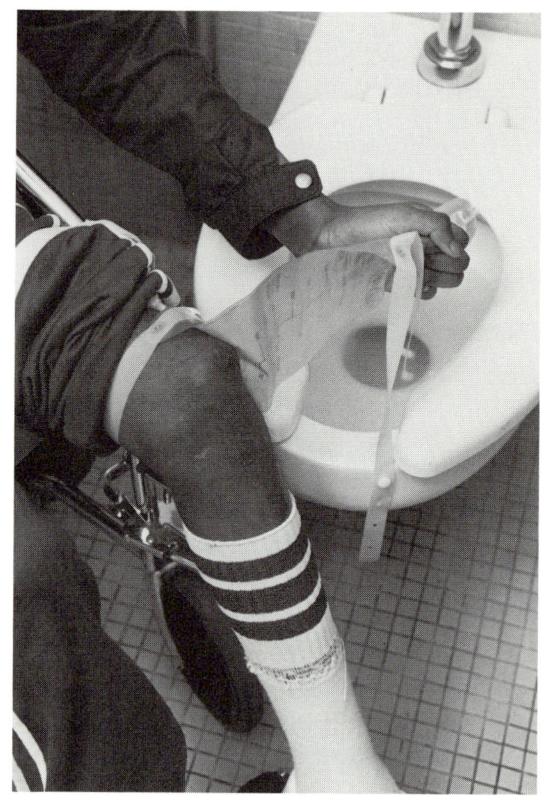

Figure 11–24 The bottom strap of the leg bag is unfastened and the drainage bag pulled away from the leg to be emptied into the toilet.

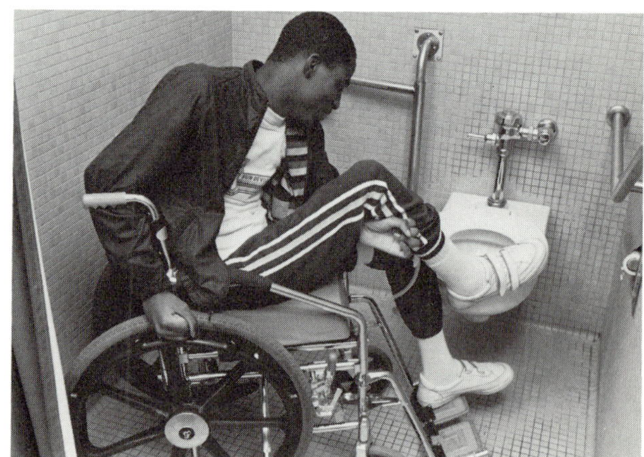

Figure 11–25 The leg is lifted onto the toilet and the drainage bag emptied directly into the toilet.

up with the biceps. If this is not possible, a McCormick loop may be attached to the back upright of the W/C for additional leverage in resuming the upright position (Figure 11–22). One arm is hooked into the loop and the patient flexes forward until he is able to reach the drainage tubing. Bilateral UE use is helpful to manage the drainage tubing and clamp. One extremity stabilizes and directs the tubing while the other operates the clamp itself (Figure 11–23). Unilateral operation may be possible with an adapted clamp. A hole can be made in the pants leg for easier access to the tubing or the pants leg can be slit and Velcro added to allow for the pants leg to open. A zipper pull or hook can be used to assist with pulling the drainage tubing from under the pants leg. The urinary drainage bag may also be lifted away from the leg and placed onto the toilet bowl for drainage (Figure 11–24). This can be accomplished by not using a strap on the bottom of the urinary drainage bag or by unfastening the bottom strap and reconnecting it after emptying. Care should be taken when not using a bottom strap that circulation is not cut off at the thigh from additional tension on the top strap. The foot itself may be lifted onto the toilet bowl and the urine drained directly into the toilet (Figure 11–25). This method usually requires C7 or C8 function and is particularly useful in the community setting.

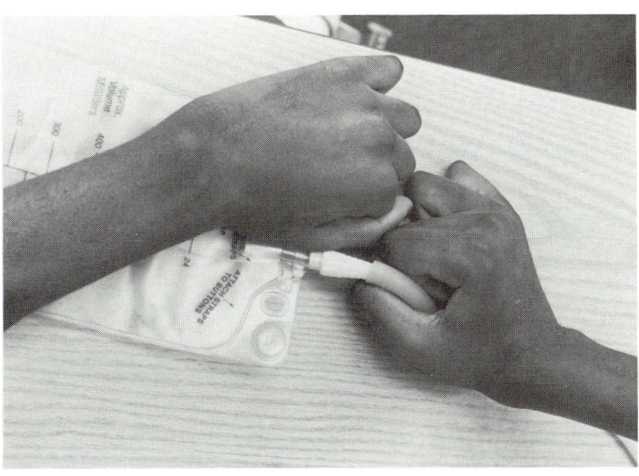

Figure 11–26 Attaching the tubing to the drainage bag or connector.

Managing the Urinary Drainage Bag

The ability to independently assemble and apply the urinary drainage bag involves five steps:

1. Attach the connecting tubing and connector (if needed) onto the top end of the urinary drainage bag.
2. Connect the straps onto the urinary drainage bag.
3. Attach the drainage tubing onto the bottom end of the urinary drainage bag.
4. Place the clamp onto the drainage tubing.
5. Fasten the urinary drainage bag onto the leg.

The equipment used (as described earlier) includes

- urinary drainage bag
- urinary drainage bag straps
- connecting and drainage tubing (if needed)
- clamp
- urinary drainage tubing stabilizer (optional)

Tubing and connectors are often packaged so that separation of two pieces is required. This step is very difficult to perform and requires use of the teeth. Urinary drainage bags are packaged with caps on the ends to preserve sterility. The caps are removed and should be saved for use when the leg bag is cleaned and stored.

Attachment of the tubing onto the urinary drainage bag ends is often the most difficult task because of the amount of strength and coordination required. A WDFH or RIC tenodesis orthosis may be required. A suggested method is to stabilize the connector or the top of the urinary drainage bag on a firm surface with the heel of the hand (Figure 11–26). The tubing is positioned so that both pieces can be pushed together. Wetting the connector or tubing acts as a lubricant and may ease the process.

A commercially available urinary drainage bag system that is partially assembled can eliminate extra steps and conserve energy. Because of its cost, however, most patients are unable to discard the equipment after one use and must disassemble it for cleaning—defeating the purpose of a preassembled drainage bag. Family members or other care givers can partially assemble the urinary drainage system in advance.

Clamps are described under equipment. An important consideration when choosing a clamp for independent use is whether or not the user is able to open and close it easily as well as attach it or remove it from the tubing (Figure 11–27).

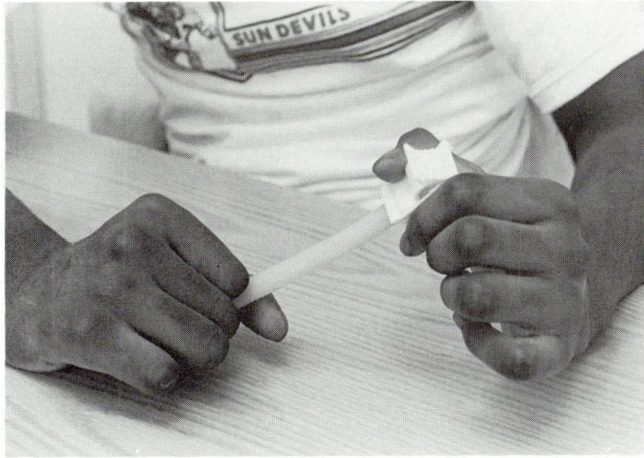

Figure 11–27 Tenodesis aids with stabilizing the tubing while the clamp is put into place.

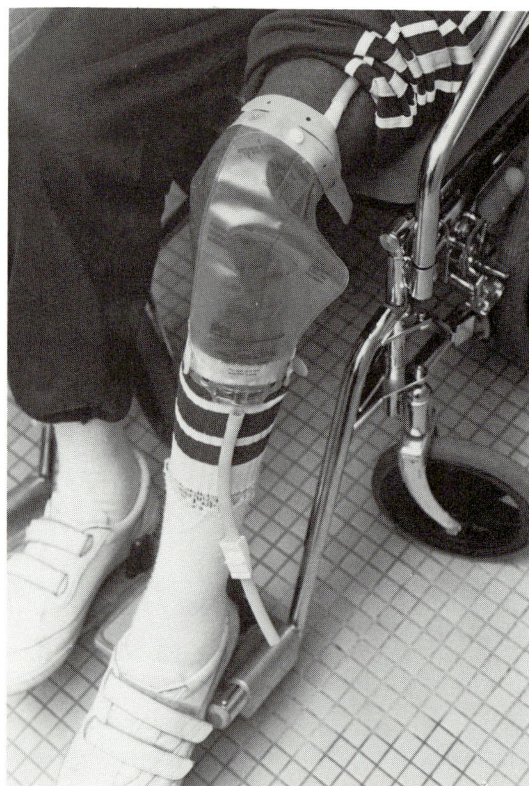

Figure 11–28 The leg bag is often worn with one strap fastened above the knee and the other below.

Urinary drainage bag straps can be attached by buttons or threaded through holes in the urinary drainage bag. A zipper pull or button hook may be used in this procedure. The latex straps packaged with most urinary drainage bags are often replaced with Velcro or Velcro combined with webbing, elastic, or foam straps, which are more easily applied by the patient.

Placement of the urinary drainage bag on the leg is determined by personal preference. In most instances it is worn across the knee, with one strap above and one below the knee or both below it (Figure 11–28). Seldom is it worn above the knee because of difficulty with proper drainage. For cosmetic reasons most patients prefer the urinary drainage bag and tubing to be hidden under clothing. The urinary drainage tubing stabilizer may be attached on the thigh to prevent excessive stress on and displacement of tubing during physical activity.

Cleaning Equipment

The nurse usually teaches the patient how to clean urinary equipment. If hand function requires upgrading or if special equipment is needed, the occupational therapist can assist by adapting syringes, adapting pans, or suggesting the use of a tenodesis orthosis.

Applying an External Catheter

For the male patient, applying an external catheter involves eight steps:

1. Open packages.
2. Attach condom to connector.
3. Attach tubing to urinary drainage bag.
4. Connect straps to urinary drainage bag.
5. Attach drainage tubing.
6. Place clamp onto drainage tubing.
7. Place external catheter, including adhesive or posey.
8. Fasten urinary drainage bag onto leg.

The process can take 10 to 30 minutes, with 15 minutes usually considered a practical amount of time to perform the technique on a routine basis. Equipment includes

- connecting and drainage tubing with connector included
- external catheter
- urinary drainage bag
- urinary drainage bag straps
- posey or adhesive
- clamp

Assembly of the urinary drainage bag was described earlier. Attaching the external catheter onto the urinary drainage bag assembly is similar to attaching tubing (Figure 11–29).

Actual placement of the external catheter on the penis requires use of bilateral UEs and can be performed in bed or in the W/C. Natural tenodesis hand function is used to place the catheter on the penis (Figure 11–30). Tenodesis orthoses are not recommended for this procedure because of the possibility of skin abrasion. Most patients find placement of the external catheter easier to perform with an erection. One extremity is used to position the penis, while the other places the external catheter onto the tip of the penis. Using the sides of the thumb or the heel of the

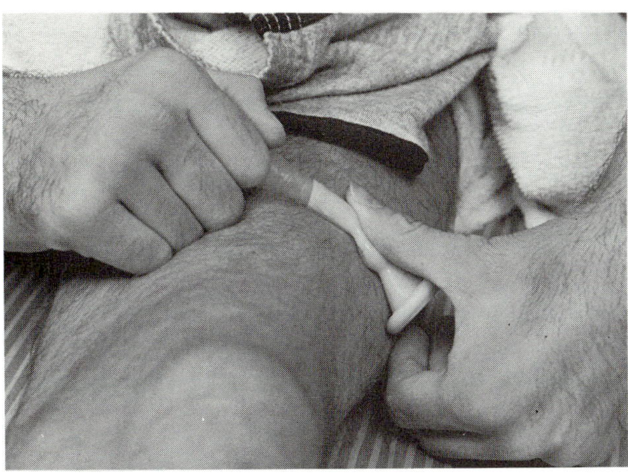

Figure 11–29 Attaching the condom to the connector with tenodesis hand function.

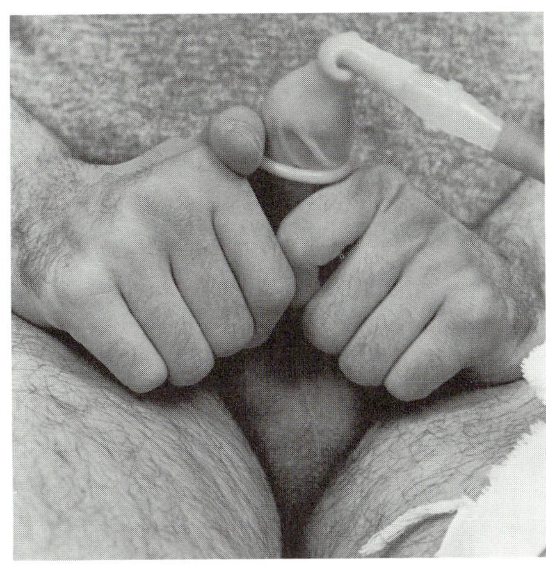

Figure 11–30 The condom is placed on the penis by using both hands with tenodesis hand function.

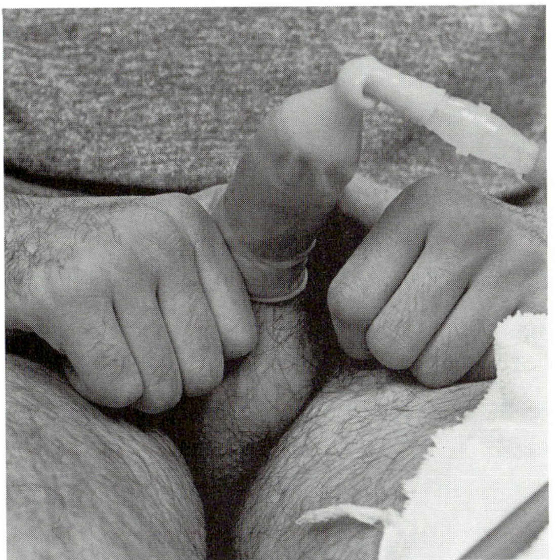

Figure 11–31 The lateral surface of the thumb is used to unroll the condom onto the penis and secure it.

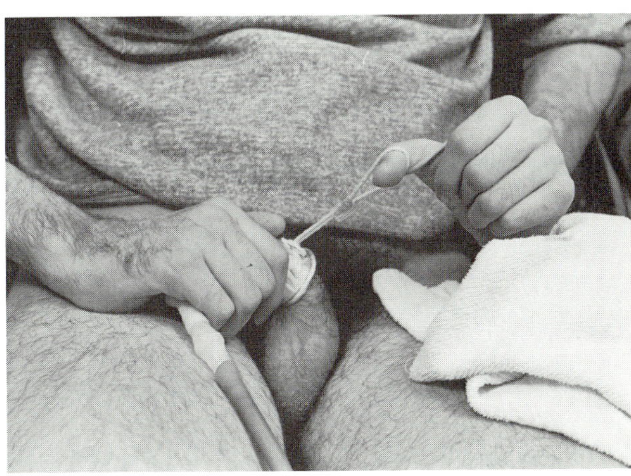

Figure 11–32 Securing the adhesive or condom catheter holder is the final step to applying an external catheter.

hand, the patient then unrolls the condom over the penis (Figure 11–31). (Care must be taken to avoid catching pubic hair under the condom.) The condom catheter holder or adhesive tape is then put in place (Figure 11–32). If Skin-Prep or Skin-Bond are used they are applied directly onto the penis before placement of the condom. The leg bag is secured to the leg after placement.

Performing Intermittent Catheterization

Inserting a urethral catheter four to six times a day for bladder drainage can be done with the sterile, clean, or nontouch sterile technique. Since the sterile technique is not frequently used for intermittent catheterization programs outside the hospital setting, training in independent performance of this technique is seldom provided. The occupational therapist is involved in providing equipment and training for independent performance with the remaining two techniques.

The clean catheterization technique is the simpler and less expensive of the two. Steps in performing this technique are as follows:

1. Prepare equipment and remove clothing.
2. Position self in bed or W/C or on the toilet.
3. Cleanse urethral area.
4. Prepare catheter tip with lubricant.
5. Position penis or separate labia.
6. Insert catheter.
7. Drain bladder.
8. Clean up.

The process can take 15 to 45 minutes, with 20 minutes usually considered practical. Equipment includes:

- soap and water
- wash mitt or cloth
- towel
- lubricant
- catheter
- urinal or other drainage basin
- table or vanity
- mirror and labia spreader for women
- leg straps or spreaders
- tenodesis orthosis or urethral catheter inserter

Equipment is set out on a clean surface in easy reach. It may be laid out on the bed to the side, on a table or vanity, or on a board projecting from under the W/C cushion. The clothing is removed. An upright or slightly reclined position is required; females require a posterior pelvic tilt, with legs abducted (Figure 11–33). (Leg abduction straps or leg spreaders may be needed to maintain hip abduction.) Whether performed on the bed, W/C, or toilet, back support is necessary in most cases for females and helpful for males. A towel under the thighs can help to achieve the pelvic tilt. A towel or disposable pad is positioned to protect clothing or sheets from possible spillage when the catheter is removed. The urethral area is cleansed with soap and water or disposable towelettes.

The catheter tip is prepared with lubricant. Tube lubricant is easier to manage than jar and can be opened

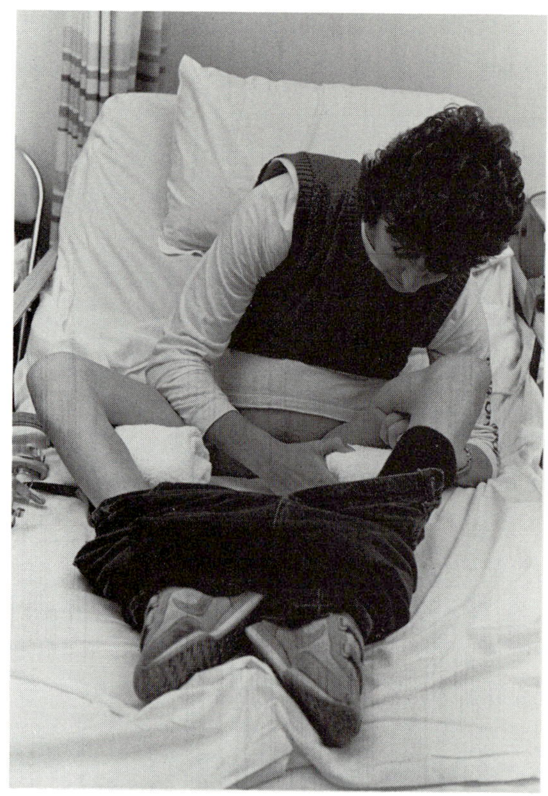

Figure 11–33 A posterior pelvic tilt, necessary for adequate viewing of the perineum, is achieved by placing rolled towels under the thigh in bed.

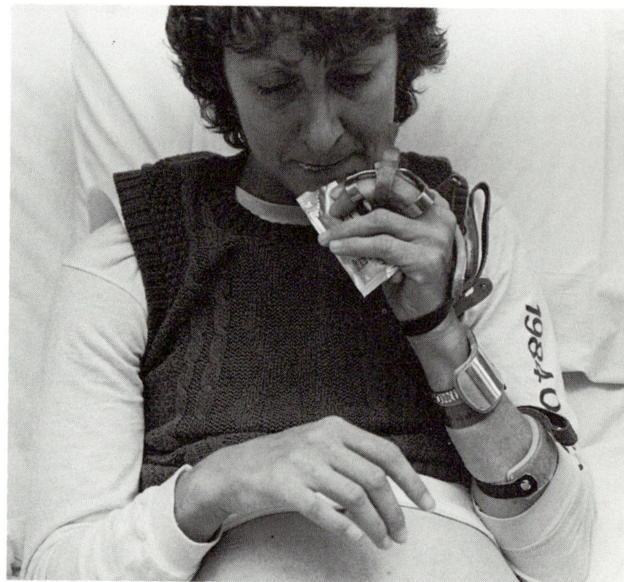

Figure 11–34 Opening lubricant package with the teeth.

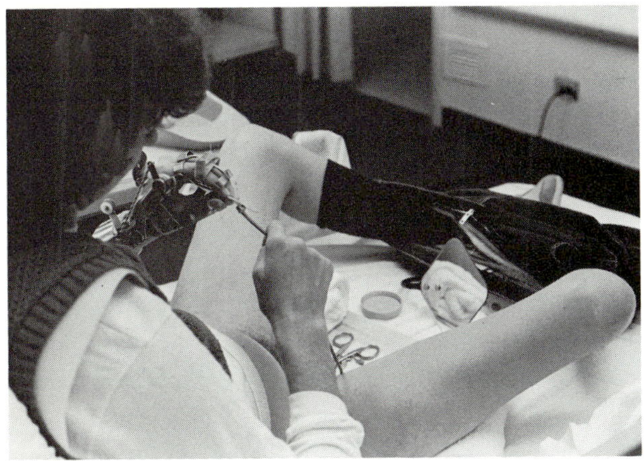

Figure 11–35 The tip of the catheter is lubricated before insertion.

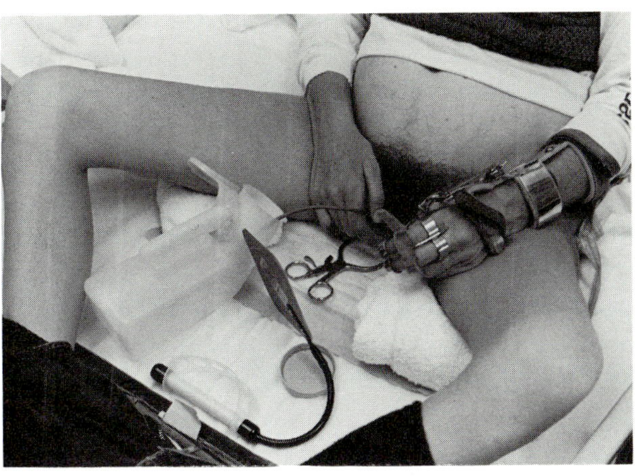

Figure 11–36 Setup for female self-catheterization includes a mirror for viewing the perineum, labia spreaders to provide unobstructed access to the urethral opening, and a collection device.

with the mouth, an adapted cap, or a tenodesis orthosis (Figure 11–34). The catheter is held 5 to 6 inches below the tip and the lubricant is applied to the top inch (Figure 11–35). It is then laid aside with the tip suspended (once prepared, the catheter tip must not touch any surface). The penis is positioned with natural tenodesis or other available hand function. Tenodesis orthoses are usually not used because of the danger of skin abrasion.

For women, separating the labia to expose the urethra may require some practice. Using the extended wrist, finger extensors, or finger flexors (if present) to put an outward and upward pull on the labia may be adequate. Only one hand can be used, as the other is needed to insert the catheter. Commercial labia spreaders positioned on the seating surface may be used when catheterizing in bed or the W/C (Figure 11–36).

Catheter insertion may require a tenodesis orthosis or urethral catheter inserter. A semirigid catheter is usually easier to insert than the flexible type. The catheter has to be long enough to reach the drainage container and must be held in place during drainage.

Cleanup includes rinsing the catheter with soap and water and returning it to its storage container. The urethral area is again washed and dried. The urine is emptied into the toilet and the drainage container is washed. If an orthosis or labia spreader has been used it should be cleaned with alcohol or soap and water.

The nontouch sterile technique with the nontouch catheter comprises the following steps:

1. Prepare equipment.
2. Remove clothing and position self on W/C, bed, or toilet.
3. Open catheter kit.
4. Straighten catheter in package.
5. Open Betadine swabs.
6. Open lubricant package.
7. Open top chamber to expose catheter without touching catheter.
8. Deposit lubricant into top chamber.
9. Prepare meatus by cleansing with Betadine.
10. Feed catheter into urethra.
11. Collect urine.
12. Clean up.

This process takes 15 to 30 minutes, with 20 minutes considered practical. Equipment includes

- nontouch sterile catheter kit (male or female)
- scissors
- garbage bag or container
- plastic-lined towel for protecting bedding or clothing
- tenodesis orthosis (if necessary)
- tube lubricant and bottled Betadine to replace the small packages in the kit

Preparing equipment, managing clothing, and positioning are performed as in the clean catheterization method.

The catheter kit may be opened using teeth, adapted scissors, or a tenodesis orthosis. The catheter tubing is packaged coiled inside a plastic sheath and must be uncoiled, with a maximum of one loop remaining, to obtain proper drainage. The catheter must be kept inside the plastic catheter guide (Figure 11–37); it is set aside while the package of Betadine swabs and lubricant are opened with both hands. Care must be taken when opening the package of swabs to avoid spilling the Betadine solution.

Opening the top chamber of the catheter to expose the catheter tip requires more hand function than is usually available for a quadriplegic, so scissors are recommended to get the package started. The teeth may be used if care is taken not to contaminate the sterile surface inside the top chamber. The lubricant is squeezed into the top chamber using tenodesis action to compress the package or by placing the package between the teeth and compressing it with the lips. The catheter is set aside while the urethral meatus is prepared with Betadine swabs. Each swab is used once and discarded. The top chamber is positioned onto the penis for males and inside the lips of the labia for females.

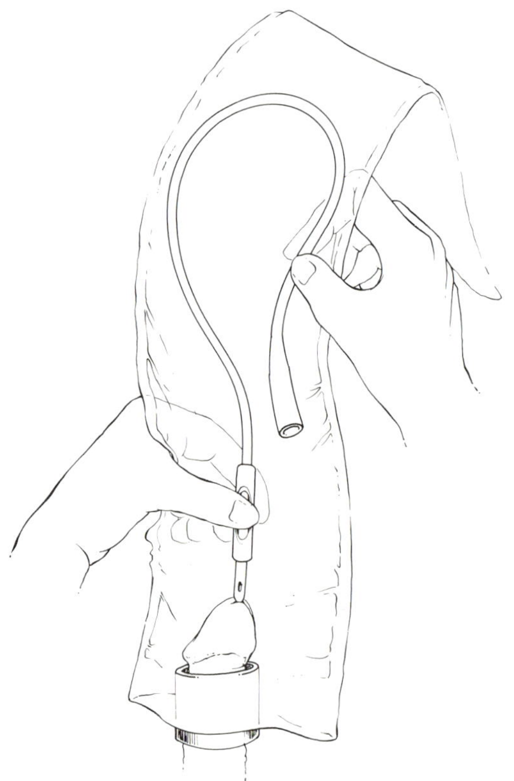

Figure 11–37 The nontouch sterile catheter kit includes a catheter guide, which assists with directing the catheter into the urethral opening (male and female).

The female catheter kit includes a sterile glove for separating the labia. Because of the awkwardness of this procedure, labia spreaders are difficult to use. Putting on rubber gloves is a difficult step for the patient with limited hand function.

The catheter is fed into the urethra by using one hand to grasp the catheter in the catheter guide (with a tenodesis orthosis) while the other hand (using tenodesis action with lateral pinch) feeds the catheter through the plastic casing and into the urethra. Patients should be encouraged to relax and take a deep breath to facilitate relaxation of the external sphincter. Once the catheter is fully inserted, the urine will drain into the plastic casing around the catheter. The catheter is withdrawn slowly to ensure proper drainage and is discarded.

Clothing Management for Intermittent Catheterization

When catheterization is performed in bed, standard clothing management techniques, as described in unit 10, are used. Women will need to almost completely remove slacks to allow external rotation of the hips and abduction of the thighs for access to the perineal area. Wearing a loose skirt makes the process easier. Clothing management is less difficult for males for catheterizing in the W/C because of easier access to the urethra. Drawstrings and elastic waistbands allow for the clothing to be pulled away from the urethral area. Side-to-side weight shifts can be used to pull clothing down over the buttocks if tighter slacks are worn. Velcro closures to replace zippers may be helpful. Extending the Velcro into the leg inseam allows even greater access. Wraparound adapted clothing can assist in clothing management as well. If there is a problem in keeping the pants away from the body, a hook that attaches to the W/C and pulls the waistband away from the body can be used.

Management of clothing for females, on the toilet or in the W/C, requires a great deal of UE strength and the ability to change positions in the W/C. In most cases, C7 or C8 function is required. Clothing can be removed in the W/C before transferring onto the toilet or while on the toilet. The W/C offers more stability for removing clothing. This can best be accomplished by removing the legrests of the W/C and placing the feet on the floor with legs extended in front (Figure 11–38). The pants are started over the hips by using lateral weight shifts (Figure 11–39). The patient slides forward in the chair as far as possible so that the buttocks are nearly off

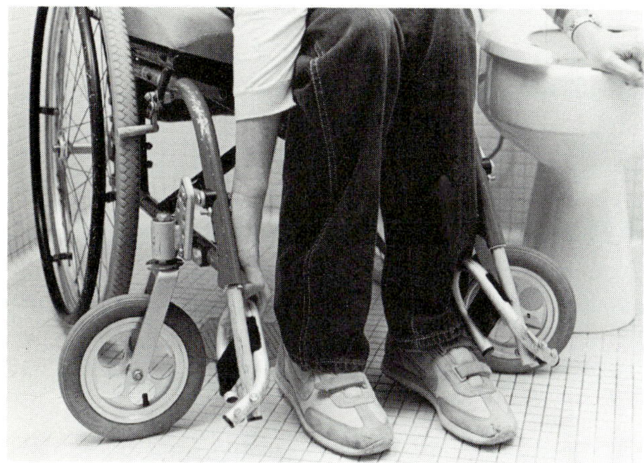

Figure 11–38 Feet placed flat on the floor provide stability when undressing in the W/C.

the seat (Figure 11–40). One extremity will be needed to hook around the W/C push handle or armrest for balance and the other extremity can handle the clothing. Once the clothing has been pushed down over the hips on one side, the process is repeated for the other. When the pants are below the hips the individual can pull herself into an upright-sitting position. This final action will slide the pants even farther down the thighs. The pants will need to be lowered to the ankles or removed from one leg. Underwear is usually not worn.

Managing an Indwelling Catheter

Insertion and removal of an indwelling catheter is not frequently performed by patients with significantly limited hand function (C7 and above). Therefore, OT intervention is seldom indicated and instruction is provided by nursing.

Irrigation of the indwelling catheter is a sterile technique seldom performed by those with limited dexterity. Equipment may be needed to make the process more efficient, even for those with weak hand function. An adapted handle may be added to the pan used for boiling equipment to sterilize it. Syringes may be adapted to make irrigation easier. Instructions in safety precautions to be used when working with hot items may be provided by the occupational therapist.

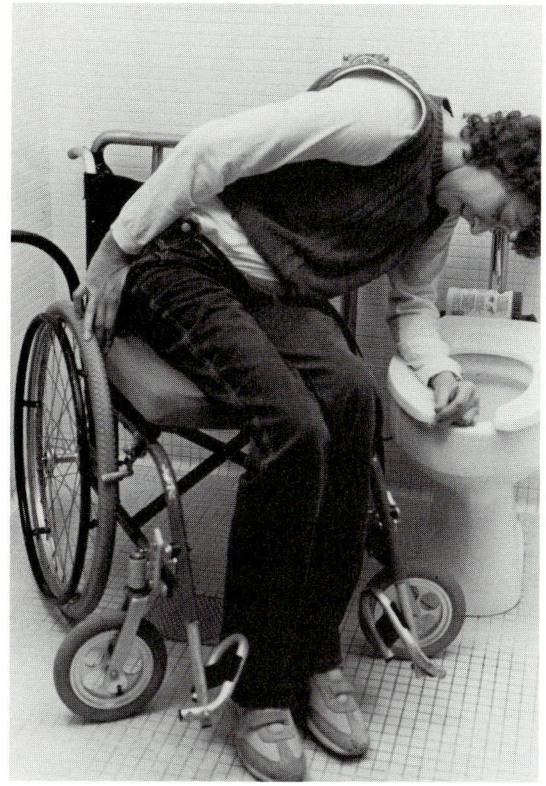

Figure 11–39 Lateral shifts in weight release pressure on the buttocks and allow pants to be pushed down over the hips.

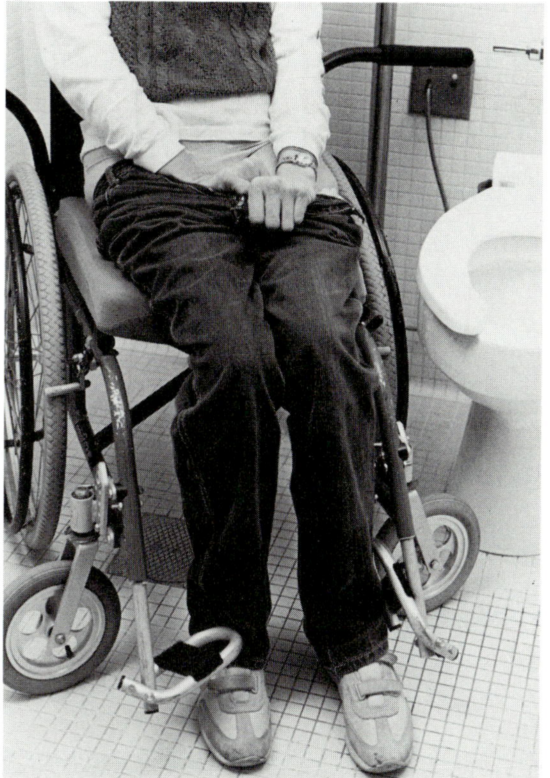

Figure 11–40 Once the pants are removed from the hips, the buttocks slide forward in the chair to allow the pants to be pushed over the thighs.

Pretraining in Techniques

Training in urinary drainage bag assembly, use of scissors, operation of clamps, and opening of packages can be performed in the clinic before actual performance. Although it is difficult to simulate these situations as they are actually performed in bed or the W/C, the patient and therapist can get an idea of problems that may be encountered and whether or not goals are realistic through the pretraining process.

BOWEL MANAGEMENT

Bowel regulation involves monitoring food intake to ensure a proper balance of fiber and nutrients and regulating elimination of waste. Once regulation has been achieved, a patient may choose to manage his program independently, thus minimizing the need for attendant care. For many, the energy expended and the difficulties encountered make self-performance of a bowel program unrealistic. Patients with C7 or lower injury are the most likely candidates for independent performance. For most, management will include suppository insertion, rectal stimulation, and cleanup.

After paralysis, proper elimination of body wastes is accomplished through a two-step process. Medicated suppositories are used to initiate peristalsis of the lower intestine while the rectum is stimulated to further facilitate expulsion of the stool. In some cases, results can be achieved by rectal stimulation alone. Positioning during performance of the bowel program may affect elimination. Some patients must lie on their side while others tolerate a sitting position. The exact position required will be determined by the individual's own bodily responses.

Specialized equipment is available to assist with inserting the suppository and in performing rectal stimulation. Successful use of this equipment requires problem solving by the patient, the nurse, and the occupational therapist. The equipment is potentially traumatic to rectal tissue, and its use must be monitored.

Position and Equipment

The position assumed will dictate the equipment and techniques needed. If a patient decides, by choice or by necessity, to perform his program on his side he will need to determine the most efficient angle to position the handle of the suppository inserter and digital stimulator and whether or not the commercially available equipment will require further modification (Figures 11–41 and 11–42). In many situations the correct angle cannot be achieved through regular adjustment, and a custom-fitted device will be necessary. The mechanical portion of a commercial suppository inserter or digital stimulator can be unscrewed from the original handle and placed in a universal cuff or a cuff made of low-temperature plastic that has been angled for the individual's needs (Figure 11–43). The correct angle is determined by having the patient assume the position and simulate insertion of the device (Figure 11–44). If the individual is unable to insert the suppository deep enough into the rectum to be effective, he can use the digital stimulator to push the suppository deeper before it begins to dissolve.

Once the suppository has been effective, rectal stimulation can be performed while lying on one's side or while on the toilet or commode chair. The model of digital stimulator used to stimulate the rectum will depend on the position assumed and the functional abilities of the user. If stimulation is to be performed while lying, the device used can be adapted in a manner similar to that of the suppository inserter. A longer handled device will be necessary for performance on the toilet or commode chair or in the case of limited arm

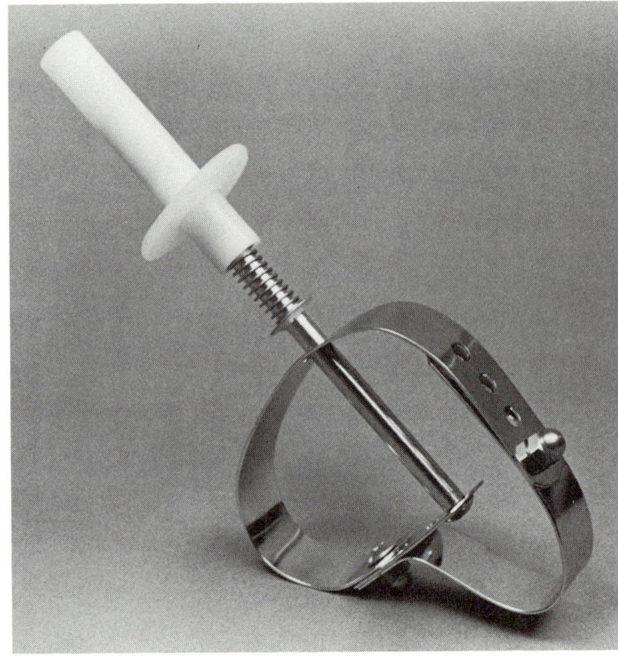

Figure 11–41 Commercially available spring-loaded suppository inserter.

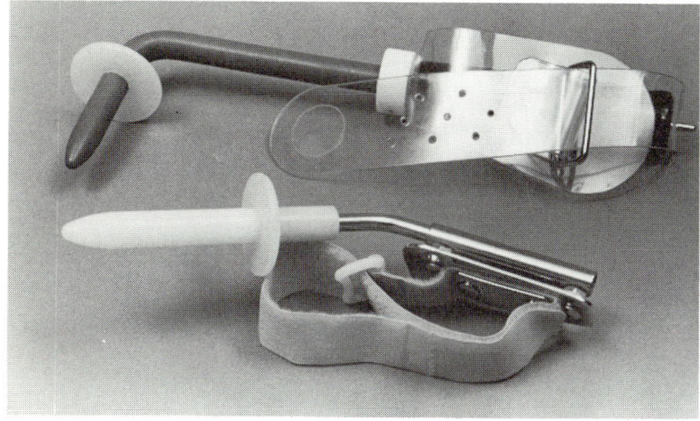

Figure 11–42 Commercially available digital stimulators are available with a variety of handle options.

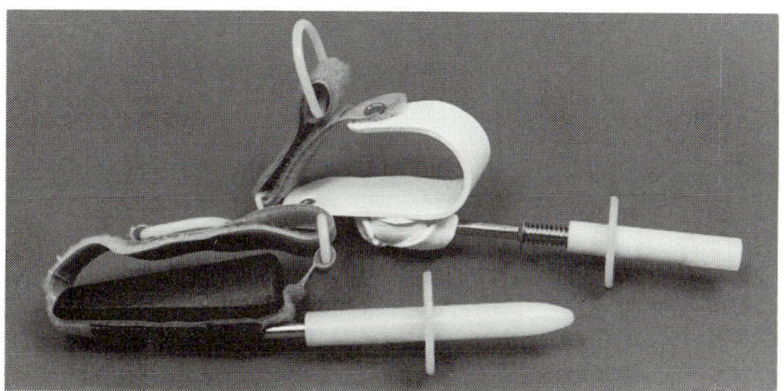

Figure 11–43 Adapted handles used for suppository inserter and digital stimulator.

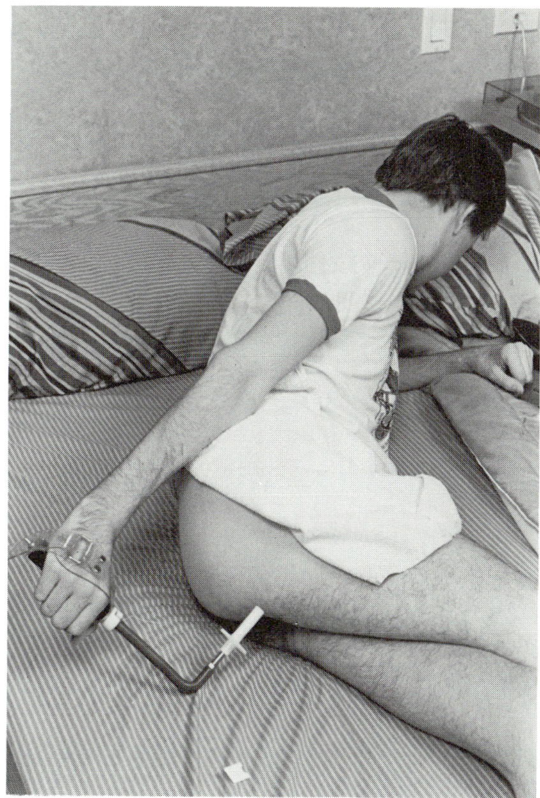

Figure 11–44 Positioning for insertion and stimulation requires practice.

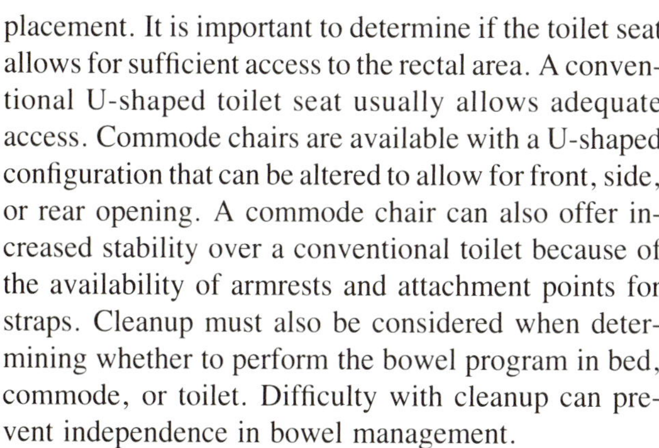

placement. It is important to determine if the toilet seat allows for sufficient access to the rectal area. A conventional U-shaped toilet seat usually allows adequate access. Commode chairs are available with a U-shaped configuration that can be altered to allow for front, side, or rear opening. A commode chair can also offer increased stability over a conventional toilet because of the availability of armrests and attachment points for straps. Cleanup must also be considered when determining whether to perform the bowel program in bed, commode, or toilet. Difficulty with cleanup can prevent independence in bowel management.

Performing the Bowel Program in Bed

If the entire program is to be performed in bed, it is important that all the necessary equipment be gathered:

- suppository
- lubricant
- suppository inserter
- digital stimulator
- disposable wipes
- plastic-lined pads
- gloves (optional)
- garbage bag or can

The plastic-lined pads should be placed under the buttocks to protect bedding and serve as a depository for the feces. The suppository is often packaged in foil and may be opened with the teeth. The suppository is small and has a smooth texture. Care should be taken to maintain an adequate grip on it so that it may be placed into the inserter as soon as possible; heat from handling will cause the suppository to melt. Lubricant should be placed on the tip of the suppository and inserter to ease entry. The hand is then placed in position to trigger the release of the suppository.

With impaired sensation in the hand, mirrors to visually place the inserter or anatomical landmarks can be used. The proper placement of mirrors may be difficult to achieve. Landmarks are used by placing the patient's hand in position for insertion, moving the heel of the hand onto the pubis, sliding the hand posteriorly around the hip until reaching the sacrum, and then gliding caudally past the gluteal slit until the rectum is located.

Once the suppository and inserter are in place, the hand is pressed internally to trigger the release of the suppository. After insertion, the patient remains in the side-lying position until the suppository takes effect. During this time, the rectum will have to be digitally stimulated at intervals designated by the individual's own bodily response. The digital stimulator is positioned in the same manner as the suppository inserter. It should be lubricated before insertion. Once placed in the rectum, a circular motion is required. The duration of stimulation will vary.

Once the feces have been expelled, cleanup must be performed. The patient will have to shift position. The rectal area may be cleansed using disposable towels and a damp cloth or moistened towelettes. Soiled towels are discarded in a trash bag or wastebasket situated nearby. Patients may choose to perform their bowel program in conjunction with bathing, completing cleanup in the shower.

Performing the Bowel Program on Toilet or Commode

The decision to perform the bowel program on the toilet or commode chair is often based on the ease with which cleanup can be achieved. Performing a bowel program in the upright position may require specialized handles on devices that will extend the reach and provide the appropriate mechanical advantages. Whether or not further modification to the handles is required will be determined by the degree of balance in forward and lateral flexion and available arm placement. In most cases, commercially available equipment will be adequate. The presence of triceps and wrist flexor function makes this procedure easier. The patient with a C6 injury may have difficulty performing the program on toilet or commode because of mechanical disadvantages, lack of wrist flexors, and poor trunk stability. If an individual's transfer skills are adequate and he prefers to insert his suppository and allow it to activate in the side-lying position, he may do so and then transfer to the toilet or commode for digital stimulation, elimination, and cleanup. This technique is frequently used by persons who achieve better results from suppositories when lying down. Again, plastic-lined towels should be placed to prevent soilage. Once the transfer is made to the toilet or commode/shower chair, additional straps may be necessary to increase stability. Webbing straps with Velcro closures may be added to the grab bars on the toilet or the upright supports of the commode/shower chair. Skin tolerance for an adequate amount of sitting time on the toilet or commode to complete the program must be determined. Pressure distribution on either is far from ideal.

Cleanup on the toilet or commode/shower chair is performed with toilet tissue, or disposable towels and moist towelettes if tissue is difficult to manage. Further cleanup may be performed in the shower after the bowel movement (unit 12).

Independent management is difficult both physically and psychosocially. Ultimately, patients must decide on the degree to which they desire to be involved in their bowel program.

SUMMARY CHART: Bladder and Bowel Management

Goal	*Indicator*	*Equipment*
Drainage Bag Emptying		
1. Independent with equipment	1. C1-C5 injury 2. Limited assisted to no arm placement 3. No hand function 4. No trunk stability	1. Pneumatic or electric leg bag clamp 2. Floor drain or litter box for drainage
	1. C5-C7 injury 2. Limited assisted to normal arm placement 3. Tenodesis to no hand function 4. Limited trunk stability	1. Adapted catheter clamp 2. Mounted, stabilized catheter clamp 3. Accessible urinal, toilet, or other drainage basin
2. Independent	1. C6 or lower injury 2. Tenodesis to normal hand function 3. Limited unassisted to normal arm placement 4. Limited trunk stability to full trunk control	1. No adapted equipment
Drainage Bag Management		
1. Independent with equipment	1. C6-C7 injury 2. Tenodesis hand function 3. Unassisted limited to normal arm placement 4. Limited trunk stability	1. Elastic, Velcro, or foam drainage bag straps with loop on ends 2. Zipper pull to attach straps to bag 3. WDFH or RIC tenodesis orthosis
2. Independent	1. C8 or lower injury 2. Normal arm placement 3. Limited natural to normal hand function 4. Trunk stability to full trunk control	No adapted equipment
Applying an External Catheter (Males)		
1. Independent with equipment	1. C6-C8 injury 2. Tenodesis to limited natural hand function 3. Unassisted limited to normal arm placement 4. Limited trunk stability to full trunk stability	1. Adapted posey 2. WDFH or RIC tenodesis orthosis
2. Independent	1. C8 or lower injury 2. Normal arm placement 3. Limited natural to normal hand function 4. Full trunk stability	No adapted equipment

SUMMARY CHART continued

Goal	*Indicator*	*Equipment*
Intermittent Catheterization		
1. Independent with equipment	1. C6-C8 injury 2. Unassisted limited to normal arm placement 3. Tenodesis to limited natural hand function 4. Limited to full trunk stability	1. Adapted scissors 2. WDFH, RIC tenodesis orthosis, or urethral catheter inserter 3. Leg separators 4. Mirror for females 5. Labia spreader for females
2. Independent	1. C8 or lower injury 2. Normal arm placement 3. Limited natural to normal hand function 4. Full trunk stability	No adapted equipment
Bowel Program		
1. Independent with equipment	1. C6-C8 injury 2. Unassisted limited to normal arm placement 3. Tenodesis to limited natural hand function 4. Limited to full trunk stability	1. Suppository inserter 2. Digital stimulator
2. Independent	1. C8 or lower injury 2. Normal arm placement 3. Limited natural to normal hand function 4. Full trunk stability	No adapted equipment

Appendix 11A
Forms

Rehabilitation Institute of Chicago
Occupational Therapy Department
Urinary Care and Bowel Management
Adaptive Equipment Checklist

Patient Name: ______________________ RIC #: ________ Age: _____ Diagnosis: __________

Orthosis:
__ Wrist Driven Flexor Hinge
__ RIC Tenodesis Orthosis
__ Short Opponens HO
__ Other

Catheter Equipment:
__ Adapted Posey
__ Quick-Clip Speed Cutter Scissors
__ Deluxe Lever Clamp
__ Adapted Deluxe Lever Clamp
__ E-Z Pull Drainage Valve
__ Flip Top Clamp
__ Durable Plastic Clamp
__ Screw Down Clamp
__ Velcro Drainage Bag Straps
__ Looped Drainage Bag Straps
__ Adapted Pants
__ Adapted Skin-Bond Can
__ Leg Spreader Bar
__ Labia Spreaders
__ Lubricant Tube Stabilizer
__ Adapted Mirror
__ Tongs
__ Adapted Sterilization Bottle
__ Adapted Syringe
__ Manual Pneumatic Clamp
__ Electric Leg Bag Emptier

Bowel Program Equipment:
__ Digital Stimulator
__ Suppository Inserter
__ Para Inspection Mirror
__ Adapted Mirror

REHABILITATION INSTITUTE OF CHICAGO
OCCUPATIONAL THERAPY DEPARTMENT
URINARY CARE MANAGEMENT
EVALUATION

Patient: ______________ RIC #: ________ Age: ______ Dx: ______________
Type of Orthosis if used: ______________ Therapist: ______________ Date: ______

KEY: 5—dependent
4—assistance
3—supervision
2—independent with equipment
1—independent

HAND FUNCTION

Left			Right	
Orthosis	No Orthosis		No Orthosis	Orthosis
		Cylindrical Grasp		
		Lateral Pinch		
		Palmar Pinch		

EXTERNAL CATHETER

Application of	Date	I.	Int.	DC
Open package				
Attach connector				
Insert leg bag				
Connect straps				
Attach tubing				
Attach clamp				
Place condom				
Fasten leg bag				

Comments

TOILETING

	Date	I.	Int.	DC
Commode use reg. or adapted				
Leg bag w/c/urinal				
Leg bag w/c/toilet				
Leg bag bed/urinal				
Suppository inserter				
Digital stimulation				

Comments

MISCELLANEOUS

	Date	I.	Int.	DC
Skin inspect.				
Sterilization				
Tampax				

Comments

MOBILITY

	Date	I.	Int.	DC
Bed Controls				
Roll Side to Side				
Sit Up in Bed				
Balance Long Sitting				
Maneuver in Bed				
Balance Short Sitting				
Return to Sit in W/C				

Comments

INSERTION OF URETHRAL CATHETER

	Date	I.	Int.	DC
Open kit				
Straighten catheter				
Open pkg. of swabs				
Open lubricant				
Open top chamber				
Deposit lubricant				
Prep. meatus				
Position top chamber				
Feed catheter				
Collect residual				

Comments

ORTHOTICS

	O	F	O	F	O	F
Splints						
Position pillows						
Spreader bar/straps						
Mirror						

Comments

Unit 12
Bathing

Robin Jones, COTA/L

Performance of all or part of one's bathing can make a considerable difference in the total amount of assistance required from family members or an attendant. The ability to participate in one's bathing routine at home is often dependent on having the necessary equipment and a properly adapted environment. It is frustrating to learn skills in the rehabilitation setting and be unable to perform these skills after discharge because of accessibility factors. Modifications may be required in the home to make the bathroom accessible. An early home visit is essential to assess bathroom facilities, make initial modification suggestions, and determine the most practical methods of bathing to teach the patient and family.

BATH EQUIPMENT

The following equipment can be used to perform the bathing program. Individual problem solving will be necessary to adapt any of these devices to meet patient needs.

- A W/C commode/shower chair is recommended for the individual who has a roll-in shower stall or whose bathroom doorways and turning radius are not adequate for the W/C. They are narrower than standard W/Cs in most cases and have a smaller turning radius for use in tight spaces. In addition, a W/C commode/shower chair may be more efficient and eliminate the need for transfer to toilet and again to shower. They can be purchased with push rims with or without projections for independent propulsion. Trunk supports or a chest strap may be added to provide more stability.
- Bath benches are available in a variety of styles and sizes. Those with a back support and side rail are recommended for the patient with poor trunk stability. Solid, slatted, or cut-out seats are available. Solid seats may provide more stability and ease during a transfer; however, they make cleansing of the perineal area and buttocks difficult. Slatted seats provide greater access to the perineum but can make placement of the hand for transferring more difficult. Cut-out seats cradle the buttocks, providing more stability. With a cut-out seat, access to the perineum and buttocks is easier; however, the transfer may be more difficult, especially if triceps function is absent. Chest straps may be added to any bench for safety.
- Grab bars may be necessary to provide a surface for support during transfers or when shifting positions to bathe all areas of the body. Placement of the bars is determined on an individual basis. They are often needed on the inside wall of the shower and on the wall where the faucets and shower head

Figure 12–1 Hand-held shower mounted for easy access, used in conjunction with long-handled sponge with adapted handle.

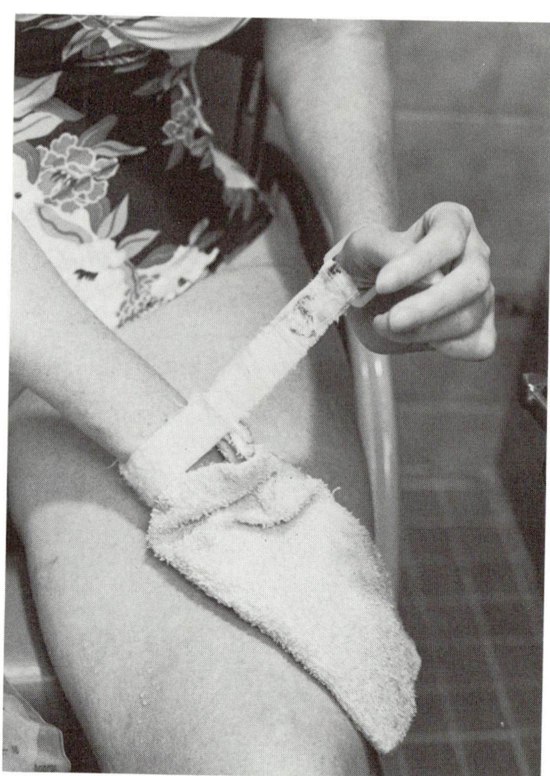

Figure 12–2 Wash mitt with Velcro D-ring adaptation.

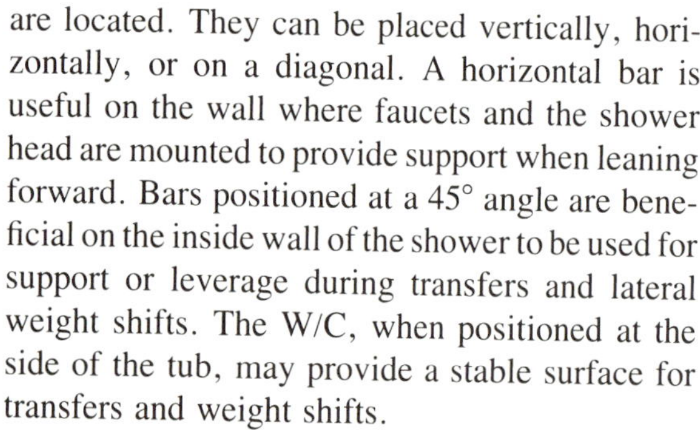

are located. They can be placed vertically, horizontally, or on a diagonal. A horizontal bar is useful on the wall where faucets and the shower head are mounted to provide support when leaning forward. Bars positioned at a 45° angle are beneficial on the inside wall of the shower to be used for support or leverage during transfers and lateral weight shifts. The W/C, when positioned at the side of the tub, may provide a stable surface for transfers and weight shifts.

- Hand-held showers allow the user control over the direction of water flow. Lightweight models with plastic or plastic-coated hose are preferable. Mounting should be in close proximity to the user (Figure 12–1). If the shower is to be used by other family members as well, a second mount may be added at a height that accommodates their needs. Handling the shower head with limited hand function may require handle adaptations; low- or high-temperature plastic handles may be added. Ease of application and removal is the main consideration when designing a handle adaptation, as it must be picked up and put down several times during bathing. It is important to keep in mind that once objects are wet and soapy they become slippery and hard to handle. Commercially available phone holders that attach with Velcro can be used. These are easily applied and removed and may be further adapted by attaching a Velcro strap to provide a more secure hold.
- Washcloths or wash mitts are used for washing. A washcloth can be draped over the hand or the thumb can be inserted into the label loop, if necessary. A wash mitt with a Velcro closure or elastic edge may be used (Figure 12–2). Wash mitts are commercially available or may be fabricated by sewing two washcloths together. Lightweight terrycloth or thin washcloths are used for easier handling.
- A long-handled bath sponge or brush that is angled to accommodate the curves of the body can be used to reach the upper and lower back and LEs. Cotton webbing straps may be added with a D-ring closure to the handle (Figure 12–1). Plastic handles may be heated to change the angle of the brush or sponge. The Magic Soaper Brush eliminates the

Figure 12–3 Squeeze bottle shampoo for use with limited hand function (C7).

need to handle soap, as the soap is stored inside the sponge. Back scrubber sponges with loops at either end are commercially available or can be fabricated from a towel or piece of terrycloth with thumb or wrist loops on either end to wash and dry the back. They are used by hooking or grasping both ends of the strap and brushing it across the back in a diagonal or horizontal direction.

- Soap can be suspended from a rope worn around the neck. Such soap may be purchased or a large bar of soap can be drilled and a nylon or cotton rope threaded through. Liquid soap is also an option. Pump-type dispensers are commercially available. Shampoo in a squeeze bottle is easy to use and reduces spillage (Figure 12–3). Gel or creme shampoos are easier to manage with decreased hand function. Commercially available body soap and shampoo dispensers that can be mounted on the tub or shower wall may also be used. They require minimal hand function and eliminate the possibility of dropping a bar or bottle of soap.
- Finger ring brushes can be used to apply pressure for scrubbing the scalp during shampooing. The brush has stiff plastic bristles and a plastic ring that can be worn on the index or middle finger.
- Octopus soap holders can be placed on the wall of the shower or bathtub to hold a bar of soap within easy reach to stabilize the soap while soaping the washcloth or mitt.
- Towels adapted with loops on the ends can be used in drying.

BATHING UPPER EXTREMITIES

Bathing upper extremities may be performed in the W/C or on a bath bench or commode/shower chair. This is a task that can be performed to some degree by patients with C5 or lower injury. The degree of participation depends on trunk stability and active arm placement. Reach to both shoulders and crossing the midline is necessary for UE bathing. Wrist stability and hand function are not necessary but make performance easier. A washcloth or wash mitt is recommended; however, some patients prefer to hold the bar of soap with natural tenodesis and use the palm of their hand for bathing (Figure 12–4).

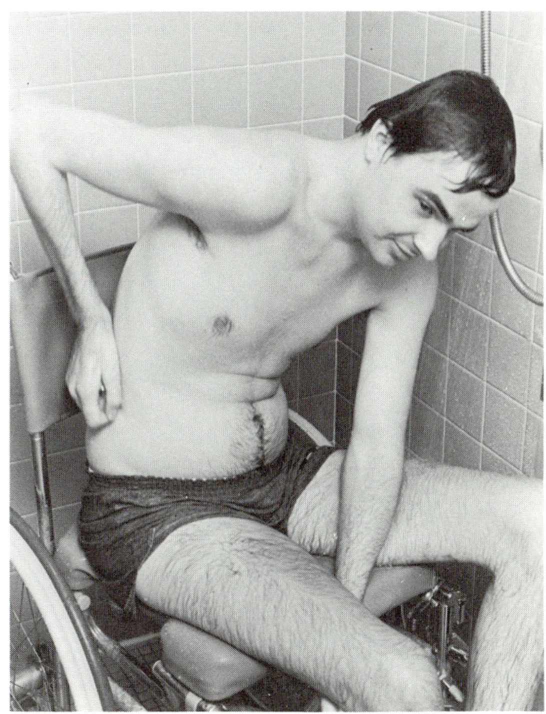

Figure 12–4 Holding soap with tenodesis to wash body.

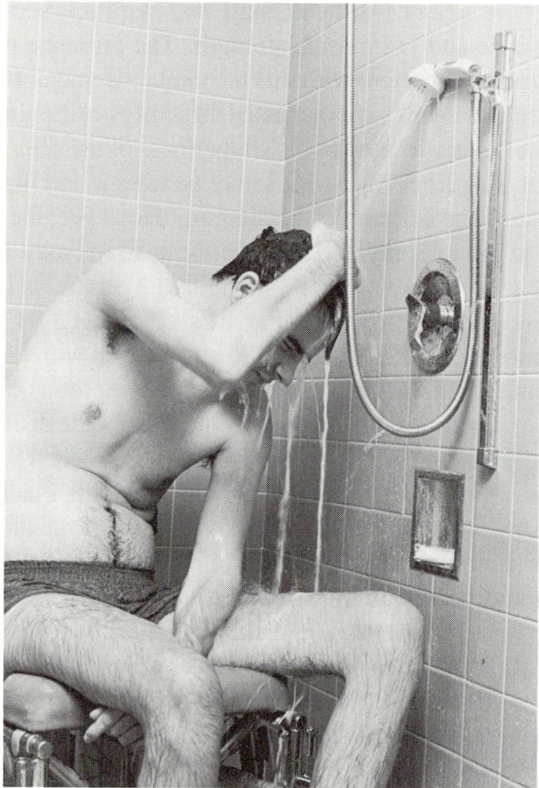

Figure 12–10 Shower nozzle placed in holder to allow use of one UE to stabilize and one to shampoo.

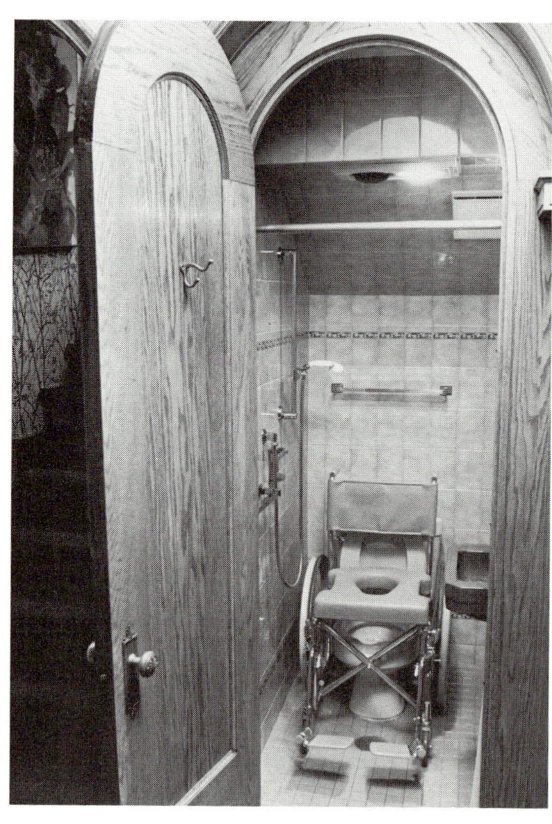

Figure 12–11 Bathroom modified to allow access to the toilet, shower, and sink from the same position.

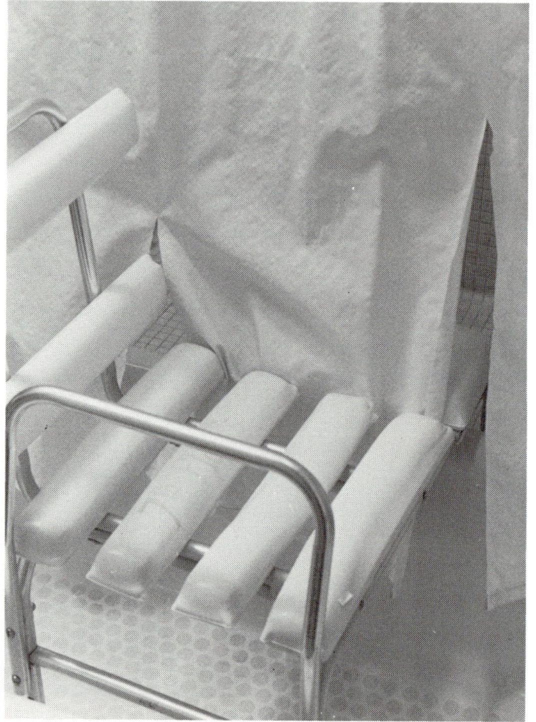

Figure 12–12 Shower curtain liner adapted to remain inside the tub.

HAIR WASHING

Hair washing is often combined with the bathing process. Arm placement to the top and back of the head is necessary for hair washing. The absence of triceps function makes this task difficult to perform; however, substitution by the external rotators and shoulder flexors may allow the patient with weak UEs to reach the top and side of his head (Figure 12–10). Leaning forward and washing the hair while the chest is on the knees is another option.

One of the main difficulties in hair washing with minimal hand function is the inability to apply adequate pressure for scrubbing the scalp. Finger ring brushes or the heel of the hand may be used to provide adequate friction. Rinsing is easily accomplished with the hand-held shower or by placing the head under the stream of water while the shower head is positioned on the wall mount (Figure 12–10). (For washing the hair at the sink see unit 8.)

BED BATHING

When accessible bathing facilities are not available, the patient will have to bathe in bed. Arm placement, trunk stability, and mobility in bed are factors in performance. A basin of water, a wash mitt or cloth, a long-handled sponge, and towels are needed. The ability to assume and maintain long sitting is necessary in addition to the ability to roll side to side. The LEs may be reached by flexing the hip and knee toward the trunk.

For the dependent individual the task of bathing is performed by the care giver. If the home environment is not accessible, bed baths or a portable bathtub are recommended. Commercially available inflatable bathtubs are often used for this level of dependence. They may be used in the bed, thus eliminating transfers, and are portable for travel; however, their use is time-consuming.

BATHROOM MODIFICATIONS

Bathroom modifications to enhance independence include widening doorways to allow the W/C or commode/shower chair to be moved inside, remodeling the bathroom to enlarge it, altering the placement of fixtures, and installing new fixtures. If the W/C is too wide to be maneuvered into the bathroom, a commode/shower chair is recommended. Bathroom fixtures may have to be moved to allow for easy access or to provide extra leg room and access to controls. A new bathroom or replacement of current fixtures may be indicated to provide a sink at an accessible height, a toilet easily accessed for transfers or with enough clearance on either side for a commode/shower chair, and a roll-in shower stall (Figure 12–11). If a bathtub is to be used, installation of a hand-held shower is usually recommended. Sliding doors on a bathtub and shower combination system have to be replaced with a shower curtain and liner to allow for use of a bath bench with extended seat for transfers. The shower curtain liner is slit to fit through the bench inside the tub, while the outer curtain goes outside the bench (Figure 12–12).

SUMMARY

Bathing is an important aspect of ADL, and self-performance of bathing can be a major factor in achieving independence. It frequently requires attendant care because of accessibility and equipment requirements. Given accessible facilities and proper equipment, SCI patients with C6 or lower function can perform this task independently. Accommodating for less than optimal accessibility often means multiple transfers, resulting in excessive time requirements or dependence. A home visit and evaluation of bathroom accessibility and fixtures are invaluable. The occupational therapist must know about equipment alternatives to make the most economical and appropriate recommendations possible.

SUMMARY CHART: Bathing

Goal	*Indicator*	*Recommended Intervention*
1. Independent with setup and equipment in UE and trunk bathing and drying	1. C5-C6 injury 2. Tenodesis hand function or no hand function 3. Limited unassisted arm placement 4. Limited trunk stability 5. Dependent to assisted in transfers	1. Adapted sponge 2. Hand-held shower with adapted handle 3. Soap on a rope or push-button soap dispenser 4. Towel adapted with loops 5. Wash mitt 6. Commode/shower chair
2. Independent with equipment in UE, trunk, and LE bathing and drying	1. C6-C8 injury 2. Tenodesis to limited natural hand function 3. Limited unassisted to normal arm placement 4. Limited to full trunk stability 5. Independent in transfers	1. Adapted sponge 2. Hand-held shower with adapted handle 3. Adapted soap dispenser 4. Towel adapted with loops 5. Wash mitt (optional) 6. Commode/shower chair or bath bench
3. Independent in UE, trunk, and LE bathing and drying	1. T1 or lower injury 2. Limited natural to normal hand function 3. Normal arm placement 4. Full trunk stability to full trunk control 5. Independent in transfers to bath bench or tub bottom	None (bath bench may still be used)

Unit 13
Leisure Skills

Kim Hurd, OTR/L

Helping SCI patients to become involved in leisure pursuits is an interdisciplinary team effort at RIC. Although therapeutic recreational specialists are responsible for focusing exclusively on leisure participation, their efforts are supported by the rest of the rehabilitation team. The practice of OT includes the use of leisure activities as well as other activity media for remediation and adjustment to physical and psychological trauma. OT's role in leisure activities, within the context of team, is to contribute to treatment by providing equipment, experience, opportunity, skills, and encouragement. Leisure participation is seen as a goal for a well-integrated life-style as well as a ladder to other physical and psychological goals.

Negative psychosocial effects of SCI may arise from separation from past life tasks. Among these tasks are leisure pursuits. It is not uncommon for the patient to withdraw from social involvement. If social deprivation persists, problems with motivation may arise and further hinder reintegration into the community. The process of introducing leisure activities to facilitate social reintegration follows a basic sequence:

1. Explore ways of participating in former leisure interests in individual treatment.
2. Introduce the patient to new leisure interests in individual treatment.
3. Provide group activities to explore and practice leisure interests.
4. Vary settings.
5. Involve families.

The occupational therapist exposes patients to leisure and community activities individually or in a group setting. This exposure builds the patient's confidence and encourages interest in additional activities. As the patient and family learn more about their options, they may be more inclined to independently pursue leisure skills (Figure 13–1). The diagram depicts the process for building a patient's confidence by utilizing successful and unsuccessful experiences. As the therapist processes both situations with the patient in a safe, supportive environment, the patient will be more willing to initiate future involvement and eventually carry these skills over to the home setting.

LEISURE ASSESSMENT

The SCI patient may begin to experience leisure activities through the occupational therapist's incorporation of basic avocational activities and gross and fine motor skill games into treatment. The patient should complete an interest checklist early during hospitaliza-

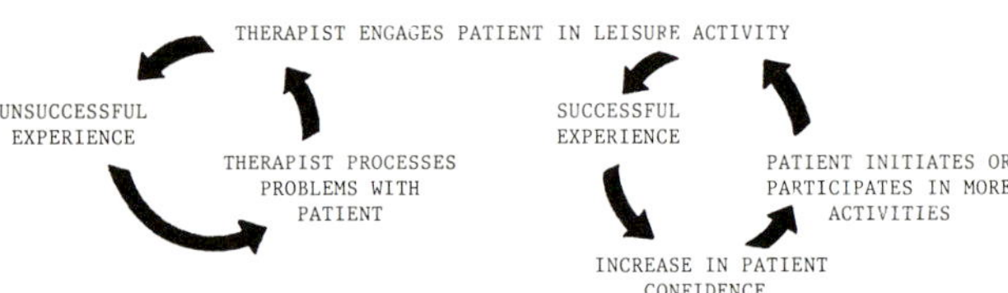

Figure 13–1 Process for building a patient's confidence in leisure activities.

tion. This provides the therapist with information about previous leisure involvement and life-style and potential new interests. This information can also be obtained from family and friends. Going over the completed checklist with the patient can be a good way to get to know the patient and to build rapport. The patient should be provided with the opportunity to attempt former leisure activities and should also be exposed to new activities. When premorbid activities are difficult and frustrating to perform, special equipment or an alteration in the extent of participation may be necessary. It is at this point that new activities may be emphasized.

EXPLORING NEW SKILLS

As functional skills are acquired they can be incorporated into leisure activities. In this way, motor skills are reinforced and self-confidence is built. The focus is not only on the outcome of leisure participation but on the process involved in getting there. Examples of ADL skills include writing, typing, using a tape recorder, and feeding; the leisure activity counterparts of these skills are doing crossword puzzles (Figure 13–2), typing letters, playing music, and eating at a restaurant, respectively.

EQUIPMENT

A primary role of the occupational therapist in working with the SCI patient to develop leisure skills is to provide adaptive equipment and social interaction for successful participation in leisure activities. As definitive equipment such as mouthsticks, BFOs, and WHOs are issued for ADL tasks, additional attachments and adaptive devices can be added to develop leisure skills.

Equipment specific to certain leisure skills may also be needed. For example, although a C6 quadriplegic patient has tenodesis hand function, he may lack the fine motor control that is needed to perform an activity such as photography. The occupational therapist can assist the patient in determining an alternative method, such as a lever system or mouth control system (Figure 13–3).

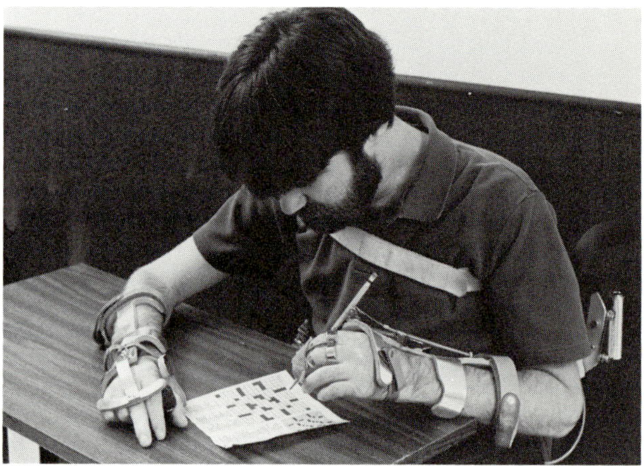

Figure 13–2 Patient (C5) using writing skill to enjoy a crossword puzzle.

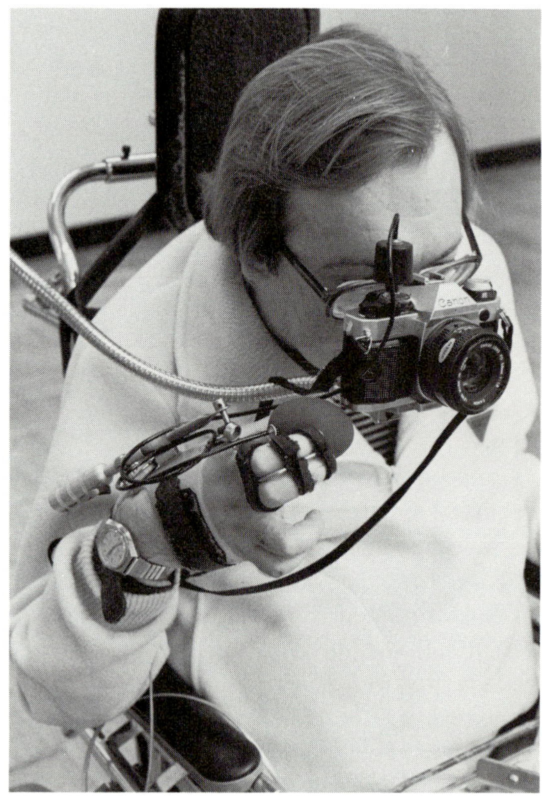

Figure 13–3 Patient (C4) using camera setup with pneumatic control switch.

INDOOR ACTIVITIES

After discharge, persons with SCI may spend various amounts of time indoors depending on their home situation and available resources. It is important to develop leisure skills for the home setting. Many OT activities done individually or in groups can be done at home. The social interaction associated with these activities is an important component of leisure. Involving family and friends in these activities while the patient is still hospitalized can facilitate carry-over after discharge. Such interaction can also strengthen or reestablish relationships.

There are many indoor leisure activities in which a person with SCI may participate. Examples include

- cards
- checkers
- chess
- Connect 4
- horseshoes (rubber)
- Simon
- Yahtzee
- pool
- word games
- shuffleboard
- Ping-Pong
- Battleship
- Score 4
- Trivial Pursuit
- puzzles
- video games

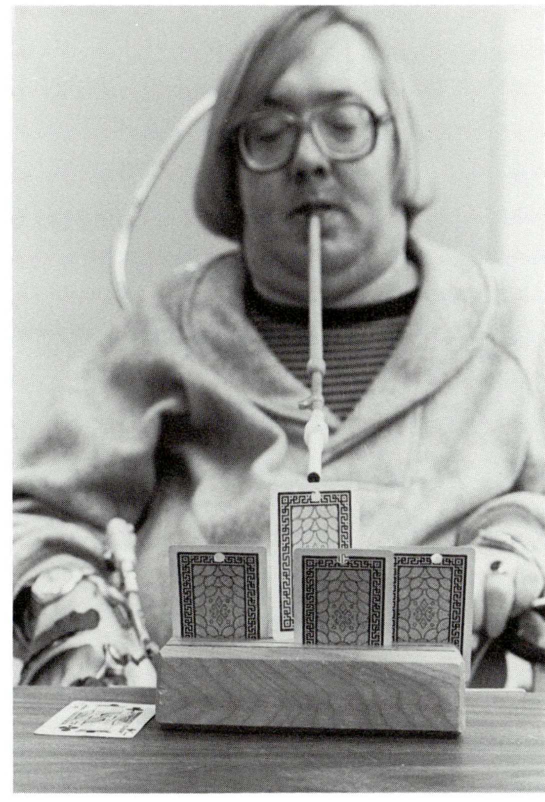

Figure 13–4 Patient (C4) playing cards using a mouthstick.

The patient with C4 function can be involved in tabletop games such as cards, checkers, chess, Yahtzee, and word games through the use of a mouthstick with pencil attachment for keeping score or writing words and a page-turning attachment for moving checkers or chess pieces. Cards can be picked up from a card holder by using a bird beak mouthstick, pincer mouthstick, or modular mouthstick system with a stickpin to insert through holes punched in the cards (Figure 13–4). Dice for Yahtzee or other dice games are "thrown" by using a mouthstick to tip over an adapted dice roller. Video games are accessed through a pneumatic sip and puff control or a chin control.

The patient with C5 function frequently uses BFOs during indoor activities for increasing UE function or endurance. Long opponens WHOs with a utensil slot and a vertical holder with a pencil are used to move game pieces, keep score, or write words (Figure 13–5). The pencil can also be used to slide game pieces on the board or to tip over an adapted dice roller. Card playing may be done by inserting a stickpin in the eraser of a pencil and placing the pencil in a vertical holder. With holes punched in the cards and a card holder, the pin is used to move the cards. An electric, cable-driven, or ratchet orthosis can also be used to pick up cards and game pieces. Video games may be accessed by adding a large knob with a Velcro strap to the joystick.

Figure 13–5 Patient (C5) playing backgammon using long opponens WHO.

Figure 13–6 Patient (C6) playing Connect 4 using WDFH.

Figure 13–7 Patient (C6) using adapted pool cue holder.

Patients with C6 to C7 function use natural tenodesis, RIC tenodesis orthoses, short opponens HOs, or WDFH orthoses to participate in indoor activities. These methods are used to manipulate cards in card holders or to move small game pieces in checkers, backgammon, Connect 4, Othello, and chess (Figure 13–6). Writing splints are used to keep score or write words in word games. A tenodesis pinch allows dice rolling without equipment. Participation in gross motor games such as pool, Ping-Pong, or horseshoes is possible by using adapted Velcro straps or handles to achieve a grasp or wrist extension to stabilize objects such as a pool cue or horseshoe (Figure 13–7). Video games are adapted with a large knob or Velcro strap for ease in participation.

Paraplegic patients are able to perform indoor activities from W/C level or from a standing position with braces.

OUTDOOR ACTIVITIES

As the range of outdoor activities performed by SCI patients has expanded, occupational therapists have collaborated with other team members to improve patients' success by problem solving and providing needed equipment. For example, in boating, if manual skills impede participation, a safety strap or hand adaptation may be fabricated to facilitate a more independent experience. Outdoor activities in which OT intervention may be necessary include boating, fishing, picnics, tennis, and Frisbee.

A person with any level SCI can enjoy participating in the social aspects of outdoor activities, such as picnics or barbecues.

Patients with C5 quadriplegia can use BFOs and feeding equipment to participate in picnics and barbeques. Sandwich holders are helpful for many foods, especially when a table is not available outdoors. For boating, a chest strap must be added for balance and Velcro hand straps must be added to the paddles to provide a grasp for rowing (Figures 13–8 and 13–9).

Patients with C6 to C7 SCI can help to prepare food at picnics and barbecues. Long-handled spatulas adapted with handles and Velcro straps or used with tenodesis orthoses aid in cooking on a grill. Patients interested in boating require the same chest strap and hand strap adaptation as mentioned for C5 SCI. If the person is interested in tennis, Velcro and plastic handle adaptations on the racket (Figures 13–10 and 13–11) and a sports chair may enable participation.

Paraplegic patients participate in many outdoor activities from the W/C level without adaptive equipment. Specific outdoor leisure resources are listed in Appendix C.

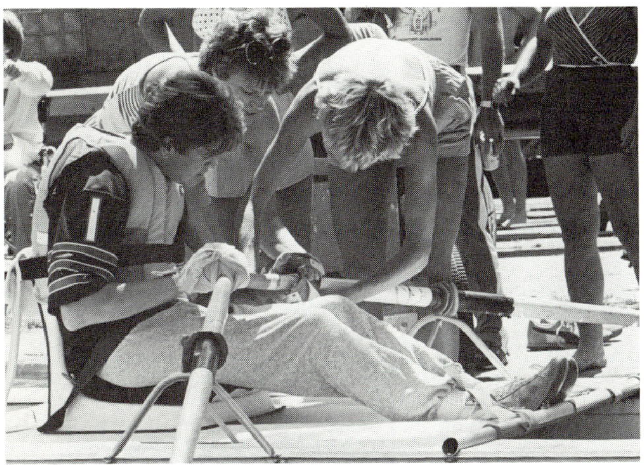

Figures 13–8 and 13–9 Patient (C6) rowing a boat using paddle adaptations fabricated in OT.

Figure 13–9

Figures 13–10 and 13–11 Patient (C6) using tennis racket adapted in OT.

Figure 13–11

CRAFTS AND HOBBIES

As premorbid and new activities are investigated, crafts and hobbies may be considered. Exploring this area of leisure may broaden the sense of accomplishment and increase the abilities of SCI patients. Craft hobbies that OT may incorporate into treatment include the following:

- woodworking
- painting
- music
- decoupage
- string art
- drawing
- weaving
- wood burning
- ceramics
- needlework
- tile trivet
- copper tooling
- leather work

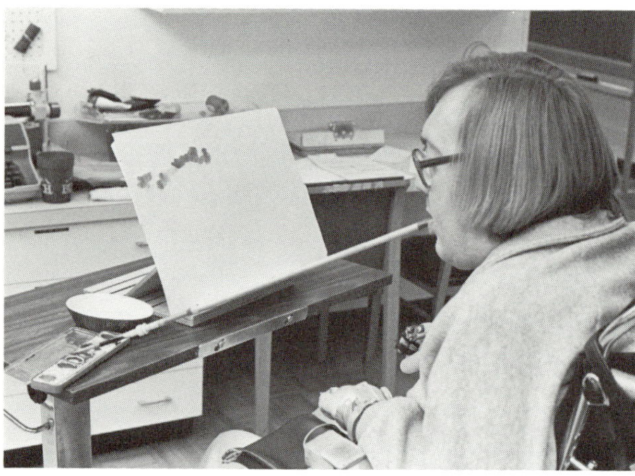

Figure 13–12 Patient (C4) using a mouthstick to paint.

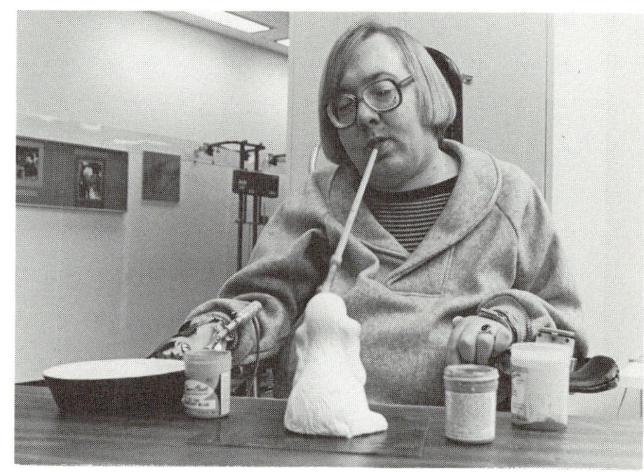

Figure 13–13 Patient (C4) doing ceramic glazing with a mouthstick.

The C4 patient may participate in craft activities by using a mouthstick with various tips. Paintbrush tips are used to paint, glaze ceramic greenware, stain, and varnish, and in decoupage. Different pencils, pens, or chalk tips are used for drawing. A bookrest or Dycem may be used to stabilize the objects (Figures 13–12 and 13–13).

Patients with C5 injury often use BFOs and paintbrushes in vertical holders to paint, stain, varnish, decoupage, or glaze ceramic greenware. A variety of pencils, pens, or chalks can be inserted into the vertical holder for drawing, or an adjustable writing orthosis can be used. An electric, ratchet, or cable-driven flexor hinge orthosis allows for ease in changing pens, pencils, and chalks throughout a project (Figure 13–14).

Figure 13–14 Patient (C5) decoupaging a plaque using his cable-driven flexor hinge orthosis.

Patients with C6 to C7 injury may use natural tenodesis, RIC tenodesis or WDFH orthoses, or short opponens HOs to participate in crafts and hobby activities. Paintbrushes can be built up with foam or placed in vertical holders to paint, stain, varnish, decoupage, glaze ceramic greenware, or apply grout to a tile project. Built-up foam on a wood-burning tool allows for a better grasp during this activity. The tenodesis pinch is used for tile trivets and macrame projects.

Paraplegics participate in many crafts and hobby projects from the W/C level, or the standing level with braces, without adaptive equipment.

COMMUNITY ACTIVITIES

A wide range of recreational, entertainment, and socialization activities take place outside the home. The community, however, presents many barriers to the W/C-bound person, such as curbs, doors, stairs, restrooms, and transportation. Personal issues such as bowel and bladder management, medications, and sitting tolerance also need to be managed.

Community leisure experiences that may be introduced during hospitalization by the rehabilitation team include the following:

- travel
- restaurants
- movies
- concerts
- libraries
- bowling
- shopping
- public transportation
- sports events
- church or synagogue
- health clubs
- museums

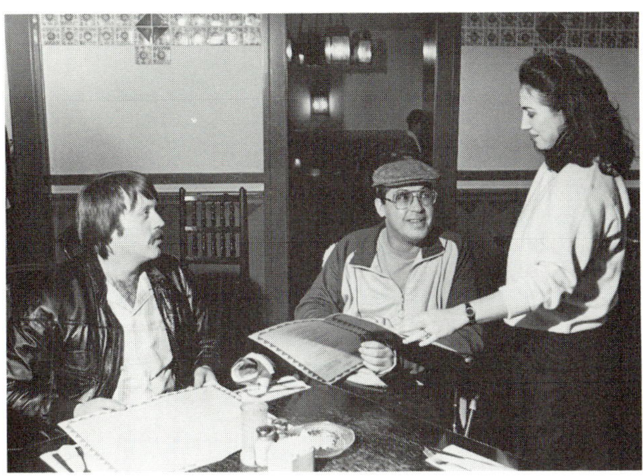

Figure 13–15 Patient (C5) enjoying a meal at a restaurant.

Figure 13–16 Patient (C6) shopping.

At the C4 to C5 level, patients must direct their care and make their needs known to others during community activities. A back pack can be used to transport equipment needed for use in the community. C5 quadriplegics are encouraged to direct their feeding equipment setup in restaurants (Figure 13–15).

The C6 to C7 patient may attend to mobility, bowel and bladder, feeding, money management, and pressure relief needs with little assistance (Figure 13–16).

Paraplegic patients are frequently independent in the community once training has been provided (Figure 13–17).

Figure 13–17 Paraplegic patient exercising at a health club.

Unit 14

Home Management

Robin Jones, COTA/L

The ability to participate in or be independent in meal preparation and other home management skills is an important goal for the SCI patient who intends to return to the role of homemaker. Preparing a beverage or simple meal on one's own can give the individual much-needed privacy. Modifications to the home environment can increase safety and independence in the performance of these tasks. The modifications may involve rearrangement of appliances to increase their accessibility or the purchase of new appliances that better suit the patient's needs.

MEAL PREPARATION

Meal preparation can be as basic as pouring a cold beverage and assembling a sandwich or as complicated as cooking a gourmet meal. The degree of participation in meal preparation varies with the individual's physical abilities, previous roles, and planned roles.

Physical Requirements

Independence is a realistic goal for patients with C6 or lower function. The C5 patient may be able to participate in simple meal preparation with a cable-driven or electrically driven orthosis. Ninety degrees of shoulder flexion and abduction, good biceps strength for adequate arm placement, and tenodesis hand function are minimum requirements for functional performance. A functional orthosis such as a WDFH may be indicated to assist with resistive activities or those requiring fine motor skills. Independence in W/C mobility, either manual or electric, is necessary to allow for maneuvering in the kitchen.

Major Appliances

In most cases it is financially unfeasible to replace major kitchen appliances and work areas with those that are W/C-accessible. Electric appliances can reduce effort and simplify procedures.

Stove-top burners are difficult to use because of their height and problems associated with positioning the W/C correctly in front or to the side of the stove. If they are used, a mirror is placed at an angle above the stove top to enable the individual to see the food as it is being cooked. New Vision, or other transparent cookware, can be used to view what is cooking. These pans tend to be heavier than those made of aluminum or stainless steel, so ability to maneuver them should be evaluated. Individuals with limited arm placement often find it difficult and unsafe to cook at the stove. A hot plate may be used in place of a conventional stove because it is portable and can be positioned at a more convenient height. Hot plates with more than one burner can be

Figure 14–1 Hot plates provide an accessible alternative to standard stove tops.

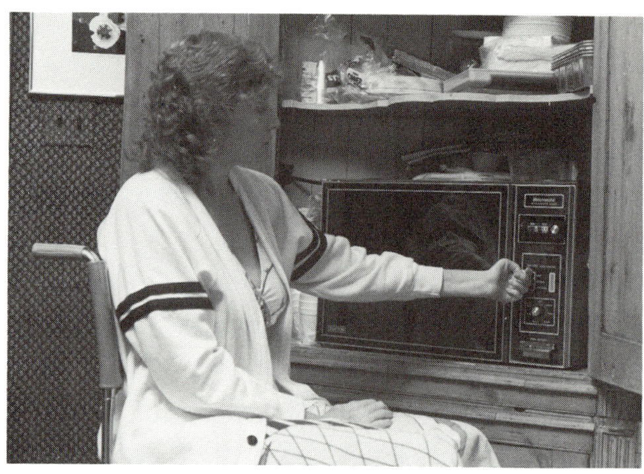

Figure 14–2 Microwave controls are evaluated before purchase. Proper height is important.

used for preparing more than one item at a time (Figure 14–1).

Electric fry pans or griddles can be operated with limited arm placement and hand function. The controls can be operated by the heel of the hand, thumb, or with an HO.

Ovens can be difficult to use because of the weight and spring action of the door as well as the problems associated with positioning the W/C to allow safe access. A toaster oven, broiler, or portable convection oven is recommended. In most cases, the door of a toaster oven is operated by lever action and the controls are easily operated with the thumb or the heel of the hand.

Microwave ovens are recommended for persons with limited hand function for use in preparing meals or heating food. They can be placed at an accessible height and require minimal effort. The door is often controlled by a button or lever and can be operated with the thumb or the heel of the hand. Wrist loops can also be attached to the door handle for easier opening. Light-touch, electronically controlled models are recommended (Figure 14–2). Microwave dishes do not get as hot as dishes used in a conventional oven but still require safety precautions in handling.

Reaching items in the refrigerator or freezer is often difficult for quadriplegics. A problem common to those with limited hand function is the inability to grasp the door handle. A wrist strap attached to the door handle may eliminate this problem (Figure 14–3). Positioning the W/C at the proper angle to allow for clearance of the doors can also be difficult. Positioning is determined by the location of the refrigerator in relation to other appliances and walls in the kitchen. If the patient can independently reverse his W/C, then he may be able to hook his arm in a wrist strap and wheel backward to open the door (Figure 14–4). An alternative method is to back up to the refrigerator, attach a strap onto the push handle of the W/C, and wheel forward. If ade-

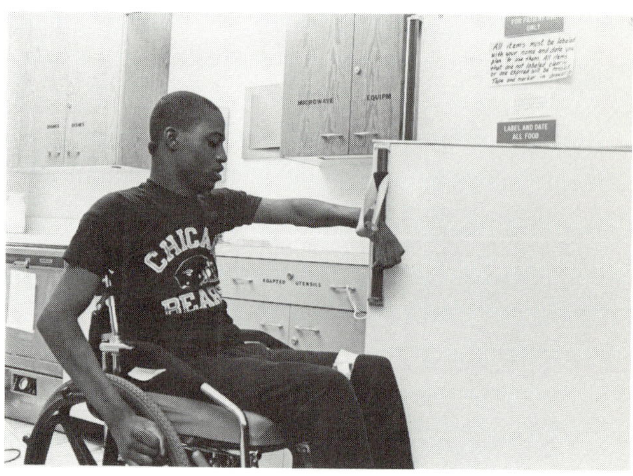

Figure 14–3 Wrist straps can be used on appliance and cabinet doors to assist with opening.

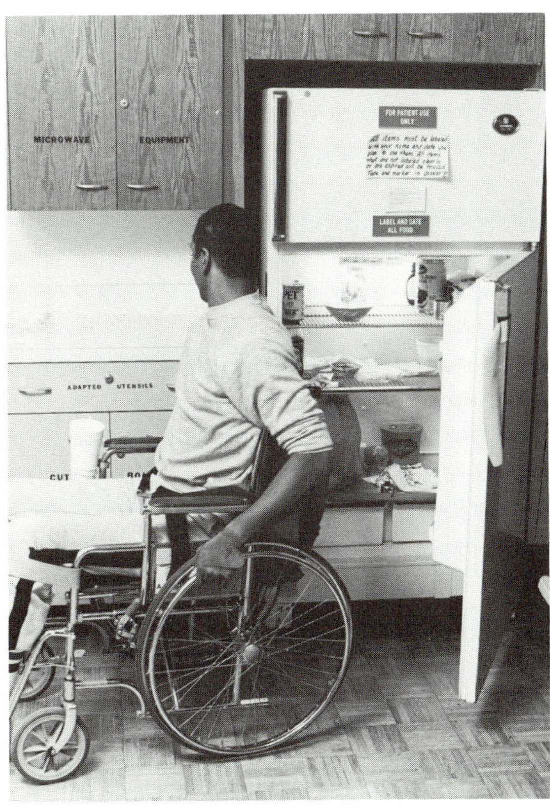

Figure 14–4 Backing into the refrigerator.

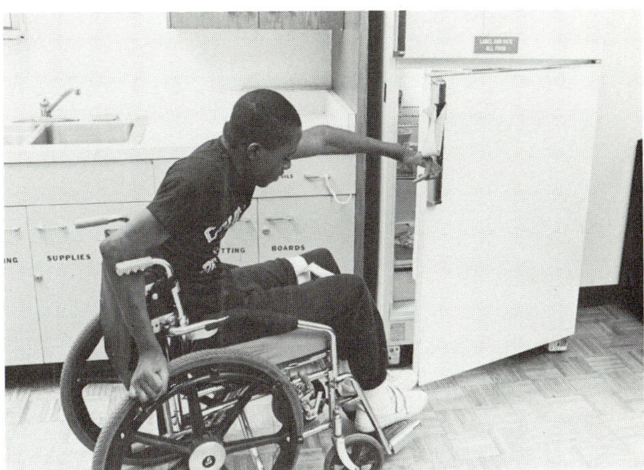

Figure 14–5 The left UE is used to pull the refrigerator door open and the right to maneuver the chair to block the door.

quate trunk stability is available, the individual may be able to position the W/C approximately 1 foot from the door of the refrigerator. While leaning forward, he hooks one extremity behind the push handle and the other to the wrist strap attached to the door. By pulling himself upright, he can open the door slightly. The W/C is maneuvered to block the door from closing and he then positions himself to open the door fully (Figure 14–5).

Reaching the freezer compartment is often difficult due to its location. If the patient has an option, it is recommended that a side-by-side refrigerator/freezer be purchased or a unit with the freezer compartment located on the bottom. As with the refrigerator, a wrist strap may be used to open the door. Automatic ice makers are also recommended, as well as units with ice and water dispensers located in the door. These features allow for independent access to fluid and ice.

Countertop Appliances and Work Area

The establishment of a work area in the kitchen that is the correct height and has sufficient space to accommodate necessary equipment is recommended. Many patients will find countertop appliances beneficial because they require less energy to operate. The work surface should be organized so that the most commonly used appliances and utensils are within easy reach.

Many of the appliances and utensils commercially available require modifications to the handles, switches, or levers to make them easier to use. Low-temperature plastics may be used to fabricate adaptations; however, the primary function of the device must be kept in mind. Low-temperature plastics melt under moderate heat, so they are not practical for adapting devices that need to be placed in the oven, used on or near the range, or cleaned in the dishwasher. High-temperature plastics that are more heat-resistant may be more practical in these instances. Metal rivets or screws must be considered carefully because they conduct heat, posing a danger for patients with impaired temperature sensitivity.

Electric can openers that are hand-held or stationary are recommended. Commercially available "one-handed" can openers with an adjustable stand to support the can are difficult for the quadriplegic to adjust, but with practice may be used effectively. If trunk stability is adequate, both UEs may be used to work a

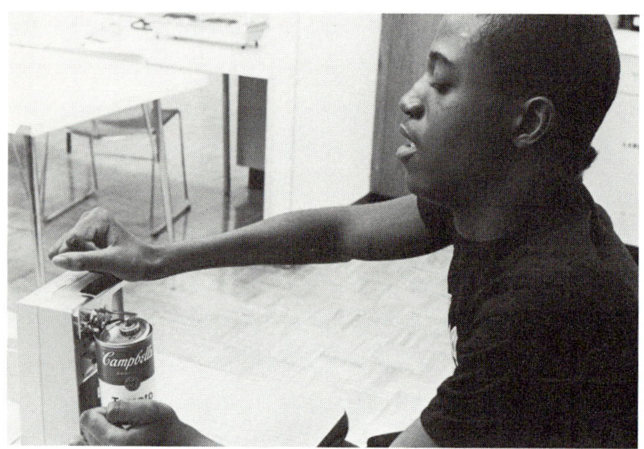

Figure 14–6 Both UEs and tenodesis hand function operate a standard electric can opener.

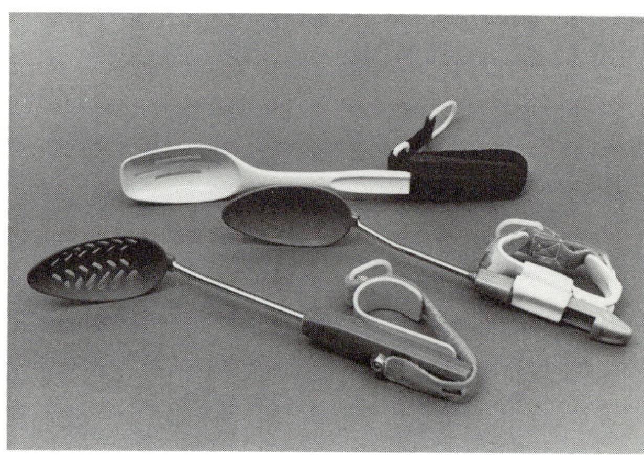

Figure 14–7 Spoons modified with orthoplast handles or inserted into utensil cuff.

standard electric can opener. The can is placed in the palm of one hand and supported against the cutting blade, while the other hand operates the switch (Figure 14–6). A WDFH orthosis may be used to hold the can against the cutting blade.

A blender or electric mixer can conserve energy while stirring and mixing. The controls on the blender should be light-touch or adapted with extended levers to allow for easier operation. Plastic blender tops are preferred over glass because they are nonbreakable and lightweight. An upright mixer with a stand is recommended. A portable electric mixer can be used if the handle is adapted with a cuff. The controls on the mixers vary, but in most instances can be operated with the heel of the hand or the thumb or by using an eraser tip in a utensil cuff. An orthosis may be used for grasping and holding the mixer itself.

Adapted Kitchen Equipment

If a blender or mixer is not available, stirring will have to be done by hand. Stirring thick batters or liquids may pose a problem for patients with limited hand function. Utensils may be adapted with cuffs or phone holders; however, the circular motion required makes it difficult to keep the hand in place and the wrist stabilized (Figure 14–7). The use of a utensil cuff with the hand in a neutral position is recommended. The spoon is inserted into the cuff on the ulnar border. Utensil handles may be cut or trimmed to fit into the utensil cuff, or a cuff can be fabricated to accommodate the handle. A built-up handle may be sufficient for those with minimal hand dysfunction.

Cutting can be performed by most individuals with C6 or lower injury. Most prefer to cut with their dominant extremity, using the nondominant extremity as a stabilizer. The angle of the knife is best determined by trial and error. Each patient will have a preference based on how much pressure he can apply and his own comfort with the task. Commercially available "quad" knives operate on a rocking principal; however, most patients prefer a sharper blade. Serrated utility knives are often recommended. These blades are sharp enough to cut meat and vegetables, yet are not as bulky as large kitchen knives. Knives or adapted scissors can be used to open boxes, bags, and packages.

A design commonly used for adapting these knives requires low- or high-temperature plastic, Velcro, D-rings, and strong glue. A cuff is fabricated that supports the palmar arch and wraps around the web space. It is left open on the ulnar side for ease in donning and doffing. The knife is placed with the blade down and projecting horizontally from the thumb. An additional piece of low-temperature plastic secures the knife to the cuff, and strong adhesives can further stabilize it. The handle of the knife should protrude far enough so that the thumb can rest on the top of the handle and away from the blade. A guard to provide additional protection may be fabricated at the point where the blade and handle join (Figure 14–8). A Velcro closure with a D-ring component is the most efficient way to secure the cuff to the hand as well as allow for independent donning and doffing. The same

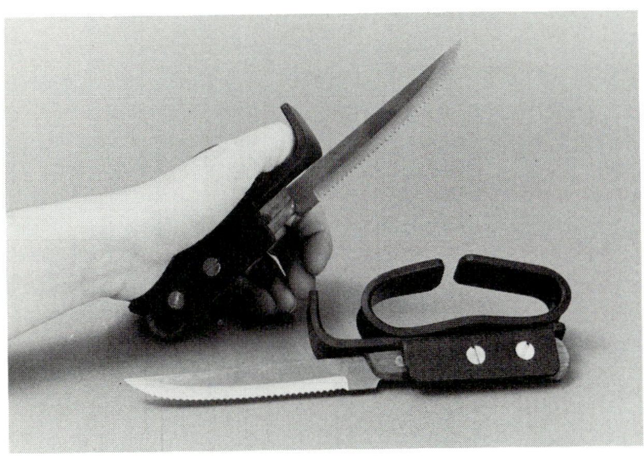

Figure 14–8 Kydex handles on serrated knives. The design keeps fingers behind the cutting edge.

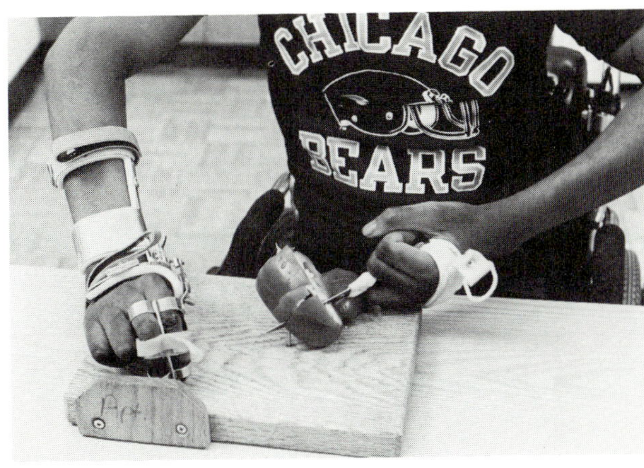

Figure 14–9 A knife adapted with the blade parallel to fingers is often preferred by C6 SCI patients.

design can be used to position the knife parallel to the fingers (Figure 14–9).

A more versatile knife system for meal preparation can be fabricated with a 2-inch wooden dowel, various-sized knife blades, a Velcro strap with D-ring closure, screws, and a set pin (Figure 14–10). This system allows the same handle to be used with various types of knives. It also reduces equipment needs and eliminates the need for donning and doffing as different knives are needed. The dowel is cut the width of the palm and a channel the width and depth of the knife handle is cut horizontally in the dowel. The knife handles may have to be trimmed to make them a uniform width. The Velcro strap with a D-ring is attached with a staple gun or wood screws. The handle of the knife fits into the horizontal groove and is secured with a set pin. The pin should have a loop on the end for ease of blade insertion and removal. Care should be taken when storing the knives to eliminate the chance of injury. Sheaths are recommended for such storage. A built-up handle on the knife may be used by those with minimally impaired hand function. A tenodesis orthosis can be used to cut with an adapted knife.

Cutting food can be done on a cutting board that has stainless steel nails to secure the food and suction cups on the bottom to provide stability (Figure 14–11). The food can also be stabilized with the other hand using a fork in a utensil cuff.

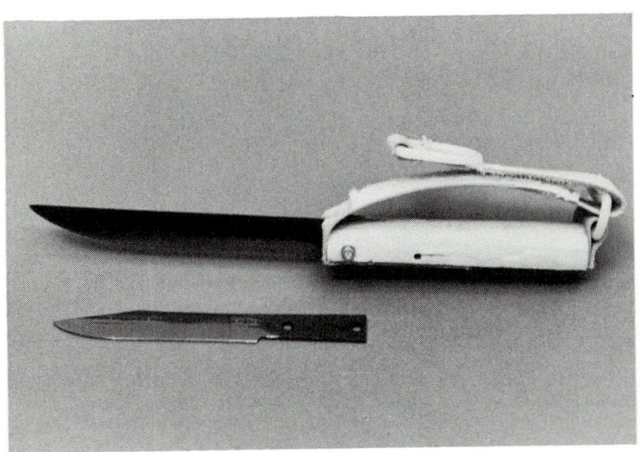

Figure 14–10 Interchangeable blade knife.

Figure 14–11 Patient with C6 SCI using WDFH to cut with serrated knife on a cutting board with nails to secure the food.

Figure 14–12 Handles make stabilization of the bowl during mixing easier.

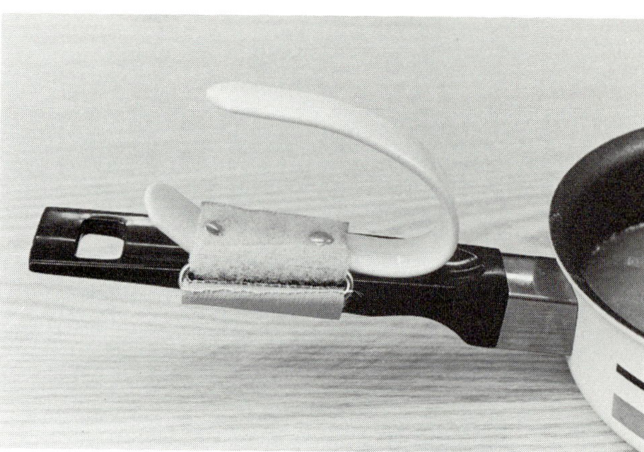

Figure 14–13 Commercial phone holder used to adapt pan handle.

Handles can be added to bowls to provide a point of stabilization, or commercially available bowls with handles may be purchased (Figure 14–12). Lightweight stainless steel or plastic bowls are recommended to reduce the chance of breakage. The bowl may be stabilized on the table with a nonstick material such as Dycem or placed in the lap for stability while stirring.

Thumb loops or larger handles may be added to measuring cups and spoons. Plastic utensils are recommended because they are lighter.

Jars can be opened with a commercially available jar opener that is mounted on the wall or under the cabinet. Bilateral use of the UEs is necessary to provide the leverage needed to unscrew the lid. Once jars are opened, they should be stored with the lids screwed on loosely. If a tighter seal is required for freshness, the items can be transferred into a plastic container with an airtight lid that can be removed and replaced with less effort.

Frying and sauce pans may be adapted for use by modifying a commercially available phone handle (Figure 14–13) with a Velcro strap that allows them to be attached to the handle of the pan. The Velcro strap can also be removed and the phone holder screwed onto the pot handle. Although this method requires one handle per pot, it provides additional stability and durability.

When even more stability is required, the phone handle can be further modified with an ulnar stop or Velcro strap, which prevents the hand from sliding out. The ulnar stop is created by bending the bottom portion of the holder 1 inch from the end in a 90° angle. The Velcro closure is riveted onto the phone holder at each end. Low-temperature plastics are not recommended for these modifications because of the presence of heat. If metal is to be used, it must be coated with heat-resistant materials to avoid burns.

Pot stabilizers can be used to secure the handle of the pot while it is on the stove or tabletop so that both hands are free to work with food (Figure 14–14). These are

Figure 14–14 Pot handle stabilizers enable both UEs to be free for handling utensils and serve as a safety device.

commercially available or can be fabricated with wood and suction cups. Wood stabilizers should not be used on gas stoves.

When transporting hot items from one place to another, the patient should slide the item along a counter whenever possible or use a lap tray. Some patients carry items on their lap, protected by thick towels, but this method should be used with extreme caution and only when absolutely necessary. Large oven mitts are recommended to protect the hands and arms.

CLEANING, LAUNDRY, AND DISHWASHING

Home management tasks such as washing dishes, doing laundry, making the bed, and cleaning the house are difficult when hand function and mobility are limited. Because a high degree of energy is required to perform these skills, they are generally not emphasized unless the individual has good arm placement, limited natural hand function, and strong motivation. If independent performance of these tasks is unrealistic, the person must use homemaker services or rely on family support or a personal care aide. The need for help, as always, varies with the patient. The process of joint problem solving and planning to meet home management objectives may occur most effectively during a readmission or during outpatient sessions, since needs can then be more specifically and realistically identified.

Light cleaning, such as washing the dishes, dusting, and wiping up spills, might be addressed first. Adaptations for washing dishes in the sink include

- automatic faucet
- faucet-mounted spray attachment
- liquid soap dispenser
- adapted scrub brush
- wash mitt
- suction bottle brush
- rubber pad to protect against breakage

Front access to the sink may be gained by removing the cabinet doors and modifying or insulating pipes to eliminate the possibility of burns. Patients may also approach the sink laterally, but this promotes poor posture and is therefore less desirable. Dishes can be air-dried to eliminate the step of towel drying. A dishwasher can also be used; however, dishwasher doors are generally difficult to open. A wrist strap may be attached to assist in opening the door.

Light cleaning and dusting of knee- to chest-height surfaces can be accomplished from a W/C with little difficulty. Large flat surfaces can be cleaned with a wash cloth mitt or an unmodified dust cloth. A handle adaptation may be added to a feather duster to aid in cleaning small objects and hard-to-reach surfaces. Floor spills can be absorbed with paper towels and a reacher used to retrieve them. A lightweight sponge mop with or without handle modifications can also be used.

Quadriplegics and high paraplegics (T1 to T2) often need assistance with heavy weekly cleaning tasks such as vacuuming and mopping. Paraplegics with lower injuries often can vacuum without adapted equipment and mop with little or no adapted equipment. A shorter handled mop and a pail on wheels are occasionally used.

Laundering can be performed by paraplegics and C7–C8 quadriplegics using front-loading machines and a basket or bag that attaches to the W/C to carry laundry. Top-loading machines can be used if the patient can lift himself to sit on the W/C armrest while retrieving clothes or if a ramped 6- to 8-inch platform is placed in front of the machine so that he can see and reach in. Reachers are sometimes suggested to retrieve clothes from machines, but this is a slow, clumsy process that most patients have not found acceptable. Accessibility of laundry facilities is often a problem for apartment dwellers.

HOME ENVIRONMENT CONTROL

Home management also includes the operation of light switches and room temperature controls. This can be done with an environmental control system (unit 17) or with commercially available devices that can be operated with minimal effort.

A wall switch can be lowered with minimal cost and effort to allow independent access. Dimmer switches can be installed in which the on/off function is controlled by applying pressure and the intensity by turning the switch clockwise. Pad and rocker switches can be mounted on the wall, and are also operated by applying

Figure 14–15 Various light switches are commercially available, making operation with limited hand function and arm placement easier.

pressure (Figure 14–15). Touch control lamps are available in most furniture and department stores. The on/off mechanism is triggered by touching any portion of the lamp. A device to convert a standard lamp to touch control is also commercially available.

Temperature regulation is important for the individual who lives independently or spends periods of time alone in the home. Computerized thermostats can be preprogrammed to alter the temperature of the home automatically. The light-touch controls can be easily operated with limited hand function. As with light switches, the height of the thermostat can be altered with minimal cost and effort. Fans and air conditioners are often more difficult to operate, but can be purchased with light-touch controls or lever-type switches that can be modified for easier use.

SUMMARY

Independence in home management tasks is considered a goal for patients with C6 or lower function; those with C8 or lower function are the best candidates. Patients not achieving independence in home management tasks can participate in aspects of a task and assume responsibility in organizing the work that will be performed by others. Discussion of home management roles, goals, and options occurs during the initial hospitalization, while training may continue on an outpatient or in-home basis. Home management roles may change throughout life depending on living situations, economic status, and prioritization of time and energy. OT intervention and training in home management skills is most appropriately provided when the person with SCI is assuming or resuming responsibility for these tasks.

Unit 15

Community Living Skills

Annette Russell Farmer, OTR/L

Community living skills include money handling, W/C mobility, shopping, recreational, vocational, and educational activities, and transportation. Most individuals thrive on daily community interactions. Community living skills can be altered by both the psychological and physical impact of SCI as well as the accessibility of the environment. During the rehabilitation process, skills are developed that allow for the resumption of previous life roles and their application in ADL for successful reintegration into the community. Community living requires problem solving and the ability to verbally direct others when assistance is required. Utilizing resources to plan ahead will enhance the patient's performance in the community.

This unit describes the training process used at RIC to facilitate development of community living skills and achievable goals for specific SCI levels. (Community recreational activities are discussed in unit 13.) To bridge the gap between skills training in the clinic and application in the community, a structured, integrated program is beneficial. During the 2-week community reintegration program at RIC, patients meet with staff for 2 to 4 hours each day. The format allows sufficient time for patients to be involved in the three components of community living skills training: planning, participating, and analyzing.

PLANNING COMMUNITY ACTIVITIES

Patient involvement is an integral part of the planning phase. The patient learns to obtain information by using newspapers, telephone books, guide books, and state and local services for the disabled. Independent living centers, such as Access Living in Chicago, run by disabled people, can provide resources for various aspects of independent living, including community living skills. They often have guides that list accessible establishments in the area. By calling a destination ahead of time logistics and accessibility issues can be worked out in advance (Figure 15–1). Next, personal and medical needs are organized. If transportation is required, the patient again does research and explores various options. These might include public transportation (bus, taxi, subway), private services (W/C van transporters), friends, family, or driving oneself.

The following list is reviewed when planning for a community activity:

1. W/C maintenance
   - tires
   - battery

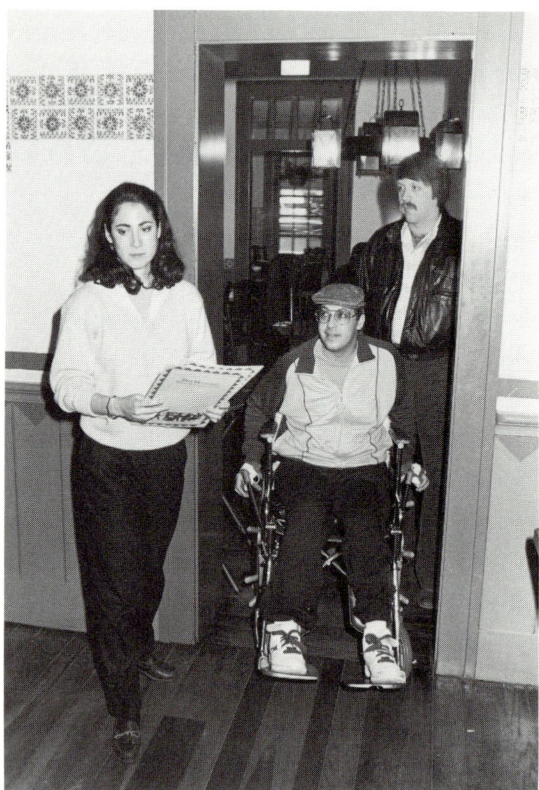

Figure 15–1 Planning: Ensuring accessibility before visiting a restaurant promotes a successful and enjoyable experience.

2. medical needs
   - medications
   - sitting tolerance
   - bowel and bladder care
   - fluid intake
   - diet
3. personal needs
   - ADL (appropriate clothing, feeding equipment)
   - money handling
   - temperature
4. preparing for difficulties that may arise
   - using telephone
   - obtaining phone number
   - using operator
5. specific difficulties
   - stairs
   - doors
   - lack of assistance
   - poor accommodations for W/Cs
   - inaccessible bathrooms
6. transportation options and needs
   - availability
   - cost
   - distance
   - availability and location of parking

Community activities are chosen to include a variety of common pursuits and to simulate activities the patient plans to be involved in after discharge as well as those engaged in before his injury. For example, if a patient is interested in van adaptations to maximize independence in transportation, the telephone book is used to locate a shop that adapts vans. Once it is located, initial information is gathered over the phone and plans might be made to visit the shop for more information and a demonstration. In this manner, several objectives are met. The patient has an opportunity to plan a community activity, use resources, and gather needed information.

In using the phone to obtain information, the patient gains experience in asking questions or directing the conversation to obtain the specific information needed. Asking only whether a sports stadium is accessible to W/Cs may not provide the necessary information for a well-planned, successful evening at a ball game. Instead the caller, after identifying himself as W/C-bound, should ask a series of questions:

- Are there any stairs into the facility or the seating area?
- If there are stairs, how many are there? Is there an alternative way that a W/C user could enter these areas?
- Is there an assigned area for W/C seating? Where is this area located (good viewing?) and is there a particular entrance?
- How can a W/C user access the bathrooms? Are they on the same floor as the seating or is there an elevator or ramp?

Common activities include the following:

- going to a restaurant
- visiting a museum
- visiting a zoo or park
- shopping for clothing, shoes, or groceries

- going to a theater
- attending a concert
- visiting a health club
- visiting an airport (some airlines have allowed patients to practice getting on and off an airplane)

PARTICIPATING IN COMMUNITY ACTIVITIES

After the necessary arrangements for the community activity have been made, the patient participates in the activity. If a step is omitted during the planning phase, the consequences are faced during the participation phase, allowing the patient to learn and to resolve the situation. For example, in going to a restaurant after neglecting to ask about the location of the bathroom facilities, the patient may discover that the restaurant's bathroom is located downstairs and that there is no elevator in the building. Options at this point include having friends "bump" the chair down the stairs, going to another restaurant with an accessible bathroom, returning to the hospital, or draining the leg bag outside the restaurant. The emphasis during this component of community skills training is on the patient acquiring the necessary problem-solving skills to improve physical, social, and leisure independence for comfortable and enjoyable performance in a community setting (Figures 15–2 and 15–3).

The following guidelines are used to objectively assess the patient's performance during the community activity:

1. responsibility
   - requests assistance when necessary
   - clearly directs others to assist
2. independence
   - does not request assistance unnecessarily
   - uses adaptive equipment
3. problem solving
   - manages the unexpected
   - makes modifications when necessary
   - generates possible solutions and chooses the most reasonable and safe one
4. self-care
   - initiates pressure relief
   - takes medications
   - monitors fluid intake

Figure 15–2 Participating: Solving money-handling problems in the community.

5. mobility
   - manages physical barriers (curbs, doorways, aisles, unlevel surfaces)
6. sensitivity to others
   - is relationship-oriented rather than self-centered

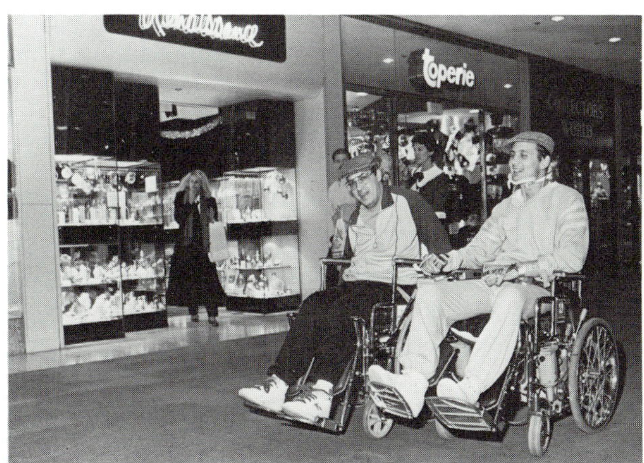

Figure 15–3 Participating: Enjoying an indoor shopping mall in winter.

- considers the needs and desires of others in problem-solving situations
- consults with others in decision making

If the patient is physically unable to perform an activity, the emphasis is on the ability to verbally direct someone else to ensure that his needs are met in the community.

ANALYZING COMMUNITY EXPERIENCES

After participating in a community activity, the patient analyzes his performance with the therapist. Appropriate adjustments in the planning or participating phases are made for the next community activity (Figure 15–4). Areas to consider in analyzing the experience are

1. problem identification
   - recognition of problems that could have been anticipated
   - recognition of problems that could not have been anticipated
2. self-evaluation
   - ability to assess performance (positive or negative)
   - ability to consider personal role in success or failure
3. idea generation
   - ability to identify alternatives for use in future situations
4. new questions
   - ability to anticipate new situations
   - ability to plan appropriately, drawing from past experiences

Figure 15–4 Analyzing: A basket to securely carry items would have been helpful!

EQUIPMENT USED IN THE COMMUNITY

Equipment for maximizing independent performance in the community includes feeding equipment, writing equipment, a reacher, and dressing equipment such as a button hook. Planning is required to ensure that all necessary equipment is taken and is carried in an accessible place.

Carrying equipment and money may require special adaptations. If a back pack is used, practice in retrieving the pack from the back of the chair may be required. Small items such as utensil cuffs, writing devices, and money may be carried in a W/C side pouch attached to the armrest of the chair for easy access and greater security. A reacher can be carried in a back pack, suspended from the handle of the chair, or kept alongside the person in the chair. These are a few common options for carrying equipment in the community. Additional needs may have to be considered. Generally the approach is to make a list of equipment that will be needed while planning the community experience and then to consider how to carry the equipment.

SUMMARY

The training process for community living skills at RIC comprises planning, participating, and analyzing the experience. This allows the patient to practice and apply the skills learned during rehabilitation to practical situations. Initial reintegration experiences are provided before discharge. Skills are learned through participation and allow for application into one's own community setting. Independence in community living skills refers not only to physical performance but also to being able to verbally direct another person when assistance is needed. As the patient becomes proficient in directing others, he can also apply these skills in the job setting, school setting, leisure pursuits, and while traveling. The emphasis is on the ability to safely and enjoyably meet one's physical and emotional needs in the community.

SUMMARY CHART: Community Skills

Goal	*Indicator*	*Recommended Intervention*
1. Independent in verbally directing care	1. C5 or higher injury 2. Dependent—assisted in self-care 3. Dependent—assisted in mobility	1. Arranging for accompaniment by family members, friends, attendant 2. Researching accessibility using communication aids, written resources, independent living centers 3. Instructing friends, family, attendant, strangers in mobility assistance 4. Learning how to handle emergency situations 5. Taking all necessary equipment for task performance in community (money, feeding equipment, etc.)
2. Independent in money handling	1. C6 or lower injury 2. Tenodesis to normal hand function 3. Limited unassisted to normal arm placement 4. Good problem-solving skills	1. Instruct patient in safe placement of money 2. Provide equipment (back pack, W/C side pouch, adapted wallet)
3. Independent in shopping skills	1. C6 or lower injury 2. Motivation 3. Good problem-solving skills 4. Limited unassisted to normal arm placement 5. Tenodesis to normal hand function	1. Provide patient with assistive devices (e.g., reacher) 2. Demonstrate mobility skills to maneuver through aisles, checkout counters 3. Demonstrate and provide opportunity for practicing methods for conveying needs to salesperson when assistance is needed
4. Independent in mobility skills	1. C6 or lower injury 2. Motivation 3. Good problem-solving skills 4. Good strength in both UEs	1. Demonstrate and provide opportunity to practice ways of maneuvering W/C through elevators, doorways, curbs, escalators

Unit 16

Play for Play's Sake

Audrey Yasukawa, OTR/L

It has been stated by educators that play is children's work. Through purposeful play a child develops physically, cognitively, socially, and emotionally. The role of toys in this development and learning process is well known to those who work with the physically disabled child. When toys are properly used they can help the child develop skills in physical control, vision and other forms of perception, cognition, language, and interaction with others and with self. Toys can also frustrate the child who is unable to use them in the ways that other children do.

Toys should be chosen to fit needs and abilities and should be challenging at each of the child's developmental levels. Learning and exploring through play must be carefully structured to best facilitate development. Challenging, developmentally appropriate play can be provided by battery-operated toys, commercially available games, and toys that require simple modification. These toys provide initial skills training for improving physical control and increasing the child's independence.

Children will pass through several stages of play: sensorimotor play, symbolic play, and play with rules (games). At each stage, the child with SCI may require special adaptations and an atmosphere conducive to development and learning. The different stages of play may overlap and they extend into adulthood.

SENSORIMOTOR PLAY

The sensorimotor period of play occurs during the first year of life. Sensorimotor play occurs for the pleasure and development of the senses and involves touching, moving, hearing, seeing, and tasting. Incorporation of movement into the child's sensorimotor experience is extremely important for exploration of the environment and for understanding cause and effect and object permanency. The child develops voluntary control of movement, becoming more aware of self in relation to movement and space. During this period the child's visual, auditory, tactile, and motor perceptions develop.

A mobile hanging from a crib will visually attract an infant's attention. The baby may accidentally swipe at the mobile and then repeat the act for the pleasure of watching it move. The infant can then anticipate swiping the mobile and watching the bright colors in action. For the baby with SCI, the mobile may have to be lowered to allow for easy reach (Figure 16–1). Brightly colored mobiles that play music and turn are especially successful in attracting the child's attention and eliciting movement.

For the child to play independently the therapist must consider proper W/C positioning, level of injury, and developmental needs. There are many commercially

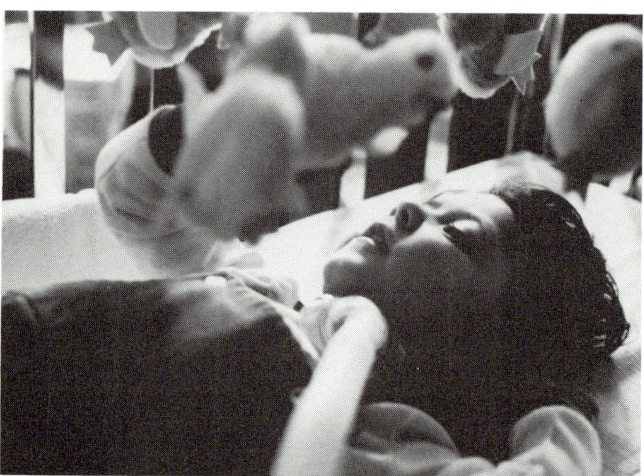

Figure 16–1 Infant playing with a mobile.

available "cause and effect" toys that may not need modification for use by the child with SCI. For example, the Happy Apple is a bright red apple. When a baby touches or swipes at the apple it rebounds and makes a pleasant ringing sound. Cause and effect toys that are large, brightly colored, musical, and visually interesting may be fun for the child with limited arm function to begin working on motor control.

The child can play with blocks using simple adaptations. Velcro straps can be made to wrap around the hand of a child with limited hand function. A small piece of Velcro can be applied to lightweight plastic blocks. This will enable the child to bang the blocks together and begin to use his hand for play with the aid of an adapted strap (Figure 16–2).

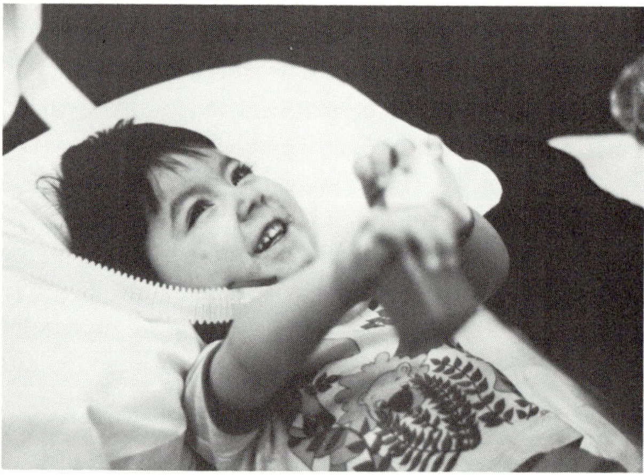

Figure 16–2 Infant playing with plastic blocks adapted with Velcro.

Figure 16–3 Battery-operated clown with tread switch.

Battery-operated cause and effect toys can be easily modified with various switches to suit specific needs. In choosing the right switch, the therapist must evaluate the child's level of function and specific motoric control. In addition, the toy is chosen to challenge the child's cognitive level. If the toy or switch is too complex, the child may feel that others should move it for him. Choosing the proper toy and switch will encourage the child to independently make a series of discoveries and give him an immediate response. The use of switches, starting with the very basic tread switch and leading to the more complex and sophisticated ECU, will enable the child with SCI to freely explore and initiate and to develop self-control at his own pace (Figures 16–3 to 16–5).

SYMBOLIC PLAY

Symbolic play begins about the second year of life. The child moves from sensorimotor play into a world of make-believe. Role playing and pretend play may assist in expressing needs, dealing with fears, and developing the ability to communicate. While pretend-

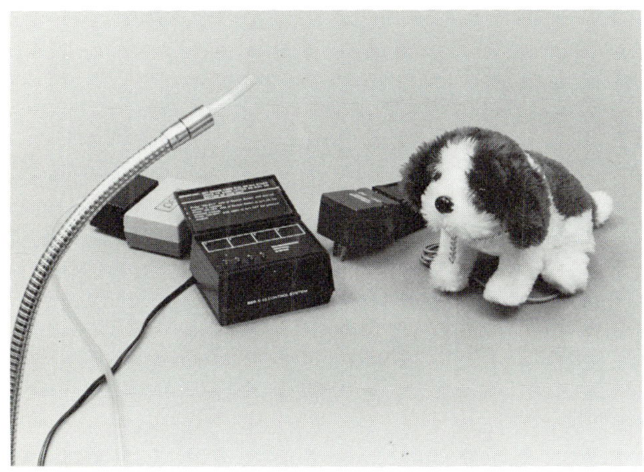

Figure 16–4 Battery-operated dog with sip-and-puff control.

Figure 16–5 Battery-operated roller coaster with Switch-it control.

ing, the child is "in charge." In this stage the child explores a broader range of feelings and emotions.

Dolls and stuffed animals provide companionship and a sleeptime partner. Dolls with changeable clothes can be used for role playing and to foster nurturing behavior. The child with limited hand function may require special adaptations for the doll's clothes in order to play independently. Velcro fasteners and loops can be sewn onto the garment. This will assist in donning and doffing the doll's clothing (Figure 16–6). Specially adapted doll clothing not only encourages and promotes motor control, it helps in the development of body image (Figure 16–7).

Colored pencils and crayons encourage creative expression and the development of eye-hand coordination. Buying a pencil box with the necessary school supplies is an important step for a child in preparing for

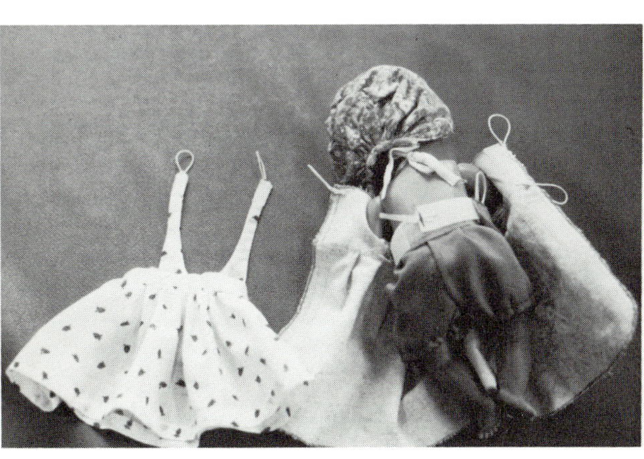

Figure 16–6 Adapted doll clothing.

Figure 16–7 Child holding doll.

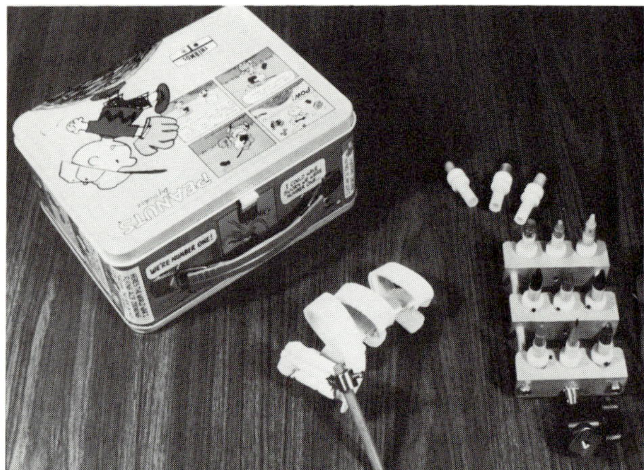

Figure 16–8 Lunch box with school supplies.

Figure 16–9 Child coloring with setup.

school in the fall. The child with limited hand function can actively participate by choosing a lunch box to be used as a pencil box. In conjunction with an adjustable writing device (unit 8), a variety of tips, such as a pencil, eraser, and crayons can be utilized (Figure 16–8). The child can independently choose and change the various writing tips without assistance. Quiet, creative play can then occur (Figure 16–9).

Many children are fascinated by science fiction and space adventure toys. The Armatron is one example of a battery-operated robot arm controlled by two joysticks. By moving the joysticks, the child can direct the robot arm to pick up, place, and release small objects. The top of each joystick can be turned clockwise and counterclockwise; to do so requires fine muscle control and palmar prehension. This may present a problem for the child with absent or limited hand function. The Armatron can easily be modified by adding an additional lever to compensate for the inability to turn the knobs of the joysticks. The movements needed to operate the Armatron can now be accomplished by pushing or pulling the joysticks and pushing or pulling the adapted lever (Figure 16–10). The child can use a natural tenodesis grasp pattern, an orthotic device, or a mouthstick to play independently.

Children enjoy pretending, creating, and fantasizing. This form of play helps a child begin to understand what is real and what is make-believe. Fantasy play provides the child with a foundation for the development of cognitive, language, and social skills, concentration, and increasing functional control.

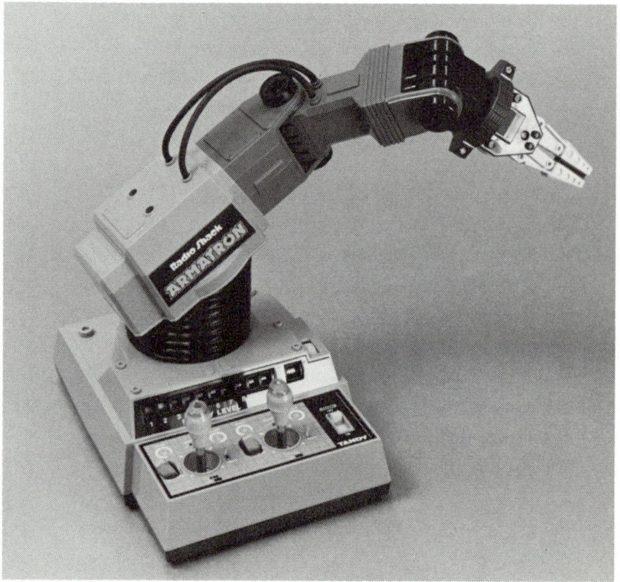

Figure 16–10 Adapted Armatron.

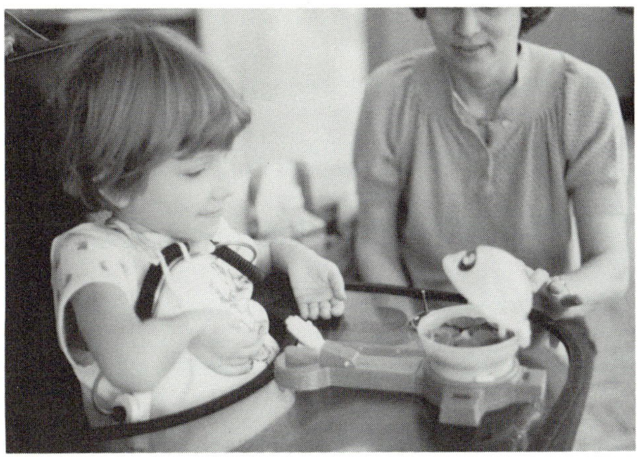

Figure 16–11 Child and mother playing with Mr. Mouth.

GAMES

Focus on games with rules generally begins at 7 to 11 years of age and continues throughout life. As the child continues to develop and learn, his attention span increases and his ability to understand and challenge himself increases. The child is now beginning to play with others, take turns, and develop a sense of order and sportsmanship. Learning to share and to take turns requires time. The child with SCI will need practice and support to become a social being. Initially, friendships may be formed by playing with adults. Gradually, relationships with peers should develop.

There are many commercially available games that encourage practice in taking turns. One is a battery-operated game called Mr. Mouth. There are four colored hands with matching tokens attached to Mr. Mouth. The object is to place the token on the corresponding hand and to press down the hand to flip the token into Mr. Mouth as he turns in a circle, opening and closing his mouth. This game requires color matching, speed, and coordination (Figure 16–11).

The list of board games, electronic toys, and video games is endless, and the possibilities for modification or adaptation are limited only by the imagination and ingenuity of the therapist, parent, or child.

Through playing games with rules the child's organization, sequencing, attention to task, motor planning, and ability to relate to peers are enhanced. This stage challenges the child's intelligence. The need to develop social skills continues throughout life. Play, therefore, continues to have value as a means of recreation, socialization, and relaxation.

SUMMARY

Play and toys are essential to the growth and rehabilitation of the child with SCI. The developmental stages of play may be used as a framework to assist the child to develop independence and confidence in exploring the world. Each stage helps to lay the foundation for the next skill level. Play must be fun, and children need to develop according to their own physical, mental, and emotional levels and at their own rate. The disabled child needs more time than others and adaptations that allow independent exploration and discovery.

Interest in some toys may be present before the child has the muscular skills necessary for their use. Toys are classified by age groups and may be suitable only for the child with normal function. The physically disabled child may not be able to play with the toy even though his developmental needs are similar to those of the normal child. Therefore, giving extra thought to choosing appropriate toys, providing special adaptations or modifications, and using special switches has many therapeutic implications. Toys can be used for increasing muscle strength, coordination, and social skills in the play situation. Besides providing fun, toys that fit the child's special needs will promote a healthy outlook and a new level of independence.

Unit 17
Technical Aids

Janet Bischof, OTR/L

Technical aids are devices designed to enhance human performance in all environments in which we live, work, and play. Many persons with quadriplegia are unable to control basic appliances in their homes. Without specialized equipment they must ask a family member or attendant to turn on a light, change the TV channel, or turn pages for them. The act of making these simple requests can reinforce feelings of dependence, loss of control, and inadequacy. Today's technology offers alternatives to these situations, making the environment more accessible to the individual with SCI at a comparatively reasonable cost.

An environmental control unit (ECU) is a technical aid that provides the ability to control many appliances, including lights, radio, TV, electric bed, and the telephone or a call alert system. Units vary in method of operation, number and type of devices that can be controlled, and ability to interface with a computer or with the W/C control. (See Appendix 17–A.)

Technical aids, when used appropriately, can offer independence at home, school, and work, resulting in an increased sense of control and self-esteem, motivation for achievement, and financial savings. Conversely, if technical aids are recommended when they are not necessary, physical and psychological dependence may be promoted.

This unit discusses the process a patient experiences when referred for a technical aid and the devices available. The technical aids described include commercially available switches, emergency call systems, telephone systems, electric page turners, ECUs, and computer keyboard emulators and adaptations. It is important that occupational therapists prescribing technical aids be current in their knowledge of available equipment and the intricacies of its operation. To meet this requirement, one or two therapists in a center or area usually specialize in technical aid evaluation and prescription.

REFERRAL AND ASSESSMENT

The referral and assessment process includes the following steps:

- referral
- evaluation
- determination of the control and device for trial
- training
- consultation with a rehabilitation engineer regarding operation and mounting of the device
- equipment ordering and fabrication
- family or attendant education
- follow-up

Exhibit 17–1 RIC Referral Form

Rehabilitation Institute of Chicago

Alan J. Brown Alternate Communication and Environmental Control Center

OCCUPATIONAL THERAPY REFERRAL FOR ECU EVALUATION AND TRAINING

Name: __________ RIC#: __________ Occupational Therapist: __________

Diagnosis: __________ Onset: __________ MD: __________

Functional Skills

Physical

Cognitive

Communicative

Needs

What needs do you anticipate being met through use of ECU? (Please include patient and family needs and expectations.)

Tentative D/C date and environment.

Would you like to be involved during evaluation and training?

Referral

Patients may be referred for a technical aid evaluation by the physician or any team member. Outside referral sources include community agencies, teachers, health professionals, vocational counselors, and physicians. At RIC, typical referral information is gathered on a referral form (Exhibit 17–1). A physician's order should be obtained.

Evaluation

The evaluation process involves analysis of four areas:

1. Function. Baseline information from the referring source should be gathered. A functional assessment rather than any one specific evaluation is performed. This includes position (W/C, bed); head and neck ROM and control; UE placement, coordination, tone, endurance, and grasp; LE ROM, placement, tone, and endurance; and use of orthotics. These areas affect the types of switches to be used and their placement. Additional positioning or equipment may be needed before trial of technical aids.
2. Psychosocial. The state of adjustment to disability at the time of evaluation is crucial to the outcome. Understanding the disability and its

implications can affect the choice of equipment. Attitudes also affect the involvement in training and procuring funding for the equipment.

3. Patient and family goals. Family, educational, avocational, and vocational needs should be assessed to determine realistic patient and family goals. For example, is the individual likely to ask the family to perform functions, regardless of ECU equipment, or will the equipment eliminate or decrease the need for attendant care? Educational and vocational goals also affect the system chosen.
4. Funding. Many insurance companies consider technical aids to be luxury items, despite the fact that they can be cost-efficient in reducing attendant care and provide vocational opportunities. This requires that the need be validated in terms that the funding sources will accept. Equipment orders submitted to third-party payers should be accompanied by detailed letters of justification and a description of the equipment. The letter should address the patient's current functional status and the effect the equipment will have on that status. It should also stress the cost efficiency of the equipment in cases where attendant care can be reduced. A photograph of the person using the equipment may also be submitted. Community resources, including various clubs, church organizations, and funding drives may provide funding options.

Determination of Device and Control for Trial

Results of the functional assessment will be the major guide in selecting the control site and switches that should be evaluated. The aesthetics of the equipment should also be considered. Patients should have a trial session with each device when possible and be given information on other appropriate equipment not available for trial. Many vendors of medical equipment are willing to loan devices to a facility for a trial period at a minimal fee.

Training

Some training is necessary to establish the most efficient and appropriate controls and devices. The patient and his family should know about all options before making a final decision. However, extensive training is not recommended before funding has been obtained.

Consultation with Rehabilitation Engineer for Mounting Devices

Individual needs vary and may necessitate consultation with a rehabilitation engineer to design a mounting system for a device or to design and fabricate equipment that is not commercially available. Some commercially available devices may require adaptations to enable maximum control, such as a key guard, extensions attached to on/off switches, and so forth. Realistic appraisal of adaptations required and estimated costs should be established before equipment is actually ordered.

Equipment Ordering or Fabrication

When all evaluations of motoric skills and needs are completed, the equipment is ordered or fabricated. The patient should be actively involved in this process to encourage development of problem-solving abilities.

Education

When the equipment is delivered, the family and patient are thoroughly trained in its operation and maintenance. Training time varies significantly with each piece of equipment as well as with the abilities of patient and family. Some equipment can be demonstrated sufficiently to enable it to be set up at home independently. Other more complex systems require the occupational therapist or the rehabilitation engineer to make a home visit to set up the system and make necessary adaptations. Many suppliers of this equipment are willing to set it up in the home for a fee. However, in many cases it is strongly recommended that the occupational therapist and rehabilitation engineer, who know about the patient's functional status as well as the equipment, set up the equipment and make modifications to best meet the patient's needs.

Rechecks

Periodic rechecks should be completed after technical aids are issued to ensure functional use of the device and to evaluate changing needs. If the person later decides to return to school or work, suggestions to expand his present ECU or computer system may be needed. The person should be educated as to appropriate resources for maintenance and repairs. In some cases the vendor may offer a replacement item while the equipment is being repaired.

CALL SYSTEMS

For most people with high-level SCI, a call system may be one of the first technical aids required. In a hospital setting the conventional nurse call system may be inaccessible to the patient with no functional arm or head movement. Four variations of call systems will be described. Emergency safety systems may be of benefit to the individual who will be home alone for periods of time or who is living alone.

1. Nurse call system. Some nurse call systems can be adapted by replacing the existing touch pad or button switch with a pneumatic, head-activated, or light-touch switch. The touch pad switches connect to the wall jack with a quarter-inch phono plug. If the new switch's plug is a different size than the hospital's existing jack, an adapter can be purchased from an electronics store. Pneumatic switches are easily mounted on the bed with a gooseneck. Zygo leaf switches can be easily attached to a gooseneck or other retractable arm and placed for head or shoulder activation. An eyebrow switch is another option. However, maintaining proper placement of the headband may be difficult.
2. Buzzer. A simple call buzzer operated by batteries may be used in a hospital or home environment when the distance is small enough to enable the care giver to hear it throughout the home or nursing unit. Low-cost buzzer boxes can be easily constructed by referring to a manual on homemade switches or battery-operated toys and are commercially available through communication aid companies. A desk call bell may meet some patients' needs. If arm placement is not adequate to reach a buzzer, it can be interfaced with a switch mounted at the best available control site. The Zygo call alarm and the Prentke Romich Company (PRC) call buzzer are two models that can be interfaced with a switch (Figure 17–1). The PRC model can also operate by light touch without a switch interface. An orthoplast holder can be fabricated to contain the buzzer and be attached to the W/C, or it can be placed in a W/C bag. For the SCI patient who is unable to phonate, a call alarm may be indicated for use in the W/C, even though the conventional nurse call system is used from the bed (Figure 17–2). When the person is using an ECU, the buzzer can be accessed through this system, negating the need for additional switches.
3. Intercom. Some people may benefit from using a wireless intercom system in their home. This enables care givers to go about household tasks and yet be confident that they are in constant communication with their charges. Wireless intercoms can be set up with stations in different locations (Figure 17–3). The individual can then

Figure 17–1 (left) Zygo Call Alarm interfaced with a tread switch. (right) PRC CS-3 Call Signal, which can be activated with or without a switch interface.

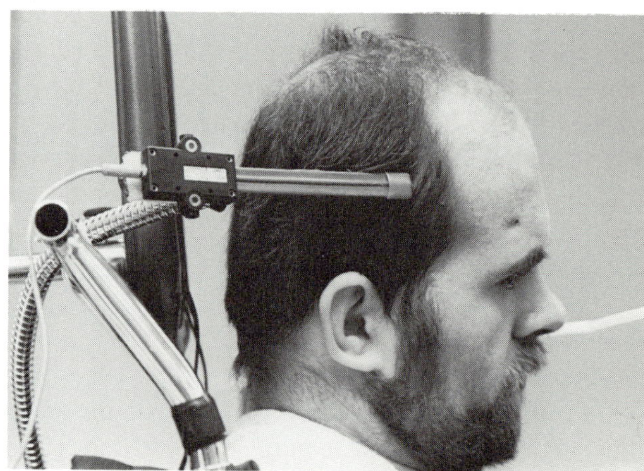

Figure 17–2 C4 patient using his head to operate a leaf switch plugged into a Zygo Call Alarm.

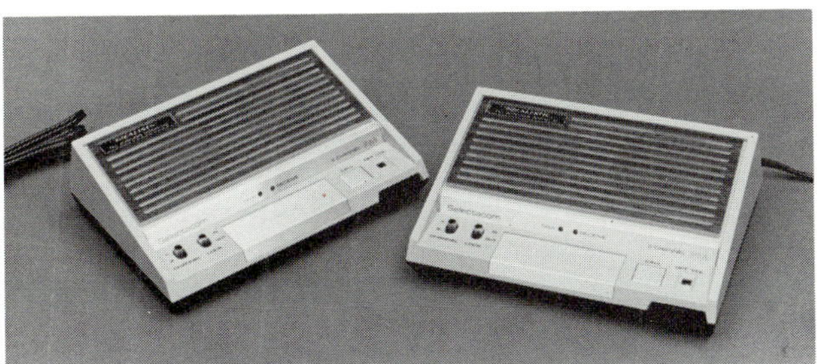

Figure 17–3 A wireless intercom system enables monitoring of person's need for assistance from another room.

communicate back and forth with the care giver by activating a touch plate. The amount of pressure required for activation varies with different products, beginning with almost zero pressure. Some devices permit locking of the touch plate for a one-way conversation. This feature benefits the person unable to activate the touch plate.

4. Emergency call systems. A variety of emergency alert systems are currently available, with new devices being added constantly. Each system varies slightly as to method of input, cost (rent or purchase), installation, and the process through which help is obtained. Most of the systems work by a pushbutton-activated transmitter worn by the person, which activates an automatic telephone dialing mechanism. A recorded message is sent to a central monitoring station. After receiving the message, some monitoring centers immediately contact an emergency medical team, while others contact family or neighbors listed in the person's file. Pushbuttons may be adapted for the person with limited hand function by building the button up, or gluing on a lever. The transmitter can be mounted on the W/C for head or arm activation. The Ezzie system detects falls and is activated through tilting of the monitor worn by the person. It can be worn in the shower. The Lifeline system works through a pushbutton transmitter and can be rented at a reasonable monthly rate. AT&T offers a pushbutton system that activates preprogrammed numbers and sends a distress message.

TELEPHONE SYSTEMS

Patients with a high level of injury often require more than an adaptation to present phone systems (unit 8). Total independence both in receiving and placing calls may require a new system. Phone systems on the market are continually being revised and new ones added as technology improves. This requires constant monitoring of the new products. Speakerphones, which allow hands-free conversation, are manufactured by many companies. The quality and price are usually directly related. It is best to have the person try out the phone before purchasing it. Some speakerphones do not allow the caller and the person using the speakerphone to talk at the same time and be heard. This characteristic, which can be a hindrance to smooth conversation, should be evaluated with each brand.

A less expensive option to the speakerphone is an amplifier. The amplifier plugs directly into the modular jack of a standard phone. Various ways to depress the switch hook are discussed in unit 8. Telephone companies, electronics companies, and general merchandise outlet stores are good resources for commercially available equipment. Two new telephone systems, a voice-activated system and a pneumatic system, which offer independent telephone use to some individuals with SCI, are described below.

The AT&T Directel allows for placing and receiving calls with a pneumatic switch (Figure 17–4). The per-

Figure 17–4 Quadriplegic operating Directel speakerphone with a pneumatic switch to place and answer calls.

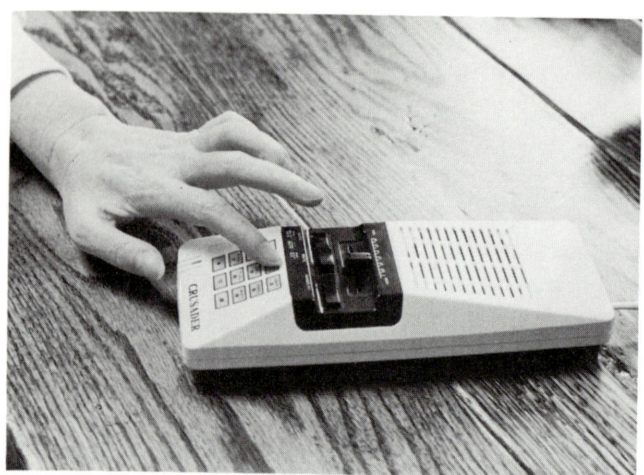

Figure 17–5 Person with C7 SCI operating a Crusader speakerphone.

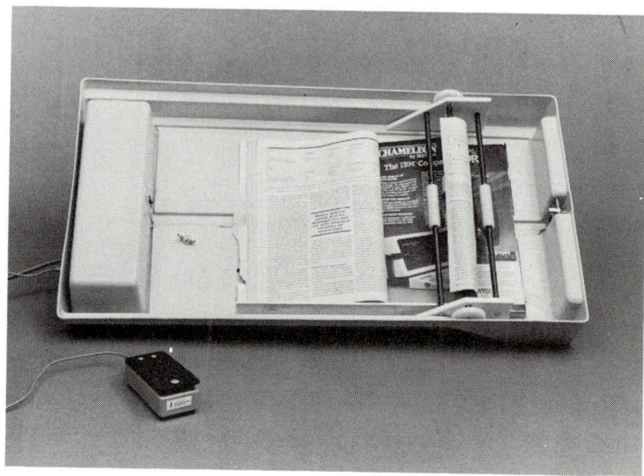

Figure 17–6 Brussee electric page turner controlled by a single plate switch.

son places a call by contacting the operator through sip-and-puff activation, then requests that the number be dialed. Calls are received and disconnected through sip-and-puff activation also.

The Crusader phone allows placing of calls through activation of light-touch, half-inch-square pads (Figure 17–5). It can be operated with tenodesis hand function without additional equipment. A person with good arm placement but no wrist or hand function may require a writing orthosis to hit the small squares. Calls are received by voice activation and automatically disconnect when the caller hangs up.

Another option for the person with SCI who travels alone in his car or van is a cellular phone. Besides being critical in an emergency situation, it is useful when the person is independent in driving and exiting from an automobile but is unable to access a building. The person can phone inside the building on reaching the destination to request assistance. A wide variety of cellular phones are available through telephone companies.

ELECTRIC PAGE TURNERS

Electric page turners automatically turn the pages of a book or magazine through single or multiple switches (Figure 17–6). They are used when limited arm placement and head control prohibit manual turning of pages with a hand-held pointer or a mouthstick (unit 8). Sitting tolerance, endurance, muscle tone, contractures, and positioning of the user (from reclined W/C or bed) are all factors that affect the selection of this device. Electric page turners have many features that should be assessed, including switch compatibility, number of switches required, ECU interface, turning direction (can device turn forward and reverse), adjustable viewing angle, size of reading materials accommodated (books or magazines), maintenance, complexity of setup, and cost. Vendors for a number of page turners are listed in Appendix B.

POWER DOOR OPENERS

There are many types of commercially available power door openers that can be easily installed and operated remotely through a variety of switches. However, these are usually extremely expensive. Less expensive adaptations to existing doors are possible through the services of an electrician, rehabilitation engineer, or someone else knowledgeable in the area of electronics and wiring. It is possible to install a lock release inexpensively, enabling unlocking of the entrance door from W/C or bed when a visitor presses a buzzer. This is similar to the intercom systems in apartment buildings that enable a resident to press a button in the apartment to release the lock on the building entrance. An electric door release and a garage door opener receiver and transmitter are required. It should be installed by a specialist in electronics or a locksmith. Two control options for unlocking and opening doors are available through Stanley Magic Door, Inc. One is operated by remote control, with a switch mounted on the W/C, and one has a wall- or table-mounted touch pad near the door.

A power door opener can be operated through some ECUs, such as Control 1 and MECCA (Mobile Environmental Control and Communication Accessory). This eliminates the need for additional switches. The vendors can be contacted for specific information, especially concerning voltage compatibility, as this can be a critical factor.

SWITCHES

A control or method to operate a device is required to access electronic equipment. The switch is the control, and the methods used to control the equipment described below entail direct selection or scanning. Direct selection is a method of input in which one selection action indicates one item. For example, hitting a computer key produces a letter on the monitor. Traditional or automatic scanning refers to a method whereby activation of a switch causes a cursor or light to begin to scan an array of items. The switch is activated a second time when the desired set of items or item is reached. In step scanning, the switch must be activated repeatedly to advance item by item. When the desired item is reached, either a second switch is activated to effect selection or a period of time is allowed to pass, without a switch closure, to indicate selection.

Two-switch input is required for commercially available ECUs, which are not of the direct-selection mode. A person having only one efficient control site for switch activation should explore computer options or contact an RE center to evaluate custom adaptations. It is possible to adapt a commercially available device from two-switch to one-switch activation. This necessitates using a slower scanning method for input. Some basic switches for ECU control are described below (Figure 17–7).

A pneumatic switch is activated by a change in air pressure above or below a set amount. Two pneumatic switches are combined to form a sip-and-puff switch. This type of switch closes one set of electrical contacts by sipping and a second set of contacts when sensing high air pressure caused by puffing.

The light-touch switch is a dual or two-switch system that resembles a 3-inch-high toggle or a joystick. Switch activation occurs by moving the toggle in either of two directions. It is most commonly operated with the UEs.

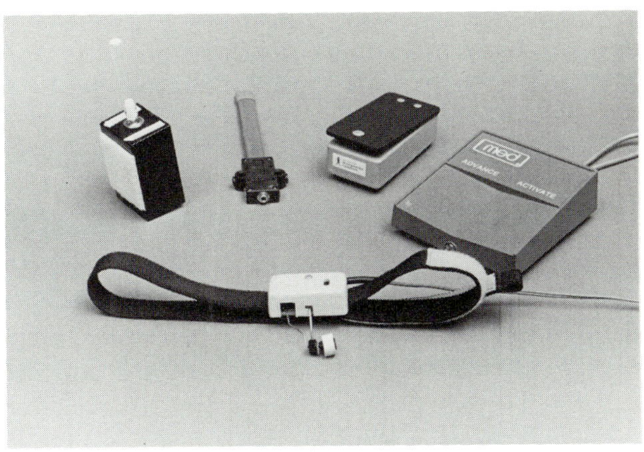

Figure 17–7 Switches: (left to right) light-touch switch, leaf switch, single-plate switch, dual rocker switch, and eyebrow switch (front).

The leaf switch is a single flexible switch activated by deflection in either direction. It can be easily mounted for use with the head, arm, hand, or leg.

The tread switch is a single switch requiring light pressure (16 ounces). It provides an audible click and spring action for sensory feedback. It may be mounted for the arm, hand, foot, or head.

A rocker switch can be a single or dual switch. Pushing the plate down on either side produces activation. The dual rocker switch is used most often with the hand and the single rocker switch is activated by head, arm, hand, leg, or foot. The chin controller referred to later in this unit indicates a W/C control switch activated by the chin.

Technology continues to offer new switch possibilities to operate technical aids, including eyebrow, eye blink, and electromyographic (EMG) switches. These switch options have not proved reliable for operating technical aids, however. For example, a person using an EMG switch to operate a computer requires someone else to place the electrode on his forehead each time he wants to use the computer. The eyebrow switch may require periodic readjustments to the headband on which the switch is mounted. An infrared switch (which can be activated by blinking) is extremely sensitive to changing light and may require a visor to minimize this problem. It also requires eyeglass frames for mounting. These switches are all extremely sensitive, and maintenance may be a problem if there are multiple care givers because they must all be well trained in placing the switch in the correct position. These switches, however, offer a method for persons unable to access other switches to communicate and to control their environment.

ENVIRONMENTAL CONTROL SYSTEMS

Various ECUs are commercially available, along with custom-designed systems developed through rehabilitation engineering centers. It is imperative that the therapist prescribing ECUs stay informed about new products in order to make appropriate recommendations. The most versatile commercially available systems are listed in Appendix 17–A. They range from simple direct-selection pushbutton systems to scanning and computer interface systems. The categories in Appendix 17–A will be defined here to provide a clearer understanding of ECU operation.

The selection method refers to the mode of operation of the ECU—direct selection, step scanning, or traditional row-column or linear scanning. The Rehab Technology ECU is the only device to pair a pneumatic switch with a direct-selection method (Figure 17–8). This simple pneumatic system consists of four switches that control four devices. Puffing on the first straw turns the first device on, and puffing again turns it off. Sipping on the first straw activates the second device; sipping and puffing on the second straw controls the third and fourth devices.

The switch options list includes the most commonly interfaced switches with each device. It is not meant to be all-inclusive.

The activation column lists suggested means of controlling ECUs at each functional level of injury. Criteria to note include the amount of equipment required at each level of injury to operate each device. Devices are not usually designed to meet the needs of a specific disability, and matching devices with a disability is not straightforward.

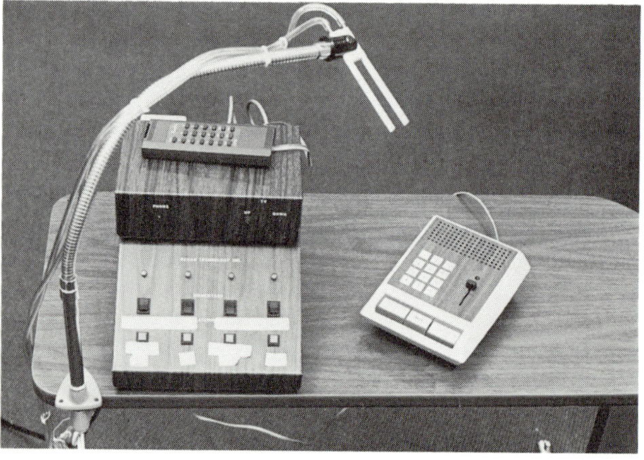

Figure 17–8 Rehab Technology ECU operated through two straws by sip-and-puff activation.

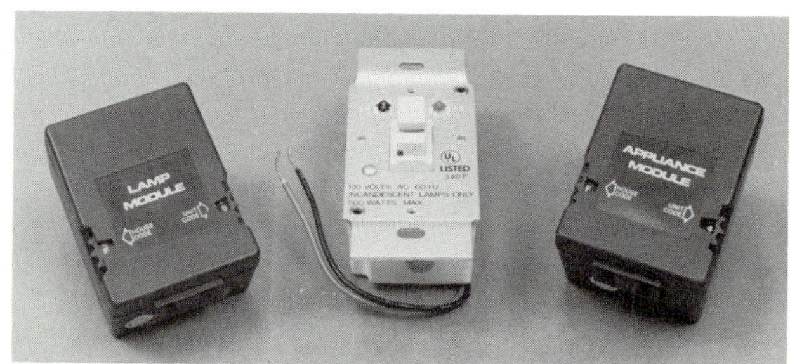

Figure 17–9 BSR modules: (left to right) lamp module, wall switch, appliance module.

Transmission refers to the way signals are sent from the user's control or switch to the ECU and from the ECU to the devices being activated. Transmission can occur via radio, ultrasound, or infrared signals. Control signals can also be sent from an ECU to a device over house wiring. Appliances to be controlled are plugged directly into the ECU in some systems. Other systems require the appliances to be plugged into a receiver, which is then plugged into an outlet. These receivers are then "remotely controlled," as there is no connection other than the installed house or apartment wiring between the appliance/receiver and the ECU, which is sending the signal. Many ECUs have BSR modules as their receivers. The three most commonly used types of BSR modules are for appliances, incandescent lamps, and wall switches (Figure 17–9). Every appliance, lamp, or wall switch to be controlled requires one BSR module. The radio, for example, would be plugged into an appliance module, and the module would then be plugged into the electrical outlet. BSR modules usually operate up to a distance of 50 feet and allow control of any appliance from any room in a house. All these modules, however, must be on the same transformer. Each module is manually set to a house code that corresponds to the letter on the transmitter (Figure 17–10). They are also set on a number (1 to 16) that corresponds to a number on the transmitter. These can be easily reset at any time.

All the ECU systems listed utilize some BSR modules, with the exception of the Switch-it, TASH Ultra-4, and Rehab Technology systems. Switch-it and Ultra-4 have their own color-coded receivers and function like the BSR modules (Figures 17–11 and 17–12). Both these systems allow for increasing the number of

Figure 17–10 BSR appliance module is manually set to a house code letter and to a unit code.

devices controlled by using identical sets of receiver modules. Three different color-coded receivers could be in each room, enabling activation of three appliances in every room in the house. The Rehab Technology model requires that all appliances be plugged directly into the main unit; while prohibiting distant control of appliances, it limits the number of outlets required.

Another differentiating feature of ECUs is the user-ECU interface. Systems are classified as having either a portable transmitter or a stationary console or both. Activation of either of these devices is what causes an appliance to turn on and off. A portable transmitter is wireless (not connected to an outlet or receiver), unlike the stationary console. It can be hand-held, like the Switch-it or Ultra-4, or wireless like the Control 1 system in which the transmitter or an electric W/C is connected to a wireless receiver also on the W/C. This allows for control while remaining mobile in the environment. Control 1's transmitter, called a CID (control input display), is mounted on the W/C and allows the user to control appliances anywhere in the house or building without being in the same room as the stationary receiver (Figure 17–13). The stationary receiver is usually set up in the bedroom to allow control from bed.

The MECCA (Mobile Environmental Control and Communication Accessory) also permits control of appliances and the phone from the W/C without being in the same room as the stationary receiver. MECCA

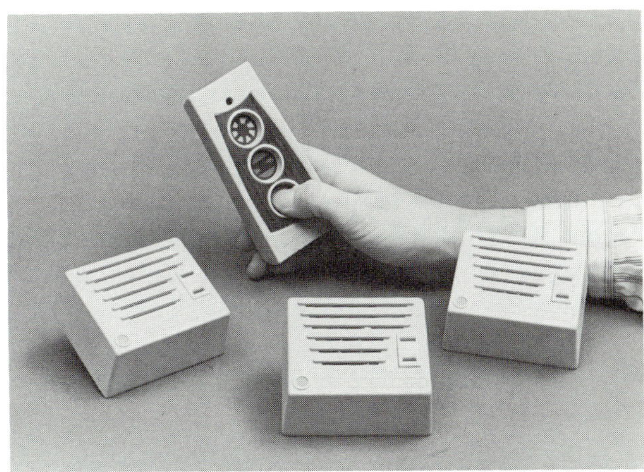

Figure 17–11 Switch-it ECU transmitter with three color-coded receivers.

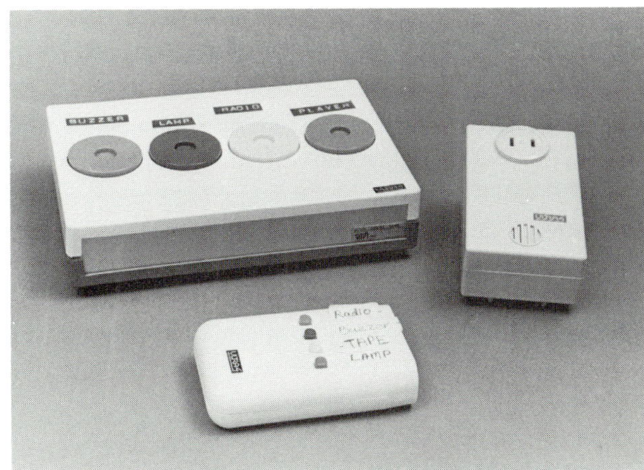

Figure 17–12 TASH Ultra-4 ECU: hand-held transmitter (front), large pushbutton transmitter (back), and one of four color-coded receivers (right).

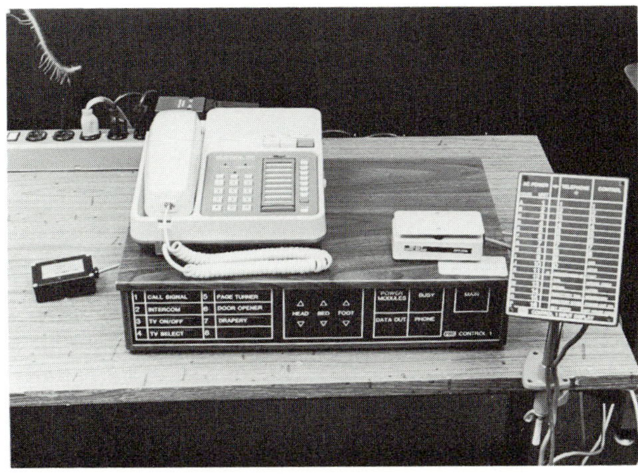

Figure 17–13 Control 1 ECU (on table) and control input display (CID) (right) allowing for remote wireless control.

operates through the telemetry capabilities of a cordless phone and consists of three subsystems: MECCA Mobile, MECCA Base, and MECCA Bedside. MECCA Mobile is a cordless phone in which the keypad has been replaced by an electronic scanning system. MECCA Base receives messages from MECCA Mobile, which is mounted on the electric W/C to control appliances. MECCA Bedside provides two-switch operation from the bed.

The MicroDEC also allows for wireless transmission from the W/C to the receiver. Although the setup is wireless, the user must be within hearing distance of the command console in order to receive auditory feedback. There is no mechanism to provide visual feedback from another room. Some people are able to memorize the sequence in order to operate the MicroDEC from another room. Transmitters are available to be connected to the circuitry of the electric W/C to allow dual control by the W/C controller (refer to next section) or to be mounted on a manual W/C. In the latter case, a dual switch would also be mounted on the manual W/C and plugged directly into the small portable transmitter (Figures 17–14 and 17–15).

Figure 17–14 Light-touch switch for ECU operation mounted on manual W/C. The switch can be used to change TV channels via light-touch switch remotely through MicroDEC.

Visual or auditory feedback when sending signals can be critical to a person functionally operating a system. In addition to a switch giving feedback (an auditory click) when activated, it is beneficial for some persons to receive immediate feedback on whether their signals were received. Some ECUs provide visual feedback in the form of a light or an auditory message; others provide no immediate feedback.

Appliances can be controlled via two modes, latching or momentary. Latching refers to switch activation in which a device remains on when the switch is activated and released and goes off only when the switch is activated a second time. Momentary refers to switch activation in which a device remains on only when the switch is held on and turns off when the switch is released.

The ability to interface the ECU with the electric W/C controller provides a more functional means to control devices and allows for less hardware on the W/C. This feature allows the user to drive the W/C and operate the ECU with the same control. For example, a MicroDEC user could drive the electric W/C with a switch controller (such as a pneumatic controller), pause, activate the reclining mechanism or safety switch, and then operate the ECU with the same controller. Activating the "forward" switch reverts the controller to W/C operation. A short-throw joystick W/C controller can be interfaced with the ECU, but a

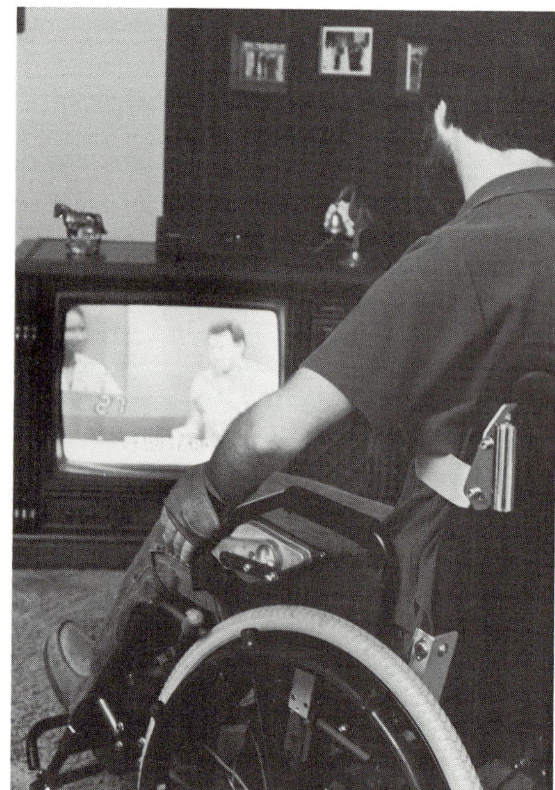

Figure 17–15 Same as Figure 17–14.

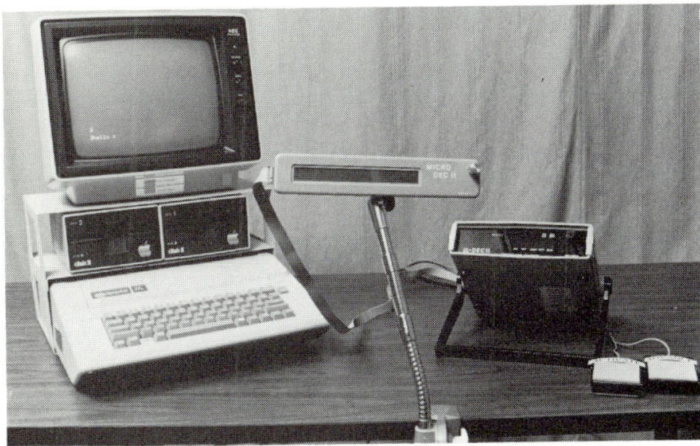

Figure 17–16 MicroDEC II ECU interfaced with Apple IIe computer and two tread switches.

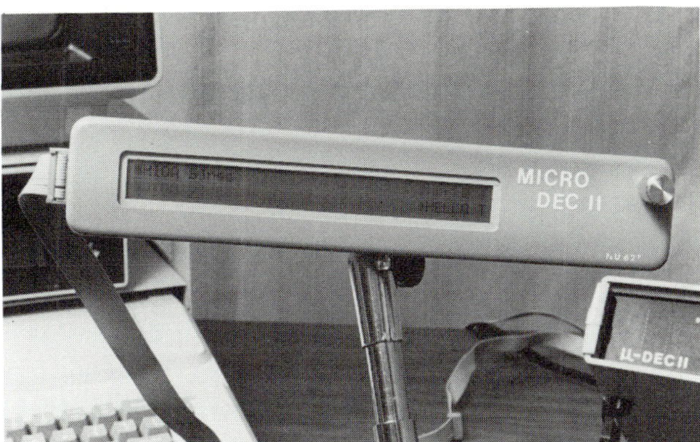

Figure 17–17 Computer input accomplished by advancing cursor to desired letter with one switch and selecting it with the second switch. Letter T is printed with light-emitting diodes and the selected letter H immediately appears next.

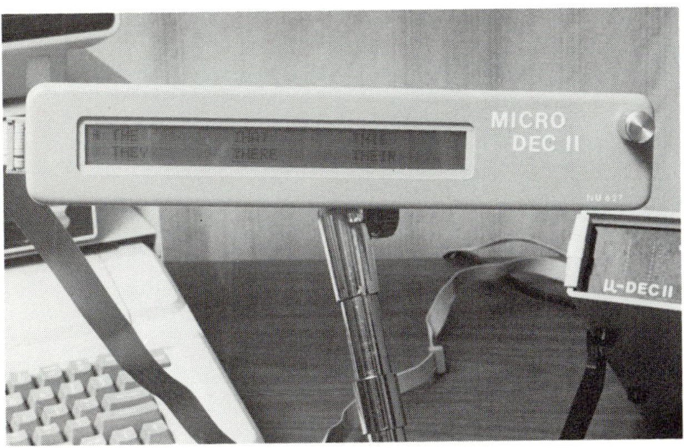

Figure 17–18 Word list beginning with TH is displayed automatically after letter H is selected.

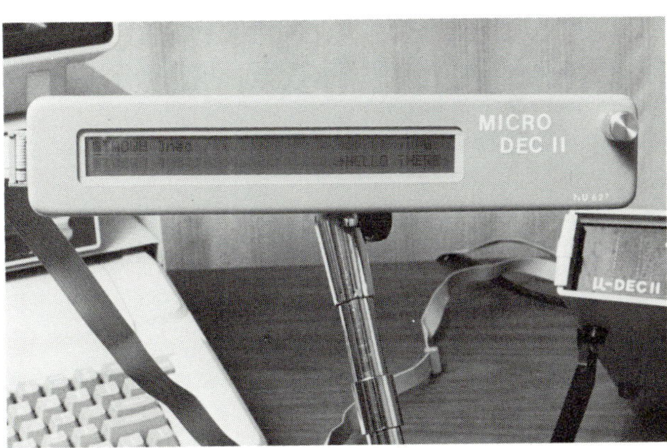

Figure 17–19 Cursor is advanced to desired word and then selected to display word on monitor.

proportional control joystick cannot. To convert other electric W/C systems, the manufacturer or a rehabilitation engineer should be consulted.

Some ECUs can be interfaced with a microcomputer to allow for control of appliances and a computer from the same input device. This allows a person using a word-processing program to answer the phone and then return to the program exactly where it was left through the same input device. Control 1 and MicroDEC II both provide the option of computer interfacing. DU-It Systems plans to produce a computer interface that can be operated simultaneously and through the same W/C controller as MECCA. The computer will not, however, be operated through MECCA, as it is through MicroDEC, but as a separate unit.

Computer access for Control 1 is available via Morse code, which operates through two-switch input. One switch represents the dot and the other the dash. The CID (control input display) converts the dots and dashes into characters recognizable by the computer, which then displays them on the monitor.

MicroDEC II provides transparent access to the Apple II+ and IIe computers for persons unable to operate the standard keyboard. Input is provided through a two-switch interface such as a pneumatic switch, rocker switch, or joystick. Its unique feature is the anticipatory letter and word selection that provides more efficient computer input than simple scanning. This system is based on stored statistical analyses of American English text and the user's own past word selections. As the user selects characters, MicroDEC II predicts the most likely letters or word to complete the selection. A 500-word fixed list is stored in MicroDEC II, which negates the need to spell out words in the list letter by letter. After the first two letters are selected a word list appears containing all the stored words beginning with those two letters (Figures 17–16 to 17–19). A learned word list of 150 words containing

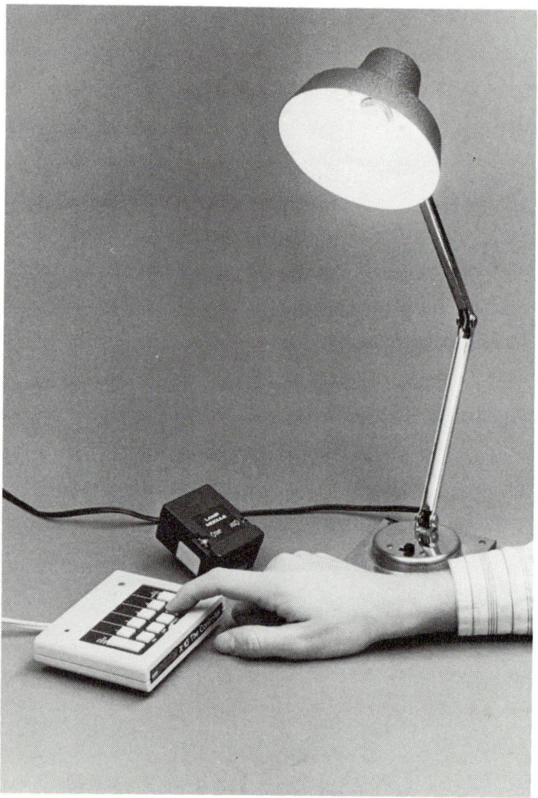

Figure 17–20 BSR Minicontroller ECU remotely controlling lamp, which is plugged into a BSR lamp module.

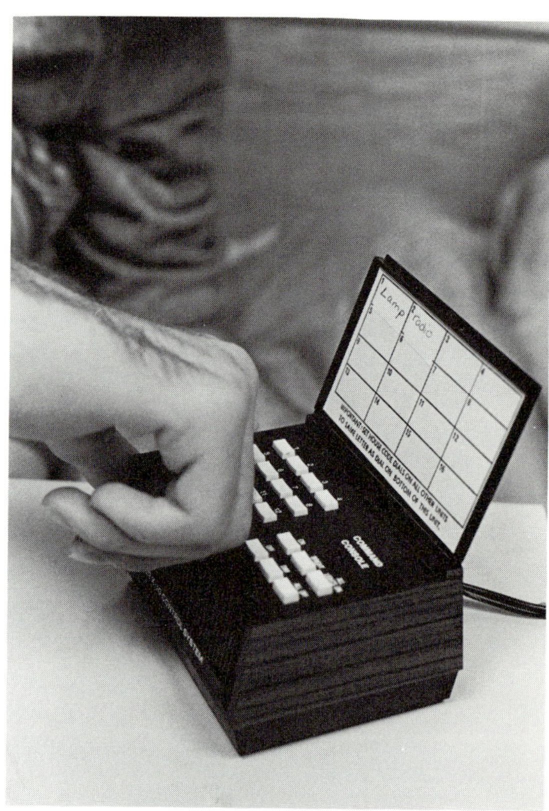

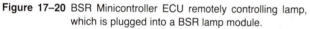

Figure 17–21 Person with C6 SCI operating BSR Command Console with tenodesis function.

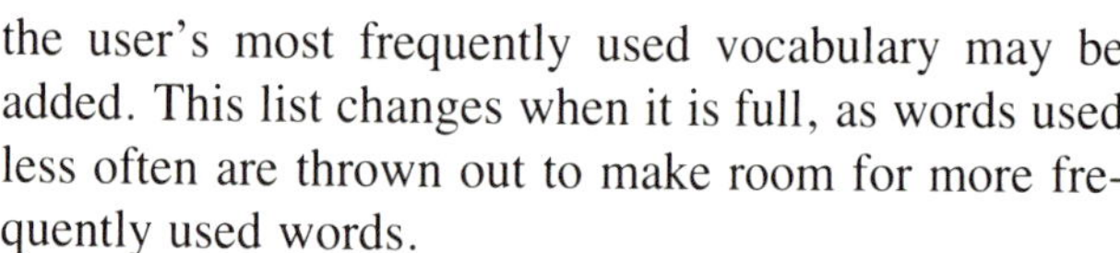

the user's most frequently used vocabulary may be added. This list changes when it is full, as words used less often are thrown out to make room for more frequently used words.

MicroDEC II and Control 1 are designed to benefit people who are unable to access the computer through direct selection. Individuals having adequate motor skills to use the standard keyboard but only in certain positions and for a limited time may also benefit. The person with a high level of SCI with limited respiratory capacity for sitting upright may prefer to use these methods rather than a mouthstick when reclined in the W/C or in bed.

Training for ECU Use and Setup

Training time in the operation and setup of ECUs varies with each device and person. An average of 30 minutes is sufficient to set up and learn to operate the Switch-it and Ultra-4 systems. The BSR Minicontroller, BSR Command Console, and BSR ECS-8 each generally require a 1-hour training session (Figures 17–20 to 17–22). The Rehab Technology system may require a 1- to 2-hour session to teach setup and operation. Two to three hour-long sessions are suggested for training a person in the operation of Micro-

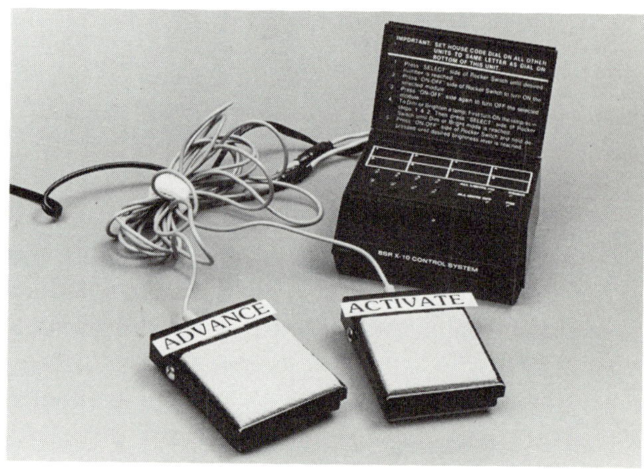

Figure 17–22 BSR ECS-8 ECU operated through two tread switches to control eight appliances.

DEC I. At least three hour-long sessions are suggested for MicroDEC II. Two to three hour-long sessions are also suggested for Control 1, with further practice required to learn Morse code. MECCA is advertised as being extremely easy to operate because of its visible menu-style display and cues that show the next step. It may require several hour-long sessions to familiarize a user with the operation and setup.

Mounting ECU Controls

Options for mounting ECUs are as numerous as one's creativity, design expertise, and cost limitations allow. A simple means of mounting the Switch-it, BSR Minicontroller, or BSR Command Console is with a gooseneck. This allows easy adjustment of the height and angle of the device for mouthstick or hand-held pointer activation. The gooseneck may require extra reinforcement because pressure from a pointer or mouthstick may cause deflection. A more rigid pole may be required. The device can also be set up on a table near the user's bed. Tread switches can be mounted on the bed with a commercially available Kydex bed rail clip.

With MicroDEC, use of the standard transmitter in bed will eliminate cords going from the bed to the command console. The distance from the switch to the receiver with the Rehab Technology device can be increased by lengthening the Tygon tubing that connects the pneumatic switch to the receiver. It is suggested that an OT/RE team set up the more complex systems (MicroDEC, Control 1, MECCA) in the home or at work to ensure functional operation (Figure 17–23).

Family Control of Appliances

Once appliances are interfaced with the ECU, it is sometimes necessary for a family member to control one or all of them. It may not be convenient (or hygienic, in the case of pneumatic control) for them to use the appliance through the switch. BSR modules, depending on the appliance, allow one to turn on the appliance without going through the ECU by turning the appliance's switch off and then on again. However, the device should not be turned off manually and left off, as this prevents control through the ECU. A cordless, hand-held controller is also available for use with the ultrasonic model of the BSR Command Console. It transmits signals to the console 30 feet away; however,

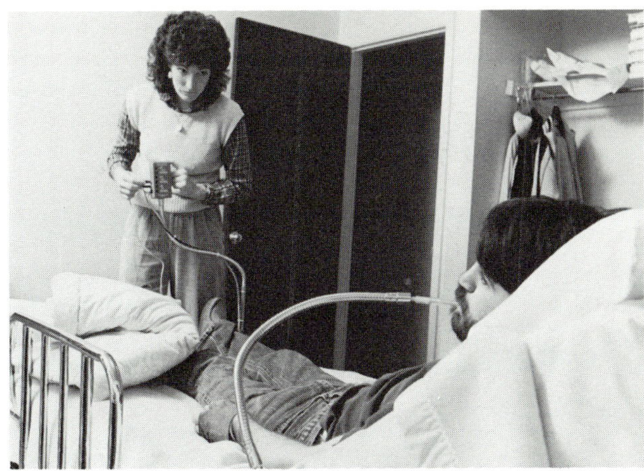

Figure 17–23 Occupational therapist setting up an ECU in patient's home for sip-and-puff operation of bed controls.

it does not transmit through walls. This cordless controller has the same features as the Command Console. The BSR Command Console or Minicontroller can be ordered for family use in conjunction with BSR control through MicroDEC, Control 1, or MECCA. The Rehab Technology console has pushbuttons on it for family control.

Concomitant Head Injury

Special consideration must be given to the SCI patient with a concomitant head injury when determining appropriate devices for trial. Features to be examined include complexity of selection method (direct selection versus scanning), type of feedback available, and number of devices operated. TASH Ultra-4 and Switch-it may be functional for the person with memory deficits, as the number of devices is limited and feedback is immediate when a button is touched. Each selection button can be labeled with the name or picture of the device. Some persons may require simple directions posted on the device for easy reference. Portability of the device may be critical because the person may need the transmitter to be constantly present to facilitate its use.

ALTERNATIVE COMPUTER INPUT METHODS

Adaptive Firmware Card

This hardware provides transparent access to the Apple II and IIe and serves as a transparent keyboard

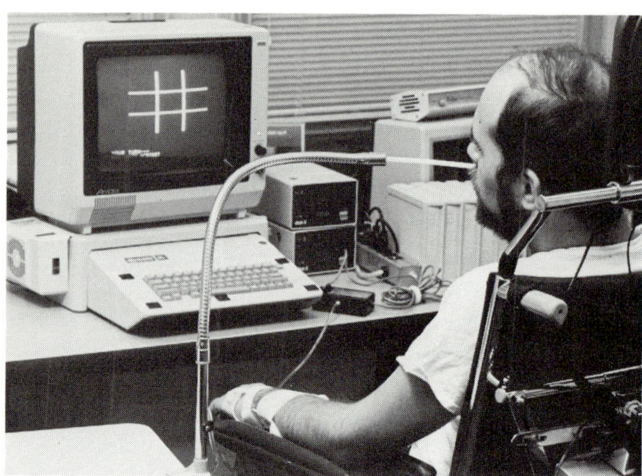

Figure 17–24 Accessing game software (tic-tac-toe) through the adaptive firmware card with a sip-and-puff switch.

emulator for those individuals unable to use the keyboard (Figure 17–24). This allows information to enter the computer from sources other than the standard keyboard, thus permitting use of all standard software for that computer. The complete interface consists of a printed circuit card that is inserted inside the Apple computer and a small plastic box that is screwed onto the side of the computer (Figure 17–25). This box contains two minijacks for switch interface and a thumb wheel that is manually turned to the selected mode of input. Sixteen different input modes are available to accommodate the various needs of the disabled. The keyboard remains active and can be used at any time.

The process cannot totally be controlled through one-switch activation. The software must first be inserted into the disk drive. The second step is to turn on the computer. The program does not load immediately, but necessitates inputting the timing or scanning rate for the selected method through the keyboard. After this, the person can utilize the selected input method through the control switch. The 16 input methods include three types of one-switch scanning, Morse code with one or two switches, two-switch scanning, and modes to accept peripherals such as a miniature or expanded keyboard. The speed of the cursor can be accelerated or decelerated at any time. The firmware card provides access to games, word processing, educational programs, or ECU functions for persons with limited arm placement and head control.

The adaptive firmware card can be activated through a variety of switches, including pneumatic, eyebrow, eye blink, and EMG. Adaptive Peripherals is the vendor.

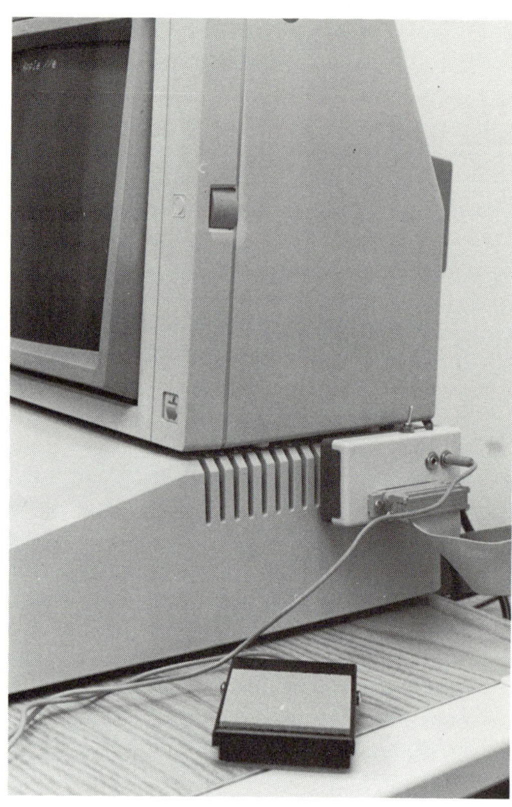

Figure 17–25 Adaptive firmware card with two jacks for switches and a jack for an expanded keyboard.

Voice Recognition Systems

Voice recognition systems (Figure 17–26) were designed to improve speed of entry and ease of learning complex software; keyboard and voice entry can be used simultaneously. Many new systems, compatible with a variety of computers, are entering the market. Some systems are designed to run only particular software, while others are compatible with all available software for a given computer. Important characteristics to consider include accuracy of voice recognition, extent of vocabulary, length of training required, and price.

The user utters a word or phrase into a microphone (also available in a headset and as a wireless microphone), and the computer recognizes and responds to the input as though it were given through the keyboard. Before running the program, the user builds the necessary vocabulary for that program and then trains the computer to recognize his voice speaking the words. In training, the user repeats each word or phrase at least three times. Further repetitions may ensure greater

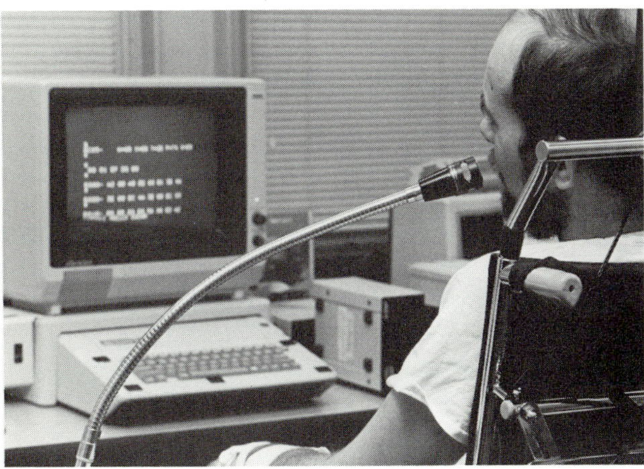

Figure 17–26 Quadriplegic (C4) accessing computer through voice recognition system by speaking into a microphone.

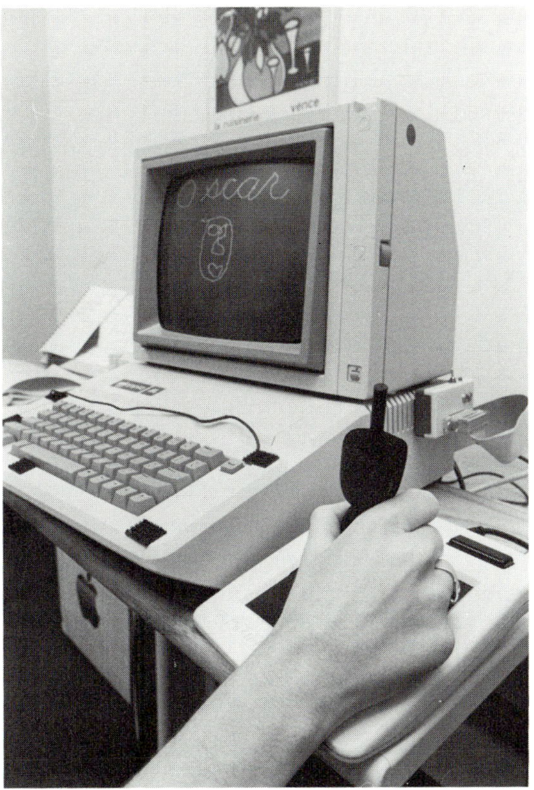

Figure 17–27 Koala pad.

accuracy in recognition. Pronunciations different from the voice patterns trained and loaded may necessitate frequent repetitions during operation and decrease the efficiency of input. For example, problems may occur if a respiratory infection results in hoarseness.

The voice recognition systems were designed to be used concurrently with the keyboard to decrease the necessity of hitting several keys for one action. However, for the disabled, input through only the voice recognition system is possible. The input time must be compared with that of other possible modes of input, such as a mouthstick or Morse code with a pneumatic switch. Voice input is not for everyone, as reliability, needs, and ability to build and train vocabulary are all significant criteria. Four systems, compatible with the Apple and IBM, are listed in Appendix B.

Voice recognition systems are activated by the user's voice. Key Tronic, Prentke Romich Company, The Voice Connection, and Voice Machine Communications sell such systems.

Koala Pad

The Koala pad is an electronic video sketch pad allowing the creation of a variety of multicolored graphics (Figure 17–27). It can be used with any Apple II series computer through a game port. A stick or a person's finger is moved across the pad. Two touch switches also need to be activated to control the programs. Tenodesis hand function may be adequate to utilize the stick with a built-up handle. The switches can be adapted with a latching mechanism to keep them depressed until they are released by pushing the latching mechanism again. This may be necessary for use with programs requiring the use of the stick while simultaneously holding a switch down. The stick can also be attached to a WHO. Pad activation requires a degree of maintained pressure not always available to users with SCI, but the Koala pad does have potential to become a miniature keyboard as it is possible to develop a customized keyboard on the pad. Available software includes education, games, drawing and graphic design, and programming.

The Koala pad is activated by direct selection through use of a pointer or finger and depression of two touch switches. The vendor is Koala Technologies Corporation.

Light Pens

Computer input with a light pen is achieved by holding the pen next to the monitor and pushing a small button on the end of the pen for activation. It is currently not a functional alternative for those with significantly limited hand function. It is possible to operate the pen with bilateral hand function, as the button can be pushed with the other hand. Fatigue may be a critical factor in holding the pen close to the monitor.

Computer activation with a light pen occurs when the pen is held next to the monitor and the button on the pen tip is depressed. The vendor is Koala Technologies Corporation.

COMPUTER ADAPTATIONS

On-Off Switch

Most computer on-off switches are located in the back of the device, making activation impossible for those with limited arm placement. This problem can be overcome simply by plugging all the hardware into a multiplug outlet that is mounted accessibly and activated through a rocker switch by mouthstick or hand.

Keyboard

Key guards mounted over the keyboard can enhance speed and accuracy of operation. They are recommended for use with mouthsticks and hand-held pointers (Figure 17–28). Key guards prevent these devices from slipping off a key or inadvertently hitting a wrong key. They can also serve as a resting place for a mouthstick or pointer, avoiding accidental key activation while reviewing or resting. Proficient users of the mouthstick and hand-held pointer may be slowed by a key guard. Key guards are commercially available for many computers, including the Apple II, II+, IIc, and IIe, Atari 800, Franklin Ace 1000, T199/4A, Epson HX 20, IBM PC, and Commodore 64. Custom key guards can also be fabricated.

Latching mechanisms for certain keys (control, shift, etc.) are built into some key guards to allow maintained key depression without manually holding the key down. The key is released by pushing the opposite end of the lever. This permits a mouthstick or single-pointer user to activate more than one key at a time, which is necessary with many software programs.

Key latches are also commercially available to easily attach to keys on the outside periphery of the keyboard, where control keys are usually located. Some of these attach with screws. The computer owner should be cautioned that disturbing the body of the device by drilling a hole to insert the screw may invalidate the warranty.

Figure 17–28 Key guard on computer helps some users of mouthsticks and hand-held pointers.

Inserting Software

Equipment is available for the person with high-level SCI to operate computer programs independently with an eyebrow switch once the software is inserted. There is an adaptation for insertion of floppy disks into non–built-in disk drives that works well for the person with good arm placement but no wrist or hand function. This is a removable Kydex stand (Heckathorne, Hedman, and Rossano, RIC RE) with a slot that is attached to the disk drive with Scotchmate (Figures 17–29 and 17–30). The disk is dropped into this slot by using two pencils in WHOs and then is pushed inside the drive with one pencil. The door may be shut and opened with

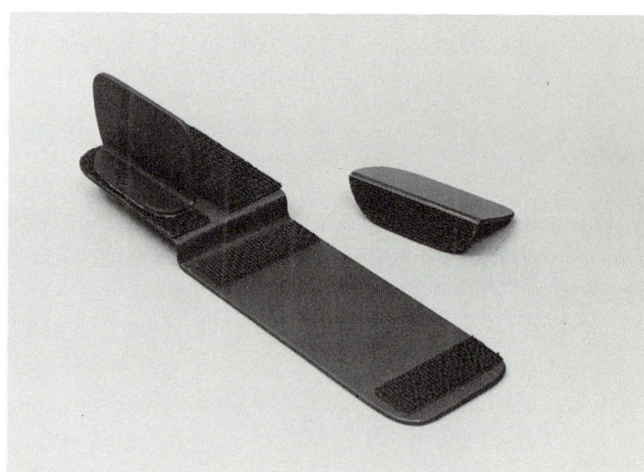

Figure 17–29 Kydex stand assists in guiding floppy disks into single disk drive.

Figure 17–30 Kydex stand attaches to disk drive with Scotchmate.

a pencil eraser. The disk is removed by pulling it out with the tips of the erasers. The disk drive can be set on its side for easy access. It may be possible for a mouthstick user to insert the disk with a pincer mouthstick while the drive is standing on end.

Wire handles are also commercially available. These are slipped onto the edge of each floppy disk. A mouthstick user can then insert the disk with a hook on the tip of the mouthstick. Commercial disk guides are available for some computers.

Positioning of Devices

Positioning of the computer and peripherals is critical for functional use by the person with SCI. It can determine a user's ability to operate a standard keyboard without a special interface and can increase the efficiency and duration of operation. Table selection for hardware is dependent on the person's W/C. Critical factors include the height and length of the W/C arms, the recline angle, the angle of the user's legs, and the method of accessing the keyboard. Adjustable height tables and U-shaped work stations generally provide good work areas. Some persons may require an elevating hospital table to bring the computer between the W/C armrests. Detachable keyboards are ideal for optimal positioning. Bookrests may be used to angle the keyboard for this purpose. Monitor arm supports are available that support the monitor, adjust it to any angle, and allow it to be swung away from the computer. These should be investigated thoroughly before purchasing to check for safety, as some arms are unable to support the weight of the monitor.

SUMMARY

Despite the many advances in the field of technical aids for the disabled, there are still many limitations. Most new technology in computers is developed without consideration of the disabled and tends to widen the gap between the able-bodied population and persons with disabilities who have work and educational potential. Rehabilitation professionals and disabled consumers can play a role in influencing computer companies to recognize the needs of the disabled in designing new hardware and software so that they have equal access. It is often less costly for both manufacturers and consumers to make these alterations in the design phase than adapt inaccessible equipment later.

Technology is providing the tools with which the person with SCI can fashion a productive and satisfactory life-style. It is the responsibility of the health professional to provide information about appropriate equipment and requisite training.

Appendix 17A

Environmental Control Units

System	Selection Method	Switch Options	Activation	Transmission	User-ECU Interface: Portable Transmitter	User-ECU Interface: Stationary Console
Switch-it	Direct selection	None	C2–C3:MS C4: MS, BFO C5: orthosis C6–C8: NE	Remote to receivers in same room (A)	Ultrasonic	
TASH Ultra-4	Direct selection for switch-activated, joystick, hand-held, and large-button transmitters	Pneumatic, light-touch	C2–C3: MS, S/P C4: MS, BFO, S/P C5–C8: NE, rocker switch	Same as above	Ultrasonic	
BSR X-10 Command Console	Direct selection	None	C2, C3: MS with key guard C4: MS, BFO C5: orthosis C6: NE, orthosis C7, C8: NE	House wiring, remote control (A,B)		Keypad
BSR Minicontroller	Direct selection	None	C2, C3: MS C4: MS, BFO C5: orthosis C6–C8: NE	House wiring, remote control (A,B)		Keypad
BSR ECS-8	Two-switch step scanning	Pneumatic, light-touch, rocker, leaf, tread	C2–C4: S/P C5: tread, rocker, light-touch, S/P from bed C6: NA	House wiring, remote control (A,B)		Connected to switches
Rehab Technology	Direct selection	Pneumatic; adaptations for other switches possible through manufacturer	C5 or higher: S/P; can have adapted to other types C6–C8: NA	Appliances plugged into ECU (C)		Connected to switches
MicroDEC I	Two-switch step scanning	Pneumatic, light-touch, tread, joystick, tongue/chin	C2: S/P C3, C4: S/P, CC C5: tread, rocker, light-touch, S/P from bed, joystick C6–C8: NA	House wiring, radio transmission (A,B)	Radio. Portable transmitter must be within hearing distance, or memorize sequence	Connected to switches
MicroDEC II	Two-switch step scanning	Same as MicroDEC I	Same as MicroDEC I	Same as MicroDEC I	Same as MicroDEC I	
Control-1	Two-switch step scanning and traditional scanning for dialing	Dual rocker, pneumatic, joystick	Same as MicroDEC I	House wiring, radio transmission (A,B,C)	Radio	Connected to switches
MECCA	Two-switch traditional scanning	Chin, tongue/lip, pneumatic	C2: S/P, tongue/lip C3–C4: S/P, CC C5: CC, joystick, rocker C6–C8: NA	House wiring, radio transmission through telemetry capabilities of cordless phone (A,B,C)	Radio	Connected to switches

Key: MS, mouthstick; BFO,balanced forearm orthosis; S/P, sip-and-puff or pneumatic switch; CC, chin controller switch; NE, no equipment or orthosis required; NA, (generally) not appropriate or necessary at this level of injury; A, appliances plugged into separate ECU receivers; B, appliances interface with main console through house wiring; C, appliances plugged directly into ECU console.

Feedback	Appliances (no.) Latch	Momentary	Either	Options: TV Channel Changer	Telephone	Computer Interface	W/C Control Interface	Source(s)
Visual	3	0	0	No	No	No	No	VSC Corporation
None	4	0	0	No	No	No	Fortress Scientific Controller	TASH
Visual	16	0	0	No	No	No	No	Radio Shack, BSR/MED, Sears
Visual	8	0	0	No	No	No	No	BSR/MED
None	8	0	0	No	No	No	No	BSR/MED
Visual, auditory	0	4	4	Yes	Yes	No	No	Rehabilitation Technology
Visual, auditory	0	0	16	Yes	Yes	No	MED Quad system can be adapted to any W/C system with four-switch controls (short-throw joystick or sip-and-puff)	MED
Visual, auditory	0	0	16	Yes	Yes	Apple II+ and IIe	Same as MicroDEC I	MED
Visual, auditory	256	0	8	Yes	Yes	Apple II, II+, IIe, IIc; IBM PC via Morse code encoding	Same as MicroDEC I	PRC
Visual, auditory	2 (for fixed-wiring appliances)	0	8	Yes	Yes	Available fall 1986	DU-It system, MED, Dufco, Abbey	DU-It Control Systems Group, Inc.
	10 (for remote-controlled appliances)	2	4					

Unit 18

Putting It All Together: Discharge Planning

Judy Hill, OTR/L

Many skills are learned by SCI patients during initial and subsequent rehabilitation hospitalizations. The true test of the rehabilitation process is the patient's ability to use these skills after discharge.

It is important to determine the postdischarge setting early in the rehabilitation process. It may not be possible, however, for the patient or family to predict placement until they have had time for initial adjustment and for participating in the necessary care. The level of independence the patient is expected to achieve in his initial 2- to 3-month rehabilitation stay and beyond is important in determining the most appropriate postdischarge setting. Other equally important factors are the social support systems available to the patient, financial resources, psychological status, and housing.

Regardless of the specific postdischarge setting, planning for the incorporation of learned skills and necessary care into a daily routine must occur. During the process discussion is needed to determine which activities are appropriate for the patient to do and who will perform the remaining care. The optimum routine for both care givers and patient must be determined.

Crucial decisions are made in discharge planning. A decision to have assistance in dressing and transfers because it is faster can have long-term impact. If the time for self-dressing is available and the patient has the necessary skills to perform the task, a decision not to carry through with dressing could result in unnecessary dependence and the need for relearning skills at a later date. However, if, after dressing, assistance is needed for a transfer into the W/C and this assistance is provided by a family member before going to work, it may be realistic to decide that dressing can be practiced only on the weekend when time is available. If other activities such as work or school are more important to the patient and require that morning care be assisted because of limited time, assisted dressing may be most appropriate.

Issues to be addressed in discharge planning include the following:

- Who will perform each component of self-care at home?
- What training will care givers need?
- What equipment is needed to meet self-care needs?
- What activities will have to be performed by patient or care giver to prevent further loss of function?
- Is the home environment conducive to meeting self-care needs?
- Is the work, school, or recreational environment conducive to meeting self-care needs?

In addressing who will perform tasks, what training care givers will need, and what equipment is necessary, each task, from feeding to hygiene to urinary care, is reviewed with patient and family. It is necessary to determine components of the task that the patient can perform as well as the equipment and setup needed. Accessibility and daily routine considerations contribute to deciding who will perform the task. Once this is decided, skill at task performance must be ensured, first in the hospital and then in the postdischarge setting. Home passes are invaluable in testing the discharge plans and making necessary alterations before actual discharge. In instructing care givers in equipment use and task setup, the patient's ability to direct care is tested, with the therapist observing and providing demonstration when necessary.

A list of commonly used pieces of equipment for each area of self-care is helpful in ensuring that the patient has all the necessary equipment at discharge. Back-up pieces of essential equipment that the patient depends on should be provided. Utensil cuffs, W/C gloves, catheter clamps, and feeding utensils are common pieces of equipment issued in duplicate just before discharge. Equipment care instructions and resources for obtaining replacement equipment should be provided.

The patient and therapist should consider carefully what activities, including self-care activities, are necessary for continued skill building and preventing further loss of function. Frequently, involvement in self-care activities such as dressing and propelling the W/C will be sufficient to maintain UE ROM and strength in patients with C6 or lower function. At C5 and above, limited possibilities for self-care will require that a minimum of passive ROM to the UEs be provided by the care giver. Activities such as self-feeding (at C5) or mouthstick use (C3) should be sufficient to maintain strength in available musculature.

There are times when a specific strengthening program is indicated in the postdischarge period. The following are indications of the need for such a program:

- Muscle function is still changing, so a strengthening program could result in achieving additional functional goals.
- Specific muscles, not yet strong enough for incorporation into functional tasks, have potential to achieve functional strength (poor to fair wrist extensors, for example).
- Specific muscles require strengthening for tendon transfer surgery.

In these cases a home strengthening program or outpatient treatment for follow-up are alternatives. As with any exercise regimen, it must be scheduled into the daily routine.

Assessing home, work, school, and recreational environments for their conduciveness to optimal independence often requires a site visit. Many detailed references on accessibility are available for research on specific measurements. General areas to be considered include the following:

- Access to parking. Width and length of parking space for unloading the chair or lift operation and access from the parking area are considered.
- Access to buildings. Particularly at school and work, access to multiple buildings may be necessary (library, classroom buildings, dormitories, etc.). Door weight, direction of opening, spring loading, lock height, and resistance are considered.
- Access to rooms at home, work, and school. At home access to all rooms is considered, with bedroom and bathroom often most crucial. At school and work access to classrooms, offices, meeting rooms, cafeteria, and bathrooms is important.
- Space for necessary equipment must be considered as a part of accessibility.
- Access to appliances and tools. Tabletop models may make access to kitchen appliances easier. Work and study stations should allow access to all necessary equipment such as typewriters, page turners, and telephone.
- Placement of light switches and telephone near the bed should be considered.
- Access to leisure activity areas and equipment. Patio, yard, garden, TV, stereo, radio, and community activities are considered. Many major metropolitan areas have accessibility guides and independent living centers that can help in researching community access.
- Access and egress in emergencies. Most local fire departments have special services for disabled

persons. Alternatives to elevators must be considered in emergency egress plans.

Site visits can offer more than objective data. Observations can be made about the patient's comfort in the environment and with family. Often, functional skills that need further refinement before actual discharge are identified and adaptations, furniture rearrangement, and equipment recommendations are made. When a need for home modification is identified, resources, including the names of contractors specializing in accessible housing, are provided.

A discharge plan that takes into consideration home care routines, home programs, and accessibility is made through discussion with the patient and family and is critical for adjustment. Inevitably issues will arise that were not foreseen and planned for. The recommendations made for such situations depend largely on the problem-solving abilities of patient and family, as observed during the hospitalization. Many patients will be able to adapt routines to fit changing needs and circumstances. They will use professional resources appropriately when problems arise. Others may require home OT to assist with problem solving during the transition phase and periodically thereafter. OT rechecks are used to assess the adequacy of the discharge plan and physical status. They are usually done 1, 3, and 6 months after discharge and annually thereafter. For high-risk patients rechecks may be made sooner and more frequently.

Persons with SCI gradually leave the role of patient to resume old roles and assume some new ones. They have gained maximally from the rehabilitation process if they are physically performing all or some of the tasks they were unable to perform on entering the rehabilitation hospital and if they are more aware of their ability to meet their own needs and control their own lives. Even when some assistance is needed for task accomplishment, rehabilitation has been a success if needs and activities have been ordered into a meaningful and satisfying pattern, if old friendships have been resumed and new ones established, if old interests are being pursued and new ones found, and if goals and ideas for becoming more self-sufficient are being realized.

Appendix A
GROUP PROGRAMS

The following is a description of the OT groups that SCI patients may be involved in at RIC. These groups are an adjunct to individual OT treatment.

QUAD GROUP

A. Purpose

The purpose of the Quad Group is to facilitate the development of functional skills, ADL, socialization, and appropriate leisure and recreation skills. The group is intended to provide basic community skills needed for transition into the Quad Community Reentry Group (QCRG) and necessary to aid in a smooth transition into the community.

B. Objectives

1. To provide opportunities for patients to improve and carry over learned skills, to solve problems, and to direct others in a group setting. The following areas are addressed:
   - meal preparation
   - communication (writing, typing, telephone, reading, etc.)
   - oral and facial hygiene
   - leisure time
   - bowel and bladder
   - feeding
   - dressing
2. To provide time for additional practice in UE functional activities:
   - UE muscle strengthening and endurance
   - fine motor control, coordination, tenodesis, and use of orthoses
   - gross motor coordination (balance, bilateral arm placement, trunk mobility and stability)
   - use of adaptive devices (BFO, mouthstick, Swedish sling, etc.)
   - avocational projects
3. To increase the patient's self-esteem and reestablish roles.
4. To promote reintegration into social situations.
5. To help patients learn responsibility to and for self.
6. To provide a group milieu for patients to exchange information and build mutual support.

C. Content

1. *Planning*. Group members are given the opportunity to plan the weekly schedules according to their interests in each of the activity areas (fine motor, gross motor, communication, community trips, meal preparation, avocation, and education).
2. *Problem solving*. Group members solve activity setup problems with group therapists.
3. *Success*. Group therapists ensure the success of group activities, especially community trips. This will increase patient confidence and future initiation of activities (unit 13).

D. Staffing

The group is staffed by two occupational therapists. Volunteers are utilized as needed. The group has three to seven patients.

E. Process

The group meets 1 hour per day, or 2 hours on community trip days, Monday through Friday. This group precedes participation in QCRG.

QUAD COMMUNITY REENTRY GROUP (QCRG)

A. Purpose

The purpose of QCRG is to facilitate the development of problem-solving skills in physical, social, and leisure functioning in a community setting. Programming is intended to supplement the patient's treatment program and is designed to incorporate the skills learned in-house into actual performance in a community setting. The program is designed to expose the patient to commonly experienced community situations and to develop problem-solving techniques that will enable him to apply similar techniques to new situations upon discharge.

B. Objectives

1. To minimize the impact of architectural barriers in community settings.
2. To maximize the ability to functionally manage time to complete ADL.
3. To maximize the application of self-care skills in the community.
4. To maximize mobility skills necessary for performing self-care tasks in the community.
5. To maximize functioning in recreational settings, including time management skills, general skills development, and resource awareness.
6. To enhance self-esteem.
7. To promote self-motivation.
8. To maximize responsibility for self.
9. To minimize the psychological impact of attitudes regarding disability.

C. Content

1. *Planning*. Participants are responsible for planning for each community experience decided on by the group. A variety of potential problem areas are discussed to develop planning skills:
   - medical needs
   - personal needs
   - W/C maintenance
   - architectural barriers
   - transportation options
   - potential social interactions
2. *Participating*. After the necessary arrangements for the community trip have been made, patients then participate in the activity. Emphasis is on acquiring the necessary problem-solving skills to increase physical, social, and leisure independence in the community setting.
3. *Debriefing*. In the first portion of each session, following a community trip, participants are involved in individual and group discussions with facilitators to identify any problem areas and successes encountered. Ideas are shared to improve individual problem solving before the next community trip is undertaken. In addition, informative lectures are provided.

D. Staffing

One occupational therapist, one nurse, one nurse assistant, one therapeutic recreation specialist, and one physical therapist serve as program facilitators. The exact staffing ratio is determined on the basis of group size, level of function, and activity. The group has five to eight patients.

E. Process

This group is held once a month for a 2-week period and meets every afternoon for 2 to 4 hours. It is included in the patient's treatment plan when he is approximately 3 weeks from discharge and is used as a transitional time to incorporate skills learned into the community setting.

COMMUNITY REENTRY GROUP (PARAPLEGIC)

A. Purpose

The purpose of this group is to facilitate the development of functional skills, ADL, socialization skills, and appropriate leisure and recreation skills necessary to aid in a smooth transition from the clinical setting to the community. It is the intent of the program to expose the patient to community situations most commonly experienced and to facilitate problem-solving techniques that will enable him to apply similar techniques to new situations upon discharge.

B. Objectives

1. To provide opportunities to improve and carry over skills learned in all therapies.
2. To minimize the impact of environmental barriers in the community by increasing awareness of barriers and resources and by planning for most limiting factors.
3. To minimize the impact of attitudinal barriers in the community by encouraging awareness of such attitudes and ways of dealing with them.
4. To maximize performance of self-care activities in the community (clothes, shopping, catheter care, etc.).
5. To maximize participation in recreational activities by encouraging awareness of resources and assisting in prioritization of needs.
6. To maximize responsibility for self by monitoring attendance, motivation, and the ability to identify and meet needs.

C. Content

Each session focuses on the development of functional and social skills needed for reentry into the community setting via in-house and out-trip activities. The emphasis of this group is to assist the paraplegic in carrying over learned skills into the community so those skills become more natural and spontaneous. The group utilizes discussions, lectures, in-house activities, and community trips. The participants will be exposed to situations that require problem solving, direction of others in care, and social interactions with others in the community. The group activities will be chosen by the participants, with staff direction. The experiences are then reviewed by the patients.

D. Staffing

The group is staffed by two occupational therapists on a daily basis, two therapeutic recreation specialists on a daily basis, and a physical therapist on an as-needed basis. Exact staffing ratio depends on group size and activity. The maximum number of members is 12, with four staff members.

E. Process

The group meets for 1 hour Tuesday through Friday. Mondays are reserved for introduction of new participants to the group. The community out-trip time will vary depending on the activity planned.

INTERDISCIPLINARY FLOOR TREATMENT PROGRAMS

A. Purpose

The purpose of these programs is to facilitate the provision to SCI patients of an interdisciplinary treatment program involving OT, PT, therapeutic recreation, and nursing.

B. Objectives

1. To provide a setting for joint goal setting between therapists and patient.
2. To foster peer support and problem solving among group members.
3. To encourage carry-over of learned functional skills to the nursing floor, social interactions, and community interactions through interdisciplinary planning, problem solving, and treatment.
4. To provide patients with skills training in all areas of self-care.

C. Content

The group includes the following:

1. Individual treatment given in a one-to-one manner.
2. Setup treatment given in a supervised manner, with the patient set up to work independently.
3. Group treatment activities.
4. Cotreatment in which two or more disciplines work together with a patient on an activity such as bathing or dressing.

D. Staff

One registered occupational therapist and one registered physical therapist serve as group leaders. The services of a therapeutic recreational specialist and nurse are scheduled periodically. The group has three patients.

E. Process

The group meets Monday through Friday for 2 hours in a common treatment area on the patient floors.

FEEDING GROUP

A. Purpose

The purpose of the feeding group is to provide the opportunity for patients to gain maximal independence in self-feeding skills, to gain skill in directing equipment setup, and to continue solving problems in self-feeding with an occupational therapy assistant.

B. Objectives

1. To provide a consistent setting in which patients can practice self-feeding skills presented in individual OT treatment.
2. To develop skill in the use of feeding equipment.
3. To provide necessary cues, supervision, and encouragement for appropriate behavior and equipment use.
4. To promote reintegration into social eating situations.
5. To redevelop patient awareness of table manners practiced in social situations.
6. To suggest methods whereby patients can be more independent in feeding.

C. Content

The feeding group incorporates the following:

1. *Directing setup*. The SCI patient is expected to direct the group leader in setting up needed equipment for feeding.
2. *Independence*. The SCI patient is expected to feed independently and request assistance if needed.

D. Staffing

The group is staffed by one occupational therapy assistant. The maximum group census is ten patients, with all diagnosis-eligible. A volunteer or aide is utilized as needed.

E. Process

The group is held at breakfast and lunch in the cafeteria, Monday through Friday. Patients participate in the group until supervision is no longer needed.

MEAL PREPARATION PROGRAM

A. Purpose

The purpose of this program is to promote compensatory and organizational skills for the development of safe cold or hot meal preparation habits for patients returning to a semiindependent or independent environment.

B. Objectives

1. To provide consistent opportunity for patients to improve and carry over learned meal preparation skills.
2. To solve skills and equipment problems arising during meal preparation tasks.
3. To direct others for equipment setup and assistance, as needed.
4. To evaluate and prepare for meal preparation needs associated with independent or semiindependent living situations.

C. Content

Patients prepare their meals in the OT clinic instead of receiving a cafeteria tray. They are expected to use adaptive equipment or compensatory techniques to complete an appropriate meal with supervision.

D. Staffing

Three occupational therapists serve as group facilitators who rotate on a schedule allowing for one group facilitator per day. The group numbers two to three, with all diagnosis-eligible for participation.

E. Process

The group meets 4 days a week at lunch time. Patients are signed up to attend at least two sessions per week.

AVOCATIONAL GROUP

A. Purpose

The purpose of this group is to provide a setting for patients to gain a variety of physical and cognitive skills by participating in independent avocational activities.

B. Objectives

Objectives are determined by the primary therapist. Possible SCI objectives include

1. Increase UE strength.
2. Increase UE balance.
3. Patient to use tenodesis for avocational activity.
4. Increase avocational and leisure interests.
5. Patient to use orthotic devices and equipment for completion of avocational activity.
6. Patient to direct needs and equipment setup.

C. Content

Patients work on crafts projects, including woodworking, needlework, metal tooling, ceramics, and leather work in a parallel group setting.

D. Staffing

One OT assistant, an OT aide, and a volunteer (when available) facilitate the group.

E. Process

The group meets 1 hour per day, Monday through Friday. This hour of therapy is provided in addition to an individual OT session. A patient attends as long as he has goals that can be met in the group and as decided by the patient and primary therapist.

Appendix B

EQUIPMENT SOURCES

The following is a partial list of sources for equipment discussed in this book. It is meant to provide common general sources for ADL equipment and specific sources for equipment that is not so generally available. The general sources are listed first, followed by sources more specific to particular units. The listings are made for informational and not endorsement purposes.

GENERAL EQUIPMENT SOURCES

BeOK!, Fred Sammons, Inc., Box 32, Brookfield, IL 60513–0032

Cleo, Inc., 3957 Mayfield Road, Cleveland, OH 44121

Maddock, Inc., Pequannock, NJ 07440–1993

Ways & Means, The Capability Collection, 28001 Citrin Drive, Romulus, MI 48174

BOWEL AND BLADDER EQUIPMENT

Dynamic Mobilities, Inc., 2068 Helena Street, Madison, WI 53704 (LUV valve)

Elizabethtown Hospital and Rehabilitation Center, Orthopedic Appliance Department, Elizabethtown, PA 17022–0710 (labia spreader)

Handi Medi Devices, P.O. Box 897, Plymouth, MA 02360 (clamp)

Medical Devices International Corporation, Gurnee, IL 60031 (leg bag)

Medical Marketing Group, P.O. Box 29187, Atlanta, GA 30359 (leg bag strap)

R.D. Equipment, 12 Herring Run Road, Harwich, MA 02645 (clamp)

ORTHOTICS

Applied Orthotic Systems, 18437 Mt. Langley, Suite E, Fountain Valley, CA 92708 (LSEO)

Jaeco, P.O. Box 75, Hot Springs, AR 71901 (BFOs, WHOs, etc.)

Orthotic Systems, 2209 Darrington, Houston, TX 77025 (electric orthosis, WHOs, etc.)

POSITIONING

Adaptive Engineering Lab, Inc., Building 2A, Unit 3, 4403 Russell Road, Lynwood, WA 98037

Alimed, Inc., 297 High Street, Dedham, MA 02026–2839

Creative Rehab Engineering, 513 Schuvier, Portland, OR 97912
Foamcraft, Inc., 947 West Van Buren, Chicago, IL 60607
Miller's Rental and Sales, 284 E. Market Street, Akron, OH 44308
Otto Bock, 4130 Highway 55, Minneapolis, MN 55422
Pin Dot Products, 2215 W. Belmont, Chicago, IL 60618
Rees-Goebel Medical Supplies, 9663 Glades Drive, Hamilton, OH 45011
STC Companies, 147 Eady Court, Elyria, OH 44035
Thompson Medical, 4301 Bryant Avenue, South, Minneapolis, MN 55409

TECHNICAL AIDS

Computer Key Guards and Latches

Don Johnston Developmental Equipment, 981 Winnetka Terrace, Lake Zurich, IL 60047
Prentke Romich Company, 1022 Heyl Road, Wooster, OH 44691
TASH, Inc., 70 Gibson Drive, Unit I, Markham, Ontario, Canada L3R 2Z3
Extensions for Independence, 635-5 N. Twin Oaks Valley Road, San Marcos, CA 92069

Computer Peripherals

Adaptive Peripherals, 4529 Bagley Avenue North, Seattle, WA 98103
Koala Technologies, 3100 Patrick Henry Drive, Santa Clara, CA 95050

ECUs and Buzzers

BSR (U.S.A.) Ltd., Route 303, Blanuelt, NY 10913
Don Johnston Developmental Equipment, 981 Winnetka Terrace, Lake Zurich, IL 60047
DU-It Control Systems Group, Inc., 8765 Township Road 513, Shreve, OH 44676–9421
Fordham Radio, 260 Motor Parkway, Hauppauge, NY 11788 (electronics catalog)
Medical Equipment Distributors, Inc. (Med), 1215 South Harlem, Forest Park, IL 60130
Prentke Romich Company, 1022 Heyl Road, Wooster, OH 44691
Radio Shack
Rehab Technology, Inc., 498 S. Plymouth, P.O. Box 185, Aviston, IL 62216
Sears
Sharper Image
TASH, Inc., 70 Gibson Drive, Unit I, Markham, Ontario, Canada L3R 2Z3

Electric Page Turners

Medical Equipment Distributors, Inc. (Med), 1215 South Harlem, Forest Park, IL 60130
Maddock, Inc., 6 Industrial Road, Pequannock, NJ 07440
J.A. Preston Corp., 60 Page Road, Clifton, NJ 07012
Touch Turner, 443 View Ridge Drive, Everett, WA 98203
Zygo Industries, Inc., P.O. Box 1008, Portland, OR 97207

Emergency Call Systems

AT&T National Special Needs Center 3, 2001 Route 46, Parsippany, NJ 07054
Independent Living, Inc., 770 Frontage Road, Suite 118, Northfield, IL 60093–9990
Lifeline Systems, Inc., One Arsenal Marketplace, Watertown, MA 02172

Power Door Openers

Dor-O-Matic, 7350 W. Wilson Avenue, Chicago, IL 60656
Lite Touch, Dorma Door Controls, Inc., Dorma Drive, Reamstown, PA 17567
Prentke Romich Company, 1022 Heyl Road, Wooster, OH 44691
Stanley Magic-Door, Inc., Division of Stanley Works, Farmington, CT 06032

Speakerphones and Intercoms

McDade and Company
Prentke Romich Company
Radio Shack

Service Merchandise
Telephone companies

Switches (Refer to ECU Sources)

Luminand, Inc., 8688 Tyler Boulevard, P.O. Box 268, Mentor, OH 44060–0268
Zygo Industries, Inc., P.O. Box 1008, Portland, OR 97207

Voice Recognition Systems

Key Tronic, P.O. Box 14687, Spokane, WA 99214
Prentke Romich Company, 1022 Heyl Road, Wooster, OH 44691
The Voice Connection, 17835 Skypark Circle, Suite C, Irvine, CA 92714
Voice Machine Communications, Inc., 10522 Covington Circle, Villa Park, CA 92667

Appendix C

REFERENCES AND READING LIST

General

Burke, D.C., & Murray, D.D. (1975). *Handbook of spinal cord medicine*. New York: Macmillan.

Guttman, L. (1973). *Spinal cord injuries: Comprehensive management and research*. Oxford: Blackwell Scientific.

Nixon, V. (1985). *Spinal cord injury: A guide to functional outcomes in physical therapy management*. Rockville, MD: Aspen Publishers.

Pierce, D.S., and Nickel, V.H. (1977). *Total care of spinal cord injuries*. Boston: Little, Brown.

Spinal Cord Injuries. (videocassette). (1980). Chicago: RIC Education and Training Center.

Trombly, C.A. (1983). *Occupational therapy for physical dysfunction* (2nd ed.). Baltimore: Williams & Wilkins.

Wilson, D.J., McKenzie, M.W., Barber, L.M., & Watson, K.L. (1984). *Spinal cord injury: A treatment guide for occupational therapists*. Thorofare, NJ: Slack, Inc.

Accessibility

Accessibility Standards, State of Illinois. Capital Development Board, State of Illinois. 180 N. LaSalle Street, No. 320, Chicago, IL 60601.

Catlin, J. (1980). *Adaptable housing*. Chicago: Access Living of Metropolitan Chicago, 815 W. Van Buren, Suite 525.

Cary, J.R. (1978). *How to create interiors for the disabled: A guidebook for family and friends*. New York: Pantheon.

Bowel and Bladder Management

Intermittent Catheterization Management. (slide/cassette package). (1984). Chicago: RIC Education and Training Center.

Urinary care management using the Rancho flexor hinge hand orthosis. (videocassette). (1980). Chicago: RIC Education and Training Center.

Equipment

AbleData. Marian Hall, national director. P.O. Box 3368, University Station, Charlottesville, VA 22903.

Evaluation

Kendall, H.O., Kendall, F.P., & Wadsworth, G.E. (1971). *Muscle testing and function*. Baltimore: Williams & Wilkins.

Mathiowetz, V., Kashman, N., Volland, G., Weber, K., Dowe, M., & Rogers, S. (1985). Grip and pinch strength: Normative data for adults. *Archives of Physical Medicine and Rehabilitation, 66*, 69–74.

Rancho Los Amigos Hospital Occupational Therapy Department. (1978). *Guide for muscle testing of the upper extremity*. Downey, CA: Professional Staff Association of the Rancho Los Amigos Hospital, Inc.

Home Management

Whirlpool Appliance Information Service. (1983). *Aids to independent living and designs for independent living*. Benton Harbor, MI: Whirlpool.

Enders, A. (1984). *Technology for independent living sourcebook.* Bethesda, MD: Rehabilitation Engineering Society of North America.

Lowman, E.W., & Klinger, J.L. (1969). *Aids to independent living.* New York: McGraw-Hill.

Leisure

The following list of resources was provided by the Therapeutic Recreation Department at RIC. Resources to which SCI patients are referred in the community are included.

Breckenridge Outdoor Education Center,
P.O. Box 168,
Breckenridge, CO 80464

National Spinal Cord Injury Association,
P.O. Box 468,
Palos Park, IL 60464
(312) 974–1103

National Wheelchair Basketball Association,
110 Seaton Building,
University of Kentucky,
Lexington, KY 40506
(606) 257–1623

Paralyzed Veterans of America,
Paraplegia News/Sports 'n Spokes,
5201 N. 19th Avenue, Suite 111,
Phoenix, AZ 85015

Vinland National Center,
3674 Indohapl Road,
P.O. Box 308,
Loretto, MN 55357
(612) 479–3555

Wilderness Inquiry II,
2929 4th Avenue South, Suite 0,
Minneapolis, MN 55408
(612) 827–4001

Orthotics

American Academy of Orthopaedic Surgeons. (1975). *The atlas of orthotics.* St. Louis: Mosby.

Burt, C.M., & Guilford, A.W. (1982, summer). The linear shoulder elbow orthosis: An innovative avenue toward independence. *Spinal Cord Injury Digest, 4,* 37–42.

Chapparo, C. (1980). *Upper extremity orthotic systems for patients with quadriplegia.* (Slide/sound training package). Chicago: RIC Education and Training Center.

Kozole, K., & Yasukawa, A. (1982). Elbow extension orthosis. *Orthotics and Prosthetics, 36,* 50–62.

Malick, M., & Meyer, C. (1978). *Manual on management of the quadriplegic upper extremity.* Pittsburg: Harmarville Rehabilitation Center.

Rancho Los Amigos Hospital. (1979). *Rehabilitation of the head injured adult.* Downey, CA: Professional Staff Association of Rancho Los Amigos Hospital.

Thenn, J.E. (1975). *Mobile arm support installation and use: A guide for occupational therapists.* Brookfield, IL: Fred Sammons, Inc.

See also Pierce & Nickel and Wilson *et al.* under General References.

Play and Toys

Burkhart, L. (1982). *Homemade battery powered toys and educational devices for severely handicapped children* (unpublished material). (Available from author: 8503 Rhode Island Avenue, College Park, MD 20740).

Burkhart, L. (1982). *More homemade battery devices for severely handicapped children with suggested activities* (unpublished material). (Available from author: 8503 Rhode Island Avenue, College Park, MD 20740).

Gilfoyle, E., Grady, A., & Moore, J. (1981). *Children adapt.* Thorofare, NJ: Slack.

Johnson, D.M. (1984). *Children's toys and books.* New York: Scribner's.

Knox, S. (1974). *"A play scale": Play as exploratory learning* (pp. 247–266). Beverly Hills, CA: Sage.

Oppenheim, J. (1984). *Kids and play.* New York: Ballantine.

Rubin, R., & Fisher, J. (1982). *Your preschooler.* New York: Johnson & Johnson Child Development Publications.

Singer, D., & Revenson, T. (1978). *A Piaget primer: How a child thinks.* New York: New American Library.

Sinker, M. (1983). *The Lekotek Guide to Good Toys.* Chicago: North Shore Lekotek.

Takata, N. (1969). The play history. *American Journal of Occupational Therapy, 23,* 314–318.

Wright, C., & Nomura, M. (1985). *From toys to computers: Access for the physically disabled child* (unpublished material). (Available from authors: P.O. Box 700242, San Jose, CA 95170).

Positioning

Andersson, G.B.J., Murphy, R.W., Ortengren, R., & Nachemson, A.L. (1979). The influence of backrest inclination and lumbar support on lumbar lordosis. *Spine, 4,* 52–58.

Bergen, A., & Colangelo, C. (1985). *Positioning the client with central nervous system deficits: The wheelchair and other adapted equipment* (2nd ed.). Valhalla, NY: Valhalla.

Brunswic, M. (1984). Ergonomics of seat design. *Physiotherapy, 70*(2), 40–43.

Butcher, B. (June 1985). Foot support with 90° knee flexion on adult wheelchairs. In *Proceedings of the Eighth Annual Conference on Rehabilitation Engineering* (pp. 407–408). Memphis, TN.

Hage, M. (1985). *Ischial and femoral weightbearing during anterior and posterior sitting postures.* Unpublished master's thesis, Northwestern University PT School, Chicago.

Hobson, D.A. (1983). *Foam in place seating for the severely disabled.* Memphis, TN: University of Tennessee Rehabilitation Engineering Center.

Hobson, D.A., Henrich, M.J., & Hanks, S.F. (June 1984). Bead seat insert and seating system. In *Proceedings of the Seventh Annual Conference on Rehabilitation Engineering* (pp. 209–211). Ottawa, Ontario, Canada.

Silverman, M.W., & Silverman, O. (June 1983). The contour-u-seating system. *Proceedings of the Sixth Annual Conference on Rehabilitation Engineering* (pp. 226–228). San Diego, CA.

Trefter, E. (1984). *Seating for children with cerebral palsy: A resource manual.* Memphis: University of Tennessee Center for Health Sciences Rehabilitation Engineering Program.

Ward, D. (1984). *Positioning the handicapped child for function: A guide to evaluate and prescribe equipment for the child with CNS dysfunction* (2nd ed.). St. Louis: Phoenix.

Zacharkow, D. (1984). *Wheelchair posture and pressure sores.* Springfield, IL: Thomas.

Sexuality

The Boston Women's Health Book Collective. (1984). *The new our bodies, ourselves.* New York: Simon & Schuster.

Mooney, T., Cole, T., & Chilgren, R. (1975). *Sexual options for paraplegics and quadriplegics.* Boston: Little, Brown.

Shaked, A. (1981). *Human sexuality and rehabilitation medicine: Sexual functioning following spinal cord injury.* Baltimore: Williams & Wilkins.

Technical Aids

Burkhart, L. (1982). *More homemade devices for severely handicapped children with suggested activities.* (unpublished material). (Available from author: 8503 Rhode Island Avenue, College Park, MD 20740).

Closing the Gap, P.O. Box 68, Henderson, MN 56044.

Committee on Personal Computers and the Handicapped 2, 2030 W. Irving Park Road, Chicago, IL 60618.

McWilliams, P.A. (1984). *Personal computers and the disabled.* Garden City, NY: Doubleday.

Phonic Ear, Inc. (1982 and monthly updates). *The many faces of funding.* (Available from Phonic Ear, 250 Camino Alto, Mill Valley, CA 94941).

Rehabilitation Engineering Center. (1982). *A guide to controls: Selection, mounting applications.* Palo Alto, CA: Stanford University Children's Hospital.

Rehabilitation Engineering Society of North America, Suite 700, 1101 Connecticut Avenue, N.W., Washington, DC 20036.

Schwejda, P., & Vanderheiden, G. (1982). Adaptive-firmware card for the Apple II. *Byte, 7* (9), 276–314.

Vanderheiden, G., Bengston, D., Brady, M., & Walstead, L. (1982). *International software/hardware registry* (2nd ed.). Madison, WI: University of Wisconsin Trace Research and Development Center.

Wright, C., & Nomnua, M. (1985). *From toys to computers: Access for the physically disabled child.* (Available from the authors, P.O. Box 700242, San Jose, CA 95170).

Index

D

E